Collector's Encyclopedia Of

Russel Wright

SECOND EDITION

COLLECTOR BOOKS
A Division of Schroeder Publishing Co., Inc.

For Ralph

The current values in this book should be used only as a guide. They are not intended to set prices, which vary from one section of the country to another. Auction prices as well as dealer prices vary greatly and are affected by condition as well as demand. Neither the Author nor the Publisher assumes responsibility for any losses that might be incurred as a result of consulting this guide.

Searching for a Publisher?

We are always looking for knowledgeable people considered to be experts within their fields. If you feel that there is a real need for a book on your collectible subject and have a large comprehensive collection, contact Collector Books.

On the Cover:
Iroquois brick red teapot, Theme Formal A.D. cup and saucer, American Modern butter dish, American Modern coffee cup cover, Mary Wright sauce boat.

Cover design: Beth Summers
Book design: Sherry Kraus

Contents

Acknowledgments 4

The Importance of Manitoga and Dragon Rock 6

Over Our Shoulder 7

Pricing in General 12

From the Beginning 13

More on Marks 27

Color Charts 32

New Uses for Metal 34

Furniture, for a New Generation 69

In a New Light 97

Wood, Early and Late 111

American Modern, the Experiment 120

Iroquois, Three Times a Day 137

Bringing Sterling Restaurant China Home 158

The Hope of Highlight 169

White Clover, Pattern for the First Time 177

Knowles Esquire, the Designer's Favorite 185

Naturalistic Bauer, Everyone's Choice 194

A New Look at Cutlery 206

Putting Plastics in their Place 213

Glass with Class 231

Fabrics, Background Material 245

Mary, her Work and Support 255

Elegance in the '60s 269

The Best of the Rest...277

Wright's American Way, Another World of Modernism 287

Chronology...297

Bibliography 298

Acknowledgments

Every writer, thanking those who have helped in so many ways, crosses fingers, and hopes that none have been omitted. I do the same, for there have been many who have helped and their names may have been lost in spite of good intentions. I have tried to keep a running list, but I over-extend my time and attention and your name may be missing. I should begin by thanking all those who have been so helpful and whose names have gotten away from me.

Space does not allow me to repeat the gratitude which I feel for so many who have added to this study and who were mentioned in previous writings. Their support has not been confined to those writings and they have added to this work in major ways.

Our photo sessions for this writing have been marathon events and Adam Anik's photography work here exceeds even the work he did on the 1990 book. I think you will agree. We were able to photograph Russel Wright's Bauer as well as Mary Wright items from Naomi Murdoch (Naomi's Antiques-To-Go, San Francisco), linens from Ted Hahn, and glass and important early metal work from William H. Strauss (Upstairs/Downstairs, New York) all while having the time of our lives in New York City. Annie Wright's wonderful dinner party brought collectors, writers, and friends together for a wonderful evening at Dragon Rock — a fine touch, a "Wright" touch. We'll all remember that evening. Time spent at Dragon Rock with Annie, Adam, and Max was very special and the thrill of the house and grounds lingers on. But I had work to do and others kept me at my computer, helping in supportive ways. At the eleventh hour, fortuity stepped in. Steve Healy, a long-time Russel Wright collector, knew of this writing and also knew that Hugh Grant (Vance Kirkland Gallery) in Denver, Colorado, was documenting and photographing his collection. He brought the projects together and made photographs of this great collection available to us. Glen Cuerden of Denver photographed the Grant collection and we have to thank all concerned for these unexpected wonderful pictures. You will agree that they were worth waiting for. Others helped in so many ways. They sent home-grown pictures, traveled many miles, loaned items, wrote notes, shared findings, consulted on pricing, and talked dishes as we shared experiences and opinions. Several stayed with me as the writing progressed, calling often, sending photography, writing encouragement, and keeping me up to the minute with their new findings and opinions. All of these are listed here, not in the importance of their contribution, not even in alphabetical order. It takes many people to write a book and these are all researchers, adding much to what is written here. They are all "Russelmeisters" (even the term has been given us by a collector) and they include: Loren Stein, Bevil and Russell Wright, Alvin Schell, Dr. Bill Burke, Barbara Endter, Andrew W. Wierengo, James R. Cooper, Rico/S.F., Joni and Monte Gordon, Susan Gose, Chuck Cichanowicz, Joe Keller, David Ross, B. J. Overby, Annie Wright, Adam Anik, The Los Angeles County Museum of Art, Bill Eppard, Joel Alpert, Bruce Arnold, Steve McMaster, Jim Drobka, Scott Vermillion, Dennis Mykytyn, John Terry, Karen Silvermintz, Gus Gustafson, Naomi Murdoch, Larry Paul, Ray Vlach, Steve Heffernan, Chad Sutton, Michael Caradine, Norna J. Lewis, Helene Guarnaccia, Diane Bridge, Jenny Gorkowski, Dan Sadwin, Carol A. Roock, Sam Chadwick, Jerry Gallaher, Robert Stacey, Allan Rupp, Shirley Schroeder, Marilyn J. Felling, Leslie Alden, Richard G. Rachetor, Carol Levison, Brad Mobley, Susanne Frantz, Doug Stanton, Lee Hay, Vic Hugo, Dianne Petipas, Pacific Design Center, William A. Straus, The Des Moines Art Center, Carmen Brady, Peggy Patrick, Bill Tanner, Chuck Rogers, Carl Gibbs, Eileen Quarels, Jeffrey Head, E. Head, Jim Wallace, Kim and Rusty Mann, Jo Cunningham, John Moses, Terry Telford, Sheri Dickson, John A. Blanton, Paul Walter, Linda Haden, Bill Ruman, Tom Kraft, Laguna, Cindy Cooper, Charles Alexander, Greg Golden, Reba Schneider, Ted Haun, James Elliott, Ralph Clifford, BA Wellman, The Corning Museum of Glass, Steve Healy, Lucille Kennedy, Mr. and Mrs. A. J. Florio, Julio Rodrigues, Paul Beedenbender, Bruce McClung, Jennie Stout, Jean Lickert, Daniel Wickemeyer, Troy Ford, Laura Kaspar, Mike Baker, Fred Palladino, Martin Seibila, Jay Johnson, Lorna Chase, Patrick Parrish, Gary McCracken, Mike Nickel.

This listing would be less than complete if I were not to include my appreciation to those at Collector Books who have been so supportive. The Schroeder family and Lisa Stroup, as well as the entire staff, have again made my Russel Wright writings possible and I thank them as often as I can, wherever I can.

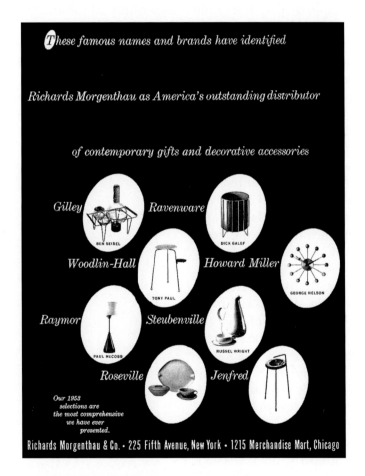

Richards Morgenthau/Raymor Advertisement

The Importance of Manitoga and Dragon Rock

This writing recognizes the collector's interest in Manitoga, Russell Wright's estate, and Dragon Rock, his home. Both the grounds and the house speak much to those of us who admire his work, but our understanding is less if we do not acquaint ourselves with the fullness of his interests as he expressed them, as he developed Manitoga and built Dragon Rock. Manitoga draws its name from the Algonquin language, signifying a spiritual home which includes 80 acres of land in the Hudson Highlands. The Appalachian Trail runs through it and the Hudson Highlands State Park is near. Wright left Manitoga to The Nature Conservancy in 1975 but in 1984, it became Manitoga, Incorporated, a non-profit corporation with a board of directors who attend to the house and grounds as they are able. They have as their goals, his goals: to promote understanding of his concept of design with nature, to offer the grounds as a resource for any who would find there a natural laboratory, and to develop there a center and meeting place for professionals involved in art, education, the environment, and landscape design. These goals are spelled out in a quarterly newsletter sent to those who are members. Such a membership provides a calendar of events which includes social functions Manitoga offers. It allows those who have known Wright well from their own collecting to become part of a larger group, one dedicated to preserving his best interests. Trails need constant maintenance, the home, so beautiful, is fragile and tenuous. Funds are largely made available by friends like you and me and there are always projects "on-hold." Your involvement is needed to join in preserving this site. There are several levels of memberships, all of which allow access to the property, the newsletter and notices of workshops, tours, and programs. While the trails are open to the general public for hiking and picnicking, one should call for hours. Members receive access at any time and the house is open for guided tours, conferences, and workshops, and by reservation. The information from which these facts are taken is the wonderfully photographed newsletter which will be yours for the membership price of a dinner plate. Individual memberships are $35.00, Seniors $15.00, and Family $40.00, but other memberships are available, all of which offer increasing benefits. For more information, write Manitoga, Garrison, NY 10524 or call 914-424-3812. Located in Garrison, NY, on the east side of route 9D, 45 minutes by car from the George Washington Bridge, up the Palisades Parkway, across the Bear Mountain Bridge, and north on route 9D. Easy access is an hour and 20 minutes by Metro North Hudson trains which leave hourly from Grand Central Station. A driving service is said to be available from the Garrison railroad station. Your membership is important for it unites those who have come to know Wright and keeps alive the expression which he valued most. I hope you will join in our dedication to this retreat.

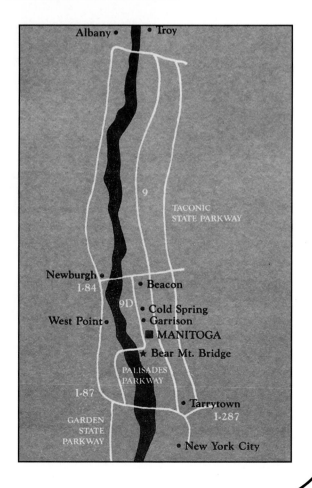

Over Our Shoulder

Ad in *Woman's Home Companion* magazine, 1956.
In warm weather Russel Wright and daughter Annie would breakfast
in the garden of his townhouse and design studio in New York City.

In 1990, with many seasoned Russel Wright collectors, almost 15 years of searching for Wright's products, and a good bit of research by myself and others, it was not expected that we would return to this study so soon. However, more information, much of it coming from collectors who are researchers themselves, has added to that which we had found and that information, new findings, and the new stories behind them called for another study.

That study came in bits and pieces, a phone call one week, a letter or two the next week. Collectors had taken my invitation to call or to write, to talk "dishes," to compare our finds. It has been a wonderful few years with so many great conversations, letters full of exciting new accounts and interesting opinions, and new phone friends to add to old ones. Storing and sharing all this information and the timing of this writing comes

at an important passage in the collecting of Russel Wright designs for many collectors have become advanced collectors, but we still search. We think of new ways to search. We're a committed group. At the same time, a new, enthusiastic group of collectors have taken to streets, fairgrounds, shows, and shops, searching out a sugar here, a table there, around the corner a casserole, and they have come home to their computer to share their findings with Internet friends. This new group sends out electronic word of findings, opinions, new ideas, prices, rarities, all the subjects that have held our interest for so long. It is all as exciting today as it was yesterday. Collecting has joined new collectors and seasoned collectors. Could it be deja vu? As we make this new examination of Wright's work, I must ask early collectors for their understanding as we revisit facts recorded before and which remain as we have come to know them. Some basics cannot be changed and it would be wrong to alter them for the sake of a new writing. At the same time, it is important to report change where it can be supported by documentation or where it adds to our understand-

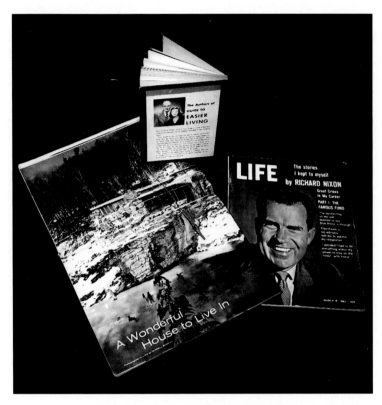

***Life* magazine with article about
the Russel Wright home.**

ing of Wright's work.

In this writing I have tried to examine areas in which Wright's work has not been found in spite of probable existence. I've pointed out where sampling, experimental, and prototype work resulted. Rarities remain to be found in this sort of study and all collectors would do well to consider such possibilities. There is reason to hope for more findings in the Paden City lines and there exists the possibility that collectors will still find items not yet seen in rare Iroquois colors. The Theme Formal and Informal lines hold out hope for real surprises and it is probably true that more of Wright's decorated lines in Sterling will be found. There is a world of Bauer in prototype glazes waiting to be recognized and early wood examples should hold exciting finds.

In the chapter "The Best of the Rest," an overview of Wright's work detailing small accounts with uncertain production, we point to many sources which should offer samples, runs, prototypes, or limited production. All of

these areas should be explored as we continue our search for Wright's designs. Not meaning to direct any personal research you may be doing, I point to these as logical areas in which you may find rewards. Such a search should be fruitful and the journey should be a joy. I encourage any who wished to do serious study on Wright's work to go to Syracuse University, examine Wright's papers, and share your findings. The files there are nirvana for those of us who study.

Some new insights continue to come from those whose interest and collections began in the 1930s when Russel was introducing his designs and his social philosophy to America. My correspondence indicates that, in those days when collecting was not the national pastime that it has since become, there was, even then, the awareness that these designs were important, that they drew a line in America's sense of style, and that examples should be preserved. Mothers of today's collectors, in many cases, saved the remnants of their Russel Wright purchases, stored them in America's attics, sure that they were exceptional. In most of those cases, the original owners remembered the story behind the items, for they had been the first generation to adopt the social concerns which Wright had promoted along with his wares. It is not unusual to hear from a first generation collector who needs a dinner plate or two, a bowl for vegetables, several pieces to complete a service for a son or daughter, and almost every day, word comes from a son or daughter, who has found the designs in the attic, at a flea market, at an antique show, or a high styled shop. These second generation collectors want the plates and bowls but they ask for more. Their interests extend to what items were made, what colors they came in, and what is rare. They want it all, rarities included, and the story behind the designs is important to them. Wright's philosophy has added importance to their collections. It is right that we return to examine the facts as we have come to know them and the findings as they have been reported.

A newness has been added to our search and now we must make room for that. Collecting preferences have changed since the '30s and we suspect that they are still changing. Rarities have evolved and scarcities have developed out of early collecting. A longer examination has had unexpected influence upon our collecting. Hands-on examinations have resulted in new favorites. So it will be — we hope for a long time. Unable to alter absolutes, we are bound to report changed collecting. We have much to look forward to.

My own interest in Russel Wright's works date to the "first time around." My attic held boxes of his work but my collecting life had not started when the *New York Times* in 1979, printed an article on Andy Warhol's extensive Russel Wright collection (1,659 pieces). It was to be a step into a new life for many of us. Fiesta collectors, of course, were a step ahead of us, but we knew that where Fiesta and Warhol had been, there would be rewards for our Wright collecting. In no time, all of New York City was searching for Russel Wright designs and many of the rest of us were cleaning our attics, looking for that box we'd saved. National antique publications repeated the *New York Times* news and soon the country had found itself involved in a search for Russel Wright designs — all of them. Our success was predictable and the size of Warhol's collection has been surpassed by many as we have become better acquainted with the varied items which Wright designed.

Our first study, begun before the Wright papers were available at Syracuse University, was based upon recollections and a small amount of documentation which could be found in Steubenville, Ohio, where Wright's American Modern dinnerware was made. Few of us knew the American Modern story and almost none of us knew the extent of the journey we would make as we searched out the extensive body of his work. However, it was a beginning and we did have some facts upon which to base our further questions. It was soon possible to conduct some meager surveys and offer an incomplete price guide aimed at the findings which were being made.

Soon, though, the George Ahrent's Research Library at Syracuse University received the extensive Wright files which had been willed to them. They were available for research almost at once and my search for information took me there quickly. I was convinced that if we were to make order out of our dinnerware findings, we could do so only with the aid of concrete, documented facts. Coming home to personal correspondence, it was possible to reply to questions as well as findings which had raced ahead of documentation. Organizing the material led to a more comprehensive study of Wright's table top designs. That writing was in 1985, and was titled *Russel Wright Dinnerware, Designs for the American Table* and was published by Collector Books in Paducah, Kentucky. The facts as presented there were based upon solid research, in contradiction to that which had not been possible in former writings, but time was to catch up with me. Collectors were finding other things, not just tableware, signed by Wright. In no time, my mail and that of Collector Books was full of "What is this?" questions. Collector Books sent me signals that it was important to look at the complete Wright work. I made two more trips to Syracuse and the files where my examination

extended to the complete body of his work. It was not an easy search. The files are confused and with no one familiar with the work it addresses, any examination has been difficult, verification of detail complicated. Early on, trying to find my way through them, I found limitations which defined my search. While the contract files have answered most questions which we ask, they are not complete. They do not cover custom work and there is little in them to supply us with the exact prototype/sampling information. We are unsure of some dates which would help us as we fit glazes and shapes into an order that would allow us a complete picture of several of the lines. The fact remains, however, that they still are the best reference point we have and actual production of lines is detailed. Perhaps we ask too much of the files, but collectors' appetites are voracious.

My research led to my last writing, *The Collector's Encyclopedia of Russel Wright Designs* which was published by Collector Books in 1990.

As I researched for the *Encyclopedia*, I was fortunate to add information found in Wright's personal files loaned to me by his daughter, Annie Wright. Those files answered questions not clear before and gave personal accounts of business dealings absent from the Syracuse files. It was a bonanza of unexpected information made possible by his family. Equally generous was the personal involvement of Adam Anik, Annie Wright's husband, a professional photographer. Adam has been tireless in the pursuit of fine photographs of Wright's work. He did the pictures in the *Encyclopedia*, and I turned to him at once for help with this writing, believing his work to be among the best in books of this type.

As we begin this new study, it seems important to revisit facts which remain important if we are to find more of Wright's work. Prototypes, samples, experimentals, and runs are important to our search and should be defined. Prototype work was done, usually at the time of contractual agreements. Prototype items were models or illustrative pieces, one of a kind or several of a kind, usually made by Wright for a client. There are a few of these, at the most, but they are part of the interesting body of rarities which exist. Experimental items have come to mean items made by the customer/client, according to Wright's specifications, and were usually done to allow for limited amounts to be used to evaluate the item, glaze, size, or other characteristics. They gave practicality to the concept and could provide all concerned with important information upon which the feasibility of production could be judged. Often these experimental items were not approved and more experimentation followed, adding to a greater number of experimental items. A run was a limited production providing examples for sales purposes. Client acceptance of these samples or runs often affected the development of a line and added to more experimentation. It is not easy to see where all these prototypes, experimental items, samples, and runs may lead us. It is certain that we have scratched the surface, but not deeply.

The files include contracts which have been called "empty contracts," referring to an agreement from which no production resulted. Experience has taught us that these contracts are fertile ground for prototypes or experimentation examples. Wright's own standard contract clause which allowed for restyling and redesigning resulted in many possibilities, many variants as production was considered, and it would be wrong to suggest that all have been found.

Fortunately, Wright was a note writer, as well as an accumulator, and while the file information does not answer all our questions, it does afford us with extensive and detailed information, confirming production as we have found it. Sorting actual production from prototypes, samples, experimentals, and runs has confused us, but the actual listings of items/glazes/shapes agreed upon contractually is specifically documented, changed only by events which are also documented. Substitution of names was easy. Persuading a manufacturer to formulate new glazes was costly and was not done except in contractual agreement.

As we search files, photos, and advertising materials, we should be cautious in interpreting the information which we find there. National advertising, beautifully conceived, may mislead readers into believing that the colors and items listed there were the only colors. They may suggest that items were the only items made at the time when the advertisement ran. Not true. The fact is that not every store carried every color, not even every item and descriptive names may have been derived from the designer's second thoughts. His imagination was as colorful as his dinnerware. We must be aware that marketing often allowed only one area store to carry the entire line while other accounts were offered partial listings. Even brochures which were give-away advertising folders listed only the items and colors which a particular store sold. Allow me an illustration of this practice. I have only a copy to offer, but it shows a picture taken from a 1941 issue of *Interiors* magazine two years after American Modern dinnerware had been introduced. The article showed several table settings by prominent designers of that year. You would recognize every item in the American Modern group *except* the bowl which is placed on top of the plates in the foreground. (See photo below.) It has not one lug handle, but two. The caption identifies all the items as we know them to be with the exception of that bowl which is described as a "lug oatmeal." With the American Modern line already established it is difficult to explain this piece which we know was not part of the line. The strange name has not been found elsewhere in documentation. Today's perspective allows us the certainty that it misrepresents the line, but it helps us examine other such misleading advertising, articles, and photo information.

Add to these practices that Wright and Mary shared a love affair with the language and seemed to find limitless wonderful names for the same color. Coral sand was another name for coral, parsley, and forest are the same color, seedless grape and curry were both chartreuse. There are other examples and you may find them in your own research. All of the dinnerware lines benefited from Wright's imaginative use of words and it would be a mistake to believe that we have found rare, unlisted colors in spite of what has seemed like persuasive evidence. An article written by Wright in 1943 describes a dinner by candlelight, listing various early American Modern items as complimenting the table. He is quoted: "The white pottery is from the American Modern line of dinnerware manufactured by the Steubenville Pottery Co. It is also furnished in gray, brown, turquoise, and chartreuse." *House Beautiful* in December 1939 lists the colors as "bone white, granite gray,

Interiors **1941 advertising photo.**

**Photo in *Woman's Home Companion* magazine, 1956.
The Wrights like to pop corn for guests
or when they're at home together.**

bean brown, seedless grape, and turquoise." Coral is conspicuously absent and we recognize seedless grape as chartreuse and turquoise as seafoam. *Sunset Magazine* in June of 1948 carried a half-page black and white advertisement for Wright's American Modern Dinnerware, glassware, and tablecloths. The colors they list are gray, teal, chartreuse, and coral. We can recognize that teal was seafoam, but where were the other original colors? In that same year, The Famous Barr Company in St. Louis, Missouri, carried a full page, color ad listing the colors as gray, blue, coral, and chartreuse, and no others. There are many such examples, many incomplete listings, but the variety of names for colors, outside the names which we know to be accurate, can lead us into confusion or error if we use any one source, original or not, as absolute. Item listings are equally suspect as the *Interiors* photograph illustrates.

Altering an item by decoration was and is a common practice. Too often, collectors are assured that designs are original and "underglazed." Workers in the potteries and home ceramists today are able to decorate and apply an overglaze. The practice of boring a hole into an item and using metal fittings to change the intended usage is also one used by workers then and now. Be very careful with these adapted items for they are neither rare or unlisted. They are not Wright's designs and while they may be lovely additions, the fact that they are not Wright's intended items, usually lowers their value. The listed items, with allowances for experimentation and prototype of the item, remain as we have found them in the *Encyclopedia*.

Where it adds to our understanding, Wright's own words have been used to add to the interest which has

revolved around his work. He was an accomplished speaker and writer with strong social concerns and he voiced his message with the same intensity as he advertised his wares. With conviction, he wrote articles in most of the leading magazines of his day, and letters to the editor were not foreign to him. He spoke regularly, and many of his speeches have come to us from the files in Syracuse. Much of the wording found in his advertising is his own and we find his words to be as creative as his dinnerware and he used them, spoken or written, to advance his product, his mission in every opportunity open to him.

Most long-time Wright collectors have had time to define their collections. So many choices have left room for much variation. Some of us acquired sets, so many that we secreted some of them for special occasions, some for seasonal use. Many moved on to one-of-a-color groupings, water pitchers, carafes, or the like, and they have challenged us as scarcities developed. We extended our collecting to Mary Wright's work and where we have recognized it, we admired and added the work of American Way contributors. Others, having met Modernism through Wright's work, look for his influence in the work of others, or in the style of Transitional Modernism which he favored. As we take time to define our own collecting, it occurs to most of us that, almost without our knowing it, Wright's social philosophy has influenced us. We have a new view of the things we use every day. We look for a certain "look," if not a "Wright look," then a "right look" and our lives have been enriched. With a changed perspective, our pleasures have increased. It should be so. We may have come full circle, but most of us are ready to go around again.

**Photo in *Woman's Home
Companion* magazine, 1956.
Annie's "blackboard" is in
the kitchen.**

Pricing in General

The person who first said "location, location, location" must have been a Russel Wright collector. The first to say "condition, condition, condition" was surely an advanced collector. No other factors influence pricing with the emphasis that location and condition do. Those of us who live between the coasts and not in large urban areas have always known this to be true as we visited larger markets personally or through trade papers. Often our collecting experiences were based on availability. We recognized that our own buying and selling figures were not representative. That situation continues. Where you are deeply affects the cost of what you buy and its price if you sell. Regional differences are more important with Russel Wright collecting than they are with many other areas of collecting.

Having said that, I must admit that I tried very hard to get suggested pricing, comments, and observations from both coasts as well as middle America. A broad sampling was taken. All these prices have been arrived at by eliminating the highest prices as well as the lowest prices and averaging the remaining figures. If these sometimes surprise you, remember that they are averages only. You may need to adjust them to your own location. They have not been offered as definitive and you should use them as a guide only.

I hear from many people who have just dug out a 1940s set of dishes, basic place settings with shakers, cream and sugar, vegetable bowl, and platter. Realizing that these are collectible, they believe them to be more valuable than they are. If this is you, do not be misled. Remember that these designs have been collectible for over 15 years and most collectors have found basic pieces. If you wish to sell them, consider that dealers can pay only about 40% to 50% of the prices for which they expect to sell items. If you hope for better prices, you should advertise them in one of the many antique periodicals. Mail-order buyers expect to pay for shipping, but you should be prepared to pack and ship properly.

Because high prices seem to get the most attention, I approached pricing with some concern. I was very aware that a new group of Russel Wright collectors were looking at yesterday's rarities, today's scarcities. I hope that prices would not be so high as to discourage those collectors. I find that I was overly concerned. Most dealers who responded evidenced the fact that they wished to sell, not display, and most collectors offered what they had paid, not what they would pay.

Regional availability adds a percentage increase for rare or important colors. Several who helped with pricing believed that I should break down color values according to popularity or rarity, giving several ranges. I tried to do so but I found much disparity and too little agreement. For this reason, I have returned to a general price range, somewhat more broad than in my last writing, but I believe you will be able to find your region, your popular colors, rarities, and pricing that applies to you and your circumstances. I have used NPD to indicate "no price determined" where items or colors are very rare. That term also applies to items never reported but which the files document. In such cases, you may be wise to trust your instincts, remembering that often this NDP indicates important, expensive pricing.

The representative prices apply to mint condition items with no damage and minimal factory blemishes. Having said that, a rare piece with minor damage, carrying an "as is" price, would be attractive to all but purists.

Specific details on items, colors, rarities, as well as pricing considerations, are discussed in the headings of each listing.

From the Beginning

Russel Wright, designer, populist, social reformer, naturalist, machine age advocate, American, came from a conservative background with which he always identified even as he brought a newness of spirit to the artistic world and a changed concept of informal living to a nation too long unsure of its self esteem, overly imitative of worlds and ways foreign to it.

Born in Lebanon, Ohio, on April 3, 1904, he came from a family with strong ties to the law. His father was a judge in Lebanon and Wright was a descendent of two signers of the Declaration of Independence, Whipple and Morris. His father's mother was one of the founders of Lebanon College. Wright felt that his mother had an early influence on his career, drawing on will power and energy. His creativity, revolt, and devotion to detail, as well as his strict adherence to social concerns, appeared to be inherent influences. While he left Lebanon as a college student, he remained close to his family, returning to visit them, writing with frequency, and never removing himself from the concern which he felt for his mother and sister after his father's early death. His correspondence with family shows us a young man with many interests — political, social, artistic — all of which he spoke to as he wrote home from a personal world very different from that in Lebanon. This family unit may well have been the only unit in which he felt secure as he carved out a life for himself in a world more complex than he could have imagined. To his credit, he never lost his moorings.

While still in high school, Wright was determined to join himself with the world of art and design, taking a part-time job in a munitions factory in order to spend his Saturday afternoons studying at the Art Academy in Cincinnati. His teacher was the respected Frank Duvanek and Russel was fortunate to have such an early and exceptional instructor. Completing his local schooling at 17, he was given parental permission to go to New York for a year to indulge himself in the study of art which so interested him. This study was to be at the Art Students League. The understanding, however, was that when he "got this art out of his system," he would enter Princeton and study law as had others in his family. While in New York at this early time, he won the first and second Tiffany prizes for the outstanding war memorial of 1929, no doubt confirming his conviction that his future was in the field of art.

In spite of that success, he entered Princeton as he had promised, but he soon neglected his studies there and showed an indifference to academic work. His father, disappointed, wrote to the Dean asking for advice about this son whose progress was poor. The reply was very important to Russel's future. The Dean agreed that Wright could and should have done better, but the faculty at Princeton with whom Russel had studied, agreed that his talents were outside the limits of legal studies. They felt he had a good future, perhaps even a very brilliant future in the artistic world which interested him so much. His work in that field was so gifted, he was so dedicated and interested in it that his instructors recognized his talents at a time when his experience and training were still not fully developed. The Wrights were reassured that this was a respectable interest, not a "loose Eastern City" dalliance, however different from their expectancy. Coming as it did from academicians whom they trusted, the advice was taken, and his family allowed Russel the opportunities to expand his interests, making no more exacting scholastic demands. With help from his instructors, he had declared his independence. Shortly after that, his father, in his early forties, suffered a fatal heart attack in court, leaving his family in debt. It was necessary for Russel to find his place in the world as quickly as possible. With the wind to his back, he raced to New York.

Interestingly, had Wright graduated from Princeton, he would have been part of the class of 1926. Not having done so, he was, never-the-less, asked to be their principal speaker when they celebrated their 50th reunion in 1976. At that time he was given their Outstanding Achievement Award. He did not go unrecognized in academic circles.

While at Princeton, he had become interested in set and production work in the Triangle Shows. There and as early as his sophomore year in school, he had begun to attract the attention of those in the world of theater in New York. Soon he was working for and with Norman Bel Geddes, the quality of his work acknowledged. His Princeton days ended when Bel Geddes asked him to go to Paris to work on the production of "St. Joan."

Not dismissing his studies, during these early years in New York, he studied at the Columbia School of Architecture and later the same subject at New York University. The twenties were a wonderful time for Wright. He was young, charming, blessed with patrician good looks, and had found a place for himself in the exciting world of theater people and artists. For a time, he felt a sense of belonging.

He was to move on from stage design, however, for it did not allow him the personal creativity which he desired. The theater and stage experiment had been an important influence, for out of it had come recognition from decorators who, in turn, spread the word to department store accounts. It was a small step, then, into the home furnishings field and accounts of his own.

Much later, he spoke of his early art studies, saying "I was very religious as an art student and my work was mixed up with my religion." While so interested in the world of art, he judged his own artistic skills to be of only average merit, explaining that he did not turn from the fine arts for the sake of making more money and that (in 1941) "My aesthetical conscience is just as energetic as it used to be. Designing articles which could be sold for use to every man seemed a more important service in my time." These words and his reflection upon them go a long way in explaining the emphasis he placed on his social concerns. Later Wright said that studio sculpture or painting would not have satisfied him for his social conscience was so much a part of his life that working in a studio alone would have made him feel "left out and misunderstood." With his work and his words, Wright would lead a cultural change not addressed by others working in the American art community at that time.

Fortunately, Mary Small Einstein entered Russel's life in 1927. They met at Woodstock where Russel was working summer stock and his marriage to her added more to his life and work than either could have imagined as they set out to storm New York and the artistic world. Coming from a socially prominent family whose fortune had been made in the ribbon and lace trades, she was to show dedication to her husband's career, always at the expense of her own. She was an early and continuing influence and his work. His social concerns became hers. Her financial and social contacts contributed to his acceptance in very real ways and she was her husband's advocate as he designed and manufactured. She sold him as well as his products and was relentless in promoting her husband's name. She could not sell his acceptance to her family, however. It was reported that her father, upon receiving the telegram of the elopement, threw his priceless collection of seventeenth century pewter down the stairs. Russel never became a part of the family into which he had married.

Wright's earliest work, of course, was one of a kind or a few of a kind, as he was able to turn them out of a converted coach house on E 53rd Street in New York City. They lived upstairs and Russel, turned artisan, displayed designs from the ground floor where a large glass window became an interesting site for passers-by, most of whom took notice that there was some interesting work being done there. In 1930, some of Russel's very early works were masks of theater and political personalities: Greta Garbo, Herbert Hoover, Mary Pickford, and more. Soon, however, he found himself designing decorative accessories in chromium, aluminum, and pewter. Limited capital, limited space, and limited accounts seemed not to deter Mary and Russel

Herbert Hoover caricature mask, 1930.

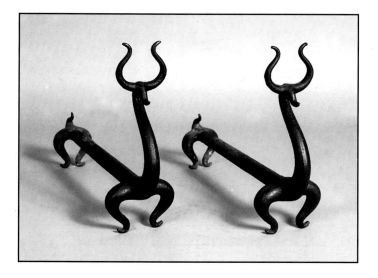

**Fire Deer Andirons, 21¼" long
x 15½" high x 6" wide.**

shocking. Mary, meeting customers daily, urged her husband to concentrate on spun aluminum serving accessories rather than upon decorative items. She made her way from shop to boutique selling his work and she had an early understanding of sales and the market place which Russel, in the coach house confines, soon saw was important if he were to succeed. She was right, of course, and it was later said that Wright had been the first to introduce home furnishings tuned to informal living and entertaining. He had succeeded upon using commonplace materials in new ways for new functions. Mary Ryan, an advocate of contemporary art objects, had put a new face on the gift business in New York and securing her account was important by anyone's measure. She endorsed Wright's work early on, selling all that Russel could produce and Mary could carry across town. The agreement between them was such that her advertisements promoted the causes which Wright had begun to define as his own. "He was an American craftsman, a patriot working only on the American market, paying taxes to the American government." Spelling it out, Mary Ryan said that modern production methods allowed him to place his artistic work in the homes of average people, in contradiction to the craftsmanship of the past which had worked to serve the needs of the wealthy. He was a modern Paul Revere, she said, as she sold his work on a commission basis. It would remain difficult to separate Mary Ryan's expression of Wright's creed from his own, to which he would give voice over and over during his working life.

Times change, however, and by 1934 there was little money in the country to be spent on whimsies or even necessities. It became clear that he must continue to develop his home accessory line. Even so, sales dropped off and it became Mary's lot to keep two sets of books; one set showed sales and profits, the other an accounting of her own finances with which she shored up their business and her husband's encouragement. Still, Wright's work attracted attention and only the size of his operation limited sales to larger accounts who were interested in ordering and stocking his line. His attractive low prices, they felt, might breathe new life into their own sluggish sales. Arrangements were made to expand production. With spun aluminum items turned out in greater numbers and new items introduced as fast as Wright could conceive them, he seemed to have made his mark, even at a time when the rest of the country was in financial distress. Surprisingly to everyone but Mary, orders began arriving from all across the country affording Wright a pulpit upon which to advocate informality and easy living. The country embraced

who were refining business policies and products which Russel was making and Mary was selling. Their experience soon taught them that chrome and pewter were difficult to work with, given their workshop tools. Aluminum was cheaper and easier to manage. Their days were rewarding as they met success with enthusiasm.

Before the Wrights abandoned the use of the more difficult metals, however, Wright produced the Circus Animal line which, together with the masks, secured Wright as an avant-garde designer. His work quickly caught on as different, new, fresh, and sometimes

Pamphlet Featuring the Circus Animals

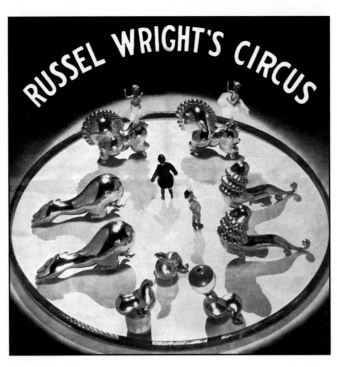

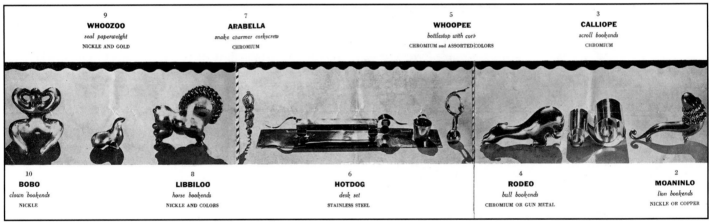

9	7	5	3
WHOOZOO	**ARABELLA**	**WHOOPEE**	**CALLIOPE**
seal paperweight	*snake charmer corkscrew*	*bottlestop with cork*	*scroll bookends*
NICKLE AND GOLD	CHROMIUM	CHROMIUM and ASSORTED COLORS	CHROMIUM

10	8	6	4	2
BOBO	**LIBBILOO**	**HOTDOG**	**RODEO**	**MOANINLO**
clown bookends	*horse bookends*	*desk set*	*bull bookends*	*lion bookends*
NICKLE	NICKLE AND COLORS	STAINLESS STEEL	CHROMIUM OR GUN METAL	NICKLE OR COPPER

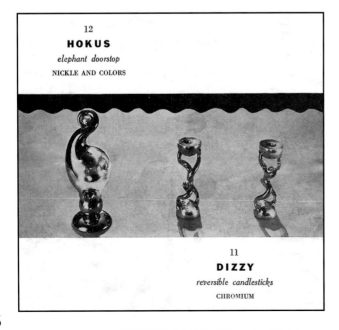

12

HOKUS

elephant doorstop

NICKLE AND COLORS

11

DIZZY

reversible candlesticks

CHROMIUM

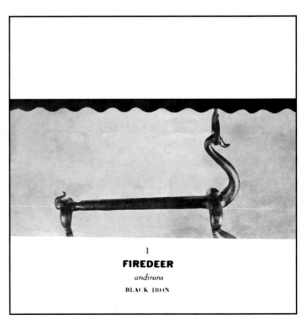

1

FIREDEER

andirons

BLACK IRON

"I believe with religious intensity that good design is for everyone." — *Russel Wright*

both concepts. Never completely at rest, he soon turned to a design for dinnerware, as opposed to accessory items. Out of that restlessness came American Modern, the wonder design which catapulted his name and his work into the consciousness of Americans in 1939. Common people with uncommon tastes came to know Wright's designs in their daily lives.

The restructuring of his designs to include dinnerware had been made possible because of the friendship and working relationship which the Wrights had established with Irving Richards, a respected business owner in Manhattan and an early admirer of Modernism with personal friendships in that field. In every way, Richards was well connected. Recognizing success from years of experiencing it, Richards joined with the Wrights in the business side of Russel Wright Inc., renamed Russel Wright Accessories. The new partners believed that colorful, functional design would be well received. They further believed that it should assume the mantel of a distinctive American design serving the needs of average people of average means, Wright's creed restated.

Out of this agreement evolved the giant Raymor firm. It is important for serious collectors of Mod-

ernism to understand the firm and Wright's relationship to it. The firm was formed as a distribution company, to sell and distribute Wright's work as well as the work of other good American designers. Business decisions were to be the concern of Mary and Richards who divided the voting stock evenly. Wright would design exclusively for Raymor for a five year period and Mary, Russel, and Richards were to be paid dividends from the profits. After the original five year period, Wright and Mary sold their stock to Richards, leaving the Raymor firm to Richards who was in sole charge of the company. Wright continued to design for Raymor, but he was paid on a royalty basis for his past work as well as the future work which Raymor distributed. The Wrights later felt that they had sold their stock too soon for American Modern sales, on the way to breaking records, would continue to do so for so many years. Hindsight, however, often distorts actuality. Russel drew royalties out of all expectations for many years and he enjoyed the freedom to work on many other designs. Collectors confuse the wonderful body of work which Raymor distributed, believing it all to be Wright's work. That is not the case. Raymor, under Richards, went on to distribute fine modern designs for many years after Wright's association with the firm had ended. While not exactly synonymous, we may consider the name "Richards Morganthau" as the Raymor firm. The working arrangement of Richards Morganthau has no bearing on our understanding of Wright's involvement with Raymor.

Both Wright and Richards, well acquainted with the world of design, were aware that there was new and exciting work coming out of the Bauhaus movement in Europe and the Arts and Crafts movement in England, and they could not ignore work in which Scandinavians were involved. These and other important art styles were exciting, finding a substantial number of followers in this country. Certainly, Wright and his friend were among them, but with some reservations. While Wright admired the functionalism and frugality of detail he found there, he did not believe that Americans were ready to accept the sterile lines of much that added to modernism. He chose to follow his own instincts always with an eye for the great changes which he expected when WW II ended. Many believed that American industries would need a great deal of time to retool once the war was over. More optimistic, he expected an immediate hunger for a better life combined with increased income in the hands of new homemakers.

Of course, he was an advocate for modernism, but not modernism which was confused with fads or outlandish styles. Metropolitan living not related to informal living and entertaining, was at odds with his cause and his designs. His modernism was a homegrown version, easy to understand and accept and he touched the urban home with a Transitional Modernism. He was later to describe his earliest works by saying: "I learned not to take the traditional or acceptable path in undertaking any project, but to search for the basic approach or reason for it and introduce an original creation of my own. This was the driving force behind all of the product designing I did in the 1920s and I always innovated. Not, of course, without consideration and study of the market. But even when I designed the largest portion of the line in terms of possible prices and possible tastes, I included a top of the line that was experimental or innovative and forward looking. Often I did this kind of work at a loss and production departments generally oppose me but this innovation created millions and millions in sales of new types of products.

Rejecting Art Deco which had been widely popular, he also turned away from styles called Modernistic, Neo Classic, and Classic Modern. Nodding to these styles, he felt that none would endure, saying that "They may have been decoratively acceptable epidemics, but cannot hold as sound examples of modern design." Edgar Kaufmann Jr. in the *American Magazine of Art* in April 1948, wrote that "Wright passed through the major design metamorphoses of the past twenty years." From the first, however, most saw a touch of the Orient in Wright's work. No one has denied that. It was an early influence which he admired, sprinkling it into his work all his life and using it extensively in his home, but this was only a minor influence. It remains true that texture and construction stressed to the degree where they substitute for surface decoration was central to his work. He felt that by the use of dramatic, but practical materials, combined with the functional lines of modernism, the handcrafted look for which he reached would result.

He knew before we did that great social changes were afoot in the world and that our old lives would never return. World War II had turned the world on end, leaving young Americans searching for their places in a changed society. Wright meant to give them the changes he believed they deserved. He told us that art belonged to all of us and that it should be embodied in the every day tools and furnishings which surrounded us, that "The best things in life should be free, or sell for a reasonable price." He was critical of our art education, saying that because that study had been so poor, our own art was imitative. His words were: "A terrific machine to belittle American culture has been built up

in American schools and colleges and it will take several generations to repair the damage that has been done." He said that we were insecure with any art, style, or design which was not an European adaptation. Calling for change, he urged us to be proud of our native heritage, our own skills and tastes. Most important, he said, was that we change our admiration for extravagance to the appreciation of minimalism. "The fear that casual living is sloppy living and that we had better hang on to traditions underestimates a lot of the things that are going on. How can you hold on to the traditions in times that are changing so fast and so radically? In adapting ourselves to this big social revolution we are naturally going through a transitional period. Our new way of living will not be tasteless. Fed by industry and the press which serves it, we have accomplished greater comfort on a larger scale than any previous civilization. Science and industry helped. Traditionalists have been afraid of change." We were making new rules, better rules, he said, and we came to know that living the lives of the past did not fit our new needs. We needed more creativity, warmth, a democratic life style. It was meaningful to us and we learned as he lectured. Even the process of our learning and accepting was new and different and we found ourselves developing a mind-set based on the principles Wright sold along with his designs. Russel Lynes, social critic of the times, said it best, "Above all, he was exactly right for his time. In the early thirties, we entered a period of informality that was very different from the starched Edwardian decades and the frenetic twenties. We put aside, partly for financial reasons, but also for humane and social reasons, a good many conceits of behavior that were regarded as 'de rigueur' by our parents' generation."

Wright told us that designers, manufacturers, and sales people were also behind the times. "Proof surrounds us. That shiny new cars are parked outside millions of shabbily furnished homes cannot be denied." The cars, he added, work, but our homes did not. He was struck with the cost and energy needed to maintain them, by the "patently projected snobbery, the concentration on impressing the visitor and disclosing the heft of the client's wallet." Too many were engaged in the buying and selling of snob appeal. Shams, pretense, and self deception no longer paid and the twentieth century would have no more room for it. He was relentless in ridding our lives of the decay of formality and we were caught in the glare of his dreams.

The work place changed direction also as these new ways became our ways and by this time he was perfectly positioned to change the market place as well. He had established a reputation for a newness of work, overwhelmingly accepted by the public. If we were name droppers, it was likely that we chose his name. With our future and his before him, he closed the Russel Wright Accessory Company to spend all his time in design work. The new firm was to be Russel Wright Associates and business practices became more uniform. The firm included a few designers and a small support group of very skilled managers. These would include Arthur Harshman, Herbert Honig, Ed Fitzwater, Don Yellin, Hector Leonardi, and Guido Barbierbi, as well as a few others. His staff was kept small since he oversaw all details. Final approval of all work rested with Wright and he watched all of the work with religious intensity, always critical, difficult to please, and injecting his own influence, insisting on details he favored. He was a hard man to work for, but the demands he exacted from his staff, his clients, and himself produced uniformly high quality products. It seems likely that he did not think of himself as a hard taskmaster.

For a time, he occupied two city houses, living in one and using the other as a studio where his staff of 10 or 12 worked. The terraced gardens were thrown together and in good weather much of the work was done at the side of windows in a glass enclosure converted to a studio. A winding outdoor staircase joined working and living quarters, bringing the outdoors inside. He used such practices wherever he could, believing that less formality in the work place relieved stress and accomplished better results. No doubt his employees agreed. It is well documented that in spite of his exacting supervision, most of those who were associated with him respected his work and considerations, and were proud to be a part of such a grand design.

Herb Honig, his business manager, and Irving Richards, his partner, are among the very few with whom he retained a continuing friendship. Honig had taken over business matters in 1950, and the order he brought to the organization proved to be very important to Wright. Irving Richards, with his fine sense of intuition and uncommon insight, was willing to deal with Wright as he found him. They were life-long friends and it appears that Richards brought some stability to Wright's fragile disposition.

He had many offers from manufacturers and suppliers who wished to use his name in connection with work in which he had no part, but he never accepted the large sums which would have come his way if he had compromised the integrity of his name or his designs in such a way.

Contracts and Wright's stipulations became more uniform as he reshaped his firm. He was to receive 5%

royalty on goods sold as first class and a lesser amount on those which were second class. This arrangement was to continue until sales fell below a specified figure, after which the contract was dissolved by both parties and the design reverted to Wright. Advertising costs were to be assumed by the clients, and they were free to use his endorsing signature in all but specified cases. His signature, by contractual agreement, was to be the largest printing on the page of advertising. Wright was diligent, his staff equally so, and they policed extensive national advertising with frequency to be certain that these advertising practices were not violated.

He studied all of his business details with the same scrutiny he used in his designs. His personal attention extended to all customer relations in spite of the fact that he saw himself as an artist, not a business man. It was no small accomplishment that by his personal attention, he established a marketing practice never recognized before, that of combining name recognition with product design. The policy he established then is common now, but using his name as an endorsement was another first for Wright.

He kept a tight control on all daily concerns and in so doing, he allowed himself some generosity with contracts where it benefitted sales. When first presenting a design to a client, he was demanding in the details. However, if, at any time, a client's line met customer resistance or sales people reported slow sales, Wright contractually agreed to redesign the line or restyle items. If it appeared that an item should be added to the line, he agreed to add that design. If an item, for any reason, seemed not to be needed in a line, he allowed the client the last word in discontinuing production. He was very aware that sales drove royalties and cooperated with clients on designs where they did not compromise his concepts. If his client relationships became difficult, the fault seemed to derive from personal differences.

His sales department was small and not as structured as it appeared to be. He used "business promoters" who received a commission of 15% less specified expenses if they were solely responsible for a sale. In most cases, these promoters sold several lines in addition to Wright's. He was slightly more generous with his own small staff of sales people, saving the most concessions for them. Sales people were furnished desk space, a phone, secretarial assistance, calling cards, research assistance, training in industrial design sales practices, and access to his records of potential customers. They received 5% to 50% commission depending upon the account which they obtained and the terms of that account. Not salaried, they received

$25.00 a week as pocket expense money. Wright restricted their use of an already established house account. We must recall that these arrangements came at a time when commerce was less regulated than now and that many were willing to work at any price in times when jobs were few. Practicing economy in all ways, Wright never wasted time or ideas. In a day's progress, he used any few spare minutes to draw, scribble notes to himself, tear magazine articles or advertisements for his files, reminding himself of things admired. His own drawings never pleased him but his papers show many of the rough drafts which he made, saved against a future time when they might be used in a design.

Neither did he waste an opportunity to speak or to write and these opportunities extended beyond that of "the trade." He addressed new graduates, made store appearances as new products were introduced, never losing an opportunity to advance his work and his causes. He and his work could not be ignored for notice of it seemed to be everywhere. As early as 1937, two years before the phenomenal success of his American Modern dinnerware, he had announced that Dillon-Wells Inc. in Los Angeles was to be his representative in the entire western area. He covered his bases early.

It is true that he recolored and reshaped the home furnishings field supported by national advertising. Breaking precedent, he directed all of this material to the manufacturer and retailer as well as the final customer — and it worked. Eating from the same plates that Nelson Rockefeller used became important and we were impressed that Mamie Eisenhower liked them also. Market research had shown that young, white collar people were those who chose American Modern dinnerware. It spoke to the youth of his times who found themselves in a world less grand, less elegant than they'd expected, a new generation, with a position empowered by war and depression. Wright translated his causes and products into a message that could not be ignored.

Photographs of Wright's homes, penthouses, and apartments often appeared in home magazines, shown as a background for a new product or design or as an illustration of his doctrines put to use, promoting his work. His life was never private, but that also, was by design. He rose to every comment on his work, and it would be wrong to suggest that criticism was not made. The *New Republic* saw in American Modern "a quality of steeliness, a nudity, a hammer-like statement-like chi-chi color." In 1946 Emily Post, the acknowledged expert on manners wrote to *Time* magazine regarding a comment of Wright's which said "I want to do something practical for the housewives. The 18th century is kept alive by Emily Post." Mrs. Post's reply said that she would like to suggest that he, himself, test the "practicability of the 18th century cup whose fine and slightly flaring rim was skillfully designed to check the escape of any drop of liquid down its sides. A thick edge, especially one curving inward defies every effort of human lips to hold back the gush of liquid which dribbles down the sides, and even makes a ring in the saucer!" Responses followed in letters which the magazine printed and many came to the defense of the American Modern cups. Wright, himself could not resist the opportunity to strike back, defending his designs, while attacking Mrs. Post and her writings which represented all that he found wrong with the conventions of the day. He wrote to Henry R. Luce, the editor of *Time* magazine, "Mrs. Post is quite right in her letter to you, in that the eighteenth century cup with fine and slightly flaring rim does not drool like the heavy-edged one which curves inward but her fine tea cup requires tender care, more time in dish washing, to avoid chipping. Mrs. Post's point, I think, illustrates very well my statement that she attempts to keep the eighteenth century traditions alive in these times which can hardly be called similar. She stands for drinking tea gracefully from a fine, flaring cup (I suppose with the pinky raised — with nary a drip). Tell Emily I stand for more drooling, less fancy 'etiquette' and less housework." *Time* made much of the comments for as long as they found readers interested and Russel benefited from some free exposure, defending his work against the social graces of other days. The last word on the subject may have been Wright's as you will find it in the Iroquois section of this writing.

Always running to keep ahead of the crowd of young designers, he often won the race. He was the first to design many things: a portable radio, a radio and phonograph console, sectional upholstered furniture, spun aluminum accessories, stove to table accessories. He was the first to use rattan, hemp rope, or wood in informal serving pieces and his blonde wood furniture became the model for furniture of modern design. Add aluminum blinds, stainless steel flatware, and Melamine used for synthetic dinnerware. While involving himself with new products and new uses for them, he also was doing a great deal of custom work which would have included showrooms for manufacturers, room displays for department stores, and whole restaurant concepts. He was in charge of the Food Exhibit Building at the World's Fair in 1939, and his work on that brought him national and international notice. His contributions were in several areas: Focal Food, Focal Fashion, Guiness Stout, Mental Hygiene, and various store exhibits.

For the Campbell Soup Company, he drew a whimsical portrait of dancing vegetables which attracted many. One of the rooms which he exhibited there bore a distinct resemblance to one in his own Dragon Rock home. He was in charge of an exhibit at the Metropolitan Museum of Art which showcased the work of contemporary American industrial designers including Deskey, Dreyfuss, Rhode, Van Nessen, Teague, Bel Geddes, Loewy, and others. Organizing an exhibit with such important designers adds to our understanding of the reputation which he had achieved. With few exceptions, he attended national and international exhibits and kept copious notes which detailed his impressions, good or bad. These often found voice or print later. It is clear that he appreciated the efficiency with which the design community could come together.

At the same time, many personal awards were coming his way. His work was included in museums everywhere. None of these, however, was more important to him than the Museum of Modern Art's International Chair Exhibit in 1938, where his Cowhide chair was singled out.

Russel Wright cowhide chair. Exhibited in the Museum of Art International Chair exhibit, 1938.

Never completely satisfied, the Wrights turned their attention to a complex merchandising program called The American Way. It was 1941 and because the country was at war, the seeds of failure were built-in. The Way was to include artists, craftsmen, designers, and manufacturers who, in concert, promoted their own

home furnishings designs, all compatible with the new informal, Transitional Modern style. A jury system was to have been developed and Wright allowed only those designs he believed the best to be included. Skillfully conceived, it was perhaps overly ambitious for it became too difficult to manage sales and production at a time when shortages of materials used in the war effort as well as transportation problems limited the scope Wright had intended. It may also be true that Wright was not, by definition of his personality, able to keep control of such a project while still active in his own firm. It did fail after two years, and Wright continued to pay for the experiment out of his own funds for 10 years.

By 1951, however, Mary and Russel, had turned to another project and they threw aside established household practices, by writing the '50s handbook on housework. *A Guide to Easier Living*. Addressing efficient

Dust jacket front to *Guide to Easier Living* by Mary and Russel Wright.

housekeeping and achieving leisure by adopting business techniques and motion management, the Wrights really believed that easier living would result. "If the American home is inadequate, it is our belief that this inadequacy must be attributed to an ill-fitting and outmoded cultural pattern." They told us that housework should be put on a 40 hour work week and gave 1,000 ways to make such work easier, more rewarding, and faster. Starting with building a home, living in it, and working it, the book quickly became a bestseller and women rushed to find the easy life it promised. We were told how to make a bed in three minutes, how to make a child's room "childproof," and how to plan a living room so it would be "self-tidying." The text was accompanied by charts, check lists, and diagrams. Wright had told us that to entertain successfully involved pre-planning and participation. We would do well, he said, to make a listing of chores which needed to be done at a social occasion and, as guests arrived, ask each to choose one of them, be responsible for it, and follow through as the occasion progressed. These might include: dust off chairs, boil water, set up tables, put out beverage glasses, empty ashtrays, slice and butter muffins. The guide addressed every aspect of housekeeping spelling it out in detail and we were given efficient instructions on everything from putting groceries in cupboards to organizing spices alphabetically. It went into three printings and became the Bible of housework. If it was not a woman killer, it surely was an obsessive study which allowed little time for life other than housework or the planning of it and it is still a marvel that we bought the concept individually and as a society.

As I have written, we were text book oriented. A generation of young men were sent to college after World War II and young wives, who had put on hold the homes they would establish, joined them in the academic approach. We were not yet aware that we would need to put all this aside and go to work outside the home if our husbands were to graduate. Instead, we studied our housework, read Gilbreath's *Cheaper by the Dozen*, and measured our children's progress by Dr. Spock's writings. Our world was much different than that of our parents and we looked to new experts to show us new ways. The company was good. Our friends, those with strong tastes and slim budgets were part of "our bunch." Certainly we were part of a much larger whole and it pleased us that we had latched on to something so great and so affordable. It would take time for us to find our own focus, to laugh at our intensity, to realize that we had espoused extremity. Early lessons linger, however, and some of us never lost all of what we had taken so seriously in 1951.

It was that year, too, that Wright became the president of the Society of Industrial Designers, a distinct honor and one of which he was proud. He had never allowed himself leisure or pleasure in the company of others. He seemed to seek few friends and found fewer. His self-perception did not match actuality and when he seemed at odds with it he turned to his work, his comfort zone. He was not at ease outside that work. Anxieties and enthusiasm were tempered there and the refinement of his creed became a substitute for the personal involvement he tried to avoid. He disdained precedence and authority, limiting relationships which might involve them. Not cosmopolitan, never allowing

himself the experiences which would add social amenities to his life, he found himself not acceptable to sophisticates who ignored him as a person but respected him as a designer.

His own design community was critical. They accused him of being "too commercial," a bitter pill. It was said that he was too profit-oriented, not taking time to perfect his work, an untruth. They said he was a "gate crasher" in their midst. The life he made for himself was not an easy one and he was solitary, well known, but a stranger, even among those who admired his work. He had adopted a lonely position and held himself apart from all except those whose cause he promoted — the average man.

Espousing rebellion in design, he also accepted that position personally. A nonconformist, hard to read, his disposition was variable and he was seldom even tempered, never secure in social situations into which he was thrust. These qualities did not overshadow the depth of his care and concern for his craft nor for his prophetic vision, for things did make a difference to him and often that came between him and his contemporaries. Surely sensitive to slights and accusations, he was not allowed the easier life he proclaimed and he kept his defenses in place. He remained competitive to the bottom line, promoting himself and his work, and managed, by his own wits and skills, to fly alone at the high altitude in which he was comfortable. He did not perceive his position as a lowly one. Mary, always first in Russel's support, died in 1952, leaving him very alone and with a very young child to raise. The fun went out of his work and it was never the same. He threw himself into the only medicine he had known which was work and it sustained him. He could not reinvent himself and the relationship between his life and his work was almost seamless. He lived to work and he discovered, in 1952, that in his struggle for answers and truth, he had found his soul in his work.

Over the years, he had become hostile, a fractious law unto himself. Admitting influence in his own work, he never admitted derivation. He often believed that he saw his own work imitated by others. Alone, he became even more withdrawn, more difficult to please. His work had been his focus and later when he found his world changed, he said he felt he had left American Design at a time when it was in worse shape than he had found it. "I am sickened when I go into a home furnishing store now." After his life-long crusade, it was a hurtful admission. Discouraged, he redesigned his life, finding other outlets for old interests. Arthur Pulos said it best: "He preferred to light his way with a lamp of his own making."

**"I am more interested in nature than
any other subject."** — *Russel Wright*

He allowed himself pleasure in a very personal way as he worked in the planning of his own home and the grounds surrounding it, a retreat which had been important to him. In 1941 he and Mary had wished for a home, a weekend retreat, and had bought 79 acres of wooded mountainside in Garrison, New York, 50 miles up the Hudson River Valley from New York City. It was an expanse of abused ground, worn out from years of mining granite from an abandoned quarry but it spoke redesign to Wright who was challenged by the site, sure that with his work and energy he would be rewarded. As early as 1945 *House Beautiful* described him as a "restless, exploratory stubborn designer who likes to take long walks through the woods, wears overalls easily, reads little, and has a preference for exotic foods, especially Oriental dishes." The Garrison grounds seemed suited for this loner. Over the years it had been an easy and pleasant drive and the change from the city invigorated him as he worked physically to reclaim quarry land. For many of those years, he worked alone, felling trees, chopping and burning brush, cleaning logging sites, replanting quarry roads, and the work was cathartic. He left each weekend feeling spiritually renewed.

The reclamation was to take 30 years but he said that he gradually found his weekend work showing up unconsciously in his regular work in the city. The work at the quarry site followed the pattern of his old work habits. He studied the area as it existed and allowed his imagination to wander through all sorts of solutions for its improvement. Healing the grounds took time and as he worked with nature, he looked for ways upon which to improve it. He became a naturalist, managing to restore balance to the land, and then to enhance the beauty of it. He seemed to have a sense of the plants and animals which had been the original occupants and whose lives had been interrupted by quarry trucks. Following old animal trails rather than the truck rutted roads, he achieved theme-oriented areas. Sunset Path was a westward walk with an area to stop and follow the sun as it was going down. Morning Path, the reverse, was directed toward the east and led through a hemlock forest which dappled the sun as it rose. A Winter Walk passed through an area of evergreens and a Spring-time Walk made the most of the riot of wild flowers he found and transplanted there. Ripe berries were there for the picking. Deer Run, an easy short walk passes through the tall hemlocks along a slope of glacially deposited stones and into the Four Corners Room. Leading to the laurel field, tulip poplars, and huge oak trees, it ends at a log bridge of stepping stones. The Appalachian trail crosses the property and walking that is a special walk. On the Chestnut Oak Trail one encounters an opening which extends to a view of the Hudson River, Bear Mountain, and West Point. He softened the stone quarry walls with moss and fern plantings, making the rock outcroppings less severe. Redirecting a small stream and allowing it to fall into the quarry pool below was made magnificent by the addition of large rock ledges adding

**"These stones, these trees, have a mood; they give
me a feeling of awe and of reverence which calms
me and puts me in relation to it."** — *Russel Wright*

majesty to the effect. He called the grounds "Manitoga," home of the great spirit. Surely a good part of his own spirit is in evidence there, certainly sacred ground as it is viewed today. When he was asked how he had found such a site, he replied: "This land which I bought...was a nondescript piece of woods...the remains of firewood operations. It was uninviting, dry, and impenetrable woods, without views or vistas. Today the land contains miles of paths, many vistas of the river and mountains, a natural pool and a waterfall. I am amused and pleased to often be asked 'How did you ever find such an unusually beautiful site?'—pleased because they think that I found it this way, and therefore I know it looks natural."

Dragon Rock, the home which he placed on the quarry wall was as studied as any design work he had ever done. Others have described it as "part pavilion, part cave." Each will find his own meaning in the home and grounds, but few would argue that it was his "pleasure dome" and that the "sparkling rivulets" of the waterfall were personal indulgences, beautifully executed. He adhered to his old easier living edicts where it pleased him, and ignored them where they conflicted with the effect he wished for. The home, chameleon-like, blends with the quarry walls out of which it is cut, a placement Wright considered with care as he studied

Dragon Rock at Manitoga.
"My goal is to bring to American culture
an intimacy with nature." — *Russel Wright*

the view of the house and from the house. Nothing was left to chance as he considered the angles and sites which were possible placements, using the Oriental principles of "feng shui" as he made choices. Anchored to the quarry wall on one side, the glass walls opposite extend from the top of the house to the bottom level, opening out on a terrace, exposing the view of the waterfall, the quarry pool, and a grassy area he called "Mary's Meadow." Wild flowers are everywhere and the view of a four acre laurel field changes with the seasons. The flat roof, planted with vines blend the home with the woods that surround it and similar vines drape the walk way between the house and the studio.

The interior, a departure from tradition, is an extension of the view and the outdoors blurs into the interior with rooms on eleven levels which are joined by steps leading from the entrance to the den, down to the two level living room, and on below to a high balcony into the dining and kitchen area. There are few absolute lines of demarcation, except for those in the bedroom wing where a sunken bath tub fills from a wall of rock, an interior waterfall of sorts, reflected in the floor made of seeded Murano glass tile in rich shades of blue set in vivid blue mortar. Doors there, open to a secluded patio. The great stone fireplace is actually cut out of a rock deposit and rises above the roof line. He chose not to disturb the rock formation, not wishing to add artificiality in any way that was not necessary. The stucco walls are a forest green with hemlock needles pressed in, presenting a facade which unites it with the hemlock grove across the quarry pool. Butterflies, wild flowers, tall grasses, and ferns are embedded in lighted panels and sliding doors, hiding necessary storage space, bringing the outdoors inside using a decorative accent. Other storage space is secreted behind copper faced sliding panels, all are concessions to the use of metal and synthetics, artistically combined, all focused on native plantings. Steps which unite the floors circle a tree which grows from the dining area to the top of the house, actually supporting the beams overhead. The steps are carved from the stone floors and have no railings, no hint of construction outside that which nature would have intended. In the spring, wild flowers grow in pockets at the steps but those change with the seasons. Ferns were favored. Rya rugs resembling pads of moss covered the floors when Wright furnished it. The giant glass walls are hung with ribbons of various colors in the spring, threaded fabric in a loose weave in the autumn, and the light refracted by them softens the rock walls and floors. Furnishings changed seasonally and added interest as they often were of Wright's own work, sometimes the work of others whom he contacted, saying that he was building an experimental house and asking if they would be pleased to donate items or materials in a project that would show-case them. Many did so. The DuPont Company sent synthetic panels with interesting lighted self pattern which divided a bedroom from the hall as well as curtains loosely interlacing clear and colored synthetics allowing for both light and privacy.

Wright had built his Shangri-la and he cared for it and the grounds surrounding it all of his later years. If others compared it to Falling Waters, Frank Lloyd Wright's masterpiece, it angered Russel, who had made Dragon Rock his own personal statement. "I wanted to prove that a house of good contemporary design could be as livable as traditional ones; that it could be romantic, sentimental, even lovable despite the use of improved technology. My second aim in designing this extensive project was to tie the house to the land by using only the native materials outside as well as inside." Today the home melds into the grounds as if it had always been there, which would have been as he hoped. It is certain that he found personal satisfaction and a never before achieved ease there. He had carved a second chance out of this land and out of his dreams and he found contentment in it. It may well be his most important design. You will find pictures of the home in the March 16, 1962, issue of *Life* magazine.

In 1955 Wright was retained by the United States State Department to survey the possibilities for developing cottage industries in South East Asia. He traveled extensively throughout the area, exploring native handicrafts in Japan, Taiwan, Cambodia, and Vietnam. He advised these workers on ways to perfect their work, how it might be distributed and sold in efficient ways. Establishing centers for the manufacturing of these products, he made an important contribution to these cottage-styles industries. He had his own American Way experiences upon which to draw as he looked to these problems, and it gave him pleasure to return to his old social concerns. Finding these meetings meaningful, Japan asked him to return in 1965 to work for over 100 companies in the same advisory role. Without question, the benefits to Wright were rich with personal rewards for it gave him more opportunities to observe the Orient, its people, and its art, another chance to crusade for democracy. Later he joined with the Johnson administration to establish a park beautification program, forming an association with public lands and their reclamation for useful means. Old lion that he may have been, he once refused to work on a beautification project when he saw that housing and food were being neglected in the area. This Washington work won him several awards and he was never far from involvement with public lands from that time on.

Interestingly, he never lost touch with the good life he had urged us to achieve. Returning from a far eastern trip he reported that he was surprised to hear several of the younger men say that their dream was to have a Japanese wife, a Chinese cook, and an American home. He thought the State Department should exploit this significance for he believed that the American home was the ideal of all the rest of the world, as original as jazz, as impressive as skyscrapers and highways, and had as great potential as atomic energy. Having achieved so much, he said, we still should resist sameness. "Living in standard designed houses, using mass-produced objects and mass communicated ideas, it is not easy to make our homes individual." Our homes, he added, should differ in detail, but not in essence, spirit, or personality. He felt it to be wrong that homes were still considered the women's domain (and he published an 11 item tongue-in-cheek list to prove it). He believed that other family members should be more involved in its creation and upkeep. Again, he showed his concern for others: "With all our material possessions we still find families drifting apart, divorces increasing, and boredom setting in. We aren't doing enough culturally with the things we have. Now I realize that I have used an old fashioned word. Like diligence, sentiment, charity, and morality, the word culture seems to make moderns squirm with embarrassment. All the same, culture is exactly what I mean. I mean beauty for its own sake. I mean creative outlets for our interests and energy. I mean whatever excites you, involves you, soothes you, renews you, reflects you, and makes you forget that other thing that excites, involves, soothes, renews, etc. — i.e. money. This is culture in my book and it can add an interesting individuality to your home. This is also involvement. Each person with the others and all with the home. It is participation with each other in common interests." His remarks are detailed and lengthy, extending to the need of each individual for space of his own in the home and the respect which is due that space. All this came at a time when his product association was completed, showing again, the depth of his feelings about the human condition and trying, once more, to give voice to the life experiences he felt so important.

Closing his own studio in 1967, he never separated himself from old interests. He became involved in the reclamation of ground fill areas in the Garrison area and using his old theatrical experience, he designed and directed two local festivals at Garrison which exhibited beauty resulting from restoration. A new sense of community, one he had never known before, united him with others of similar interests and he found in the Garrison area, the place for himself he had never recognized or accepted before. His old medicine still at work, he had thrown himself into new projects and found a new life, a new art form.

Wright's death came in 1976, and that was only a short time before his work was sought after for the "second time around." He was 72 and had fought cancer for a year before he died of a heart attack. Many feel that this work was timeless and that those who found it first never allowed it to fall from favor. He had been too important to our generation, touching our lives with beauty, assuring us of the worth of our ways. His work brightened our days as well as our homes with an art that concealed art and his legacy to us may well be that he made us aware of the need for beauty in our daily life. No other such influence had come into his time and the changes he made were ingrained in our lives. We were not alone. Major museum exhibits have centered upon Wright's work and it has been included in many permanent exhibits as well. We should not be surprised. His life influences spoke to our times as few others had done and his place in the design history of our times continues to influence us as we examine the enduring impressions he made upon his century.

SELLING HIMSELF, RUSSEL WRIGHT EPHEMERA

Condition is very important with these fragile items and this pricing applies to items in good to fine condition. Our position on original magazine advertising has changed from our 1990 judgements. Interesting and informative, new collectors often refer to it as research material. While not a substitute for file documentation, it does add to our understanding of Wright's work and we list a price range here for the first time.

Guide to Easier Living, first edition
with dust jacket..$150.00 – 200.00
Guide to Easier Living, second printing ....$125.00 – 150.00
Guide to Easier Living,
with autograph, either edition.....................................$225.00
Iroquois Pottery Advertising Ashtrays............$150.00 – 200.00
Iroquois Pottery or other Advertising Plates ..$150.00 –200.00
Brochures ....$35.00 – 45.00
Original cartons ....$35.00 – 45.00
Cookware signs, large and complex ....$300.00+
Full-page color advertisements ....$5.00 – 10.00
Black & white advertisements ....$3.00 – 5.00

A meal is done ahead and left in the refrigerator. Labels make it easier.

Russel Wright serves a "don't get up" meal through the kitchen pass-through.

Spices are easy to find with shelves labeled alphabetically.

More on Marks

Our new study of marks adds much to what we have known, so much that we must develop a new set of guides to allow for new marks to be included in the numbered series which were shown in the 1985 dinnerware book. In an attempt to preserve the order which was previously established, the newly added marks will be shown with the 1985 mark, but will be listed with a letter. For example, if mark #1 is an American Modern Steubenville mark shown before as mark 1, any additional marks would be 1a, 1b, 1c.

Dating marks and understanding the information in them is made even more challenging by the introduction of many new marks presented here. There remain minor differences in some of them — the addition of U.S.A. or the presence of a period, trivial to some, very important to others. I am pleased that our search has yielded so many additions for it indicates the depth of our interest.

In 1985, we felt safe in the position that there was only one Steubenville, American Modern mark. We were wrong. Added here is 1a, a new mark incorporating USA as part of the mark. Another, 1b, shows a variance in size and placement of "USA." There is said to be a slight variation in the letters "S" in Russel and that letter in Steubenville, but the variance is so small that it does not reproduce as I would like it to do. Be aware, as you study these marks, that some minor variation can be accounted for by mold ware. Both marks are incised and some irregularity may have resulted from that process. The pottery was handmade, and glazes often ran into the incised mark, all but obscuring parts of it. Not all marks are as pristine as we would like.

Most American Modern is marked — unless the item was too small for a mark. Mark 1c identifies Wright's American Modern glassware, made by Old Morgantown. It is a gold sticker. In the American Modern photographs you will find a bowl with an experimental glaze and mark. Several of these in different colors have been found but none were clear enough to reproduce here. They were numbered with meanings only to those concerned at the time. If you find one, treat it gently for they are rare. I should be careful not to assume that there are no other American Modern/Steubenville marks. As I write, I expect to hear from some mark researcher who has found a Steubenville mark with periods after the "USA." It is predictable.

Russel Wright
MFG BY STEUBENVILLE

Mark 1

Russel Wright
MFG BY STEUBENVILLE
USA

Mark 1a

Russel Wright
MFG BY STEUBENVILLE
USA

Mark 1b

AMERICAN MODERN
by *Russel Wright*
HAND BLOWN

Mark 1c

The Harker Mark 2 remains the only mark reported. It also is an incised mark and glaze runs did alter signature and company name. Harker had a short history and it is possible that our findings may be limited to the mark. Let me know if you can add to this information.

HARKERWARE
by *Russel Wright*

Mark 2

Surely, I thought, the six marks we had seen on Iroquois would be the total, but they were not. There is a 4a which is very close to the 4 mark but has a slightly different "I" in Iroquois. This difference adds to the seven Iroquois marks. The 3 through 8 marks are as we have known them, and it seems that we have placed them in the order of their production. The first two marks appear identical except for the letter "I" in Iroquois. The 3 mark with the "Loopy I" as we have named it, is the earlier of the two and the 4 mark with the straight "I" followed soon after. These will be found in dark blue and brown on the heavier, foamy early ware. Later marks, including the word "Casual" have been found in varying sizes even on identically sized pieces. Additionally they are found in several colors, usually pink, green, or brown. Not only the redesigned ware carries this late "Casual" mark. Any piece made late in production, even of original design, may have been so marked. The small code numbers contain manufacturing information which we still cannot decipher. Comments in the files which refer to marks mention "eye appeal," and that may be more of a factor with these marks than we had first thought. Only the smallest of the Iroquois items are not marked, but they are difficult to read on some of the darker colors.

In 1985, we had three Paden City/Justin Tharaud/Highlight marks. Now there are three more. Because there seems to be no better place to present it, 9a is added to show the sticker on the Paden City Snow Glass. 10a shows no period after Pat and shows the abbreviation for "pending" to be more uniform. 11a eliminates all information below Wright's signature.

Mark 9   Mark 9a

Mark 10   Mark 10a

Mark 11   Mark 11a

Mark 3

Mark 4

Mark 5

Mark 6

Mark 7

Mark 8

The 12 Sterling mark is usually found incised but we know that it is also found in raised relief as is the 13 mark. Much Sterling is not marked and some of that which is marked is done so imperfectly that glaze fills the incised letter. Paper stickers replaced marks in some cases, appearing on items that were known to have had the incised mark. Both marks 12 and 13 are marks which Sterling used on the early line done for their customers. Our new mark 13a is the mark which Wright used in patterns which he did as part of his whole concept theme for his own customers. This 13a is used on the Polynesian shape. Other stamps used in the Wright/Client concept as opposed to Wright/Sterling may be found.

STERLING CHINA
by
Russel Wright

Mark 12

STERLING by *Russel Wright* CHINA

Mark 13

Mark 13a

Mark 16

Mark 16b

SHINKO SHIKKI

Mark 16a

Knowles patterns are marked with a gold stamp and identification is made easier because the pattern is usually named in the mark. Our Knowles markings remain as we have known them.

Mary Wright's signature changed from item to item, time to time, and it seems that she was developing her own marks. Do not be suspicious if you find a signature different from the one shown in mark 17. We can expect, however, that this mark 17 signature is the one which she had come to use as standard.

Russel Wright
by *Knowles*
Queen Annes Lace
MADE IN U.S.A.

Mark 14

Knowing that little Yamato Theme Formal and Informal was made lulled me into a not-so-safe position for we now have more Yamato marks. The mark 15 Stoneware/Informal shown here lines-up Wright's signature. 15a may be a rejected mark for it does not emphasize the signature as Wright would have required. 16a is the raised mark found on the Shinko Shikki enameled Bakelite which was part of the Theme Formal line. 16b is the stickered mark found on Yamato glassware in the Theme Formal line.

Country Gardens

Mary Wright

Mark 17

The 18a signature is an early one, used on wood items done out of Wright's own workshop in addition to its use on Oceana. Both 18 and 19 are Klise Oceana marks. Signatures on these wood items may not be all-inclusive. They all represent early work and much of it came at a time when Wright was developing his signature as integral to his designs.

Russel Wright

Mark 18

Russel Wright

Mark 18a

Mark 15

Mark 15a

designed
by
RUSSEL
WRIGHT
"Oceana"
carved
wooden
ware
made
KLISE

Mark 19

29

More on Marks

The marks on Wright's synthetic dinnerware, 20, 21, 22, and 23 seem standard — for now. We have added two Ideal Ware marks, both found on the child's toy pieces and name them 23a and b.

Russel Wright
RESIDENTIAL
by
Northern
BOSTON 27

Mark 20

Russel Wright
FLAIR
by
Northern
BOSTON 27
2

Mark 21

DESIGNED BY
Russel Wright
FOR
HOME DECORATORS. INC.
NEWARK
NEW YORK STATE

Mark 22

MELADUR
by
Russel Wright
PATENT APPLIED FOR

Mark 23

Russel Wright
IDEAL
MADE IN USA

Mark 23a

Russel Wright
IDEAL
MADE IN USA

Mark 23b

Bauer items are marked as shown in mark 24, lightly incised with the signature sometimes filled in with the extremely heavy glaze. Look for vase bottoms to be heavily irregular, Wright's concept of a built-in flower frog. That often left little room for the signature but is an identifiable feature.

Russel Wright
BAUER

Mark 24

Mark 25a is the Hull Stainless Steel mark as shown on the Hull Pinch line made by them in Japan. That

ware made by Hull in this country shows the signature, the words "Hull Stainless," and a patent number. All are the same Pinch line, reflecting only a change of location for Hull.

JAPAN HULL STAINLESS *Russell Wright*

Mark 25

Marks 26, 27, and 28 are marks used on Imperial Glassware made to accompany the Iroquois line. As late as this, 1946, the signature was still developing as shown here. Marks 26 and 27 are black, with gold metallic printing on Mark 27. Mark 28 is a bright red with white lettering and banner. All are enlarged for clarity.

IMPERIAL
AMERICAN HAND MADE
by
Russel Wright

Mark 26

Imperial
BY
Russel Wright
U.S.A.
HAND MADE

Mark 27

IMPERIAL
BY
Russel Wright U.S.A.
HAND MADE IN U.S.A.

Mark 28

IMPERIAL
AMERICAN HAND MADE
by
Russel Wright

Mark 29

Heywood Wakefield Furniture, made for only a year, was marked in various ways, all incorporating the Mark 30 which was a standard mark of the company. All was to show Wright's name but we should study any highly styled veneered furniture for the Heywood Wakefield mark.

HEYWOOD-WAKEFIELD
HW
EST. 1826

Mark 30

The Conant Ball mark is shown here as Mark 31. This is burnt into the wood, perhaps inside a drawer or in an otherwise inconspicuous place.

Mark 31

Mark 32 is the Statton Furniture mark and is found in very small amounts due to limited production.

Mark 32

A bright blue sticker, the American Way mark, incorporated the name of the designer in each product. This 33 mark was used in several sizes in proportion to the product. It dates from 1941.

Mark 33

The Sovereign Pottery Mark 34 identifies the pottery made in the "Wright Shape" as first designed for Knowles. Some time after Knowles production was discontinued, Wright gave this shape to Sovereign Potteries in Canada, a firm with family connections. The glazes were Sovereign's, not Knowles, and probably not Wright's.

Mark 34

The ware only now being found and marked as International China Company is in the Knowles Esquire shape. It is identified as Mark 35. This is believed to represent remainders taken by Wright when his contract with Knowles ended. It does not amount to any large sum, nor does it imply a different line than we have known it in the Knowles patterns. This seems to have been a convenient way of rescuing stock for which there were no orders.

Mark 35

The variant Mark 36 signature is as found on early Century Metalcraft items. It shows clearly that Wright was changing his signature/trademark as he developed his products. Contrast it with the early 18a and the polished 37 which became the most popular signature of the 1940s.

Mark 36

Mark 37

The square printed sticker which is enlarged here is Mark 38, one of the earliest of all these marks. It is a 1⅛" square, used on several different items all produced from early Russel Wright Inc. or Russel Wright Accessory Company. It followed a mark which was the initials "RW," as well as Wright's name spelled in block letters. Mark 39 is a 1950s mark not used on Oceana.

Mark 38

Mark 39

Color Charts

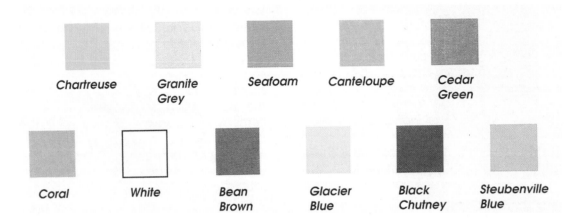

Chartreuse   Granite Grey   Seafoam   Canteloupe   Cedar Green

Coral   White   Bean Brown   Glacier Blue   Black Chutney   Steubenville Blue

American Modern Dinnerware

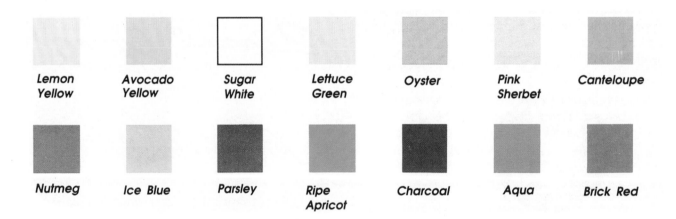

Lemon Yellow   Avocado Yellow   Sugar White   Lettuce Green   Oyster   Pink Sherbet   Canteloupe

Nutmeg   Ice Blue   Parsley   Ripe Apricot   Charcoal   Aqua   Brick Red

Iroquois Casual China

Ivy Green   Shell Pink   Suede Grey   Straw Yellow   Cedar Brown

Sterling China Company

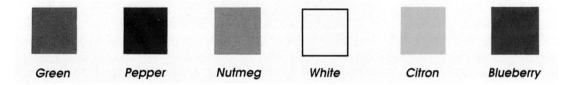

Paden City Dinnerware

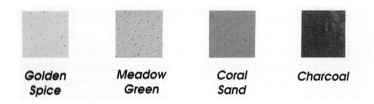

Harker White Clover

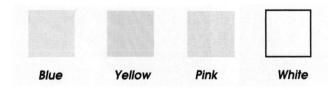

Knowles Esquire

New Uses for Metals

Wright's work as a home furnishings designer brought him immediate recognition with little time for breath after his stage-set experience. His earliest commercial work was with various metals, involving pewter, copper, brass, chromium, and spun aluminum, often combined with the use of organic or ceramic materials, a departure from most of the metal work of the 1930s.

While the work was extensive, the large body of it was done under difficult conditions. The Great Depression, closely followed by war-time restrictive use of metals limited the amount of work which Wright could accomplish. Additionally, most of the metal work was done out of his coach house work area with limited facilities and limited experience. Add to that, the fact that the earliest metals were sold store to store as Mary could manage. Shops and stores required back up inventories and were constantly asking for more of these inexpensive items. Wright's concept of the line differed from that of decorators/buyers and he tried to achieve variety often making few of a kind in favor of depth of production. Proven selling items were repeated as space and time allowed but the tendency, in the beginning was to produce a shallow line of many items. Refining it was left for another day. That might have been accomplished if production had not been aborted quickly by war-time shortages, but by that time, others had joined in the prosperity of spun aluminum and Wright never returned to it after World War II.

What we can definitely attribute to Wright's early metal work, is metal marked with his block signature or his initials RW. Other items bear a paper sticker similar to #38 in the marks section. Seemingly identical items with no markings, may be the result of worn or washed stickers. All else must remain as suspect in spite of similarity of line or concept.

As we identify these Wright metal pieces, we will do well to avoid the Art Deco look. Wright's work used less of that style and leaned strongly toward the amorphous modern style which he translated in his own ways.

Chase Corn Set

Working with chromium or chromium-plated steel, Wright's metal and the treatment of it fell into direct competition with the more expensive and formal silver. It was more affordable, easier to care for, and the sleek lines appealed to those who admired silver produced in our own colonial period. It was possible to buy chrome with less expense and use it with less concern. Some of that work as well as items involving pewter, copper, and brass was contracted out, too difficult to handle in his limited coach house facilities. This early work amounted to small lines covering small time spans and representative items are difficult to add to a collection. The aluminum was easier to work with and a great deal more was produced. That early coach house metal period was an exciting time for the Wrights.

Ad in *House Beautiful*, April 1936.

The very limited and very early work included the masks of famous people which were mentioned in the biographical material. These were sure-fire attention getters and those who watched Wright's coach house show windows were certain to watch for the latest caricature. At the same time, he was producing several groups of animals and these remain among the most sought after of his work. Made of various metals, they are found with his RW initials, sometimes placed in obscure places. Of various sizes, most are substantially weighty with amorphic lines. Whimsical, they appear to have been named with tongue in cheek, often with meanings known only to Mary and Russel.

Another animal group, a Noah's Ark assortment, consisted of an elephant, seal, lion, a hippo with a cigarette holder in his stomach, and seal bookends sitting on black glass sea. These may be more difficult to recognize or find than the circus animals and no information exists except for this listing. None have been reported and it would appear that they may have been made in even smaller amounts than the circus group. A third group of animals only slightly less easy to locate would include tropical bird centerpieces, horse and turtle dove place card holders, a dachshund desk set, a penguin and swan nut cups. The swan nut cups are the most often found of all the animals, but they are often found in bad condition. Salted nuts have left them pitted and the bowl finish is often found with damage. One in good condition is to be prized, as are all of these animals. So few have been found that it is again necessary to show catalog prints to illustrate them.

Animals!
Libbilou horse bookend, Whoozoo seal paperweight in gold finish, and swan nut cup.

There was more early coach house work, of course, and it was an exciting time for the Wrights. Early custom work, done as one of a kind for wealthy clients or for firms with special needs, was a part of the early '30s production and it remains true that we may never know the extent of that work. The Bain Marie and the Samovar, both custom pieces were very special examples. The Samovar was Wright's adaptation of an old Russian Samovar and was well insulated to protect furniture. The urn was fitted with a "scientific percolator contraption" and a cover placed over the top of the urn. Coffee could then be drawn from the spigot below. If you wished to use it for tea, the urn was used for hot water and "strong brew" kept in a "very amusing-looking teapot which rested snugly on the top of the urn so that it is kept warm." Wright fashioned the piece for Emaline Johnson of the Johnson pharmaceutical family. The Bain Marie was designed for a member of the Vanderbilt family and came with or without a base which could be used as a buffet table griddle. It is certain that other such pieces were done during this time and a buffet popcorn popper may be an example of that work. Complete with a stove, heat adjuster, and snuffer, the top half was said to be a sphere "reminding you of St. Peter's dome or the White House." Protruding from the top was a handle with a walnut knob which controlled a propeller inside the mechanism. The corn popped as the handle turned. Two walnut side handles applied to the bucket made all ready for serving. It was said to have been inspired by a music box! Since file information referred to the clients for which these pieces were made, it was first believed that they were one-of-a-kind commissioned pieces. Subsequently received advertising material, however, describes details such as those just stated and it now seems possible that these may have been items made to order for other clients as well.

Wright's designs for the Chase Brass and Chrome Co. was very fine work, for Chase showcased the work of the best designers of the times. It was not their custom to use the designer's name in their advertising and that practice has left collectors confused as to Wright's work for them. All Chase designs bear their own mark, not Wright's signature or initials.

**Spun aluminum mint julep set
with cocktail shaker.**

Wright's work with Chase dates from 1935 to 1946, war-time years, and both the designer and Chase were restricted in the use of metal during those years. As proposed and accepted contractually, in 1935, Wright

agreed to submit designs from which 10 would be selected by Chase. He was not to design similar work for another manufacturer but he was permitted to work with lamps which were already in his own early chrome production. By the terms of the agreement, Chase was to hold the patents for all the designs of which they approved, but all rejected designs were to revert to Wright. The short list which Chase gave to Wright suggested items they would like to consider: candle holder, mint julep set, baby cactus pot, deep casserole, flower bowl, hanging flower vase, over bed lamp, desk lamp with side arm, curved bed lamp with side arm of brass pewter, vanity lamp, ashtray, fish tank, and bamboo vase. This listing takes on meaning since we know that some of the items, rejected by Chase, did, later appear in Wright's own line.

Chase researcher, Richard Kilbride in his Art Deco chrome book fills in the missing blanks in our file information and we are able to use his listing to identify Wright's work with that company. Kilbride's documentation fails to identify Wright's Bain Marie as the one made by Chase. It is possible that Wright's piece was developed for another source. Wright's Chase designs as presented by Kilbride consist of:

#09014 Blue glass chrome-trimmed coaster/tray to accompany pancake set
#09015 Tray to sphere sugar and pitcher set (*#9091*)
#17108 Antarctic ice bowl with tongs
#28002 Ice bowl with tongs
#28003 Pancake & corn set
#28004 Salt & pepper spheres to *#28003* pancake set
#28005 Pitcher to *#28003* pancake/corn set
#90025 Devonshire beer pitcher
#90046 Tray to liqueur set (cups not Wright's design) This tray may be the *#9014* tray.
#90071 Cocktail ball
#90072 Olympia saucer (underplate to cocktail ball *#90071*)
#90073 Individual coffee set
#90078 Sugar sphere
#90161 Salt & pepper spheres (May be the *#28004* set.)

From 1940 to 1944, Wright is known to have done some accessory work for Century Metalcraft. Given war year's production, it is doubtful that much work resulted but prototypes and some samplings. Tumblers, including old fashioned glasses and pilsners were listed in the contract, as were a punch bowl and cups, a cheese board, an ice bucket, a 10" salad bowl, ashtray, 8½" salad plate, an 11" centerpiece, and a cocktail shaker.

No where in these metal listings is there a spot into which we can place the crystal-handled chrome salad servers with absolute certainty. For a time, we placed them as part of Wright's glass work but continued to question their identity. It now seems probable that they were part of his own early chrome work.

Out distancing all of Wright's early work, that which was done in spun aluminum took Wright from his shallow metal line into an extended production and gave him recognition beyond decorators and buyers in fashionable boutiques. It was a benchmark in his work. This new metal seemed born out of America's union with technology for it had been first used in manufacturing, finding its way into kitchens in the twenties. Wright was directly responsible for translating the material into high-style informal pieces, brought out of that kitchen and into the informal entertaining world of the 1930s. It was an easy turn for Wright for he took this less expensive metal, much more manageable and with permanent integral color, and turned it into a completely new product. It was the first of his "firsts." Now, with a material that required little more than a spinning lathe, he could achieve a larger line with the depth for restocking inventories. Larger orders with re-orders could be written. Each order brought a suggestion for a slightly different item and the line grew like a spring garden. No one seemed to notice that it scratched easily and dented often. If they did, they were told that plain steel wool rubbed in the direction of the spinning grooves would erase scratching and keep the aluminum bright. Recognized as the pioneer in this field, he was soon visited by the Aluminum Company of America people who wanted to see this new accessory line for themselves. They entered the market with their own Kensington Ware, but Wright was the undisputed leader in this spun aluminum accessory field. This work brought many clients to his door, many with interests beyond spun aluminum.

With a changed production, new business practices were quickly put into place. The line was divided into three categories which included a stove to tableware group, an informal serving accessory group, and an interior accessory group including household items such as lamps, smoking accessories, and book ends. A sales catalog, for the first time, seemed important. Wright came to know the problems of a manufacturer, a salesman, and a distributor, all good experience for complicated times ahead. He made as many items as he could imagine and Mary took as many orders as he could make. She was making store demonstrations, organizing and executing sales coordination, and composing free advertising for customers. They needed help. Mary Ryan, who was well acquainted with Wright's work and with national advertising agreed to

distribute the new articles. She was replaced soon for it was at this point where Wright's career crossed that of Irving Richards and out of their joint venture came the Raymor Company.

**Early spun aluminum cheese board,
Simtex Modern Cloths.**

Irving Richards said later that it all started with a cheese board and that from the beginning they could not make enough cheese boards or enough variants of them. They bloomed like dandelions into a larger line than either Wright or Richards had expected. All was to be sold as "open stock" with interchangeable usage though an ensemble concept was suggested. It proved to be a concept Wright would return to many times. A "sixtette group" was offered at a savings for the customer. Since this reduced the retailer's profit (but increased the designer's profit) retailers were given a 60 cents incentive refund on all sixtette sales in order to guarantee their mark-up. These sixtette sets were composed of a bun warmer, ice pail set, ring canape tray, buffet platter, sandwich humidor, and a double decker stand. Sold as a group they were priced at $10.95. Individually, they were $1.95. Other ensembles were called Sunday Supper, Beer Buffets, Cocktail Hour, Midnight Snack, Popcorn Picnics, Sunday Breakfast, After Bridge. These ensemble names, all Mary's choices, gave the Wrights an even more important sales tool for the future.

It is not difficult to understand the attraction of this new metal. With slightly exaggerated forms, it seemed to flow into spherical shapes, circular lines, curvaceous corners. Only the material itself limited the new forms. Colorless, and easy on the eyes, not bold or hard, it quickly made a place for itself.

A complete listing of the spun aluminum is impossible, but we are able to add many pictures to those which have been shown before. Do not assume, however, that these are all that may be found for the line changed

**Spun aluminum
Frankie and Johnny beer set and pitcher.**

Spun aluminum ice pail.

constantly. Most of these items are signed with the Russel Wright name in block letters, but, as with his other metal, it may take a search to locate it. On some covered items, the mark is on the underside of the cover, a potential problem for those owning only the bottom section. On cheese boards or sandwich humidors a red ink stamp may be found on the wood. Navy and white labels as well as string tags could still be in place, if you are lucky!

Plantene with a ripple finish of uneven circular lines deeply engraved upon a heavier gauge aluminum was a line different from the larger body of aluminum work. The surface of the item was burnished to a very bright sheen, giving it a "liquid glow resembling quicksilver." Supporting sales information said that it could be given the same care as spun aluminum and that the burnished luster would last indefinitely. Very little plantene has been found and reported, but the files list the following items:

Chinese bowl with cane handle, 6½"
Syrup set with 1½ pint pitcher and 7½" tray
Ball pitcher with reed handle, 2¼ qt.
Thermos, 1½ quart with cover and bowl
Punch bowl, blond maple handles, 7", 6 qt.
Ladle for punch bowl
Four piece casserole pot and cover, liner and cover, walnut handles, 1½ quart
Fruit basket, 11", light reed handle
Round tray/server with reed handle, 15"
Round tray/server with reed handle, 12"
Tray, blond maple handles, 21"
Ice bucket and tongs, light reed or maple handles
Bamboo handled salad fork and spoon
Two-tiered tidbit tray with rattan handles
Cheese and cracker board with maple cutting slab, 13"
Large ball vase, 11"
Condiment pitchers with blond maple handle, 5 oz., 3 oz., 2 oz.
Beverage set with six-cup pitcher, 16" tray, light cane handles
Nested bowl set 10", 9", 7", sold separately or as a set, all with light cane handles
Bowls, 11", 9½", 7"
Mint julep or highball tumbler, 5"
Water goblet/old fashioned glass, 3"
Service plate/canape platter, 10½"
Candy dish, blond maple handles, 7½" x 3"

Be cautions as you examine a possible Plantene item. Each of these above items has a duplicate in the regular spun aluminum line.

The spun aluminum line which Wright produced was his ticket to the future, but WW II brought an abrupt stop to this work. It had achieved local, even national distribution for him and he enjoyed an up-and-coming reputation for quality and excellence. It set his informal concepts in place and by working with this new, affordable material he was able to further identify with the people of average means for whom he would design in the future. It had been called "the age of metal in design" and it never regained its popularity after the war. His own work, however, set his course and it held much promise.

We are able to picture parts of several early Wright Accessory catalogs here. These are photos of photos and the written description may be difficult to impossible to read. Because of that, we also add all available price listings with item identification. There will be some overlapping of items, but there is enough additional information to justify inclusion.

ENTERTAIN IN A SMART WAY WITH RUSSEL WRIGHT ACCESSORIES

SUNDAY NIGHT SUPPER Includes: No. 98 and 104 for cheese and crackers; No. 156 and 157 for pretzels, pickels and salami; No. 158 for eggs or meat; No. 140 for ice cream or fruit; No. 111, 126 and 152 for salad; No. 153 for spaghetti, curry or chop suey; No. 139 and 151 for vegetables, soup or meat pies; No. 130 or 152 for serving plates; No. 127 and 147 for hors d'oeuvres; No. 120 for nuts; No. 124 for tidbits, sandwiches; No. 170 for potato chips; No. 70, 128, 137, 138, and 110 for beverages; No. 149 and 114 "carry-alls" for serving drinks, ice, bottles, etc.

BEER BUFFET Includes: No. 156 and 157 for pretzels; No. 70, 143, 110 and 128 for beer; No. 137 for cooling beer; No. 153 for sauerkraut and hot dogs; No. 130 for serving plates; No. 124 for canapes, sandwiches; No. 87 for pickles or hot dogs; No. 98 and 104 for cheese and crackers; No. 111 and 152 for potato salad; No. 170 for pretzels or potato chips; No. 172 from which to serve.

COCKTAIL HOUR Includes: No. 100, 110A for cocktails; No. 146 for punch; No. 70, 102, 110, No. 143 and 114 for stronger drinking; No. 98, 104 and 124 for cheese, sandwiches or canapes; No. 127, 147 for hors d'oeuvres; No. 156 and 157 for pretzels; No. 172 from which to serve; No. 87, 138 and 174 for ice.

MIDNIGHT SNACK Includes: No. 72 for fruit; No. 98, 104 for cheese and crackers; No. 148 for bar le duc; No. 158 for bacon and eggs; No. 110 for drinks or milk; No. 172 from which to serve.

SWEDISH SPREAD Includes: No. 127 and 147 for hors d'oeuvres; No. 158 for meats; No. 111, 126 and 152 for salads; No. 153 and 154 for serving spaghetti, salads or fruits No. 139 and 151 hot hors d'oeuvres; No. 87 and 138 for pickels and olives; No. 146 for punch; No. 70, 102, 110, 143 and 128 for stronger beverages; No. 130 for serving plates; No. 124 for tidbits; No. 98 and 104 for cheeses, breads and crackers; No. 172 from which to serve.

SUNDAY BREAKFAST Includes: No. 158 for bacon, eggs, ham, hash and pancakes; Nos. 176, 177, 178 for keeping toast or rolls warm; No. 140 to keep grapefruit or berries cold; No. 151 for cereals; No. 154 for berries or sliced fruit; No. 148 for English muffins or breakfast rolls with jam and marmalade; No. 153 shaker for sprinkling cinnamon and powdered sugar; Nos. 111, 126 salt shakers.

AFTER BRIDGE Includes: No. 100, 102, 110, 143 and 128 for beverages; No. 98, 104 and 124 for cheese, sandwiches and canapes; No. 156 and 157 for pretzels; No. 170 for potatoe chips; No. 172 from which to serve; No. 149 general "carry-all."

PORCH PICNIC Includes: No. 149 for easy service; No. 146 to protect your lemonade, punch, iced tea or iced coffee from the insects; No. 140 to keep your ice cream cold; No. 138 and 87 for olives and pickels; No. 158 for cold meats; No. 153 for spaghetti or salad; No. 111, 154 and 152 for salads; No. 151 and 139 for hot food; No. 130 and 152 plates for unbreakable useage; No. 170 for pretzels or potato chips; No. 70, 110, 143 and 128 for beverages; No. 172 from which to serve.

COUNTRY MEAL Includes: No. 139 and 151 for vegetables, stews, etc.; No. 154 for berries, rice, etc.; No. 152 and 111 for salads; No. 153 for spaghetti, curry, chop suey and vegetables; No. 150 for steamed clams or oysters on half shell; No. 110 for lemonade, ice water, etc.; No. 158 for bacon and eggs, fried eggs, creamed eggs, meats; No. 140 for grape fruit, berries, ice cream, jellied soups; No. 127 and 147 for hors d'oeuvres; Nos. 139, 151, 176, 177, 178 to keep foods hot.

TENNIS REFRESHMENTS Includes: No. 146 for lemonade, iced coffee or tea; No. 174 for hot dogs; No. 170 for potatoe chips, small cakes and crackers, pretzels and peanuts; No. 138 for olives; No. 87 for pickels; No. 182 for sandwiches; No. 137 for cooling bottles; No. 124 for tidbits; No. 127 for relishes; No. 143 for beverages; No. 172 for serving from the sidelines; No. 149 for carrying things to the court.

IMPROMPTU GUESTS Includes: No. 114, 149 and 172 for a quick set-up; No. 138 and 87 for olives and pickels; No. 156 and 157 for pretzels; No. 170 for potato chips, crackers; No. 153 for spaghetti; No. 111 and 152 for salad; No. 151 and 139 for serving hot food right from the stove; No. 70, 110, 143 and 128 for beverages; No. 158 for cold cuts; No. 154 for fruit and desserts; No. 98, 104 and 124 for cheeses and crackers; No. 148 for rolls or crackers with cream cheese and jams.

Various group suggestions as listed in *New York Times* magazine, Nov. 20, 1932.

Two table settings.
See catalog for item identification.

Spun aluminum two-tiered server.

Spun aluminum
thermo holder, cocktails,
and ice bucket on Fruitwood tray.

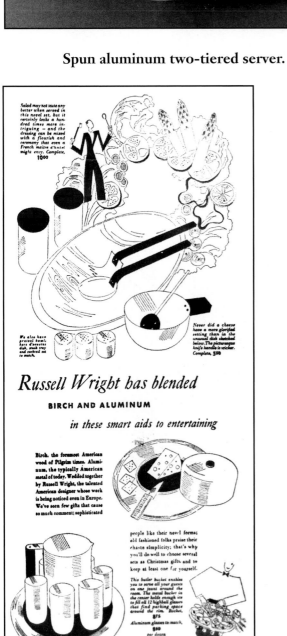

Spun aluminum punch set.

Early advertising.

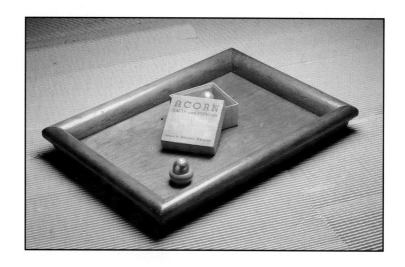

**Early Hood hostess tray
and acorn shakers.**

Bun warmer with rattan handle and maple knob.

Popcorn set consisting of 11½" bowl and four 5¾" bowls (not signed).

Spun aluminum covered sandwich tray with unusual knob shape.

Bun warmer with Bakelite handles.

Tea set consisting of teapot, sugar, creamer, and tray.

Spun aluminum punch set consisting of 11½" bowl, eight cups with maple handles, 18" tray, and bamboo handled ladle.

Spun aluminum sherry pitcher.

Ice bucket with lid and tray.

Lemonade pitcher.

Spun aluminum
centerpiece bowl, 12¼".

Nesting bowls, 10", 9", 7".

21" relish rosette.

Spun aluminum, early handle design on both
the 11" fruit basket and the two-tiered tidbit.
Cheese knife with reed trim.

#249 double boiler, handled sauce
server, aluminum with walnut handles.

Spun aluminum, 15" and 12" shallow
nesting bowls, reed handles.

Salad fork and spoon with walnut handles.

Chrome and aluminum ice bucket, salad
servers, chrome dice shakers (early).
Shakers were reproduced by the Metropolitan
Museum of Art in 1993.

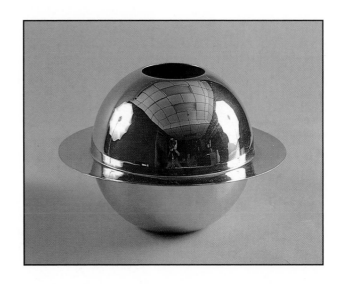

Saturn vase, 7" high x 10" wide.

Crystal ball vase with cover made into
punch bowl 11", ⅛" thick.
Also used as an aquarium.

Salad servers, salad bowl, and
relish tray.

Mark on back of salad
servers illustrates the
signature used on
early items.

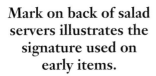

Concentrating on copper

Satin finished copper Bain Marie made for Chase (white porcelain inserts).

Spun aluminum tea set from Wright's own line. Other items not his designs.

Early metal accessories: pewter fruit basket, cocktail set, cigarette holders with striker strip, coasters, copper flower pot/vase.

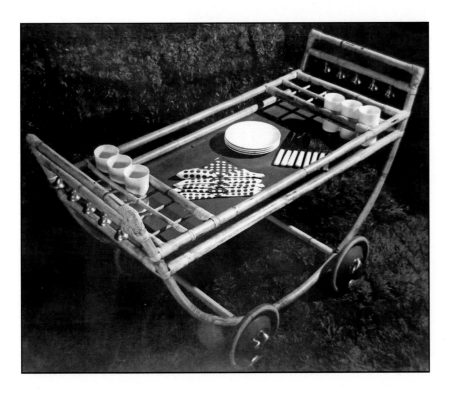

Roly poly cart,
length 32", height 36", diameter 30½",
bent bamboo hoops connected with caning wrap to
double-decker wooden trays with a Chinese red lacquer finish; wheels in matching red with spun aluminum hub caps and hard rubber tires.

Aluminum cart with bamboo trim.

Jingle cart,
bells ring as cart is pushed.

Jam jar, complete with 8 oz. jar, cover, and spoon, 4½" height x 3" diameter.

Pretzel basket, 3½" height x 9½" diameter.

Combination cocktail tray, 14¾".

Cheese and cracker board, 17".

Large canape ball tray, 14" diameter.

Small canape ball tray, 12" diameter.

1½ quart thermo, 2 piece,
complete with cover, 7½" diameter.

Flower tube,
14½" length x 2" diameter.

Items from Interior Accessory Group

Baby cactus pot,
2¼" height x 4¼" top diameter.

Flared vase and ball vases.

Early Catalog Items Showing
Chrome, Wood, and Spun Aluminum

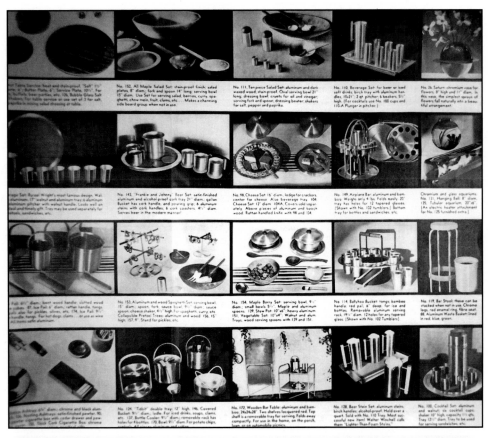

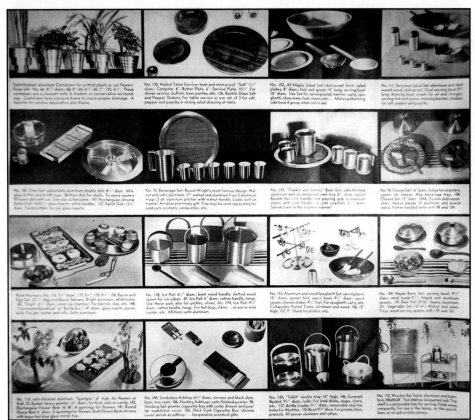

Sheet from Early Advertising Material

**Russel Wright's Stove to Table Ware
and Informal Serving Accessories Catalog**

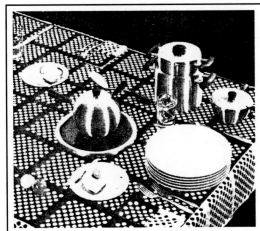

"STOVE TO TABLE WARE"

How to be smart efficiently, and efficient smartly, is the modern housewife's perennial problem. For this problem Russel Wright presents a solution.

He solves the problem with his "Stove to Table Ware"—cooking utensils that come into the dining room. Made of aluminum, they have solid walnut handles that are heat resistant. In appearance there is nothing "kitcheny" about them. They are as chic and well designed as a gown by Chanel.

The trend today is toward the "short cut," and this service is a "short cut" to the table from the stove. Combining two functions in one, these utensils are sturdy enough for cooking and good looking enough for serving.

"Stove to Table" utensils save time, bother and space. Besides being entirely suitable for the larger home, they are ideal for the small apartment. They put grace and ease into kitchenette-dinette hospitality. For the chafing dish expert, who loves to perform before an admiring audience, they are an especial boon. They are a "Godsend" for the carefully planned informal meal, as well as the more casual buffet party, the impromptu snack and the "trumped up" Sunday night supper.

In addition to these utensils for cooking and serving, Russel Wright has designed a whole family of cannisters and other kitchen and pantry accessories to match. They are also of aluminum with walnut trim, and have the same sleek simplicity of line as the cooking-serving utensils, mentioned above.

Ever since aluminum was discovered, its advantage for cooking utensils has been obvious. Aluminum is light, and safe for cooking, and because it is not plated or enameled, there is nothing to peel or chip off.

A scratch brush finish has been used throughout the entire group. This finish is entirely practical, as it is only necessary to wash in soap and water and rub with plain steel wool along the direction of the tiny scratch brush grooves. Thus with little attention, the initial lustre may be preserved.

The pieces in this group, singly, or in combination make delightful gifts—gifts that are at once unusual and practical, and if there is no excuse for giving them away they make the best possible presents for one's self. PAGE I A

PAGE II A

#248   CHAFING DISH: diam. 12¾".* Aluminum and walnut. For preparing, serving and keeping food warm. Besides using as complete unit, Covered Pan (top), and Water Chamber (middle), may be used together as separate "steamer" unit. Both make useful cooking-serving dishes. Electric 3-heat Griddle (base), may be used alone, for frying, as hot plate, etc.

#237B, C   BUFFET SERVICE SPOONS: 11" long. Aluminum with walnut handles. B has deep bowl. C has flat bowl.

#221   SERVING TRAY: diam. 20". Aluminum and walnut. May be used with #237 Bain Marie, and #237A Covered Pan (see below). For general use in the kitchen and for buffet service. Serves a large number of drinks or sandwiches.

#237A   COVERED PAN: diam. 17½". Aluminum and walnut. For cooking and serving roasts, stews, spaghetti, etc. This is the #237 "Bain Marie" Water Chamber, used with Cover to replace Rack-Cover for pots. (See directly below.)

#237   "BAIN MARIE": diam. 17½". Aluminum and walnut. For preparing, serving and keeping food warm. Besides using as complete buffet unit, Water Chamber, and three Covered Pots (which fit into removable Rack-Cover), may be used as separate "steamer" unit. Pots alone make useful cooking-serving utensils. Water Chamber may be used with extra Cover (see #237A, directly above). Electric 3-heat Griddle (base) may be used alone, for frying, as hot plate, etc. A complete cooking outfit for the bride.

#180   SOUP TUREEN with Tray and Ladle: Tureen 12½" diam., capacity 7 qts. Aluminum and walnut. For soups, chowders, stews, hot punch, etc. Also for cold punch, etc.

#139   BEAN POT with Tray and Serving Spoon: Pot 10" diam., 6" high. Aluminum and walnut. For preparing and serving baked beans, stews, etc.

#151   VEGETABLE POT with Tray and Serving Spoon: Pot 10" diam., 4" high. Aluminum and walnut. For preparing and serving stews, vegetables, etc.

#256   GRAVY PAN with Spoon: Pan 6" diam.* Aluminum and walnut. For preparing and serving gravy, sauces, etc.

#249   DOUBLE BOILER: 8" high. Aluminum and walnut. For preparing and serving foods. For buffet service, lower chamber may be filled with hot water or ice to keep contents in upper chamber hot or cold.

* See inside of back cover.

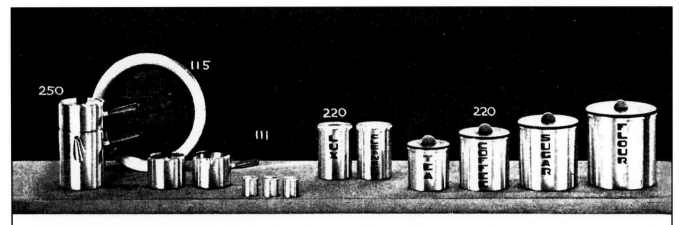

#250 DRIP-COFFEE POT with Creamer, Sugar and Tray: pot 9" high, tray 12" diam. Aluminum and walnut. 6 cup coffee pot may be used for making and serving coffee. Lower half of coffee pot may also be used for making and serving cocoa, tea, etc. Cover fits both upper and lower parts of coffee pot. (Shown with #115 tray. See directly below.)

#115 TRAY: diam. 12". Aluminum and walnut. This tray is also sold with #139 Bean Pot Set and #151 Vegetable Pot Set. (See page II A.) Separately it makes a convenient tray for general kitchen and buffet service.

#111 SHAKERS: diam. 1½". Aluminum. For salt, pepper, paprika, etc. May be used with salad sets (see page IV A). For general kitchen and buffet use.

#220 CLEANSER AND LUX SHAKERS: diam. 3¾". Aluminum with walnut letters. Besides using in the kitchen, use on the bath room shelf.

#220 FOUR-PIECE CANNISTER SET: "flour" 7¼" diam., 8" high. Aluminum with walnut letters. Luxury containers for household necessities. This set with #220 Cleanser and Lux Shakers (see directly above) make an unusual bridal gift.

#220 BREAD BOX: height 8". Aluminum and walnut. Besides storing bread and cake in the kitchen, may be used on the buffet table for hot rolls, etc. May also be used to keep platters of food warm.

#220 BREAD BOARD with Knife: Board 12" x 17". Aluminum and walnut. Knife has stainless steel blade. For use in the kitchen. Use also on the buffet table for cutting sandwiches, serving cheese, etc.

#335 ROUND VEGETABLE SERVER with Spoon: Server diam. 6½". Aluminum and walnut. For preparing and serving vegetables, creamed dishes, sauces, etc. For warming up left-overs, etc. A refreshing departure from the conventional shape, this pot requires a minimum of water, thus preserving natural juices and flavors. Looks exceedingly well on the table.

#325 ASBESTOS SERVING PLATE: diam. 11". Aluminum and brown asbestos. May be used with #335 (see directly above) and with many of the other serving containers listed here. Useful in serving extremely hot dishes directly from stove to table. Protects the table.

#182 RAREBIT DISH with Serving Spoon: Dish diam. 10". Aluminum and walnut. For preparing and serving rarebits, scrambled or fried eggs, warming up left-overs, etc.

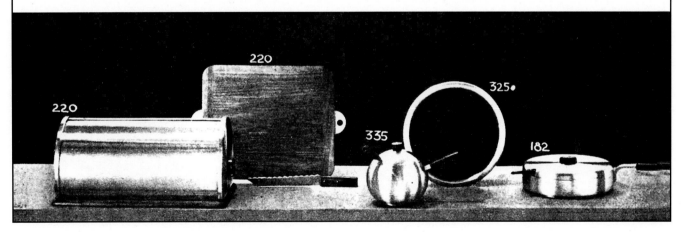

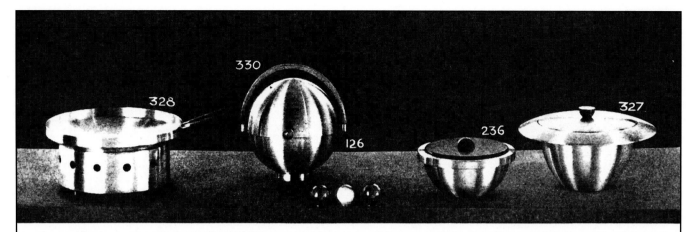

#328 "CRÉPE SUZETTE" SET: pan, 12¼" diam. Aluminum and walnut. Top pan for serving and saturating "Crépe Suzette" in flaming sauce. Lower stand has place for Sterno Can or for an alcohol lamp. Either part may be used separately for many purposes. Especially adapted to "al fresco" dining, and impromptu parties and picnics.

#330 BUN WARMER: diam. 10". Aluminum, cane handle and maple knob. May be placed on top of stove (not on flame), to warm buns, hot breads, etc., then may be used directly for serving. Cane handle and knob stay cool for serving. Also for cookies, pretzels.

#126 "BUBBLE" GLASS SHAKERS: diam. 1¾". Clear glass. Contents always visible, no chance for mistakes or for empty shakers. They harmonize with various types of table settings. Use sets of three filled with salt, pepper and paprika.

#236 "THERMO" DISH: diam. 8½". Aluminum and walnut. The hollow vacuum sides, and tight fitting cover, keep food hot or cold for at least three hours. Food may be warmed but not cooked in this container. Also use as ice bowl.

#327 TRIPLE-UTILITY SERVER: diam. 12½". Aluminum and walnut. For cooking, serving and keeping food warm. Unit includes two separate containers, one resting invisibly within the other, and a cover to fit either dish. Either dish may be used separately. When unit is used together, for serving, the air space between dishes acts as insulation and keeps food hot or cold for considerable time.

#111 SALAD BOWL with Fork and Spoon: bowl 21" long. Dark wood and aluminum. For preparing and serving salad at table. Also for fruit, berries, corned beef hash, etc.

#340 SALAD BOWL: 13" diam. Maple. Family size. For preparing and serving salad at table. Also for fruit, berries, spaghetti, etc. Use with #152A. Fork and spoon (see directly below).

#152 SALAD BOWL: diam. 15". Maple. For preparing and serving salad at table. Use either #152A Aluminum and Maple Fork and Spoon, or #153 Maple Fork and Spoon (see directly below). Also for fruit, corn on cob, steamed clams, spaghetti, etc.

#153 FORK AND SPOON: 14" long. Maple. (See directly above.)

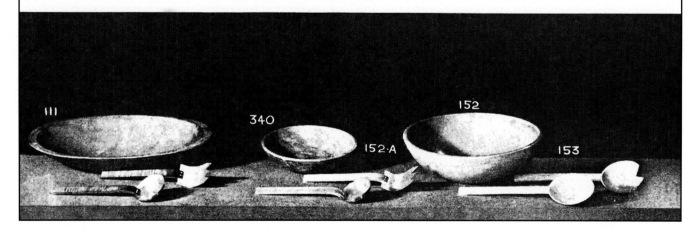

"INFORMAL SERVING ACCESSORIES"

Not so long ago, entertaining was either stripped down to picnic level or else it was swathed in all the trappings of ceremony.

There was nothing between paper plates and gold embossed china. But today, so many of the more casual parties lie between the two extremes, and require a special kind of service, which is neither paper plate nor priceless china.

Casual parties require the sort of service Russel Wright has designed especially for them—cheese and cracker boards, combination cocktail-canapé trays, jumbo relish "rosettes," beer sets, etc.—he calls these pieces "Informal Serving Accessories."

Most of these accessories are made of spun aluminum, a medium which Mr. Wright was the first to develop, in connection with its present day use in the home. To give life and warmth to the aluminum, wood, cane, rattan and cork are used for trim.

These informal serving accessories are well designed, well made and entirely practical. The total effect is one of smartness, freshness and informality. Ever since the first items appeared, they have had an astounding popularity.

With his "Informal Serving Accessories," Mr. Wright is directly responsible for bringing this type of informal service into its present vogue. Mr. Wright's work here is significant, largely since it marks the beginning of a new American etiquette—a new manner of serving and entertaining that is rapidly finding acceptance.

Because the pieces in this group are designed on the ensemble basis, they not only match one another, but can be combined and interchanged to make all sorts of fascinating new sets. Many of the pieces may be used for a variety of purposes. Scores of uses and combinations will occur to the enterprising hostess. Many of these pieces are in themselves a complete service; thus, one set may be used compactly, instead of a whole series of miscellaneous objects.

Besides being unbreakable, the material used is light, which makes these accessories "handy" for serving. This feature is a special attraction to the hostess who serves for herself. In short, these pieces are designed to give maximum efficiency with minimum effort. These "Informal Serving Accessories" are planned to be used with "Stove to Table Ware" (see page I A)—besides being ideal for buffet suppers, Sunday morning "brunches," outdoor affairs, bridge and cocktail parties and midnight "snacks," they are also indispensable for all impromptu occasions—for even everyday food takes on a festive air when presented in this attractive way.

In addition to making desirable holiday, wedding or anniversary gifts, these "Informal Serving Accessories" solve the most difficult gift problem of all—the "man's gift." Not only the cocktail sets and ice buckets, but many of the more unusual pieces, are sure to be cherished by the man who does his own entertaining.

PAGE I B

#333 "SOFT CHEESE" TRAY with Scoop: tray 9" diam. Aluminum with maple handled scoop. Hollow center may be filled with Cream cheese, Cottage, Edam and Stilton cheeses, etc., with crackers placed on the rim. Use also with cocktail glasses on rim, and olives, cocktail sausages, etc., in center. May also be used for caviar service. Makes an inexpensive, unusual bridge prize. The first cheese board of its kind.

#160 CHEESE TRAY with Knife: tray 11" diam. Aluminum, maple center with rattan handled knife. Use also as cake plate. #160A Matching Cover may be bought separately (see directly below).

#160A COVER: diam. 9½". Aluminum with maple ball. Matching Cover for #160 (see directly above). Use also as plate cover.

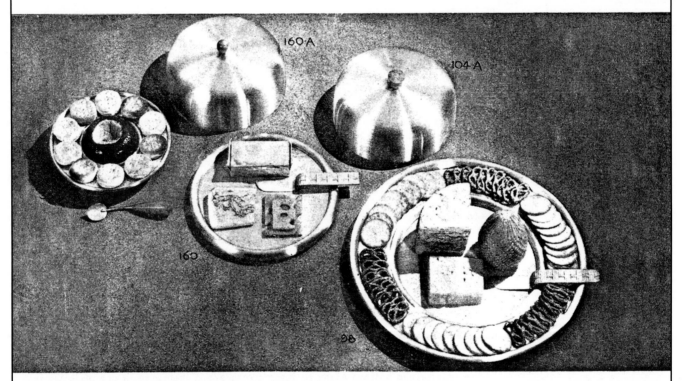

#98 "CHEESE AND CRACKER BOARD" with Knife: tray 17" diam. Aluminum rim and maple center, with rattan handled knife. . This is the original "Cheese and Cracker Board," Russel Wright's most famous design. . The center is usually used for cheeses, with crackers on the rim. Beer glasses may also be used on the rim with cheeses in the center. Center may also be filled with canapés, etc., with cocktail glasses on the rim. The combinations are endless. An ideal "quick set-up" for impromptu guests. The perfect buffet accessory. #104A Matching Cover may be bought separately (see directly below).

#104A COVER: diam. 9¾". Aluminum with maple knob. Matching Cover for #98 (see directly above). Cover is especially useful when #98 is used outdoors. Use also as plate cover.

PAGE II B

#212 CANAPÉ "ROSETTE": diam. 17". Aluminum. The three banked levels make this tray an ideal preference platter for serving canapés, sandwiches, hors d'oeuvres, etc. Also makes an excellent "cold cut" platter. The narrow circular corrugations prevent food from sticking to the surface of the tray. An ideal serving accessory for "after bridge" and for afternoon teas.

#339 COMBINATION COCKTAIL TRAY: diam. 14¾". Aluminum (shown with #326 Cocktail Cup, see next page). This tray may be used a number of ways; for instance, the outer rim may be used for cocktail glasses, the middle groove for relishes, the flat hollow center for canapés, etc. Used this way, it is a complete cocktail service in itself. Use also without Cocktail Cups, just for serving various combinations of food.

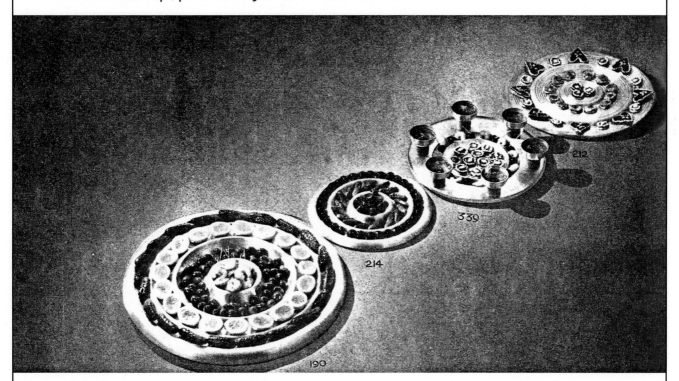

#214 SMALL RELISH "ROSETTE": diam. 12¾". Aluminum. May be used for a variety of relishes and hors d'oeuvres. The simplest relishes, such as olives, pickles, etc., take on a festive air when served in this new way. May also be used for jellied salads, hot hors d'oeuvres, etc. An unusual bridge prize.

#190 LARGE RELISH "ROSETTE": diam. 21½". Aluminum. May be used for a variety of hors d'oeuvres and relishes, small rolled canapés, etc. Ideal for the large party, as its generous capacity eliminates the necessity for frequent "refills" of food. Its extreme lightness makes it exceptionally easy to handle. Causes enthusiastic comment wherever it is used. Excellent for cocktail or buffet parties. A "quick set-up" for impromptu occasions. A week-end gift that is sure to be appreciated.

PAGE III B

#210 BAR SET including Tray and six Mugs: diam. of tray 14". Aluminum, brown cane and rattan. The handles form a double rail, which crosses the center of the tray, thus preventing beer bottles from tipping and slipping. May also be used with White Rock, Soda and Ginger Ale bottles, etc., with highball glasses placed on either side.

#70 BEER SET including Pitcher, Tray and six Mugs: diam. of tray 17". Cap. of Pitcher 2¼ qts. Aluminum and walnut. This set may be used for ice water, ice tea, lemonade, cider, etc. Aluminum pitcher keeps iced beverages cold for long period. This pitcher, 2 mugs and #115 tray (used with #250 Drip Coffee Set, see page III A) make an excellent ice water set for the night table.

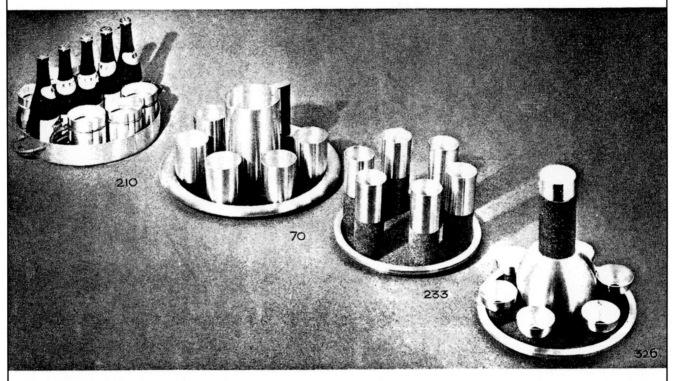

#233 MINT JULEP SET, including six Beakers and Tray: diam. of tray 12½". Aluminum and cork. The outside lower half of these beakers is cork, which acts as insulation and prevents the hand from becoming chilled. A useful good looking beaker for any long cold drink. . . . For a very big party use #143 tray (see page VIII B) to serve a large number of these beakers.

#326 COCKTAIL SET, including Shaker, Tray and six Cups. Aluminum and cork. Diam. of tray 12½"; cap. of shaker 2 qts. Shaker is leakproof and has detachable strainer. Neck of Shaker is wrapped in cork, thus preventing the hand from becoming chilled, while pouring. Cocktail cup has detachable cork ring around hollow base to facilitate cleaning. An excellent "man's gift."

PAGE IV B

#110 LEMONADE SET, including Pitcher, 6 Beakers and Tray: tray 10" x 21". Aluminum and maple. Use also for beer, ice water, etc. Beakers may be used for any "long," cold drink and make good looking water tumblers for the table.

#196 "TANTALUS" SET: 11½" high. Chromium and crystal. Two frosted crystal decanters have vertical ½" lines left clear, to show remaining quantity of liquor. Tiny chromium lock, key and chain, to keep your favorite "brand" in the decanter. Decanters may also be purchased separately (see directly below).

#196A DECANTER: capacity one-fifth. Frosted Crystal with chromium cap (see directly above).

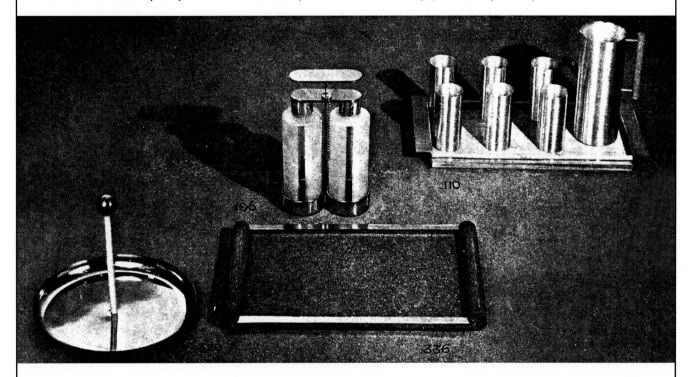

#336 RECTANGULAR SERVING TRAY: 20" x 13". Cork and polished copper—a new and pleasing combination of materials. This general serving tray is especially designed for preparing and serving "old fashioneds." The slight springyness of the cork protects the "old fashioned" glass while sugar is being ground. This tray looks very well in the modern living room. Use also for breakfast tray.

#320 SERVER: diam. 12¼". Polished copper tray and ball, with white enamel rod. May be used to serve cocktail glasses or hors d'oeuvres, small canapés, relishes, candy, etc. Set of two may be used as compotes on the dining room table. Looks extremely well in the living room. An appropriate holiday gift.

PAGE V B

#244 MARTINI MIXER with Stirring Spoon: Mixer cap. 1½ qts. Aluminum and cork. Cork covered aluminum shell keeps cocktails very cold for a long time. Cork provides a slip-proof grip and prevents the hand from becoming chilled while pouring. Used for many types of cocktails which should be stirred, not shaken. This and #218 Cocktail Shaker (see directly below), are related in design, and complementary in use; together they make a popular gift combination.

#218 COCKTAIL SHAKER: cap. 2 qts. Aluminum with cork cap. Leak-proof. Detachable strainer to facilitate cleaning. Aluminum shell keeps cocktails cold. Streamlined in design, it is one of the best looking objects here.

#166 DOUBLE HANDLE TIDBIT STAND: height 13". Aluminum trays, rattan and cane handles. Used for same purposes as #124 (see directly below).

#124 TIDBIT STAND: height 13", diam. 8". Aluminum tray, rattan and cane handle. May be used to serve canapés, small cakes, etc. Or cocktail glasses may be placed on both tiers, or on one tier, with food in another, etc. A very popular gift. One of the most useful all around serving accessories listed here.

#170 PRETZEL BOWL: diam. 9½". Aluminum with cane handles. May be used for serving pretzels, potato chips, fruit, cookies, nuts, etc. May also be used as large capacity ice bowl.

#318 COPPER FRUIT BOWL: diam. 12". Copper has high polish. Also use for serving canapés, cold cuts, relishes, hors d'oeuvres, etc. It is also very effective when used as a shallow centerpiece filled with gardenias, waterlillies or dahlia heads, petals, etc. Looks well in the living room.

PAGE VI B

#245 CHAMPAGNE COOLER: height 9". Aluminum with chromium band and rings. Swinging rings to be used as handles for carrying cooler. The aluminum shell keeps ice solid for a considerable time. Very dignified in design, this champagne cooler is absolutely suitable for the most formal occasions as well as for buffet parties, etc. An appropriate holiday gift.

#226 WINE COOLER: height 9½". Aluminum. Ice stays frozen for a long time in this cooler. May also be used as a tall vase.

#137 BOTTLE COOLER: diam. 10". Aluminum with rattan covered pail handle. Has detachable inner rack which holds four bottles securely in place. May be used for cooling White Rock, soda, gingerale and beer bottles, etc. Aluminum shell hastens chilling and keeps contents cold. Suitable for outdoor use, as well as indoor. Makes a good picnic accessory.

#174 LARGE ICE PAIL and Tongs: diam. of pail 10". Aluminum pail with rattan covered handle. One piece aluminum tongs. The aluminum shell keeps a large quantity of ice solid for hours. May also be used to serve hot dogs or pickles, steamed clams, potato chips, etc., at the buffet party or picnic.

#87 ICE BUCKET and Tongs: height of pail 6" (not including handle). Aluminum with rattan covered bucket handle. One piece aluminum tongs. The aluminum shell keeps ice cold for considerable time. May also be used as pickle pail, etc.

#138 ICE BUCKET and Wooden Slotted Spoon: height of pail 5" (not including handle). Aluminum with dark bent wood handle. Dark wood slotted spoon. The aluminum shell keeps ice cold for considerable time. May also be used to serve olives, pickles, potato chips, etc. Popular gift.

PAGE VII B

#149 "AIRPLANE BAR": diam. 22", height 25" (including handle). (Shown with #102 Aluminum Beaker. See directly below). Aluminum and bamboo, with red enamel metal braces. Very light to carry. Weighs only 4 lbs. Folds easily to facilitate storage in the closet. Upper tray has 12 holes into which most any slightly tapered glass will fit. Ice bucket may be placed in the center of upper tray. (Shown with #87 Ice Bucket. See page VII B.) May also be used with #174, #138 Ice Buckets, or with #137 Bottle Cooler, or with #170 Pretzel Bowl, in center of either tray. Bottom tray for "hot dogs" or sandwiches in the rim with napkins or bottles in the center. Excellent for outdoor and indoor service. A complete buffet "set-up."

#102 ALUMINUM BEAKER: height 4½". May be used with #114 "Ballyhoo Bucket" (see directly below) and with #149 "Airplane Bar" (see directly above). Also fits on rim of #98 Cheese and Cracker Board (see page II B).

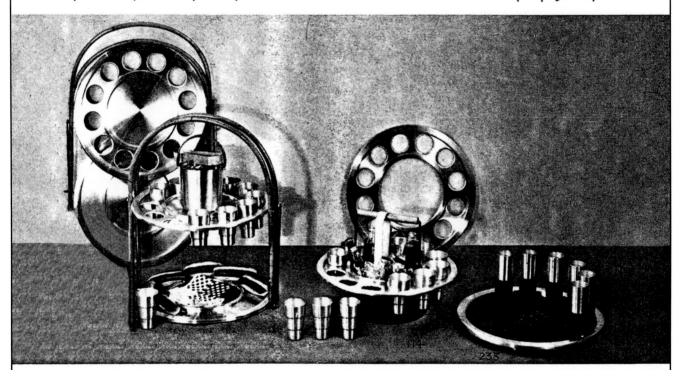

#114 "BALLYHOO BUCKET," including Tongs: diam. of rim 20". Aluminum rim, red enamel metal pail with bamboo handle. One piece aluminum tongs. (Shown with #102 Aluminum Beaker. See directly above.) The removable aluminum serving rim has 12 holes, into which most any slightly tapered glass will fit. Removable rim may be slipped off the bucket and used to serve the filled glasses. Pail may be filled with ice and bottles, or just with ice. The "Ballyhoo Bucket" may be used in a number of ways; for instance, with hot dogs in the pail and beer in the glasses. Excellent for outdoor as well as indoor service.

#143 LARGE CORK TRAY: diam. 20". Aluminum and cork. Very light to handle. A useful serving accessory. Serves a large number of drinks or sandwiches. (Shown with #233 Mint Julep Beakers. See page IV B.)　　　PAGE VIII B

RUSSEL WRIGHT STUDIO
165 East 35th Street
New York, N. Y.

P R I C E   L I S T

All prices subject to change without notice.

All prices F. O. B. factory New York, N. Y.

Terms 2% ten days, net 30 days.

Claims for breakage, shortage, etc. must be made within ten days.

No merchandise will be accepted for return unless authorized by the Russel Wright Studio.

A minimum charge of fifty cents will be added to all invoices for orders under $15.00.

The prices listed in this catalogue are net wholesale.

Sales tax not included in any sales prices. Any sales tax existing or to be enacted will be added to our invoice.

"STOVE TO TABLE WARE"

No.	Name		
#111	Salad Set Complete		2.10
	Bowl		1.00
	Fork		.60
	Spoon		.50
#111	Shaker		.35
		doz	3.60
#115	Tray		.75
#126	"Bubble" glass Shakers	doz	7.20
#139	Bean Pot Set Complete		2.75
		each, per ½ doz	2.50
	Pot		1.75
	Spoon		.30
	#115 Tray		.75
#151	Vegetable Set Complete		2.00
	Pot		1.20
	Spoon		.25
	#115 Tray		.75
#152	Salad Set complete		2.75
	Bowl		1.65
	#152A Fork		.60
	#152A Spoon		.50
#153	All wood Fork and Spoon	pr	1.80
#180	Soup Tureen Set complete		4.00
	Bowl and Ladle		2.85
	#70 Tray		1.65
#182	Rarebit Dish & Spoon		2.00
#220	Bread Board & Knife		2.25
	Board		1.65
	Knife		.65

"STOVE TO TABLE WARE" (Continued)

NO.	NAME		WHOLESALE
#220	Cannister Set (Four Piece)		4.50
	Flour		1.50
	Sugar		1.35
	Coffee		1.35
	Tea		.85
#220	Cleanser and "Lux" Set		1.90
	Cleanser		1.10
	"Lux"		.85
#220	Bread Box		5.00
#221	Serving Tray		2.50
#236	"Thermo" Dish		1.75
#237	"Bain Marie" complete with Griddle		15.40
	"Bain Marie" without Griddle		7.65
	small pots	each	1.35
	Electric Griddle		7.75
	electric cord		.35
#237A	Covered Pan		4.35
	Pan		3.45
	Cover		.90
#237B	Buffet serving Spoon, (deep bowl)		.60
		each, per ½ doz	.55
#237C	Buffet serving Spoon, (shallow bowl)		.60
		each, per ½ doz	.55
#248	Chafing Dish complete with Griddle		6.75
	Chafing Dish without Griddle		2.45
	Electric Griddle		4.30
	electric cord		.35
#249	Double Boiler		3.00
		each, per ½ doz	2.75
#250	Drip Coffee Set complete		5.00
	Drip Coffee Pot		3.00
	Sugar and Creamer	each	.75
	#115 Tray		.75
#256	Gravy Pan and Spoon		1.50
#325	Asbestos Serving Plate		.75
#327	Triple-Utility Server		2.25
#328	"Crêpe Suzette" Set complete		3.50
	Pan		1.75
	Stand		1.75
#330	Bun Warmer		2.00
		each, per ½ doz	1.75
#335	Round Vegetable Server and Spoon		1.85
	Server		1.25
	#256 Spoon		.60
#340	Salad Set complete		2.50
	Bowl		1.40
	#152A Fork		.60
	#152A Spoon		.50

"INFORMAL SERVING ACCESSORIES"

No.	Name		
#70	Beer Set complete		4.50
	Pitcher		1.65
	Tray		1.65
	Mugs	doz	3.60

NO.	NAME		WHOLESALE
#87	Ice Bucket and Tongs		2.00
	Bucket		1.60
	Tongs		.50
#98	Cheese and Cracker Board with Knife		1.75
	each, per doz		1.50
	each, per ½ gross		1.35
	each, per gross		1.25
	Knife		.50
	each, per ½ gross		.35
#102	Aluminum Beaker	doz	4.20
#104A	Cover		.85
	each, per ½ doz		.75
	each, per ½ gross		.60
#110	Lemonade Set complete		4.00
	Pitcher		1.50
	Tray		1.50
	Beakers *	doz	2.40
#114	"Ballyhoo Bucket" & Tongs		3.50
#124	Tidbit Stand		1.30
	each, per ½ doz		1.20
	each, per 3 doz		1.05
#137	Bottle Cooler		2.25
#138	Ice Bucket & Slotted Spoon		1.25
	each, per ½ doz		.90
#143	Large Cork Tray		2.00
#149	"Airplane Bar"		6.00
#160	Cheese Tray & Knife		1.50
	each, per ½ doz		1.25
#160A	Cover		.85
	each, per ½ doz		.75
#166	Double Handle Tidbit Stand		1.30
	each, per ½ doz		1.20
	each, per 3 doz		1.05
#170	Pretzel Bowl		1.25
	each, per ½ doz		1.00
#174	Large Ice Pail and Tongs		2.25
	Pail		1.75
	#87 Tongs		.50
#190	Large Relish "Rosette"		2.50
	each, per ½ doz		2.25
	each, per 3 doz		2.00
#196	"Tantalus" Set		6.00
#196A	Decanter		1.10
#210	Bar Set complete		4.00
	Tray		1.30
	Mugs *	each	.45
#212	Canapé "Rosette"		1.50
#214	Small Relish "Rosette"		1.25
	each, per ½ doz		1.00
	each, per 3 doz		.90
#218	Cocktail Shaker		1.75
#226	Wine Cooler		1.50
	each, per ½ doz		1.25
#233	Mint Julep Set complete		4.00
	Tray		.85
	Beakers *	each	.55

NO.	NAME		WHOLESALE
244	Martini Mixer & Spoon		2.55
	Mixer		2.00
	Spoon		.55
#245	Champagne Cooler		2.75
#318	Copper Fruit Bowl		1.50
#320	Server		2.25
#326	Cocktail Set complete		5.00
	Shaker		2.50
	Cups *	doz	3.60
	#233 Tray		.85
#333	Soft Cheese Tray & Scoop	doz	7.20
	dozen, per gross		6.00
#336	Rectangular Serving Tray		4.00
#339	Combination Cocktail Tray		1.00
		doz	9.00

"INFORMAL SERVING ACCESSORIES" (Continued)

* 6 to a set

66

PRICES FOR EARLY METAL, CHROME, AND SPUN ALUMINUM ACCESSORIES

Condition and rarity, both important considerations, influence all of Wright's metal work, chrome, copper, pewter, and spun aluminum. Dents, corrosion, scratches too deep to be removed, all reduce the value of items by 25–50%. Prices here are for items in fine to mint condition. Sets with component parts have been difficult to find with all pieces intact and several have been listed as NPD. That same term covers items too rare for contributors to evaluate.

EARLY METAL

Chrome ball candlesticks ....$160.00 – 175.00
Chrome cocktail shaker set ....NPD
Chrome cocktail set, shaker, tumblers, tray........................NPD
Chrome & glass salad servers..$600.00
Chrome smoking stands ....$500.00 – 700.00
Chrome and Bakelite desk accessories:
    Pencil tray $500.00
    Ashtray $400.00
Swan nut cup, good condition ....$150.00 – 250.00
Fire deer $1,500.00
All circus animals ....NPD
Dice salt & peppers ....$100.00 – 175.00

CHASE ITEMS

#9014 blue glass tray for corn set ....$150.00 – 175.00
#9015 tray to sphere sugar & pitcher set........................$75.00
#17108 Antarctic ice bowl with tongs.............................$200.00 – 225.00
#28002 ice bowl with tongs...$150.00 – 175.00
#28003 pancake and corn set ....$400.00 – 650.00
#28004 salt & pepper spheres to #28003 ....large $100.00, small $75.00
#28005 pitcher to #28003 set ....$100.00 – 125.00
#90025 Devonshire beer pitcher....................................$225.00 – 250.00
#90046 tray to liqueur set only ....$150.00 – 175.00
#90071 cocktail ball (with rubber ring bottom) ....$100.00 – 125.00
#90072 Olympia saucer (underliner for cocktail ball)........$50.00
#90073 individual coffee set ....$250.00 – 300.00
#90078 sugar sphere ....$100.00 – 125.00
#90078 salt & pepper spheres ....large $100.00, small $75.00

PLANTENE

Items in plantene are difficult to distinguish from their counterparts in the spun aluminum line. Where they can be identified, they should be 25% higher.

SPUN ALUMINUM

Wright's spun aluminum work is more extensive than this listing suggests but this is a representative sampling from which you should be able to evaluate your items. It is important in doing so to compare the complexity of pieces. You will find some of those which combine several pieces listed as NPD, reflecting the near impossibility that they have survived in tact. Condition remains important. Wright suggested that steel wool, rubbing in the direction of the spinning grooves would eliminate scratches and that may help, but deep scratching is difficult to remove. Dents are difficult to impossible to repair. Severe scratching and dented items should be priced substantially lower than the low range given below.

SPUN ALUMINUM

Bain Marie with griddle bottom.........$400.00 – 500.00
Beverage set:
    (pitcher, tray, 6 tumblers) ....$400.00 – 500.00
Bowls ....$75.00 – 85.00
Bun warmers ....$65.00 – 75.00
Candelabra ....$225.00 – 350.00
Casseroles ....$150.00 – 200.00
Cheeseboards ....$75.00 – 100.00
Cheese knife ....$75.00 – 100.00
Cooking items.................................$150.00 – 200.00
Flower ring ....$125.00 – 150.00
Fruit bowl, rattan handle ....$125.00 – 150.00
Gravy Boat ....$150.00 – 200.00
Hot relish server with ceramic
    inserts.................................$200.00 – 225.00
Cold relish server with glass inserts
    and ice pool bottom......................$200.00 – 225.00
Ice bucket ....$75.00 – 100.00
Ice fork ....$75.00 – 100.00
Muddler.................................$75.00 – 100.00
Peanut scoop ....$75.00 – 100.00

Pitcher with round handle ....$175.00 – 200.00
Portable bars ....NPD
Punch sets (bowl, cups, tray) ....NPD
Relish rosette:
    small $75.00, medium $100.00, large $200.00
Sandwich humidors..............................$125.00 – 150.00
Serving accessories:
    large $175.00 – 225.00, small $100.00 – 125.00
Serving carts (roly poly and others).......................NPD
Sherry pitcher ....$250.00 – 275.00
Smoking stand.................................$400.00 – 450.00
Spaghetti set ....$500.00 – 600.00
Tea set ....$500.00 – 700.00
Thermo items ....$250.00 – 300.00
Tid bit tray:
    single $85.00 – 125.00, double $150.00 – 200.00
Vase, 12" ....$150.00 – 175.00
Vase, round ball:
    large $300.00 – 400.00, small $150.00 – 200.00
Vases and flower pots (small) ....$75.00 – 125.00
Waste basket ....$125.00 – 150.00

EVERLAST GOLD ALUMINITE

All Rare

Bowls ....$125.00 – 150.00
Cream ....$50.00 – 60.00
Pitcher ....$200.00 – 250.00
Plate.................................$45.00 – 65.00
Sugar ....$65.00 – 75.00
Teapot ....$300.00 – 350.00
Tray ....$75.00 – 100.00
Tumblers ....$65.00 – 75.00

Furniture for a New Generation

Wright's work in the furniture industry was sizable but not nearly as large as he had hoped it to be in 1934. That work, however, gives us insight into patterns and habits to which he would return often. In front of the pack, his favored position, he proposed altogether new concepts. When he met resistance, he turned to friends in high places for help. Where it seemed right to hold with older, more friendly styles in favor of cold newness for the sake of newness, he sensed the right direction. Where challenged with extensive resources and given a free hand, he showed that his imagination could incorporate characteristics not considered practical before. Initially, he faced overwhelming burdens of tradition in the furniture industry.

For many years, Americans had looked to European styles in selecting furniture and their choices were reduced to copies, usually poor ones, as they attempted to imitate period furniture on average incomes. The furniture market was in a continual state of depression for most new homes were furnished with hand-me-downs from family attics, second-hand items from resale stores and auctions, and cast-offs of any sort that would allow for time and cash to afford more or better. Claiming that we were antique collectors gave respectability to our inability to buy new items, adding status to questionable styles, mixed, matched, and combined as it came our way free or almost so. Previous generations, by custom, convenience, and income, were said to change furniture only once after establishing their homes, leaving many furniture retailers forced to turn to a second occupation to provide enough sales to survive. Wright understood this situation and saw the war in Europe as an opportunity to advance his desire to improve the lives of Americans while profiting by changing their buying habits. He was aided, indirectly, by European events.

By the late 1930s, most European manufacturing had been suspended, except that production necessary to the war effort. What manufacturing facilities remained were being destroyed and their rebuilding would take time and capitol, both difficult to come by. Not all would survive. Wright and his fellow American designers knew that. They recognized that the newness in style would be further cause for retooling most manufacturing facilities, and while these many changes were being carried out, American manufacturers would be able to step into the situation, assuming leadership quickly since our factories and shops were not destroyed as were those in Europe. The success of Wright's designs, especially his furniture designs, evolved from that assessment of the war and its influence on mass-produced home furnishings. He believed that the demand for furnishings, delayed for almost five years, would overwhelm any shortsighted suppliers. It was important to look into the future for it appeared promising to those who were prepared.

The American market seemed ill prepared, however. An assessment of the furniture industry in America showed it to be dismal, depressed, and imitative, in real need for change. The Industrial Revolution has produced furniture which showed little creativity and very little distinguishable craftsmanship, but pre-war design changes in Europe had signaled a newness of style which had found an initial, but limited acceptance on the American market.

In addition important work had been done in England by William Morris, also a social reformer, who believed that fine craftsmanship could only be achieved by reforming the standards of design and elevating the position of workers, allowing for pride in workmanship. Morris used a guild concept, uniting workers who individually completed each article on which they worked. He found no redeeming qualities to the industrial method of mass production and abhorred the leveling of dignity it forced upon workers.

Called the Arts and Crafts Movement, it took

root in this country where Gustav Stickley and Elbert Hubbard produced very simple and functional furniture, a style not imitative of older European styles. Given the term "Mission" in this country, it was handmade of oak, with little machine work and less surface ornamentation. Stickley had been one of the first Americans to give voice to the form-follows-function concept in furniture. It was received here with restrained praise, buyers recognizing it to be an important benchmark in the industry.

Not entirely American, it was held to be so by adventurous Americans who chose it as they could replace older styles. It had been used in the Wright home in Lebanon. It clearly influenced Wright, who, 30 years later, saw a willingness to change from the overdone over-ornamented European Art Nouveau copies it replaced. His own belief that "less is more" was validated and the guild concept with its reformed work practices attracted him. He would return to that attraction later when he established his American Way program. Other influences, schools, movements were to impact Wright and the young designers of his days.

A brief tour seems indicated. The Bauhaus in Germany, which was born in the 1920s influenced the design world internationally. Its disciples were also looking to forms, shapes, a newness of design. They established what was called the International Style. Simple, stark lines with complete abstinence of ornamentation except for the lines of the piece itself was basic. Wright had seen the style himself and admired it but he believed that Americans were not ready to accept such a departure. L'Art Decoratif Moderne (altered and named Art Deco in the United States), another European concept, was luxuriously detailed with fine finishes and combined the use of rare and various materials with exotic woods, often incorporating the use of geometric detailing. It had been shown at the Exposition des Art Decoratifs et Industriels in Paris in 1925. Though the style did not have a long influence, its inherent objective of bringing beauty into everyday living was one which had a great impact on Wright. America, not exhibiting at the exposition, had no modern art to contribute according to President Hoover at the time. If not (and surely not), Americans associated with styles and design flocked to the showing but came away not much more impressed than had been Hoover. When Art Deco came to our shores, it was slow in finding its place, probably because it seemed lost in a crowd of other new "schools" and styles. Only the best would find wide acceptance as Americans considered these new concepts. Moderne evolved from the International style and was the name given to American mass-produced

furniture. Not so angular as the International Style, Moderne was conceived with the form/function lines, highly polished surfaces with various materials incorporated as trim. Modernist represented simple mass-produced items similar to the International style. Modernistic was said to have been a term which the Museum of Modern Art used to describe overdone exaggerated designs incorporating geometric ornamentation. Sorting these similar terms and the limitations of the styles they represent was difficult then, problematic now. Wright, aware of these Moderne/Modernist/Modernistic styles, was to define his own concept as "Transitional Modern." It has become known simply as Modern with no apologies to those schools from which it was derived. Modern, as Wright defined it, cannot be said to be derivative of any of these movements in design, but it is certainly true that they each had influence on his work and America's acceptance of it.

By 1934, with war behind us but still in the grips of the Great Depression, the business world looked for incentives to stimulate business. Heywood-Wakefield, with an impressive reputation in the furniture business was willing to take a chance on Modern design and contracted with Wright to design a 60-piece group which would be displayed in room-like settings in Bloomingdale's in New York. It was to be a complete Wright concept, with his rugs, lamps, and accessories featured. A different approach to merchandising, it stressed the element of flexibility.

Wright expressed dissatisfaction with the contracted line at once. His concept centered upon uncomplicated

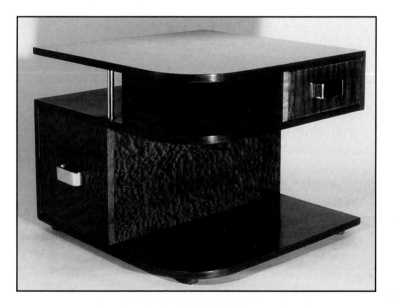

Corner end table, walnut veneer with zebra-wood veneer on most vertical surfaces including drawers, chrome pulls and chrome pipe bracing, smaller drawer opens both ways.

pieces of solid maple or birch construction to be used informally. Heywood-Wakefield insisted upon the use of veneers in imitation of the European work done in the Moderne style, popular in France. The style proved difficult to design, expensive to manufacture, and was not popular with customers.

Problems appeared soon after the work began. The veneers were difficult to work with and care for, and upholstered pieces were oversized and overdone with a combination of two or more fabrics on each item. The items seemed overworked. Wright had attempted to incorporate a flexible form which would include a sectional piece which could be arranged easily in any room concept. The idea was not fully understood or accepted by H/W or the public. Delivery problems developed and furniture stores joined customers with complaints. The company had been a manufacturer of traditionally styled solid wood furniture and their experience with this changed line left them with dissatisfied accounts. Anxious for the line and for his own reputation, Wright felt the line should be changed and offered to do a line of solid maple modern furniture which he felt Heywood-Wakefield's customers would accept. The company completely rejected his offers to change the line and his contract was not renewed after the first year. The timing left Wright with no client for the solid wood work he had hoped to send into production and too little time to prepare for the spring furniture shows. To have his work so repudiated was a severe blow.

In spite of this, Wright's H/W line has endured as some of his most interesting and sought-after work. The last word was his for he lived to see that company successfully manufacture modern furniture very similar to his designs, clearly adopting the style that they had refused to consider in 1934. This later about-face has left collectors uncertain as to whether or not H/W solid maple or birch furniture is Wright's work. We must keep in mind that the H/W line desinged by Wright was veneered, of the sort pictured here. It is high styled, elegant, and formal, usually combining two woods in the same piece with the distinctly Moderne appearance. It illustrates that Wright had a clear understanding of this style, though he did not admire it. It would have carried the H/W mark but we cannot be certain that the signature was included. H/W blond furniture is not Wright's work.

In spite of H/W's dismissal and termination of his contract, Wright believed in the timeliness of his work and approached friends who might help him. Charles Shaunessy, then the vice president in charge of home furnishings at Macy's in New York, was an old hand, well acquainted in the furniture business. Learning of Wright's problem, he suggested that they turn to the Conant-Ball Company, another manufacturer of solid wood furniture.

Shaunessy had a close relationship with Conant-Ball's president, Charles Brooks, Sr., and had influenced him to enlarge his plant at one time. Recognizing that the furniture business was adrift in 1935, and aware of the fact that Early American furnishings were out of step with the times, Shaunessy brought Wright and Brooks together. The meeting turned out to be important to all parties.

Conant-Ball agreed to manufacture this modern line and to further enlarge their facilities to do so. The hurried arrangement put Wright's work on the market sooner than he had expected and Macy's became an important outlet at once.

Conant-Ball chest, northern rock maple.

Made of solid northern rock maple, the new line was of good proportion and fine finish. With no veneer and no surface detail except for handle placements on cabinet pieces, the clean wood grain and soft lines were typical and met a receptive market. At the time of its introduction, the wood was left in its natural tawny red shade, but the parties soon agreed to further set it apart from other designs by bleaching the wood, giving it the name "Blond." Mary named it so. Quickly, it took its place as one of the most important furniture changes since the turn of the century and the wood treatment set standards of modern design for the industry at that time. It was divided into two groups in a attempt to attract all buyers. One group, more conservative than the other, allowed it to slip into furnishings already owned, blending-in without extreme contrast. The other, more modern, was a complete break-away from what had come before. Macy's and Wright were selling a new idea in home furnishings and if they could convince buyers to throw the old away to make room for the new, it would be for the better, they believed.

Traditionally, furniture had been sold in living room

suites and bedroom suites, but a new type of merchandising came into being with this line. A flexible feature allowed customers to buy one or several pieces, using them individually or in groups of their own choosing. Sets and suites would never completely return to furniture buying as the open stock concept was put into practice for the first time.

Early production was an instant success with the public. Called "Modern Living," Macy's introduced it in a nine room "Modern Maple House" in its New York store. Wright had designed every item in the house, a total concept. It was advertised nationally and Wright learned the value of applying his own name on his work and in his advertising.

Wright renamed the line and it became "American Modern." Simple and direct, it was altogether different than any furniture on the market in 1935. The clean rounded edges and corners were sold as "Cushion Edged," another new application of design. The furniture had soft and natural lines with no tricky ornamentation or cute detail. The legs were often replaced by slabs of solid wood, adding to the substantial appearance and intending to keep bed clothes from being "kicked off." Flush pulls were used because it was felt that they would prevent accidental damage as one brushed against them. Loose cushions, covered with simply designed fabrics were used on upholstered pieces in an effort to achieve a less heavy look. Many items had built-in dual uses which allowed owners to adapt them to their own purpose. The sectional sofa was joined by a sectional book case, drop leaf tables, and extension tables. This was Transitional Modern design as Wright had hoped to promote it. New, but not shocking, it was directed at

contemporary living. The line sold well, appealing to those average income Americans who could not afford expensive modern imported furniture. Marshall Field's in Chicago soon added it to its inventory as did J. L. Hudsons in Detroit and Rich's in Atlanta. Popular in most metropolitan areas in the east, transportation costs restricted the amount sold on the West Coast.

The original 1935 listings, as well as a supplemental listing of those items which were added the following year, are included here with the hope that stock numbers as well as sizes will be helpful. You may expect to find many more pieces than those listed here and you should find them with the Conant-Ball mark, but not always with Wright's signature. The American Modern attribution would not have appeared on the very first of the line, but it was soon added. The absence of Wright's name represents work done after his contract had expired, the same principle which we find in his contracts with dinnerware lines.

"Young American Modern" which came later than the original line was equally popular. Wright's file pictures will show it to be of at least two styles and one photo has remnants of a notation that it was designed by Russel Wright. While we cannot say that it was a redesign, this Young group was probably meant to update the older line. You will find catalog pages here.

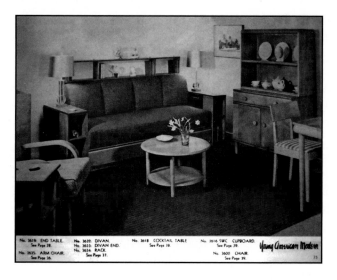

Young American Modern furniture.

Modern Mates, another Conant-Ball line dates from 1949, and seems typical of the 1950s period in which it was made. It came in eight birch finishes and customers could order it in black or black birch, which Conant-Ball offered at an increased price. An original catalog list which was not illustrated is shown here but the line changed from time to time. The long period with which Wright was associated with Conant-Ball allowed the addition of many pieces and

Conant-Ball American Modern

**Modern Mates by Conant-Ball, buffet,
30" x 15" x 44", original dark wood finish.**

Old Hickory Americana.

variants of them. The same marking principle applies to Wright's Modern Mates. The files indicate that Wright's name was used only for the term of his contract but that royalties were to be paid for the duration of the production. You will find the signature markings before his contract expired. The same item, after the contract expired, will not have the signature.

The Old Hickory Company of Martinsville, Indiana, was not a newcomer to the furniture world in 1941 when it approached Wright to design a line of informal, rustic outdoor or porch-style furniture for them. Their pieces were sold at major department stores and the firm had a permanent display room at the Merchandise Mart in Chicago. Their furniture was used in national parks as well as many other resorts areas. They were suffering from competition from come-lately inexpensive aluminum styles and they wanted to refresh their lines as well as their image and felt that an association with Russel Wright might be the answer to their problems. Wright, seeing an opportunity to enter another area of design, was quick to call attention to the similarities between this work and the causes which he promoted. He said that Andrew Jackson had a favorite chair made of hickory and that Jackson's use of his chair showed it to be tough, back to basic, no-nonsense furniture. He said it had been indigenous to America, strong and enduring, and that American settlers had used hickory saplings to hold covered wagons together. It had been used in spin-

ning wheels in earlier times. With native materials as well as design and workmanship, it was a "truly American" product. He seemed to have understood The Old Hickory Company's position, gilding the lily only slightly. He called it "Americana" and used it as a pulpit for his own creed.

The line was divided into an indoor group and outdoor group. Unadorned and light in weight, the outdoor group was left the natural hickory color but treated with an insect and rain repellent. The listing in Wright's files remains as we have come to know it: a sofa, love seat, a tavern chair with arms, bridge chair with no arms, a dining extension table, a bridge table, and a coffee table. The indoor group was very much the same except for sail cloth upholstery in plain colors or muslin which could be covered with the customer's choice of fabric. Intended for use on a summer porch or screened-in area, it was of a tawny finish and included: a love seat, sofa with a chair which matched, wing chair, coffee table, chaise lounge, bridge table, bridge chair with or without arms, and a low chair. Having met this market with Americana, Wright was not ready to leave it, and added a line called "American Provincial" made of chestnut and pine. Another line was "Modern Maple." These were the lines with which Wright was involved. Markings are uncertain and the line is seldom seen outside of resort facilities where it has been protected from the weather.

The Statton Furniture Company, a manufacturing concern owned and operated by Helen and Philo Statton contacted Wright in 1950. They planned to open a retail outlet in New York City and engaged Wright to design living room and dining room items. They had an understanding of the furniture business and a good sense of the needs of customers, and were open minded and willing to produce any interesting or exciting idea. They had done market research, studied trends as well as the work of their competition, and were willing to consider any direction which Wright proposed. Excited with the free hand which they extended to him, Wright seemed to have found a like-minded manufacturer. Solid colored veneers, marble, glass, terrazzo, and other laminates used in conjunction with wood would add interest to anything then on the market except for very expensive imported lines. The finishes upon which the Stattons and Wright decided were to be called "Satin Sycamore"

Statton furniture.

and "Golden Griege," a beige with a muted gray undertone. Joints were to be pegged, a sign of quality construction. Slip covered pieces were to be standard, allowing for customers' fabric preferences. Most pieces had dual uses and there were many interesting extensions of that practice. Nightstands held drawers, a chair had an arm with a magazine holder extending down to the seat, the buffet had adjustable shelving, a wood topped coffee table had sliding or moving trays for extensions, a card table expanded to seat eight for a meal.

First calling the line Modern Age, they intended it to become part of a larger concept to be called Easier Living. Helen Statton evaluated and approved each item. She required at least two samples of each item before giving it her acceptance. The item was then given a stock number and became a part of the line. Previous studies have included pictures of these items. Some late information has established an actual order from the Statton Company to the Modernage Furniture Company in New York City and it is

possible now to offer that order along with a list of the items and corresponding stock numbers. This is an old copy dated 1/29/51 and not in the best of condition, but it does add authenticity to the little we know of the production. *McCall's* magazines from the 1951 period picture and give supportive information including direct reference to Statton as the manufacturer. Our own information ends there, however, for no one has reported a Statton find and the author knows of none with the exception of the chair with magazine holder which Wright owned. His associates have indicated that the retail store never developed as the Stattons had expected and that this extensive line, so carefully planned was never produced in the amounts that Wright and the Stattons hoped. The details surrounding the production are still not clear, nor is it clear why furniture with such promise, featured in national magazines seemed to end in obscurity.

Furniture made by Sprague and Carleton, in Keene, NH, in maple with a new finish called "Sun Tan" was done for the American Way. Our information comes from listings of that work. The production included a small group of dinette items, table and chairs, a sun room group assortment of chairs, sofa, and four round and rectangular coffee tables. Another line of maple furniture made by Master Craftsmen in Flushing, NJ, consisted of a bedroom unit with a bed, dresser, chest, vanity, night stand, and bench. The living room unit contained a kneehole desk, straight book case, secretary top, buffet base, corner book case, and secretary case. The listing implies flexible usage of items, the sort of work which Wright favored. Collectors would welcome any information about the Statton, Sprague and Carleton, or Master Craftsmen lines.

Also part of the American Way program was a line of assemble-yourself furniture produced for Sears. The line consisted of living room, dining room, and bedroom units and was a complete departure from furniture previously sold. Interestingly, black japanned furniture was considered by Sears but our information ends with that mention.

Wright's involvement with furniture was an important one. His excellence of design, combined with the integrity of solid wood set this blond finish apart. It was a watershed in American furniture production and future generations would never again look at imitative European designs as they had before Russel made American Modern the standard.

SA-185   **PRICE 25c**

Famous Designers
DO-IT-YOURSELF PLANS

A SERVING TABLE-CART

designed by
RUSSEL WRIGHT

RUSSEL WRIGHT's products have sometimes caused such a sensation when first shown that the police have had to be called out to handle the crowds. A Vice-President of R. H. Macy said that his 1934 American Modern furniture was "the greatest influence on American furniture in our time." *Gourmet* magazine said: "In the shapes he creates, Mr. Wright combines grace with a superb functionalism." Wright "firsts" include blond furniture, modern dinnerware featuring the rimless plate, stainless steel flatware, stove-to-tableware, aluminum serving accessories, colored table linens, and Melmac for the table. He has designed clocks, luggage, houses, pianos, radios, and vending machines. His designs have been sighted for "Good Design" by the Museum of Modern Art every year since the exhibit began.

Front cover of pamphlet for Do-It-Yourself Plans.

Inside of pamphlet showing construction for the table-cart.

with the drop leaves down . . .   *. . . and with the leaves up*

THIS ATTRACTIVE SERVING TABLE-CART HAS MANY USES IN THE HOME

This ingeniously designed serving table-cart can be used as a buffet table, a tea table, a movable bar, or a dining table for an intimate party of two. When not in use, it adds a decorative note as a side table in the most finely furnished room.

As planned here, power tools are needed to cut the miters and grooves. The setting of blind dowels also calls for a certain amount of experience. Although this is the ideal way to build a table of this quality, these construction methods can be modified so they can be done without power tools. The shelf box, for instance, instead of being put together by a mitered-and-feathered joint, can be made with a simple butt joint, with the shelf placed down on the side panels. The grooved drawer-slide cut into the sides of the shelf box can be replaced by hardwood nailing strips fastened by screws and glue to the bottoms of the side panels. And the blind-dowel construction can be replaced by dowels bored through or even by long screws countersunk in ⅜-inch holes and then covered over with ⅜-inch plugs cut from the actual wood from which the table is made.

No matter which method you choose for the construction, you will be able to make a beautiful and useful table of which you and your family can be proud. It will cost you only a fraction of what you would have to pay for such a table in a retail store.

Mr. Wright recommends that this "Do-It-Yourself" table be made from Weldwood African Mahogany plywood with legs of solid Mahogany and a drawer bottom of green Micarta No. 732. You may, of course, use any of the other beautifully grained Weldwood panels such as Walnut, Korina, Rift Oak, or Birch.

Your local lumber dealer will be glad to help you select the *right* Weldwood panel for the job. Make sure that the panel you select carries the Weldwood label. It's your *guarantee* that you are buying a *top-quality* plywood panel.

Gluing the table frame together with long clamps

**Salesmen's samples of Modern Mates furniture.
All 1" – 4" high.**

It seems important to explain the Modern Mates photography found here. These small salesmen's samples came from a friend who realized how much they would mean to me. With line drawings before me, it was apparent at once that these were, indeed, the salesman's samples. My friend had recognized them at once since her family had used Russel Wright Modern Mate furniture in their home and she knew at once that these were not toys. I have never bought any doll-sized furniture and had never considered that there could be such items. Had she not said what these pieces were, I would have passed them by. I believe, now, that all of the Modern Mates line can be found as salesmen's samples and it seems likely that American Modern and Young American Modern furniture samples exist also.

Photo from Conant-Ball catalog.

ON PRICING FURNITURE

I am often questioned about furniture pricing and it is by far the area in which I have the least experience. Location really impacts furniture values and I am located in an area where all blond wood is treated as second hand furniture. Even my travels do not allow me much furniture price comparison. For that reason, specific requests for pricing are often referred to others. Where you locate your furniture finding may have an important bearing on its price. If you are in a trendy city shop where knowledgeable dealers recognize and value style, the costs will be high. At an estate sale or fairground, however, you might almost get it for the taking. Taking, however, may add to costs. If you must ship it, the value escalates with the miles.

You should consider in advance whether or not you can accept the condition in which you find it. Original finish is important to some, while others may wish to consider refinishing if the piece is priced to reflect that need. Pieces with altered finishes, stripped and treated with clear lacquer have been acceptable to all but the purist. Take a long look at Wright's Heywood-Wakefield line for veneers are fragile and do not take well to refinishing. Contributors have declined to value the rare Heywood-Wakefield Deco designs so they will have to remain NPD, but the value should be *high*. Consultants advise that Conant-Ball's American Modern and Young American Modern should be about double the price of comparable Heywood-Wakefield look-alikes. Conant-Ball's Modern Mates should be priced at about the same as the H/W blond furniture. Statton items should be regarded as NPD for now. Samsonite chairs in excellent condition can be valued at $50.00 – 125.00, tables $50.00 – 75.00. In poor condition, these are difficult to sell and expensive to restore.

FURNITURE PRICING EXAMPLES

Book case with drop front	$600.00 – 700.00
Book cases, 3 shelves	$250.00 – 350.00
Mirrors, vanity or decorative	$200.00 – 250.00
Desk chair, original finish and oilskin cushion	$400.00 – 600.00
Vanity	$600.00 – 700.00
Vanity stool	$150.00 – 200.00
Bed	$550.00 – 700.00
End tables	$350.00 – 400.00
Three tier shelving unit	$300.00 – 400.00
Corner cupboard	$550.00 – 650.00
Night stands	$250.00 – 350.00
Dining table, no leaf, signed	$600.00
Dining chairs, signed	$100.00 – 150.00
Arm chair, signed, original upholstery	$500.00 – 600.00
Corner sections	$200.00 – 300.00
Chest, 5 drawer	$600.00 – 700.00
Chest, 3 drawer	$350.00 – 500.00

Heywood-Wakefield Furniture

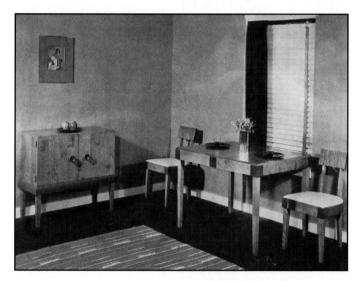

American Modern Furniture

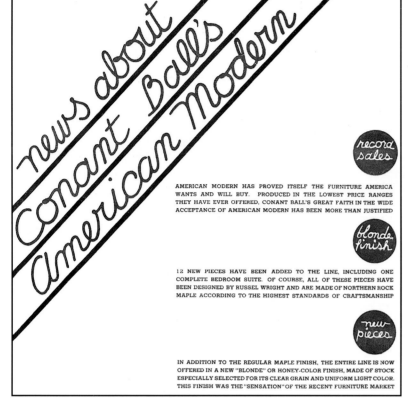

No. 3060: OTTOMAN. Uphol-
stered Reversible cushion
Height 15½. Top 15 x 21.

No. 3070: CORNER CUP-
BOARD. Cabinet Below with
adjustable shelves. Ht. 56½
depth 15, width and front 29.

No. 3071: DAY BED END
TABLE.   Two shelves.
Height 23   Top 10¼ x 30.

No. 3059: COCKTAIL TABLE.
Height 16.   Top 17 x 36.

AMERICAN MODERN HAS PROVED ITSELF THE FURNITURE AMERICA
WANTS AND WILL BUY. PRODUCED IN THE LOWEST PRICE RANGES
THEY HAVE EVER OFFERED, CONANT BALL'S GREAT FAITH IN THE WIDE
ACCEPTANCE OF AMERICAN MODERN HAS BEEN MORE THAN JUSTIFIED

12 NEW PIECES HAVE BEEN ADDED TO THE LINE, INCLUDING ONE
COMPLETE BEDROOM SUITE. OF COURSE, ALL OF THESE PIECES HAVE
BEEN DESIGNED BY RUSSEL WRIGHT AND ARE MADE OF NORTHERN ROCK
MAPLE ACCORDING TO THE HIGHEST STANDARDS OF CRAFTSMANSHIP

IN ADDITION TO THE REGULAR MAPLE FINISH, THE ENTIRE LINE IS NOW
OFFERED IN A NEW "BLONDE" OR HONEY-COLOR FINISH, MADE OF STOCK
ESPECIALLY SELECTED FOR ITS CLEAR GRAIN AND UNIFORM LIGHT COLOR.
THIS FINISH WAS THE "SENSATION" OF THE RECENT FURNITURE MARKET

record sales

blonde finish

new pieces

Cover from Conant-Ball's American Modern catalog.

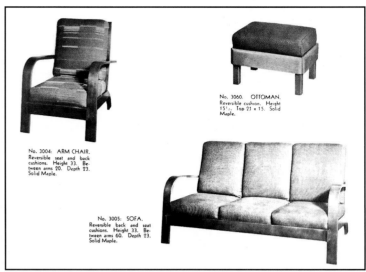

No. 3004: ARM CHAIR.
Reversible seat and back cushions. Height 33. Between arms 20. Depth 23. Solid Maple.

No. 3060. OTTOMAN.
Reversible cushion. Height 15½. Top 21 x 15. Solid Maple.

No. 3005: SOFA.
Reversible back and seat cushions. Height 33. Between arms 60. Depth 23. Solid Maple.

No. 3528: ARM CHAIR.
Height 32. Width between arms 17½. Seat depth 17. Solid Maple.

No. 3021: DROP-LEAF TABLE.
A new type of sliding leg. Height 29. Top 42 x 18. Open 42 x 51. Solid Maple.

No. 3016: CHAIR.
Height 31. Seat depth 17. Solid Maple.

Conant-Ball's American Modern Catalog Prices from 1935 – 1936

AMERICAN MODERN - LIST PRICES
DECEMBER 31, 1936 - SUBJECT TO CHANGE WITHOUT NOTICE

UPHOLSTERED PIECES

Pattern No.	Wood	X	XA	A	B	Description	Yardage 50"	36"	Page
3001	Birch	$31.50	$34.50	$37.50	$40.50	Chair	2½	3¼	2
3002	"	66.00	75.00	84.00	93.00	Sofa	7	9¾	2
3003	"	47.50	53.50	59.50	65.50	Love Seat	4¾	6½	2
3004	"	29.00	32.00	35.00	38.00	Chair	2½	3¼	4
3005	"	66.00	75.00	84.00	93.00	Sofa	7	9¾	4
3006	"	46.00	52.00	58.00	64.00	Love Seat	4¾	6½	4
3007	"	41.50	44.50	47.50	50.50	Adjustable Chair	2½	3¼	5
3009	"	19.00	20.00	21.00	22.00	Pull Up Chair	1¾	1¾	3
3060	Maple	12.00	13.00	14.00	15.00	Ottoman	⅔	1¼	
3084	Birch	32.00	35.00	38.00	41.00	Chair	2	3¼	
3085	Birch	69.50	78.50	87.50	96.50	Sofa	6	9¾	
3091	Maple	40.50	45.00	49.50	54.00	Corner Section	3	4½	
3092	Maple	49.50	55.50	61.50	67.50	Center Section	4	5½	

DINING GROUP

No.	Wood	Price	Description	Top	Height	Page
3011	Maple	$33.50	Trestle Table	60 x 30	29	8
3012	Maple	12.50	Bench	60 x 14	17	8
Set		58.50	Table and two Benches			9
3013	Birch	16.50	Extension Table — Open	46 x 28	29	9
			Closed	38 x 28		
3014	Birch	6.00	Chair, Seat 17 x 15		29½	9
Set		40.50	Table and four Chairs			9
3015	Birch	21.50	Extension Table — Open	52 x 30	29	6
			Closed	42 x 30		
3016	Birch	10.50	Chair — Slip Seat 16 x 16		30½	6
Set		63.50	Table and four Chairs			6
3017	Maple	40.50	Buffet	42 x 16	36	6
	Maple	27.00	Buffet Top	42 x 11	28	
3018	Birch	32.00	Table — Refectory — Open	62 x 30	29	7
			Closed	42 x 30		
Set		74.00	Table and four No. 3016 Chairs			7
3019	Maple	32.50	Buffet	42 x 17½	29½	7
	Maple	14.50	Buffet Top	42 x 11	29	7
3070	Maple	38.50	Corner Cupboard	Width 28	58½	

LIVING ROOM

No.	Wood	Price	Description	Top	Height	Page
3021	Maple	$38.00	Drop Leaf Table, 42 x 18	Open 51 x 42	29	2
3022	"	35.00	Flat Top Desk	40 x 22	29	5
3023	"	53.50	Kneehole Desk, 6 Drawer	46 x 22	29	3
3024	"	12.50	Coffee Table	26 x 17	16	4
3025	"	15.00	Coffee Table, Square with Drawer	22 x 22	16	2
3026	"	11.00	End Table	24 x 14	22	4
3027	"	20.25	End Table with Compartment	28 x 14	22	4
3050	"	68.00	Secretary Bookcase	36 x 16	50½	2
3051	"	41.00	Bookcase, 4 adjustable shelves	36 x 16	50½	2
3052	"	14.50	Sectional Bookcase	39 x 10	30	4
3057	"	19.00	Sofa End Table, 33 x 10	Open 20 x 33	23	3
3059	"	14.50	Cocktail Table	36 x 17	16	
3071	"	16.00	Side Table	30 x 10¼	23	
3088	"	18.50	Lamp Table	19 x 19	26	
3089	"	18.50	Bookcase	24 x 12	37½	
3090	"	22.00	Bookcase	36 x 12	37½	

PRICES QUOTED ARE IN No. 77 FINISH - BLONDE FINISH 10% EXTRA

No.	Wood	Price	Description	Top	Height	**BEDROOM**
3030	Maple	$31.00	Bed H. Board 31½, F. Board 21, Widths 3'3" and 4'6"			Illustrated on pages 10 and 11
3031	"	45.00	Chest, 5 Drawer	32 x 19	46½	
3032	"	42.50	Dresser, 4 Drawer	32 x 19	33	
3033	"	15.00	Night Table	16 x 14	22	
3034	"	22.50	Dressing Table	36 x 18	29	
3035	"	9.00	Bench	21 x 14	15	
3036	"	14.00	Mirror Glass 34 x 18			
Set	"	132.50	Bed, Chest, Dresser, Mirror (4 pieces)			

No.	Wood	Price	Description	Top	Height	**BEDROOM**
3061	Maple	$52.00	Chest	33 x 18½	46	
3062	"	48.00	Dresser	45 x 18½	34	
3063	"	20.50	Dresser-Mirror (Glass 44 x 18)			
3064	"	17.50	Light Stand	18 x 14	22	
3065	"	38.00	Bed: Head Board 34", Foot Board 22", Widths 3'3" and 4'6"			
3066	"	18.00	Vanity Mirror (Glass 36 x 20)			
3068	"	52.50	Vanity	48 x 18	25	
3069	"	9.00	Bench	21 x 15¼	15	
Set		158.50	Bed, Chest, Dresser, Mirror			

No.	Wood	Price	Description	Top	Height	**CHILDREN'S GROUP**
3058-M	Maple	$12.00	Mirror (Glass 28 x 18)			
3067	"	8.00	Chair (Seat 12 x 12) (Height to Seat 15)			
3075	"	14.00	Table	24 x 24	22	
3076	"	8.00	Chair (Seat 12 x 12) (Height to Seat, 13)			
3077	"	34.00	Dresser	38 x 17	28¼	
3078	"	39.50	Chest	29 x 16½	37	
3079	"	47.50	Chifforobe	38 x 17	37	
3080	"	27.50	Desk	34 x 18½	26	
3081	"	28.50	Toy Cabinet	38 x 15	29	
3082	"	27.50	Youth's Bed: Head Board 29¼". Foot Board 21½". Width 34¾" between Rails			
3083	"	40.00	Crib (Spring Size 51 x 27)			

CONANT-BALL CO., GARDNER, MASS.
SHOW ROOMS

67 SUDBURY STREET
BOSTON, MASS.

WATERS-KLINGMAN BLDG.
GRAND RAPIDS, MICH.

11 EAST 31ST STREET
NEW YORK CITY

Conant-Ball #3001,
American Modern chair in
early tawny color.

AMERICAN MODERN LIST PRICES

· ISSUED SEPTEMBER 1935 ·

SUBJECT TO CHANGE WITHOUT NOTICE

Prices apply on #77 finish only, other finishes add 10%.

DINING GROUP

Illustrated on pages 6, 7, 8, and 9

No.	Wood	Price	Description	Top	Height	Page
3011	Maple	29.00	Trestle Table	60 x 30	29	8
3012	Maple	11.00	Bench	60 x 14	17	8
Set		51.00	Table, two Benches			9
3013	Birch	14.50	Extension Table—Open	46 x 28	29	9
			Closed	38 x 28		
3014	Birch	5.50	Chair, Seat 17 x 15		29½	9
Set		36.50	Table, 4 Chairs			9
3015	Birch	18.50	Extension Table—Open	52 x 30	29	6
			Closed	42 x 30		
3016	Birch	9.00	Chair-Slip Seat 16 x 16		30½	6
Set		54.50	Table, 4 Chairs			6
3017	Maple	36.00	Buffet	42 x 16	36	6
	Maple	24.00	Buffet Top	42 x 11	28	
3018	Birch	28.50	Table—Refectory—Open	62 x 30	29	7
			Closed	42 x 30		
Set		64.50	Table, 4 Chairs (3016)			7
3019	Maple	29.00	Buffet	42 x 17½	29½	7
	Maple	12.00	Buffet Top	42 x 11	29	7

Confidential
Trade Discount
50%

LIVING ROOM

Illustrated on pages 2, 3, 4, and 5

No.	Wood	Price	Description		Top	Height	Page
3021	Maple	34.00	Drop Leaf Table, 42 x 18	Open	51 x 42	29	2
3022	"	31.50	Flat Top Desk		40 x 22	29	5
3023	"	48.00	Kneehole Desk, 6 Drawer		46 x 22	29	3
3024	"	11.00	Coffee Table		26 x 17	16	4
3025	"	13.50	Coffee Table, Square with Drawer		22 x 22	16	2
3026	"	9.50	End Table		24 x 14	22	4
3027	"	18.00	End Table with Compartment		28 x 14	22	2
3050	"	61.50	Secretary Bookcase		36 x 16	50½	2
3051	"	37.50	Bookcase, 4 adjustable shelves		36 x 16	50½	2
3052	"	13.50	Sectional Bookcase		39 x 10	30	4
3057	"	17.00	Sofa End Table, 33 x 10	Open	20 x 33	23	3

All prices quoted apply to wood pulls — metal pulls — 4¼" size furnished at 60c each extra.

UPHOLSTERED PIECES

Pattern No.		Grades X	Grades XA	Grades A	Grades B	Description	Yardage 50"	Yardage 36"	Page
3001	Birch	26.50	29.50	32.50	35.50	Chair	2⅓	3¼	2
3002	"	57.00	66.00	75.00	84.00	Sofa	7	9¾	2
3003	"	41.00	47.00	53.00	59.00	Love Seat	4⅔	6½	
3004	"	25.00	27.50	30.00	32.50	Chair	2⅓	3¼	4
3005	"	57.00	66.00	75.00	84.00	Sofa	7	9¾	4
3006	"	40.00	46.00	52.00	58.00	Love Seat	4⅔	6½	
3007	"	36.00	39.00	42.00	45.00	Adjustable Chair	2⅓	3¼	5
3009	"	16.50	17.50	18.50	19.50	Pull Up Chair	1¾	1¾	3

BEDROOM

Illustrated on pages 10 and 11

No.	Wood	Price	Description	Top	Height
3030	Maple	26.50	Bed H. Board 31½, F. Board 21, Widths 3' 3" and 4' 6"		
3031	"	39.00	Chest and 5 Drawer	32 x 19	46½
3032	"	36.50	Dresser 4 Drawer	42 x 19	33
3033	"	12.50	Night Table	16 x 14	22
3034	"	19.50	Dressing Table	36 x 18	29
3035	"	7.50	Bench	21 x 14	15
3036	"	11.50	Mirror Glass 34 x 18		
Set	"	113.50	Bed, Chest, Dresser, Mirror (4 pieces)		

BEDROOM

Illustrated on pages 12 and 13

No.	Wood	Price	Description	Top	Height
3037	Maple	17.50	Bed, H. Board 33, F. Board 20, Widths 3' 3" and 4' 6"		
3038	"	29.00	Dresser 3 Drawer	40 x 18	33
3039	"	33.50	Chest 4 Drawer	30 x 18	45
3040	"	17.00	Dressing Table	34 x 18	30
3041	"	7.00	Bench	20 x 12½	17
3042	"	11.00	Night Table	16 x 14	23½
3058	"	10.00	Mirror Glass 28 x 18		
Set	"	90.00	Bed, Chest, Dresser, Mirror No. 3058		

BEDROOM

Illustrated on pages 14 and 15

No.	Wood	Price	Description	Top	Height
3043	Maple	9.50	Mirror Glass 34 x 16		
3044	"	32.50	Dresser 3 Drawer	40 x 19	32
3045	"	23.50	Bed H. Board 33, F. Board 21½, Widths 3' 3" and 4' 6"		
3046	"	36.00	Chest 4 Drawer	32 x 19	44
3047	"	19.00	Dressing Table	36 x 18	29
3048	"	7.00	Bench	22 x 14	16
3049	"	10.50	Night Table	16 x 14	22
Set	"	101.50	Bed, Chest, Dresser, Mirror No. 3043 (4 Pieces)		

CONANT BALL CO.

87 SUDBURY STREET · BOSTON, MASS.

New York Office:
11 EAST 31st STREET · NEW YORK CITY

Factories:
GARDNER, MASS. · TEMPLETON, MASS.

ISSUED MARCH 1936	**LIST PRICE**		SUBJECT TO CHANGE WITH-OUT NOTICE	
	ALL WOOD IS NORTHERN ROCK MAPLE			
No.	Price	Description	Top	Height
3059	13.00	Cocktail Table	36 x 17	16
3060	10.50 X Grade / 11.50 XA Grade / 12.50 A Grade / 13.50 B Grade	Ottoman Yardage 50″–⅝, 36″–1¼	21 x 15	15½
3061	45.00	Chest	33 x 18½	46
3062	41.00	Dresser	45 x 18½	34
3063	17.50	Dresser-Mirror (Glass 44 x 18)		
3064	15.00	Light Stand	18 x 14	22
3065	32.50	Bed (Head Board 34″. Footboard 22″. Widths 3-3 and 4-6.)		
3066	15.00	Vanity Mirror (Glass 36 x 20)		
3068	45.00	Vanity	48 x 18	25
3069	7.50	Bench	21 x 15¼	15
3070	35.00	Corner Cupboard	Width 28	58½
3071	13.50	Side Table	30 x 10¼	23

Blonde Finish can be furnished on any American Modern Piece at an Extra Charge of 10%

CONANT BALL CO. 67 SUDBURY STREET, BOSTON, MASS. 11 EAST 31ST STREET, NEW YORK CITY FACTORIES: GARDNER AND TEMPLETON, MASS.

American Modern blond maple dresser,
46½" h x 20" d x 32¼" w.

American Modern blond maple night stands,
original finish,
22¼" h x 15¼" d x 16" w.

American Modern blond maple bureau,
original finish,
33" h x 20" d x 42" w.

Conant-Ball American Modern

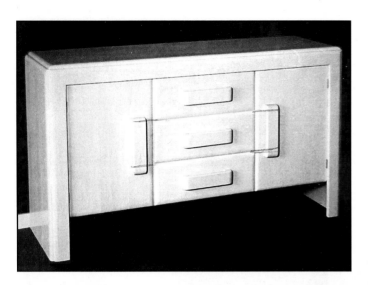

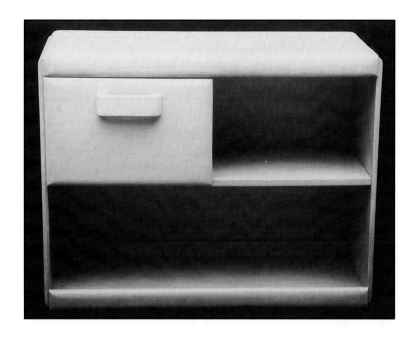

American Modern secretary bookcase,
solid copper hardware, shelf is positioned behind door
which drops to horizontal level.

#515 knee hole desk, 28½" x 19" x 43".
#515 night table, 26" x 16" x 10½".
Russel Wright line designed for Sears that was like
American Modern by Conant-Ball with easier access
and less expensive. Ca. 1946 lamp attributed to Russel
Wright (spun aluminum with walnut) shown with
Bauer vase.

Conant-Ball American Modern chair,
29" high, 24" wide, black vinyl upholstery,
limed finish is original.

Young American Modern Catalog Pages

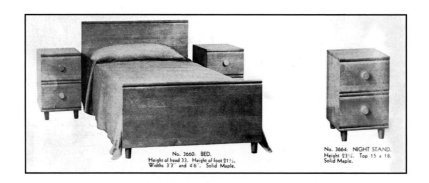

No. 3660: BED.
Height of head 33. Height of foot 21½.
Widths 3'3" and 4'6". Solid Maple.

No. 3664: NIGHT STAND.
Height 23½. Top 15 x 18.
Solid Maple.

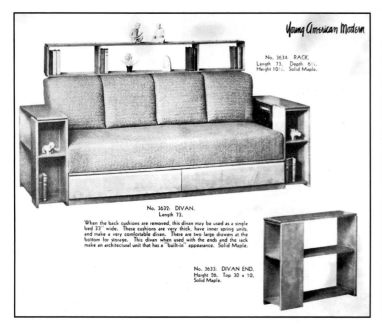

Young American Modern

No. 3634: RACK.
Length 73. Depth 6½.
Height 10½. Solid Maple.

No. 3632: DIVAN.
Length 73.

When the back cushions are removed, this divan may be used as a single bed 33" wide. These cushions are very thick, have inner spring units, and make a very comfortable divan. There are two large drawers at the bottom for storage. This divan when used with the ends and the rack make an architectural unit that has a "built-in" appearance. Solid Maple.

No. 3633: DIVAN END.
Height 26. Top 30 x 10.
Solid Maple.

No. 3609: MIRROR
Glass 34 x 28. Solid
Maple.

No. 3519: BOUDOIR CHAIR.
Height to seat 14½. Height over-
all 24½. Between arms 19.
Seat depth 21. Solid Maple.

No. 3625: VANITY BASE.
Height 26. Top 48 x 18.
Solid Maple.

No. 3626: BENCH.
Height 15. Top 23
x 15. Solid Maple.

Young American Modern

No. 3621. CHEST.
Height 45. Top 32
x 19. Solid Maple.

No. 3623. MIRROR.
Glass 32 x 20. Solid
Maple.

No. 3622. DRESSER.
Height 34. Top 41 x
19. Solid Maple.

Young American Modern

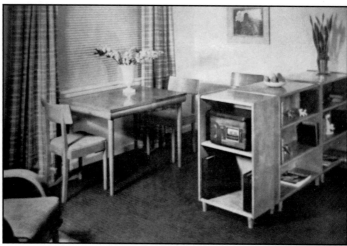

No. 3616 SCC. CHINA.
Height 62. Width 36. Depth 18.
Sliding glass doors. Solid Maple.

No. 3611. BUFFET.
Height 33. Top 58 x 18.
Six drawers. Solid Maple.

Young American Modern

No. 3602. CHAIR.
Height 31. Seat width 16½.
Seat depth 15½. Solid Maple.

No. 3616 SWC. CUPBOARD.
Height 62. Width 36. Depth
18. Solid Maple.

No. 3641. TABLE.
Height 29. Top 42 x 30. Top
open 52 x 30. Solid Maple.

Modern Mates by Conant-Ball

Modern Mates by Conant-Ball,
#8001, end table, 21½" x 26" x 15",

#5401, night table, 22" x 18" x 16".

Modern Mates by Conant-Ball,
#8505, corner desk with drawer,
30" x 30" x 30".

Modern Mates by Conant-Ball
shows how pieces were to fit together
by designing them 30" tall and 18"
deep, called "good plane common
sense" in advertising.

**Modern Mates by Conant-Ball,
#3385, rectangular coffee table, drawer
opens on both sides, 15" x 46" x 21",**

**#3390, oval coffee table, lip on back of
table, 16½" x 50" x 22½".**

**Modern Mates by Conant-Ball,
#6003, Drop leaf table, 30½" x 42" x 65"
open, shown with Bauer vase, American
Modern chartreuse dinnerware, and
American Modern steel flatware.**

**Modern Mates by Conant-Ball,
#8004, three nesting tables,
24" x 26" x 20½",**

23" x 25½" x 17",

**22" x25" x 13",
shown with spun aluminum tea set.**

Modern Mates by Conant-Ball,
desk and chair original upholstery and finish.

#5001, full-size bed, head board 33",
foot board, 21½", 4' x 6" wide,
#5204, dresser, 32" x 48 x 20,
#5703, mirror, 47½" x 39½".
#5702, mirror, 40 x 30".
Reflected in mirror is spun
aluminum torchiere lamp, 63" tall.

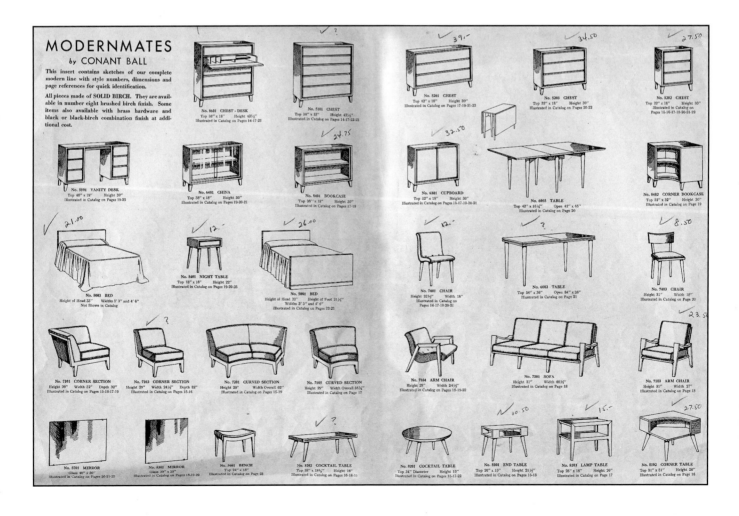

Old Hickory Americana

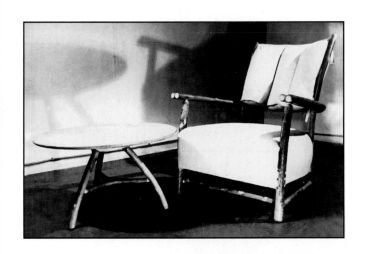

Statton

In a New Light

Wright's Transitional Modern design permeated his work with lamps as it had his metals. These lamps, which Wright named "Informal Modern," seemed to provide a logical compromise, finding their place in informal home use and harmonizing with furnishings. They date from the 1930s and they show real change from lamps on the market then. Table lamps, involving the use of cork, wood, ceramic materials, chrome, spun aluminum, brass, and copper typified this work. Student lamps, desk lamps, bridge lamps, and floor lamps, often described as reflector or torchere types, all were part of Wright's early work. An entirely new lamp called an extension reflector which had a curved stem, projecting the bowl out into the room may have been the most dramatic.

Never content to sample a market, Wright entered the lamp market with a small grouping, intending to establish himself as a pioneer in lamp design. He enlarged the line many times to be as inclusive as described here. Known for his ability to transform commonplace material into new and brilliant designs, he hoped to set a new standard in the lamp industry. Unfortunately, they did not meet with the approval which he had hoped for.

Many of Wright's lamps were planned as part of his American Way program distributed through Raymor. These should have included markings, but that may have been done with stickers or labels. A few examples of his early work with metals are known. We have records to tell us that his Chase contract allowed him to continue to produce metal lamps which were already in his chrome line. The limited Accessory Company work was followed by a great deal of client work and it is this which is most often found today. In 1946 a contract existed between Wright and the Mutual Sunset Lamp Company. He was to design 20 or 30 lamps within a specified price range and he was not to design competitively priced lamps for other clients while his contract was in effect. Under the terms, however, he could continue to keep the accounts with which he was already working. Almost at once, problems resulted and Mutual returned the designs, telling him that they were releasing him from his contract. Wright felt that this action was outside the agreements made, that he had extended himself in all ways, and that a good bit of work had been done for which there would be no product and no payment. He claimed the contract which they had signed obligated them to produce. The matter went to arbitration with a decision in Wright's favor. Mutual Sunset appealed the matter to the Supreme Court of New York State. In the end, he prevailed and the company paid him for his work, returning his designs, but not agreeing to deal with him further. These samples may be found, but they are almost certainly not marked. We cannot know whether or not

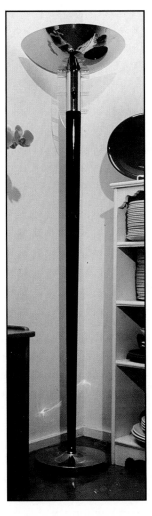

Reflector lamp, 65" tall.

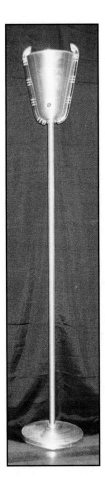

Spun aluminum torchere lamp, 65" tall.

97

the lamp designs were offered to other clients at a later time but it would have been consistent with his practice of saving products for future use.

While Wright was working on an art pottery line for Bauer in Atlanta, he proposed to include two lamps. These lamps were difficult to produce with any degree of glaze uniformity. They were part of the line shown at the Atlanta show in 1941 but no orders were taken and Bauer made the decision to discontinue the entire line. Samples, however, must exist. Look for these in Atlanta Brick, Stone Mountain Gray, and Bybee Brown. A finding would be a significant one.

Wright was asked to design several lamps to be manufactured by the Acme Lamp Company and sold by Sears Roebuck and Company. The agreement was that he would submit 12 designs and would allow his name to be used on the approved lamps. With the signature clause as part of the agreement, it is difficult to understand why these lamps have not been found unless they, like others, had stickers or tag markings, destroyed by time. All these lamps date from 1946 – 1948.

In 1949 Wright contracted with the Colonial Premier Lamp company and agreed to design 16 lamps of glass and ceramic. Restricting the use of his name on some of the advertising and production, he permitted it on specified items. He was to be paid his standard royalties and that was extended to second quality lamps sold. He stipulated, however, that any reduced price sales would result in a review of the entire contract. In a rare moment of generosity, he agreed to work with them exclusively and agreed to add to the designs yearly and to "refresh" the designs as requested. After the first year's association, Colonial informed him that they were not able to continue. They were fair in the matter, paying him for work done and agreeing to renew his contract when they found themselves in better circumstances. Whatever the problems Colonial experienced, the dissolution was accomplished with mutual understanding. With some certain production, these lamps should be found. Again, the absence of tags and stickers may limit findings.

Later work distributed by Raymor in 1951 included lamps made by the Fairmont Lamp Company and involved The Statton Furniture Company. The line, an extensive one, was called "Lamps for Easier Living," incorporated into the Statton firm's "Easier Living" line. These lamps were to have been made in several metallic colors of baked vitreous enamel and combined materials such as split bamboo, brass, copper, walnut, cork, oak, pewter, ribbed plaster, and glass. Shades were equally interesting. In some cases plain colored rope entirely covered the shade. Others used a dark rattan, a new cellophane and cotton fabric, a ribbon made of silk and spun glass, wool yarn, and a patent leather fiber made out of pine pulp. Initially limited to 10 items including both table and floor lamps, the number was to be increased often. Fairmont was told that if they wished exclusivity, the contract would need to be renewed annually and he would submit new designs on that basis. With considerable work done on this line we have many examples and will include them as space allows. That there were no more is explained by the fact that Fairmont proved difficult to please and both parties sent their differences to arbitration with Wright awarded $1,000.00 in yesterday's dollars.

Lamps, apparently done in a 1950s style, but not attributed to Wright, have been found in Steubenville glazes. With no mention in the Wright files, it seems probable that this is another example of the practice of using his glaze formula, not his designs. In such cases, he did draw royalties, of course, but they cannot be considered as examples of his lamp work.

Be careful of any lamps which incorporated a piece or part of a piece of his dinnerware. No where in the files is there any mention of such adaptation and no consideration was given to prototype or sample such items, but such combinations have been formed by those who would make their own "Russel Wright lamp."

Fortunately, archival records show many pictures illustrating characteristic features which direct us to Wright's work. Those would include the exaggerated use of texture rather than surface ornamentation, often accompanied by the use of a variety of materials in the same lamp. By concentrating on those features, our identification is directed toward work which may not be identifiable in other ways.

Completely different in style from other lamps of the time, Wright's lamps seemed very modern, very cold, to buyers in the '40s. The public had grown accustomed to period pieces with heavy surface ornamentation and traditional shapes and lamps seemed to share the slow-to-change market which prevailed in the furniture industry. Customers felt the newness too much of a departure. By contrast, today's collectors find them more ordinary, not high styled, and less innovative. Functionalism, Wright felt, had failed to serve the lamp industry. In spite of that, his lamps added a new direction to lamp selections and the impact on the industry may have had a general influence not recognized at the time when they were made.

Early metal table lamps and floor lamps may be found with the signature, his initials, or identifiable credit on the underside of the base deeply embedded in the metal. This may be difficult to locate. Look closely and examine all surfaces, no matter how obscure. This early work is worth the search for it is exceptional, much more interesting than the commercial lamp work of its time.

Wright's floor lamp and spun aluminum accessories shown in his penthouse living room.

ON PRICING LAMPS

Table lamps remain difficult to price because it is difficult to attribute the rather plain, unmarked lamps to Wright. Stories have been reported where they have been identified from photos shown in 1990. Alert collectors have bought them, placing their own values on them at about $125.00 – 150.00. Other, more interesting table lamps may be priced from $200.00 – 400.00. Floor lamps, more often with the Wright signature molded into the base attract more interest and have been reported sold at $500.00 – 600.00. Torcheres, also usually identified with the signature, are difficult to price. Some of the more ordinary types have been sold for $500.00 to $600.00, but more unusual ones, those involving other materials in addition to the metal found happy homes at $1,000.00 each plus shipping.

Signature and condition remain the prominent factor in lamp pricing. Unsigned lamps, with no signature remain suspect and collectors are unwilling to value them beyond thrift shop prices. Signed items, in poor condition, lose value, as do bridge lamps which have lost their shades. On the other hand, some very wonderful lamp work has been found and some deserve the high prices asked for them.

Russel Wright Accessory Company Lamps

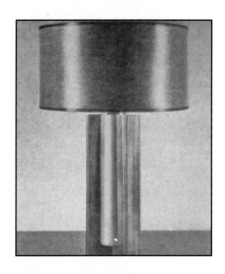

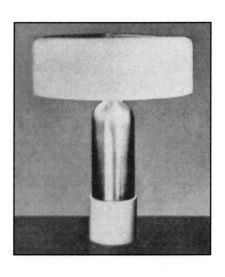

#916, Glass and metal lamp, 14" high, 13" shade diameter, 1 light, brushed copper, glass, white baked enamel.
#975, same with brushed brass, glass, with blond maple stem.
#976, same with aluminum, glass, with walnut stem.

#914, walnut fin lamp, 20" high, 13" wide shade diameter, 2 light, walnut and aluminum, shade of brown and ivory woven luggage material over parchment, trimmed with flat brown leatherette.
#972, same in walnut and brushed copper, tan luggage cloth shade.

#935, all metal lamp, 21" high, 18" wide shade diameter, 2 light, oyster white enamel, finial and small stem at bottom are brushed aluminum.

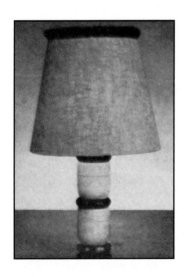

#962, stoneware lamp, 20" high, 11" wide shade diameter, 1 light, putty colored unglazed pottery and walnut, shade of ecru yarn over parchment with brown trim.

#481, pottery and reed lamp, 17" high, 15½" wide shade diameter, 1 light, highly glazed sand colored pottery, dark brown reed, shade of coarse beige over parchment.

#700, table reflector, 14" high 10" reflector diameter, aluminum and walnut.

#917, glass shade lamp, 15"
high, 12" shade diameter, 2
light, oxidized gun-metal and
white baked enamel.
#977, same with brushed brass.

#924, bowknot boudoir lamp,
14" high, 9" shade depth, 1
light, brushed copper, white
baked enamel, peach toned
parchment covered with net.
#978, same with brushed brass
base and bow, ribbed net shade
over white parchment.
#979, same with aluminum base
and bow.

#961, earthenware lamp, 20"
high, 12" widest shade diameter, 1 light, highly glazed rust
pottery and waxed maple, shade
of maple veneer over parchment, trimmed with brown
leatherette.

#914, walnut finish lamp, 20"
high, 13" wide shade diameter, 2
light, walnut and aluminum,
shade of brown and ivory woven
luggage material over parchment,
trimmed with flat brown
leatherette.
#972, same in walnut and brushed
copper, tan luggage cloth shade.

#960, diamond boudoir
lamp, 17" high, 9" shade
depth, 1 light, brushed
brass and faceted crystal,
shade of white moire over
parchment, trimmed with
gold and white silk braid.

#926, copper and reed lamp, 18"
high, 17" wide shade diameter, 2
light, brushed copper, natural light
colored reed, tan rough flecked
cotton fabric over parchment,
trimmed with heavy white braid.

#474, bamboo lamp, 23" high, 17½" wide shade diameter, 2 light, light colored natural bamboo, brushed brass, shade of rough textured ivory colored fabric over parchment.

#921, bull's eye lamp, 17" high, 12" shade diameter, 2 light, aluminum and chocolate brown baked enamel, shade of natural colored pongee over parchment, trimmed with flat brown leatherette and topped by aluminum cover.

#930, desk lamp, 14" high, 13" shade diameter, 2 light, aluminum and walnut.

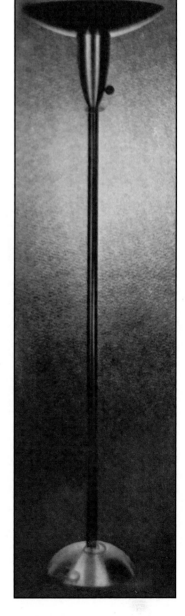

#929, reflector, 65" tall, 18" reflector diamter, brushed copper socket-housing and base, shade and stem in baked ivory enamel.
#928, same in brushed copper and baked brown enamel.
#702, same in brushed aluminum and baked brown enamel.
#725, same in brushed aluminum and baked white enamel.

 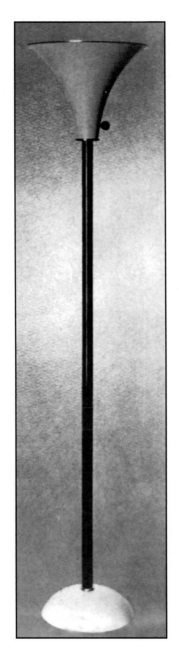 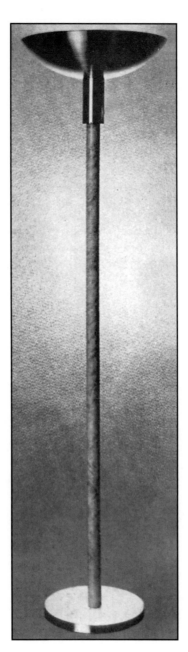 

Left to Right:

#488, reflector, 65" tall, 17" reflector diameter, maple, brushed brass, ivory glass reflector. #708, same with walnut and brushed copper with ivory glass reflector. #726, same with maple and brushed copper with ivory glass reflector.

#915, reflector, 63" tall, 13½" reflector diameter, baked white and brown enamel, aluminum trim, walnut switch. #973, same with baked white and terra cotta, aluminum trim and walnut switch.

#478, reflector, 65" tall, 18" reflector diameter, walnut stem with brushed aluminum base, reflector, and socket housing. #707, same with walnut stem, brushed copper base, reflector, and socket housing. #927, same with maple stem, brushed brass base, reflector, and socket housing.

#913, reflector, 63" tall, 11" reflector diameter, brown and ivory baked enamel, ivory Catalin switch. #971, same with blue and white baked enamel with red catalin switch.

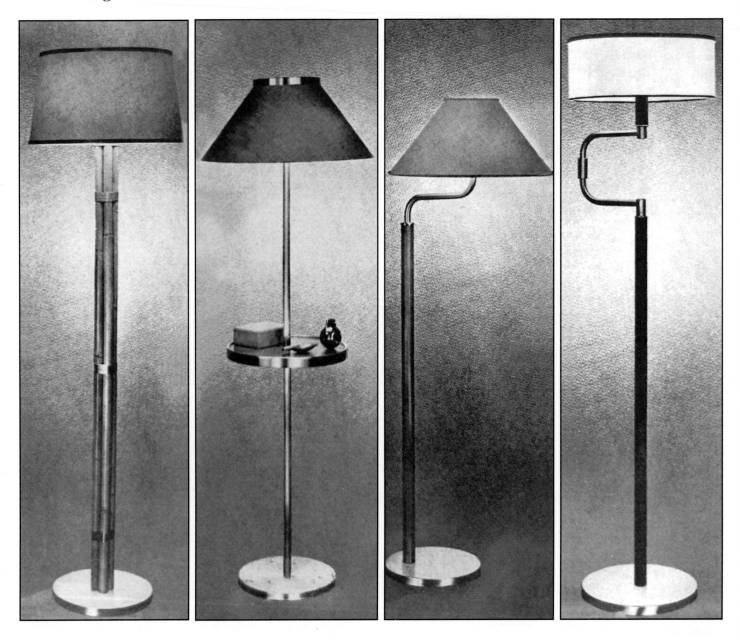

Left to Right:

#473, bamboo lamp, 61" tall, 20" wide shade diameter, 12" shade depth, bamboo, brushed brass, shade of rough textured ivory fabric over parchment with brass wire trim.

#933, swinging bridge lamp, 54" tall, 18" wide shade diameter, 2 light, matte finished cadmium base and arm, walnut stem, shade of tan pongee over parchment, bordered with brown leatherette.

#957, shelf lamp, 45" tall, 18" wide shade diameter, 12½" shelf diameter, 2 light, brushed aluminum base and shade cover, walnut shelf, baked brown enamel stem, shade of beige pongee over parchment.

#923, adjustable reading lamp, 52" tall, 14½" shade diameter, 2 light, matte cadmium arm and base, baked brown enamel stem and cover for shade of clear frosted "Clair de lune."

Russel Wright Fairmont Lamps

68" torchere, tapered wooden shaft, brass base and column, glass shield in metal top diffuses light for reading.

Brass, 27" bird cage lamp.

Heavy brass-plated base with swivel in base, tube colors chartreuse, pear green, Chinese red, gold baked enamel.

105

Stationary lamp with 2 light cluster, brass desk lamp, 16" brass-plated metal tubing in chartreuse, Chinese red, pear green, gold baked enamel, adjusts to 35".

Tripod floor lamp, 55" high, 14" brass-plated tray, chartreuse, Chinese red, pear green, gold baked enamel, table lamp, 30" high, same colors.

19" vanity or desk lamp, eggshell plastic shade, ivory or brass-plated base.

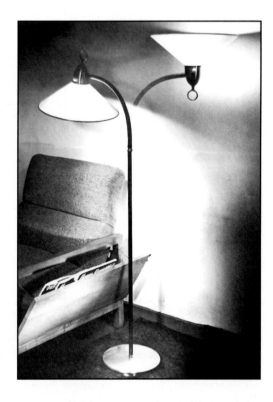

TV and reading lamp, 26" brass-plated base, tapered milk glass tube, perforated metallic parchment shade.

Floor lamp with adjustable levels, 49" – 67" high.

Adjustable goose neck lamp, brass base, goose neck and tubing covered with plastic vinyl, same colors.

27" table lamp.

#130 adjustable chromium-plated
goose neck lamp.

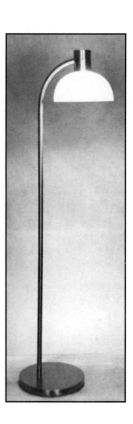

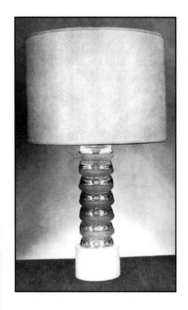

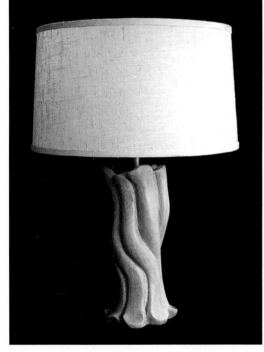

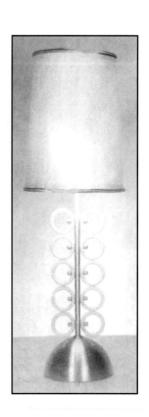

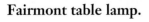
Fairmont table lamp.

#12, natural cane and rust colored pottery, 1 light harp, 12" shade with rust fabric over parchment with natural cane strappings.

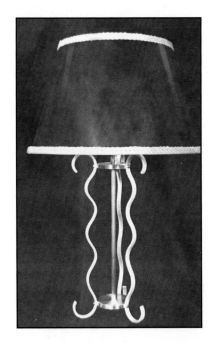

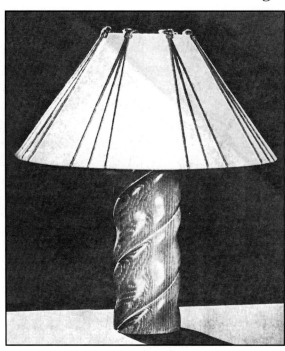

#705, 23½" table lamp, shade at bottom is 16½", base of natural rattan sticks and emeriled brass, canopy covering top of shade emeriled brass.

Wood,
Early and Late

Wright's work with wood evidences a reverential respect for that material, exemplified by the meticulous concern with which he selected various woods for accessory items using them in ways not common before. Observing the care which he used as he fashioned informal pieces allows us to see him fashioning woods with the same painstaking effort that he would later exert over glaze choices.

As early as 1932, in his coach house shop, he was able to turn out simple wood serving items. Almost plain, they might have escaped the notice of buyers except that they fit his concept of informality, resulting in an entirely different product from the metals which occupied much of his resources at the time. Mary sold these and they received attention in articles in *House and Field* which became *House Beautiful,* as well as other magazines with national distribution.

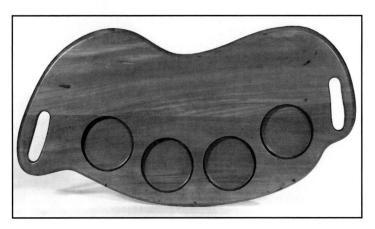

Oceana serving tray.
Courtesy of Brooklyn Museum Gift of Arthur Drummond.

With few tools to extend the variety of his wood line and with no catalog to illustrate what he was able to create, he did not work with wood for long, claiming to have been forced out of it by the intensive competition of his own ideas in the hands of others. True or untrue, it was an accusation he would level many times during his working life. Seemingly, he felt the market was overcrowded with sameness. Collectors today, find too few of his examples of this first work, perhaps because it is not easily separated from the mass-market work done by others during the same time period. Examples would have included cheese boards, relish trays, shaker sets, bowls, and platters for various uses. While a complete listing is not available, collectors should refer to distinguishing characteristics to guide them. Items were of substantial weight and usually of hard woods, easily distinguished from the common wood items imported to this country in the 1950s. Using more than one material in the same object was typical of much of the work. We find that principle put to use in the wood Lazy Susan which held Gladding McBean ceramic inserts for relishes or appetizers, serving trays which held glasses, and other items which combined spun aluminum and wood.

The most exciting work was done in a way others could not imitate. In 1935, designing for the Klise Wood Working Company of Grand Rapids, Michigan, he developed his Oceana line. A marine motif identified these Klise pieces. Of various woods, cherry, gum, blond maple, and hazelwood, each piece showed the grain and color of the wood to its best advantage. Wright was able to experiment with the use of free form with results that appear to be hand carved and finished, wood sculptures. They were not, of course, but Wright, with sculpture studies in his background, was able to make them appear so. He claimed these Oceana pieces to be art in wood "leaving behind the stereotyped geometrical cliches which constitute so much of our present day modern picture." Drawing their shapes from shells and strange sea plants, they were abstract representations of those forms. They captured the imagination of modernists at once and Oceana items were considered to be natural forms adapted to art by all who touched them.

111

Oceana snail relish and Oceana leaf relish.

Conceived to be part of the American Way line, Wright enlarged the line until the Way program was discontinued, bringing an end to this important work. It can be said that the general public seemed not to understand it, unsure just how to fit this thematic work into their homes. In 1941 buyers, hesitant with the new informal concept, may have felt it to be intended for beach or resort entertaining and its use never caught on with them. The production was very limited and Wright, once more, felt his work not appreciated as it deserved.

Modernists, however, understood this Oceana and admired its elegance lifting it to award winning status. The centerpiece bowl which we show here was used on a 1940 Museum of Modern Art catalog and it was said to have been the most sculpturally beautiful item in the line. In retrospect, Wright learned that the line had been aborted too soon. It came to enjoy such respect in the artistic community that it seemed possible that patience with the line, as well as better advertising, might have resulted in a more marketable product.

Collectors prize Oceana, considering it to be a rare, significant part of his work. It made much the same statement as did his Bauer art pottery, but it is rarer. If it seems not to have found homes with more collectors, it may be that there is simply not enough for us to enjoy.

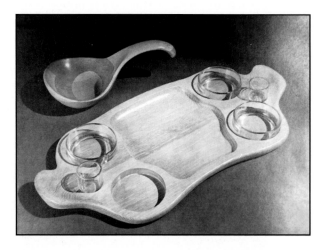

Serving spoon not listed but pictured as Oceana, 14" x 7½". Hostess tray with glass inserts.

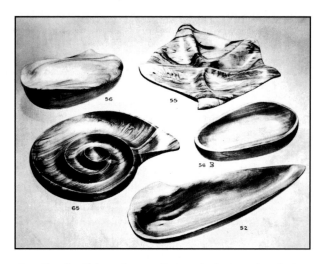

Buella shell bowl, starfish relish, snail relish, flat shell salad bowl, and one-handled bowl.

The sculpturally beautiful centerpiece bowl.

Our Oceana listing remains open ended but it originally included:

One handled relish for canapes or snacks, 6¼" x 17"	Wave salad bowl, 11", 13", 15"	Flat shell salad bowl, 12"
Fluted salad bowl, 4½" x 9"	Pearl plate, 9"	Snail salts
Wing shell bread tray, 6"	Shell plate, 9"	Jelly set
Buella shell bowl for fruit or salad, 13" x 8"	Seaweed relish, 4½" x 19"	Centerpiece bowl
Starfish relish, 13½"	Lazy Susan, 15"	Small shell dish
Reversible rosette, relish side, and cheese/cracker side	Combination serving tray/salad bowl, 10" x 18"	Salad fork and spoon
Shell candy box, 3" x 9"	Hostess tray with glass inserts, 11" x 24"	Leaf tray
	Small nut bowl, 2" x 5"	Relish, 4 compartments
	Small relish dish	Bowl
		Bowl with two compartments
		Deep bowl

Oceana items are signed with the burnt wood signature found in the marks sections. Some will also include a turquoise American Way sticker. In spite of the marine theme, not all items were as suggestive of that and collectors would do well to examine any interesting piece of wood for the signature. We are still finding some items for the first time and it is possible that pieces of Oceana are still hiding in cupboards of original Wright collectors.

Wright designed a later line for Klise in the 1950s. These informal serving items were styled in typical '50s fashion and not thematic. Made of the popular frosted oak, there were to have been buffet serving items for informal occasions as well as accessories, cigarette boxes, bowls, and occasional pieces. Lucite, glass, or chrome was to have been incorporated into the designs. Again, very little of this has been found and we find confusing markings. Some items known to be Mary's work, but with Russel's name, have appeared and these have left us with unanswered questions as well as uncertain listings. Fifties collectors, only beginning to look at frosted oak finishes, seem likely to be the first to recognize these pieces.

Wright, in 1957, found himself without the Oceana items he had been so proud of and wrote to Klise to ask if any items could still be purchased. The reply came that Wright was welcome to borrow any of the nine pieces which the chief officer owned, but that none were for sale. Later Wright considered having them cast for use in the Formosa family business with which he became involved in his Asian handicraft program, but it was not done.

Oceana had taken art from the sea and placed in the modern homes of the 1940s and it sings a siren song to collectors who recognize its beautiful grains, soft finishes, and sculptured lines. If collectors do not seek it with the frequency that drives them to Wright's Bauer art pottery, it is because art pottery appeals to a more diverse collecting group. Seldom found, you will value it as a pearl from the sea if it washes ashore on your beach.

Oceana leaf tray, small snail dish, nut bowl, jelly set, wing shell bread tray, and salad fork and spoon.

Wave salad bowl, fluted salad bowl, centerpiece bowl, and serving tray.

113

PRICING EARLY WOOD AND OCEANA

There is much interest in Wright's early wood. Unfortunately, little of it is found and it may be that it was not regarded highly when it was made, never preserved as we would have liked it to be. It may be among the rarest of Wright's work, coming early and abandoned quickly. Unfortunately, it came at a time when records were not kept as religiously as they were later and our information on it remains fragmented. A handsome five-tiered planter/flower container made of walnut and lined with copper, said to have been designed by Aline Bernstein and executed by Wright, was made as early as 1932. Other work, very similarly designed included desk and smoking accessories and small animals. This work was accompanied with information which said it to have been "assembled" by Russel Wright. Any of this work would be rare and that Wright had a connection with it, mentioned in national advertising, adds to collector's interests. All of it would compare with his early wood pricing. We would do well to look for his initials as a mark, and to regard any unusual pieces as possibilities, priced closely to the early wood items listed below.

Oceana, on the other hand remains a classic, a popular one, and today collectors love it for the beauty intrinsic in the wood as well as the design. With a short production time, and a limited number of items, Oceana seems not to have been made in an amount which would satisfy today's admirers. Some parts of the country claim to have seen only a few examples, but those are said to have sold at high prices, going into collections of those with an eye for the best. Keep your eyes out for Oceana and expect these prices to go higher soon for this work is sculpturally fine.

All wood items are priced in excellent condition, with original finish. Stripping which alters the original finish reduces value by at least 50%. Any damage from water or surface scratching further devaluates these prices.

OCEANA ITEMS

Add $50.00 – 75.00 for Oceana sticker.

One handled relish ....$500.00 – 600.00	Salad fork & spoon........................$275.00 – 350.00
Buella shell bowl..........................$600.00 – 800.00	Seaweed relish ....$700.00 – 800.00
Shell covered candy box.............$800.00 – 1000.00	Shell plate ....NPD
Centerpiece bowl ....$800.00 – 900.00	Snail shakers, pair......................$175.00 – 225.00
Flat shell salad bowl ....$500.00 – 600.00	Starfish relish ....$450.00 – 500.00
Fluted salad bowl ....$500.00 – 600.00	Snail relish (large).....................$600.00 – 800.00
Hostess trays with glass inserts ....$350.00 – 400.00	Snail relish (small) ....$500.00 – 600.00
Jelly jar with tray ....$350.00 – 400.00	Wave salad Bowl........................$600.00 – 800.00
Leaf relish tray ....$600.00 – 800.00	Wing shell bread tray..................$350.00 – 400.00
Pearl plate ....NPD	Other items ....NPD
Reversible rosette ....$800.00 – 900.00	

WOOD ACCESSORIES,
not related to Oceana

Bowls for serving (early) ....$300.00 – 350.00	Lazy Susan with ceramic inserts..$750.00 – 900.00
Frosted oak bowls ....$300.00 – 350.00	Nut bowl with chrome..................$350.00 – 400.00
Frosted oak dice shakers ....$150.00 – 200.00	Relish, small ....$250.00 – 300.00
Frosted oak platters ....$250.00 – 300.00	Relish, 2 compartments ....$300.00 – 400.00
Frosted oak relish dishes ....$250.00 – 300.00	Serving tray/salad bowl ....$400.00 – 600.00
Individual canape trays ....$75.00 – 80.00 each	Steak tray with carving tools ....$350.00 – 400.00

Oceana bowls.
Large bowl, 13" across, 3½" high.
Medium bowl 11" across, 3" high.

Oceana leaf relish.

Undocumented Oceana bowl,
13" wide, 3½" high.

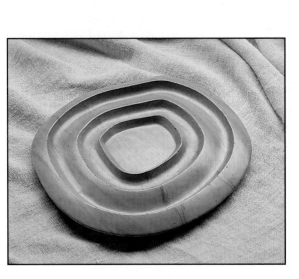

Two views of Oceana reversible relish
rosette.

Early wood believed to be
prototype piece for Oceana.

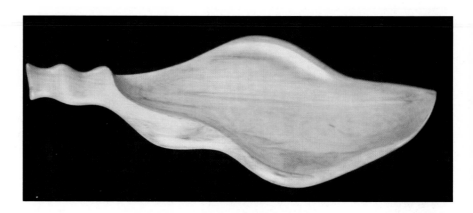

Serving tray/salad bowl.

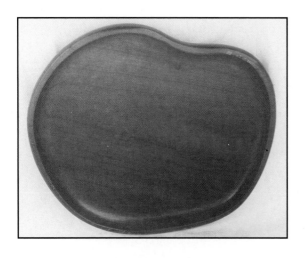

Oceana individually sized tray, probably sold
in groupings, late additions to Oceana work.

Wave salad bowl on Simtex Harvest cloth.

Oceana fluted salad bowl.

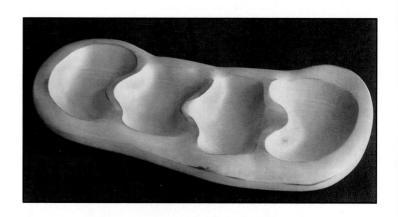

Oceana four-compartment relish.

shown open

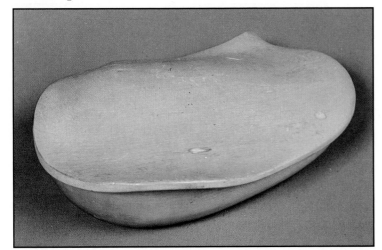

shown closed

Oceana candy bowl.

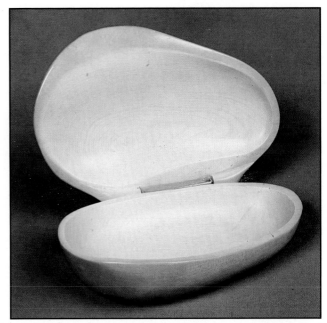

bottom

shown open

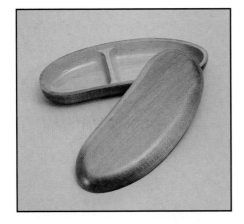

Three mountaineers covered divided box.
(We feel this could be an American Way entry
and possibly Mary Wright.)

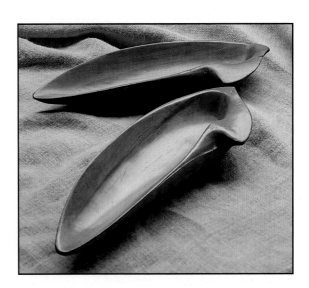

Oceana one-handled bowls, cherry finish.

Wood, Early and Late

Late Klise Frosted Oak Designs

Klise late frosted oak bowls.

Late Klise frosted oak items:
four-compartment relish, 12" square,
three-compartment relish, 11 x 6¾",
jelly jar 6" high, nut bowl, 10½" x 8".

Klise frosted oak giant dice shaker, 3⅜" cube,
steak platter, 18" x 10¼".

Oceana snail relish.

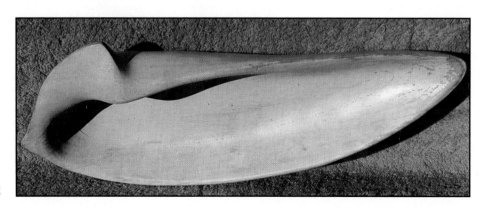

Oceana one-handled bowl
with frosted oak finish.

Oceana starfish, five-compartment relish,
with original American Way sticker.

Frosted Oak "porthole tray" with holes for napkins
and compartments for drinks or bottles,
partial label on bottom.
Glassware: American Modern wine,
double old fashion, and Pilsner.

Photo from *Home and Field* magazine, November,
1932.
Walnut box designed by Aline
Bernstein and executed by Russel Wright, has
metal containers so that it may be used for plants
or flowers.

Photo from *Home and Field* magazine,
November, 1932.
Steak set and nut bowl in walnut with chromium plate
designed by Russel Wright, the former for W. Lang-
bein & Bros. Walnut waste basket, ashtrays, gumwood
bird, large horse in tiger wood, small horse in holly
wood, Rena Rosenthal, Amboyna tray, Mrs. Ehrich.
Harewood cigarette box, R.H. Macy & Co., Inc. Roll-
top box, Abercrombie & Fitch Co.

American Modern, the Experiment

Introducing metal as informal serving items, designing furniture in avant-garde styles, fashioning wood with the appearance of sculpture, writing for national magazines, speaking alongside the important designers of his time, winning awards for his work, conceptualizing his strong beliefs and spelling them out in *The Guide to Easier Living*, all that went before was minimized by the tremendous commercial success of Wright's American Modern Dinnerware. It would catapult him into the position of the best-known designer of his time and his term "American Modern" became thematic because of it. It is a success story, a willingness to take his designs to the American public with confidence. Looking back it seemed to be an all or nothing bet on a sure thing in 1939. It was Modernism come-of-age and Wright found himself preaching to the choir as his American Modern dinnerware proved to be a miracle of Modernism. He was quoted as saying that he had no interest in keeping traditional design alive and this altogether new style drew a line in the sand.

Mass produced, American Modern was affordably priced, bringing it within the financial reach of most buyers. That, combined with innovative shapes and altogether new glazes gave emphasis to Wright's conviction that art could be part of everyone's every day life. All worked together and generations then and now took to it and the vision behind it, proving that good design is timeless and can be affordable. As early as 1941 it was awarded the best ceramic line of the year by the American Designer's Institute.

The position had not been an easy one for the Wrights to achieve, however, for the Ohio river potteries had passed their prime positions and foreign competition was bringing the industry to its knees. None of the potteries saw success in the line Wright was trying to promote. They were sure that it would fail for it was not at all the sort of thing which they had produced successfully in the past and none of the foreign imports was similar. This design, they felt, was outrageous, too harsh, certainly not beautiful. They knew the dimensions of the pottery business and this new design simply did not measure up in any way, nor was it practical to produce it. One by one they dismissed it as some "Eastern fellow's" fool-hardy attempt to change a market they had established and understood.

If it is an exaggeration to say that Wright met the Steubenville Pottery in the bankruptcy court, it is not much of an exaggeration to say that

***House and Garden*, January 1948.**

Dinner plate, salad plate, bread and butter plate, Woodfield salad fork and spoon.

ing for each sales person. Unprepared for the demands, they wrote hundreds of orders for which they had no stock and the Steubenville Pottery immediately went on an over-time operation. Altman's and Bloomingdale's in New York, as well as other large stores, opened to crowds so large and demanding that it was necessary to use supermarket practices to handle the sales. Hudson's orders were shipped by boxcars in an effort to keep enough stock to fill orders and still keep inventory on hand. Smitty's Fish Market in Baltimore bought a carload of "seconds" several times a year and sold it directly from the railroad car. Police had to restore order as customers crowded to get closer. At least one Wright family named their son "Russell" and it is said that some bridge clubs used only Wright designs for prizes. Magazines reminded us that Eleanor and Mamie used American Modern and the effect was as Wright predicted. It was exciting to find our tastes similar to those in high places. We were modern Americans, having lately been joined by depression and war, now joined by convictions which spoke to us of art in our daily living and of the democracy which afforded us that place.

American Modern was first sold through Russel

they met on the courthouse steps. Steubenville was in severe financial straits because of foreign competition and their position on this new work was one Wright had heard over and over. Only after Russel and Mary agreed to finance the production and J.L. Hudson's, the large Detroit department store, made a personal request and promised orders, did Steubenville agree to manufacture it. All who were concerned with American Modern from that time were rewarded for many years. It was made from 1939 to 1959, grossing $159,000,000.00 and became the largest selling dinnerware ever produced, a phenomenon in the dinnerware industry. Steubenville had to expand two times to keep up with the overwhelming orders which were written. Competitors, seeing the success, took a closer look and added their own contemporary lines but none were so successful. The Potter's Union used the generic term, "Russel Wright shape" to describe all these modern lines and they estimated that half of the production of dinnerware sold as late as 1950 was comprised of the Russel Wright type.

The success story of American Modern cannot be ignored. Newspapers carried the words "Mob Scene over Modern." In New York, in 1946, seven years after it was introduced, Gimbels had printed a 2" x 4" advertisement saying that American Modern would be for sale, war-time shortages were over. Not expecting a crowd, the store opened to a block long queue of customers which had formed. In the rush to buy, several people were hurt and it was estimated that there was a constant 100 customers wait-

Cream pitcher, water pitcher, cup and saucer, and covered sugar.

Wright Accessories, but the need for national distribution was soon recognized. Joining with Irving Richards, Russel and Mary formed the Raymor firm which was to market and distribute in a more efficient manner than could either Wright or Steubenville. At once, a nationwide plan for advertising was put into operation by Raymor. Steubenville, itself, continued to advertise and the designer put himself in any position open to him, praising American Modern as he went. Department

praising American Modern as he went. Department store advertising was extensive and these, together, with the Raymor advertisements were works of arts in themselves, appearing frequently in full color in the leading home furnishing magazines over many years. One was not likely to overlook American Modern dinnerware but there was no tendency to place advertising which was so "arty" that the average buyer would lose touch with it. Campbell's Soups ran ads showing bowls-full, serving bowls held Dinty Moore's Stew, and The French Mustard Company, advertising their spices, showed tables set with American Modern serving pieces. Russel continued to advance his concerns that art belonged to us all. Art for the masses, not the classes, he reminded us.

Chop plate, child's plate, relish rosette, covered butter dish, tumbler, salad bowl, and after dinner cup and saucer.

New marketing helped to promote sales. "Open Stock," which simply meant that one did not have to buy a set of American Modern, allowed buyers to buy a place setting for one or several, an extra plate when one was broken and serving items as they were needed or afforded. This policy followed the same principles long used in the sales of glass and silver, but it was a new concept in dinnerware. It put owners in the position of becoming continuing customers. A starter set consisting of four plates, four 6" bread and butter plates, and four cups and saucers was boxed and offered at a special price. No salad plates, you will notice. Almost at once, buyers realized that they needed salad plates. The practice of combining small groups allowed for larger sales though all items continued to be sold as open stock.

Wright directed these groupings to new entertaining themes, particularly as those concerned informal uses. There were groups for every day, patio or barbecue parties, bridge clubs, television entertaining, buffet suppers, brunches, and cocktail parties. Not confining these groups to social occasions, he combined items with others which seemed to make a group. The tumblers and covered pitcher, was called a "mug group," the children's items became "children's groups." The lists were revised and renewed often.

These groups tell us much about our changing times after WW II and tell us also what Wright knew would change for us. His own work was based upon his anticipation of these changes and he read the tea leaves in American Modern cups. He realized that a large number of new home owners would result from families parted during the war years. He recognized the impact that would have on the home furnishings field. New families, with financial government support as they bought their first homes, would be ready to buy after years of waiting. He meant to influence that buying for the better, understanding our new needs before we did. We now found ourselves with "family rooms" as we discovered technology and the wonderful television sets which would change our lives. Soon, we found ourselves eating, not only in front of them, but also in front of the fireplace and out on the patio. No longer was the kitchen the center for the family and our changed lives called for changes after a long wait.

Covered pitcher, patterned plate, platter, shakers, child's bowl, child's tumbler, and Old Morgantown dessert bowl.

American Modern had none of the angular or geometric lines of the Art Deco dinnerware which had been popular. With a streamline look, it was not cold or extreme but instead it had a curvaceous quality, inviting relaxation. Form did follow function, and its biomorphic shapes hinted at surrealism. Still, it was not shocking or eye assaulting, not pretentious. Wright had incorporated his idea of Transitional Modern into this new American Modern dinnerware in just the right serving for mid-century tables. It was to remind him often that standardization and self expression were difficult to combine, that it might not be achievable, but he tried and we tried to understand the grander experiment which he was developing. Primary to him were: function and form must be related, no surface detail beyond the shape, no detraction from a lean line. Economy of line must accomplish a pleasing result, sensuous, not severe. Items must relate in an informal way, coming together to form a group with the related qualities expressed in single items.

The shapes, as originally conceived, did not change and no general redesign was done on the line. Only the carafe appears to have been restyled. The items successfully illustrate the concern for individual excellence Wright tried to accomplish. The coupe shaped plate was an entirely new concept when Wright incorporated it into the American Modern line and its use throughout the entire ceramic industry established it as a staple. Other designers recognized its attractiveness and it was widely copied.

The curved-in salad bowl was altogether different from the round salad bowls of the 1930s and those found today, for it was designed functionally to keep salad from being tossed onto the table as it was being used. Wright photographed it in table settings as a centerpiece bowl. The flat curled-leaf celery was so innovative that it deserves a place in a listing of Wright's most important pieces. The versatile chop plate with its curled corners seemed to be equally useful as an underplate for a tea or coffee service. Others used it an an accessory item aside from table use. The one-handled sugar bowl was a new concept and the Aladdin's lamp creamer with its tight lip was a small marvel. The ceramic relish rosette with its origins in his spun aluminum line was Wright at his abstract best. Similar in concept to a deviled egg plate, the beauty of the Wright rosette is that by combining various foods, color added interest to the rosette itself. Very different from the small bowls of other lines, Wright's tab-handled fruits and soups were more functional than most. The stack set served many uses, a cookie jar, a catch-holder, or a covered sectional vegetable bowl. Magazine pictures

show it with a candle warming unit, though such use would be risky. The small, elusive ice box jars nestled together easily to become individual serving containers, nicely designed to form groupings on a buffet table. Difficult to find, the covered ramekin was an easy piece to use for any small serving or snack. The bowl section without the cover was the child's bowl, listed as a separate item. The carafe/stoppered jug, perhaps more suitable for wine than other beverages, had a handle just right for a host to serve guests who were standing. We seldom see its myrtle wood stopper, long-lost, we suppose, but the piece remains a prize with or without the stopper.

Individual covered ramekin, coffee pot, divided relish, ice box jar.

The restyle work done on the jug involved a version with a lip slightly more ridged that the other. The platter, oblong and easy to hold would do well as a steak plate at an outdoor affair where helpings were generous and guests needed fewer dishes to deal with. The sauce boat easily served soup or stew in generous servings, adding to its first use. From the first, the demi-cups were sold as after dinner cups or as children's cups. Coasters hold sauces for dipping today, but they could just as easily have held ashes or after dinner mints in the '30s. Salts with five holes and peppers with four were small neat and low. Other items, functional and new, fit easily into the informal living of the times and of these times. They made a statement for Modernism, but it was an easy statement, a genteel one and not offensive to those who were more conservative.

The rainbow seemed to belong to the Wrights as they selected new glazes for this modern dinnerware. Many glaze samples were tried and it is safe to say that Wright's personal preferences for these glazes derived

Covered casserole and open vegetable bowl.

from his comparative studies using food on various colors. He wanted this line to differ in every way from the "paint job look" of what had come before. The pottery, on the other hand, was concerned with chemical ingredients. Doris Coutant, Wright's glaze consultant, seemed to test glazes all day and write reports to him all night. She and the staff at the pottery tried to achieve the glazes he specified, over and over. The work was difficult and the files show written correspondence reflecting displeasure at this sample and asking for a bit less of this and a bit more of that in the next runs. With an inquiring nature and a good bit of luck, one collector was able to locate old glaze samples which had been stored at a retail outlet in Steubenville. Fortunately, we have these and some supporting data to illustrate the extent of the experimental glazes which were tried. It is clear that trials were done on a green, brighter than cedar, a bright lavender, unlike any other Wright color, and a deep rust, like brick red in the Iroquois line, but more orange than bean brown. It appears that a high gloss gray was considered also and that chartreuse was sampled extensively. Bean brown samples ran the limits of dark, light, foamy, and variations of each, including an example which may have become chutney later. All of the samples were done on plates with numbers identifying the samples. They exemplify the study and consideration given to each color, making them especially interesting to collectors.

The glazes which Wright approved were muted deep pastels, not high glossed but earthy. There is an underlying textural feeling with variegated self tones, all as different as the shapes had been. Originally the colors were seafoam blue, granite gray, chartreuse curry, coral, bean brown, and white. Made to work together in a mix and match palette, the gray is a stone shaded gray with an egg shell finish. Chartreuse curry, with the interchangeable name of seedless grape, was unlike any color in the dinnerware field at the time. Bean brown was a chemical mixture of brown drawn from burnt umber to a dark tete-de-negre. A rusty brown, it had to be discontinued during the war and Steubenville, not able to duplicate its formula ingredients, replaced it in 1950 with black chutney, a foamy glaze more black olive than brown. Cedar joined the palette at the same time. The white was a warm, creamy white with an understated elegance that stands as one of the most important colors in the line. Seafoam blue, slightly darker and bluer than the usual pale turquoise tint, was up to the minute in shading but it, as well as chutney and cedar green, was discontinued in 1956, available by special order two times a year. Today's collectors find a distinct variance in this seafoam and have divided it into categories which they call "seafoam blue" or "seafoam green." The files show no reason to believe that these were to have been two colors. It is possible, though, that the exact formula, achieved by the use of chemicals ordered from different sources over such a long time, could not be controlled to provide exact results. On the other hand, a run every six months, as was done with seafoam after it lost its place in the line, could have had unsatisfactory results, and been sold to jobbers who bought seconds or remainders. The 1955 colors of glacier blue and cantaloupe became popular at once and they are equally popular today, difficult to find because of the late production. Both are bright, jewel tones, and they add a great deal to the effects which can be achieved by mixing and matching them with older colors. Collectors find themselves surprised at results of this practice, but it remains that Wright knew that these glazes would work together. Nothing had been left to chance. Another variant of seafoam was produced in enough numbers that the name "Steubenville blue" has been used to refer to it. This blue is a bright deep color with no green in it. It is believed that this was another seafoam gone wrong, but it would appear that more of it was made than usual, perhaps a run, possibly a bit more. Little of it has been reported in the western part of the country. Certainly we cannot consider it among those colors which were actually part of the line. In spite of that, collectors jump for an example of this unusual Steubenville blue.

All of the American Modern glazes were popular, then and now, with the exception of chartreuse. It was *the* color in 1939, and its popularity continued for a long time but it has never found a place for itself with collectors. Current fashion magazines are advising readers that chartreuse, renamed acid green, is an important color. Since home furnishings follow fashion trends, watch for a resurgence of chartreuse popularity. Dealers who sell in volume have already noticed increased interest. Collectors, experimenting with these glazes, have found that a bit of chartreuse adds "zing" to a combination. We remind users to expect crazing if they trust chartreuse and white to dishwashers.

Attributes of the line went beyond shape and color. Wright expected pricing to make it affordable and it was also important that it stacked compactly allowing for extra cupboard space. The shapes were designed to be easy to handle as they were washed adding economy of use which Wright extolled as he promised us the good life. His work always made room for his causes.

Where the possibility of the use of his glazes was concerned, he allowed it, drawing royalties on any derivative of his work. Steubenville used Wright's glazes on their own Woodfield design, a leafy shaped pattern. The Woodfield salad fork and spoon, in Wright's glazes, were sold as companion pieces to American Modern from the beginning. My own experimentation with the Woodfield rust color dead-ended when I compared it to American Modern's bean brown. However, I found it to be exactly the color of Wright's Iroquois brick red and I've wondered if Wright had taken a long look at Woodfield rust and tucked the color into his memory. American Modern coasters were glazed in many Steubenville colors and can be found decorated with monogram or logos. Conveniently sized and priced for advertising purposes, Steubenville found many customers and Wright found royalties growing out of all of these sales. Most companies were allowed the same practice, with the same provisions. Collectors must be careful as they recognize Wright's glazes. There are *no* rare, unlisted pieces and the Woodfield line cannot be attributed to Wright.

Other copies have been found and it seems that Wright was unaware of these items for correspondence would surely have resulted. Luncheon plates, only slightly smaller than Wright's dinner plates have appeared in look-alike colors. Tab-handled bowls, a bit over sized for the American modern bowls they imitate, have been found in colors close to Wright's. They are not his but the chutney and chartreuse are such similar glazes that one could be confused. Demi-cups and child's cups have been found in what seems to be bean brown — until one holds them side by side. The copy has more blue in it than does the more red bean brown. These pieces seem obvious attempts to deceive. A

pitcher, signed, but with an unfamiliar glaze, can be explained by the color choices of those who worked at the pottery, but one of a small size, seems too much to attribute to an old mold change. Even as we came to the end of this writing, a stoppered jug appeared with

Covered vegetable dish.

an unexplained white lining. We must remind ourselves that pottery workers, as a matter of practice, were permitted their own lunch-hour time to experiment as they pleased. This has led to confusing pieces in all pottery production since as long as the molds existed, an identical item could be made in any color which was available to the worker. In the case of an old mold, it could be altered also. We are fortunate that not a lot of this has come down to us, but enough has survived to raise questions. Since it is impossible to know the extent of this work, our own perception of the line is better guided by the documentation in the files and the supporting findings by collectors over almost 20 years. Guard your purse when the facts do not fit your findings.

A small amount of decorated American Modern was a surprise when found five years ago. A complete set combining chutney serving items with place setting items decorated in a naturalistic leaf pattern raised eyebrows and questions followed. Soon, a white plate with a matchstick/straight pin decoration was found as was a coral scroll pattern and another pattern which appeared to resemble a broken grass leaf. Fortunately, Wright's photograph files made references to these lines not found in the Syracuse files and though the references were vague, it seemed likely that Wright had a hand in them. The questionable chutney leaf pattern was easily accounted for as it was a motif which he turned to many times and we find it in his linen lines, papers, and personal notes. Since that first finding, another set has been found with patterned serving items and matching linens. The scroll pattern, we found, was called Spencerian but the other patterns remain nameless. What we know with certainty is that if a set of the leaf pattern existed, there is the possibility that the other patterns were planned, but it is equally certain that not much was made and that probably it was restricted to sampling. Do not expect the patterned American Modern to be more extensive than those lines discussed here. Any other would likely be the work of a pottery worker or a home ceramist.

Steubenville's American Modern, premier of Wright's dinnerware lines had an intrinsic flaw. The clay from which it was made was of inferior quality or, as new information suggests, the PH level of the water mixed with the clay may have been wrong. Ceramic chemists offer the information that clay, bonding with water, must have a balance between acids and alkalis. For whatever reason, American Modern broke and chipped easily and several of the glazes were prone to crazing. These factors caused problems for Wright who saw that his future work with dinnerware must address and overcome these problems. Steubenville's claim that these problems were the result of "handmade" dinnerware was not adequate. This poor quality accounts for the amount of American Modern which has survived. Most collectors, armed with these facts, begin their collections with this design, but are likely to save its use for special occasions, choosing to use his Iroquois designs for every day.

Because so many have recognized the classic appeal of American Modern, it is more difficult to assemble a dinner service, and even harder to locate some of the serving items. As with many other collectibles, pieces have found their way into private collections and are no longer easy to find at shops and shows. Other influences, rarities, experimental items, and short productions limit our findings and scarcities exist in items that early collectors found plentiful.

As we study production policies our understanding of the line takes perspective and we find ourselves with a better understanding of Steubenville's production as well as the advertising done by them, Raymor, and retail clients. Not all accounts carried all colors or all items, and the advertising done in a retail account's name reflected the line as they carried it, often differing from that of the entire line. Be cautious as you study the wonderful advertising you find. It often reflects a limited view of the line and it is not possible to base judgements concerning the extent of the line or its colors on dated advertising. Some items were the victims of short production, never again part of the total line. Other items went in and out of production. The carafe, coffee pots, soups, the divided relish, the relish rosette, and the demi-cup and saucer all illustrate that practice. By 1951, new items became part of the line such as the covered pitcher, stack set, the individual ramekin, the coffee cup cover, divided vegetable, hostess plate and the mug. You should not find these in bean brown. The after-dinner coffee pot, sauce boat, the covered butter dish, and the children's items were added by the late 1950s and probably were not made in all colors. The loosely structured line with difficult-to-understand production can be explained by the war years and the long time span over which it was made. Steubenville found themselves prospering in an industry which was floundering and balance in business practices was difficult to achieve. Entrenchment often seemed wise, in spite of success, and there had been success. By 1952, it was estimated that there were 90 imitations of American Modern. The count went on.

American Modern made and kept a place uniquely its own. It cut a swath through our lives and defined a newness which a generation could not fail to recognize as important. It came at a time when patriotism was high and its concept, its name, and its style influenced us as we reached out for a place of our own in the midmark of this century. The timeless appeal has not been lost and it has become an American legend in a tea cup, a style attracting our children as it did us.

Fruit bowl, divided vegetable bowl, and stack set.

Gravy on liner (pickle dish).

ON PRICING AMERICAN MODERN

Pricing American Modern, I believed, would be easy. We have watched the American Modern line and its colors for almost 20 years of collecting and I felt that prices were stabilized, perhaps higher, but not much, and in a predictable way. I was wrong. Almost all consultants saw prices as considerably higher on serving items, many of which have all but disappeared as we turned our attention to other lines. Much of what was common 10 years ago has shifted to "rare," barely stopping at "scarce." Those items will be designated in the following listings. A few general words about the popularity of the colors as reported by contributors: All agree that average collectors want the original colors to be used in mix or match services with only a few exceptions. There is no dispute that chartreuse is the least liked color, but dealers with volume sales report that this on-again off-again color is finally reaching for a respectable position in the American Modern colors. Repeatedly, I hear that seafoam is the "hot" color. It has not yet become rare, but most agree that it has become more difficult to find, even scarce in some areas. Coral and gray, original colors, are common and found most easily. Black chutney, and cedar remain interesting to collectors and it seems they should enjoy a middle position in our range. White and bean brown are still very desirable colors and have enjoyed a good position from the first. Glacier blue and cantaloupe have the highest value, based upon rarity. Glacier may actually be more difficult to find than cantaloupe and it is believed that it was not made in the same amounts as cantaloupe. Glac-

ier dinner plates may be the most difficult to find items in the entire line. Neither of these late colors is believed to have been shipped to the West Coast for sale in any great amounts, though jobbers in Portland, Oregon, bought second quality items by the box-car load. Steubenville blue, a confused color in our spectrum is "off the chart," as it was off Wright's color choices. In spite of the fact that he had nothing to do with the selection of this color, rarity elevates it to a position which it seems best to describe as NPD. The text and the chronology offer more information on glazes, items, and dates which may add to your understanding of the line.

Item popularity deserves a few words. Salad plates, those missing items in the starter sets are still missing as today's collectors search for them. They are difficult to locate in any color. The covered casserole has not been a favorite, and its low price reflects that circumstance. Plates, cups, and saucers have not been raised in pricing, but there seems to be a constant demand for them with new collectors as well as older ones needing replacement items. Soups and fruits with tab handles easily broken seem to be always needed. The water pitcher, a favorite from the first, is one of Wright's classic pieces and a collection of a water pitcher in each color is enviable; celeries, carafes, and coasters only slightly less so. American Modern collecting can go on and on as collectors have moved from dinnerware sets to one of each color collecting.

PRICES FOR AMERICAN MODERN

Plate, 6" ....$5.00 – 8.00	Coffee pot, 8" x 8½"** ....$165.00 – 200.00
Salad plate, 8"* ....$12.00 – 15.00	Shaker single ....$6.00 – 8.00
Dinner plate, 10" ....$10.00 – 12.00	Covered vegetable ....$60.00 – 80.00
Cup...$8.00 – 10.00	Coaster* ....$15.00 – 20.00
Saucer...$3.00 – 4.00	Gravy, 10½" ....$20.00 – 25.00
Lug soup ....$15.00 – 20.00	Pickle dish ....$12.00 – 18.00
Chop plate ....$30.00 – 45.00	Small baker* ....$30.00 – 40.00
Salad bowl ....$75.00 – 100.00	Hostess set with cup** ....$75.00 – 100.00
Celery..$22.00 – 30.00	Coffee cup cover** ....$150.00 – 200.00
Divided relish** ....$175.00 – 250.00	Covered individual ramekin** ......$175.00 – 200.00
Relish rosette** ....$165.00 – 200.00	Divided vegetable* ....$85.00 – 120.00
Carafe (jug) ....$165.00 – 200.00	Stack server** ....$200.00 – 250.00
Covered casserole ....$40.00 – 60.00	Mug (tumbler)* ....$75.00 – 100.00
Covered ice box jar** ....$150.00 – 200.00	Covered pitcher** ....$200.00 – 250.00
Sugar ....$15.00 – 20.00	A.D. coffee pot............................$100.00 – 150.00
Cream ....$12.00 – 15.00	Sauce boat ....$35.00 – 50.00
Teapot, 6" x 10"* ....$100.00 – 125.00	Child's plate** ....$50.00 – 60.00
Lug fruit.......................................$15.00 – 20.00	Child's tumbler** ....$60.00 – 80.00
Vegetable bowl (open) ....$20.00 – 25.00	Child's bowl** ....$60.00 – 80.00
Platter, 13½" ....$25.00 – 35.00	Covered butter** ....$200.00 – 250.00
Water pitcher................................$100.00 – 135.00	Salad fork & spoon as set* ....$125.00 – 150.00
A.D. cup/saucer ....$25.00 – 30.00	

**Rare Items. *Scarce Items. Patterned items should be 25% lower than prices listed here. Cedar, black chutney, and seafoam are at the high end of this scale. Add 50% for bean brown, white, glacier blue, and cantaloupe.

Coaster, covered baker, sauce boat, and gravy on liner.

Hostess plate and cup on Leacock cloth.

After dinner coffee pot, jug/carafe, teapot.

Lug soup and lug fruit.

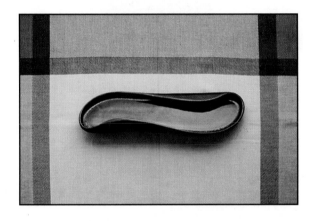

Celery on Simtex cloth.

Soup on Leacock linen cloth.

Rare American Modern patterns.

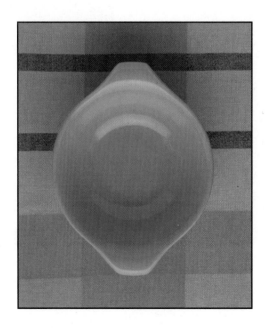

Small baker on Leacock linen cloth.

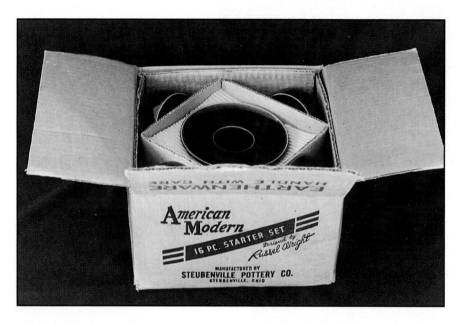

Sixteen piece starter in original box.

American Modern original boxes.

Child's set in original box.

Original
American Modern brochure.

Campbell's soup ad using
American Modern Dinnerware.

1954 recipe booklets
(Culinary Arts Institute, Chicago)
showing pictures of American Modern
dinnerware. Creamer contains catsup and
sugar contains mustard.

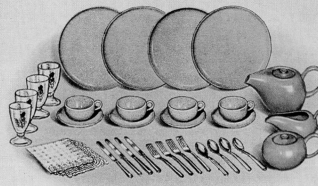

52-piece Russel Wright Modern American Dinner Set for Six

Created by a famous designer for little hostesses. Wonderfully tough plastic, takes lots of hard play. Modern mottled pottery colors stay bright. 6 each of plates, cups, saucers, metallized cutlery, goblets, napkins. Creamer, teapot, sugar bowl, gravy boat and stand, casserole with cover, large platter.
49 N 944—Turned-edge plates, 6¼-inch diameter. Shipping weight 2 lbs. 14 oz...... $4.78

Just like the Russel Wright Set mommy has

33-piece Russel Wright Modern Set for Four

Pottery-colored plastic tea service . . gives little hostesses the "feel" of really fine service like mother's. Consists of 4 cups, 4 saucers, 4 plates, creamer, sugar bowl, teapot, 4 napkins, 4 sets of metallized cutlery, 4 clear goblets. Plates 6¼-in. diameter, others in proportion.
49 N 942—Gift box. Shipping weight 1 pound 10 ounces.................. $2.78

Ads for toy American Modern made by Ideal Toy Company, from Sears 1959 Christmas catalog.

Ad for toy American Modern made by Ideal Toy Company, from Sears 1961 Christmas catalog.

Just like mommy's Russel Wright Set $4.44

Dinner Set for six created by a famous designer especially for little hostesses. Wonderfully tough plastic in mottled pottery colors that stay bright. Set includes 6 each turned-edge plates (6¼-in. diam.), cups, saucers, metallized cutlery, clear plastic goblets, napkins. Also sugar bowl with cover, creamer, teapot with cover, gravy boat with stand, large platter and casserole with cover.
49 N 944—58-piece Set. Shipping weight 2 lbs. 14 oz............. $4.44

Steubenville blue on
Leacock crossmatch cloth.

Illustrations of American Modern rare
designs Spencerian and Matchstick.

This is it! The stopper for the American
Modern carafe shown "in place."
Perhaps most rare accessory.

Another view of the stopper for the carafe.

Glaze Trial Samples

#2175 – gray

#2157 – lavender

#2494 – color unknown

#2484 – green

#2471 – red

American Modern. One-of-a-kind collection.

American Modern's classic statement.

**Cedar green, chartreuse,
glacier blue, a start on
one-of-a-color collection.**

**One-of-a-color
celery collection.**

135

Another load at another time, 1939.

Iroquois, Three Times a Day

Having given his first dinnerware the name "American Modern," unifying the product with his creed, Wright revisited his causes, and incorporated them in naming his next work "Casual." It was done for the Iroquois China Company of Syracuse, New York, in 1946. He was well aware that it was important for Casual to address the problems of American Modern, specifically crazing, breaking, and chipping. It was not by accident that he turned to the Iroquois company for they had an established reputation for producing durable high fired china. Fortunately for him, his hopes were sustained and a relationship with that company resulted in a line which could be advertised as resistant to breakage with normal usage. A refinement of style combined with this new quality resulted in a line which would be only slightly less popular than American Modern. It was written that "American Modern was the experiment, Casual was the refinement." Never completely satisfied himself, and always willing to cooperate if the manufacturer requested changes, he restyled the original production very soon after it had begun. Major redesign came later, resulting in what is often distinguished as so different that it is almost two separate lines.

Production policy showed that Casual was fired at 2300° F. and possessed thermo-shock properties. In spite of its durability, it was advertised as a true china, a finer product than earthenware. Aggressively promoted, even during testing and samplings, Casual was announced as a break-through in dinnerware. Privately, Wright, pleased with Casual's testing, declared that this new Iroquois line would scandalize the fine china industry. Both the designer and Iroquois guaranteed that Casual would not break with normal use if bought in a service for four people. At the time of purchase buyers were given individual certificates, signed and numbered, validating a personal relationship between the buyer and the retailer, acknowledging and authenticating the properties, a good faith expression that this product would not chip/craze/break as had American Modern. Claims that it would go from the stove to the table and back to the refrigerator were spelled out in print as well as in public appearances by Russel and Mary. They were pictured

Warranty Registration Certificate for Iroquois Casual China

washing Casual in an eye's wink, throwing all on a metal table, with only one cup handle damaged; proof in advertising.

Open stock continued to be an important concept as Wright adapted it to this new product. That these items could be stacked neatly in limited storage space and that many of the items could be used for several purposes encouraged investment in "some now, more later." The feature was to help Casual as it had done with American Modern. The large bowls could be used for hot foods, salads, or centerpieces in spite of the fact that there were specific items designed for many of these uses. The small bowls adapted well to many purposes. The wonderfully designed carafe could be used as a vase. The large platter was a natural underplate holding a coffee service and the gumbo held much more than soup. Using the large casseroles as soup tureens, punch bowls, or salad bowls made them versatile. It all amounted to a very large line, serving almost every dining requirement.

Garrison Products was chosen to distribute Casual, a departure from the successful Raymor choice. Contractual details were complicated from the first and difficult arrangements between Wright, Garrison and Iroquois were immediate and on-going. Out of them came intricate and involved line changes. At the outset Iroquois was to produce and sell to Garrison 100,000 pieces of dinnerware composed of 12 flatware items to one serving piece. The first order was to be replaced by monthly orders, adding to 8333 dozen pieces. Iroquois agreed to produce within a year, barring an act of God. Wright allowed his name to be used on all pieces which were large enough to carry it and agreed that he would not develop another line of china or earthenware with a similar number of items at 70% above or below the cost to retailers. Exceptions would cover buffet serving pieces, the Steubenville line, which was still in production, as well as a dinnerware line (not named), said to be earthenware and not similar to Casual. He agreed not to send that proposed line into production until after December 1947. Protecting his interests, Wright further had a clause inserted which voided his own restrictions if Casual sales fell below 200,000 pieces for any 12 month period. If Garrison became bankrupt, or it for any reason, the terms of the contract were breached, Garrison agreed to sell the designs and tradename back to Wright for $1.00. With all eventualities apparently agreed upon, trouble began almost at once. Completely out of patience with Wright's interference in sales, Garrison soon wrote: "Keep in mind that I will finance and take the responsibility for the distributing company and must have a considerable area within which to do that

job as I see fit. If you do not want me to do that job, or if you do not want to allow me the elbow room in which to do it, then our basic set-up is wrong and YOU should finance the distributing company, operate the distributing company, and provide the factory to supply the distributing company. I am perfectly satisfied that this is no more your intent than mine." We find Wright attempted to attend to business details about which he cared a lot and knew little, and limited by his social skills which troubled many of his relationships.

No real understanding of the roles each would play in this arrangement developed and in 1948 Garrison exercised its option and withdrew as the distributor of Casual. Since Wright's problems had been with Garrison only and because sales were very good, Iroquois was eager to work with him on any fair basis.

Another contract was drawn up involving only Wright and the manufacturer. Clearly, Wright sought an agreement more favorable to himself and these new terms provided that royalties, already established, would cover second quality ware. Wright had learned from his Steubenville production that the amount of these extended royalties was not small change. In the new contract, he demanded that he be allowed to design one earthenware line which would bear his name as well as one which would not. Another important concession allowed him to design a line of thin china if it were priced to sell at retail prices of no less than 50% higher than Iroquois. He made what were to amount to generous concessions himself, and agreed to restyle or redesign as sales showed need. Casual would take on a new life as well as a new look.

Garrison had been assertive in advertising casual and equally aggressive in obtaining accounts for it. Newspapers reported each new change in the line and full-page advertisements were placed in the leading home furnishings magazines, most in full color and works of art in themselves. One of the most interesting is a full-page advertisement for Nescafe Instant Coffee dated September 1955. The photographs show a picture of Emily Post (the same Emily Post who previously, in *Time* magazine, had taken Wright to task over the impracticality of American Modern cups) along with directions on how to make barbecue "company coffee" accompanied by a picture of Iroquois original mugs together with a coffee service which was not Wright's. Garrison's expertise had been recognized and Wright continued to market the line in the same manner. Twelve years after it was introduced, and with original marketing practices still in place, it continued to take on newness of design, to add interesting items, and recolor itself, still selling in record amounts.

Advertising made the most of the word "China" and it was emphasized that this was of superior quality. In cities it was sold to large accounts, but with selectivity. One department store might be chosen as an exclusive account. If there seemed to be room for more than one outlet, the new account was given a changed or limited color selection, even a slightly different item listing. In smaller towns, prestigious jewelry stores were often accounts with limited inventory, selling special order items and colors. These distributing practices have caused problems for collectors. Much of the advertising listed the items and colors which the advertiser carried and cannot be assumed to define the entire line. Additionally, these advertising pieces often show names for colors which vary from those which are listed in the Wright files, attributable to Wright's ingenious application of new names for old colors. The color "teal" appeared in one advertisement and there are other examples of this confusing practice. Conflicting information which suggests a difference in the original colors is typical. The files, referring to correspondence between Wright and the pottery, have listed them to be sugar white, lemon yellow, and ice blue. The 1946 August issue of *China Glass and Decorative Accessories* lists them as did the files. However, another researcher has found an article from the publication *Every Day Art Quarterly*. The article which is from the fall 1946 issue lists the original colors as different from Wright's correspondence and the trade paper above. These *Art Quarterly* colors are said to have been oyster white, brown, powder blue, and chartreuse yellow, all names with which we are unfamiliar. Further confusing is a *New York Times* article from December 1946, which listed the original colors as white, ice blue, avocado yellow, and nutmeg brown. More than many of us have looked at these listings with questions attempting to determine the truth of the matter. My own thoughts find oyster white a strange name for the Iroquois white which we know is a sugar white, not the creamy white which oyster white suggests. I find the chartreuse yellow an unlikely choice for avocado yellow but they clearly are the same color. Powder blue seems not to be the sort of sophisticated name Wright would use. I would be reluctant to think it was a name of which he approved. The ice blue of the *Times* article written a few months later, seems to be the blue term with which we are acquainted. We know that Wright had not been pleased with the early blue glaze trials and accused Garrison of releasing a glaze which he had not approved and that may account for these different names. They also had differences over nutmeg, and it would seem reasonable to believe that Garrison could have released the name brown, renamed nutmeg quickly. These findings, I believe, may not be as divergent as they seem and it is possible that some of our confusion may be the result of Garrison's advertising done early and at a time when Wright was less than certain of colors and names. Mustard gold, as seen in some late advertising has been especially problematic since some of the avocado yellow does certainly seem more mustard than avocado. They are the same colors and Wright may have used the changed name when avocado yellow fell from favor as such colors do. Perhaps the most important lesson here is that these are all the colors with which we are familiar and that we are all very close in our findings despite what seems to be contrary information. I would be hesitant to differ with contractual agreements found in the file documentation. For more details on this matter, see the "Over Our Shoulder" introductory chapter.

Early in my examination of all this, I questioned color variances and turned to a chemical engineer for explanations. Each supplier, I was told, furnished their own chemicals and they could differ, giving unpredictable results, colors not quite the same in spite of the fact that they conformed to the same formula. The files tell us that retailers were told to expect a 20% difference in the degrees of color.

Proof of extensive glaze studies exists. Glaze sample plates have been found ranging in what appears to be a lemon yellow through two brown shades to a color very similar to brick red. The plates are unglazed on the back, but bear the #8 mark with Q4 (in all cases) in place of the letter/numbers seen on #8 marks. The colors have glaze numbers, ranging from light to dark and are 19943-5, 19942-3, 19934-4, 19945-4. I am unable to interpret this information, but I offer it, hoping that you can add to our understanding of the glaze/mark situation.

Nutmeg, avocado yellow, and parsley green were early additions to the original line, perhaps coming sooner than we had originally believed. Lemon and parsley were dropped after short production but were later restored. In 1951 oyster, charcoal, ripe apricot, pink sherbet, lettuce green, and cantaloupe joined the earlier colors. Aqua and brick red were both late colors and we still do not have a date for them. We can be sure, though, that they were made in short amounts, probably less of brick than aqua. They remain colors not seen by many collectors but it has been suggested that, with their late production, they may still be in cupboards. It is wonderful to anticipate!

Iroquois popularity among collectors has changed since we looked at the line in 1990. Ice blue and nutmeg seem to be commonly found, with pink sherbet not far behind. Ripe apricot and nutmeg are not as popular as they were in 1990 and little has occurred to enhance avocado yellow, as the least favored color. That is qualified only by the fact that Franciscan Starburst collectors have turned to Wright's less expensive avocado serving pieces. As the color green has become popular in the '90s, so Wright's lettuce and parsley have gained ground with today's collectors. Trends have developed which favor combining colors in pastel groupings or earth-tone groupings rather than contrasting colors. Interestingly, it has been reported that many people with no interest in collecting use Casual for every day use because they find it so attractive, so easy to use, so affordable. On the other hand, collectors with dinnerware sets completed have turned to collecting one of a color items. Carafes, coffee pots, covered pitchers, all these attract those who are developing collections around items, not dinner services.

Casual's glazes, aside from the colors, were equally innovative. Wright, having come to terms with Steubenville's glaze problems, had turned to Alfred University where ceramists interpreted his vision for the line and accomplished an early Casual which differed totally, in weight and appearance, from what would come later. The

Stacking shakers, single salt, pepper mill, tea cup/saucer, coffee cup/saucer, after dinner cup/saucer.

first Casual items are those which are about ⅜ of an inch thick, and of almost restaurant weight. The glazes were foamy, with irregular effect, no two items exactly alike in the oil spot appearance. Crystallization added to the weight, giving it the handmade appearance Wright hoped to achieve. When collectors, turned researchers, first found these early pieces they believed them to be second quality items for they lacked the uniformity of mass-produced dinnerware. Finding its rightful place in the several modifications of Casual, this early work, made in limited amounts, is very popular today.

From the first, Casual drew attention. Home economics classes in the San Francisco Bay area, chose pink and blue for their classes, finding it sturdy and easily replaceable. *Country Gardens* magazine in May of 1952, featured "The kitchen a congregation built at the Second Presbyterian Church in Flandreau, South Dakota." Pictures show Wright's dinnerware designs, but the article explains that the cooks could stack and store items conveniently, fitting them neatly into blond birch cabinets especially designed for the dishes. It seems certain that someone in the congregation owned a copy of *A Guide to Easier Living* for the concepts were followed, word for word.

The original shape in the Iroquois line is that which shows rounded surfaces, seeming to be more molded than curved and with the recessed handles integrated into the body of the piece, loaning the name of "Pinch" to the line. There were no protruding handles or grips, no rims or grooves. It stacks easily. All findings indicate that before major redesign work was done Wright restyled the line in 1948, adding pieces and doing away with the original foamy glaze, substituting a more sleek refined finish while making the items less heavy, less molded in appearance. The several cups, as well as the small bowls, reflect his willingness to work with each piece until he achieved the forms which reflected their function. Sorting them has been a problem. Lids to bowls were sold separately from the first and that practice extended to pots as well. The covered casserole with no lid obviously became the

**Three early cup handles in what appears to be the order of production.
Cup #4 is the coffee cup, discontinued early and rare. Cup #5 is late redesigned tea cup.**

open casserole. A coffee pot with no lid became a pitcher. Each item had its own identity not dependent upon a lid. The cover for the soup bowl has a steam opening while the gravy cover has a ladle slot. Wright pushed dual usage to his own ends as he enlarged the Casual line.

Restyled water pitcher, family size cream, and after dinner coffee pot. All rare.

In 1951, five years after it had been introduced, Wright redesigned the line as he had agreed to do if sales showed that such work should be done. The thick shapes had disappeared already, except for back stock, and the mottled glaze had been changed to a more polished appearance in the restyling. Now the newly redesigned items would depart in a major way from what had been standard. Knobbed handles replaced pinched ones. Bowls seemed to be almost footed, and handles with a loopy applied appearance extend-ed to the body of cups and pots. The original coffee pot was never replaced and a wonderful redesigned teapot was sub-stituted. A water pitcher added depth to the line. Even plates seemed to have a suggestion of a foot and finding that feature led collectors to look at all the flat pieces. While difficult to detect as one examines a plate, stacking shows that they were redesigned. Original plates do not stack well with redesigned plates. Altogether, the line took on an Oriental influence, a positive departure from the handmade appearance which had been so important at its inception.

With such attention to detail in design, it is clear that there was confusion in the market place. Old items were still being sold along side redesigned items and new tops were sold with older bottoms. Making the most of their inventory, both Iroquois and the retailers combined what was at hand in an effort to sustain sales and avoid back stock. A year after the redesigned work was done, advertisements still showed the pinched look together with the redesigned style. Today's collectors, more selective than 1950s customers, would not be taken in by a redesigned top on an original bowl, but it seemed to matter little then and the line grew with questionable possibilities as styles were mixed.

By 1955 Casual needed a new face and Wright attempted to supply it by adding pattern. Redesigned sets composed of eight dinner plates, 6" plates, cups and saucers as well as cereal bowls, a sugar, creamer, 8" open

Redesigned covered casserole, fruit, and redesigned fruit.

Redesigned teapot, carafe, and gumbo soup bowl.

vegetable bowl, and a platter were offered. Obviously, these new patterned lines would not be available as open stock. The patterns were copper plate engraved with underglazed naturalistic patterns very different from dinnerware sold at the time. Nasturtium, introduced to the trade at Wright's home was the first patterned Iroquois. Others followed as Wright was able to design them. They would include: Shepherd's Purse with white, beige, and green flowers on a ripe apricot glaze, White Violets, a violet veining with white blossoms and green leaves on ice blue, Orange Flower, on a lemon yellow glaze, Woodhue on cantaloupe. Nasturtium was on ripe apricot and featured orange blossoms and green leaves. Gay Wings, on pink sherbet, was a fantasy treatment of pink flowers and deep pink veining. Pepper Tree, another orange flower and green leaf pattern is identified by its lemon yellow base. Babies Breath traced white flowers on pink sherbet. All of these patterned designs were done on the redesigned shapes, the delicate designs adding to the Oriental influence.

Much care was given to the detail involved in each item and no two pieces shared the same design, departing only a bit for interest. A plate might include an elaborate spray of flowers while cups or bowls would be treated with a sprig of the same design. So different from other dinnerware then on the market, it can be viewed as an important change in the development of pattern in dinnerware. Very different from his earlier work, it added dimension to his concept. Wright extended himself in every way to make this new patterned ware acceptable, but it was never as popular as he had hoped, never as popular with today's collectors.

Additional patterns may have been done by the Sheffield Pottery Company in Sheffield, Massachusetts. These were to have been country motif designs of inferior detail. While Wright was aware of them, we must not consider them as his patterns. His own work would never make room for this more traditional treatment.

Cookware was another innovative late addition to Casual. Items were especially designed to be used on a stove or in an oven. A pinch item would be the work of a potter with his own preference and no pinch item should be used on a stove. Typically much heavier than items in the regular line, the cookware is said to have been made in the late colors as well as white. Findings show that ripe apricot appears more often than other colors but none have been reported in large amounts. Look for the Dutch oven, covered fry pan, electric serving tray, percolator, covered sauce pan, hot plate, and three casseroles. All are signed and care instructions are clearly marked on each piece. If you *must* use yours, follow these instructions carefully. Advertised as "Range Proof," they are not

range-friendly and if you do not find the asbestos pad which was to accompany your piece, do not try to use the piece without it. If you are fortunate enough to have found the original pad, or are confident that you can use a replacement, *follow directions*. I speak from bad experience. The photograph files have provided us with the information that the Imperial Glass Company perfected the coated glazes of this rare cookware and collectors have reported that all items as we list them have been found.

Some Iroquois items stand out as rare or special. After dinner cups, so difficult to find, had been reported in ice blue, parsley, and avocado yellow. We can now add that they have been found in ripe apricot, nutmeg, pink sherbet, charcoal, and oyster also. We had previously thought that these after dinner cups were the most difficult to find of the Iroquois pieces but that should be updated. The after dinner saucers appear to be more rare than the cups. These small cups and saucers were not popular items when they were made, probably because the practice of serving after dinner coffees seemed formal, even sophisticated to many. Today, they are very sought after, not only because of their appeal and rarity but because what went around has come around. Americans are increasingly interested in after dinner drinks. The small platter remains very elusive. The gumbo soup serves many uses and, if priced affordably should be bought in any color. The small covered pitcher, also a useful piece, is without parallel in Wright's other lines. A brochure is shown here which includes the use of basketry with serving items. Few examples have been reported in spite of the fact that they were made in enough amounts to be used in advertising. Coffee pots, shown with raffia wrapped handles seem to be part of the general grouping and there is advertising evidence that it was used on original as well as redesigned items. In spite of that, little of this basketry detail has been found and it appears to have been a late addition to the line. No one has explained why stacking creamers are found in larger numbers than the sugars, but the fact remains. The family-sized cream and sugar still surprises us, for we do not see it often. Some suggest they were the original ones and they may be right. We are uncertain.

Given so many items, restyling, redesigning, the Iroquois line would seem to answer most of the needs of mid-century Americans, but variations and rarities confuse us. Our stand-by cup handle picture remains, reprinted here, but reports have come of another cup, clearly an early one made in the foamy glaze. I have not examined it, but it is said to be thicker and bigger than the one shown here. New cup styles seem never to surprise collectors. No doubt the work of a potter, a stacking cream and sugar have been located with the sugar replaced by the not-pinched body of a cup with handle removed. This could only be the work of a worker with a personal preference. A coffee pot, said to be 6" taller than the one with which we are familiar has been found. It is correctly signed, correctly shaped, but larger over all, probably the result of prototype or sampling. Some items have been reported to exist with three pinch indentions though we know they should have only two. These may have been the result of prototype work as the line developed. Look-alikes, some made by Iroquois and dipped in Wright's colors, can be found and may persuade you that you have found a rarity. Egg cups were found early and I hear from those who are still finding them, including one which incorporates a handleless cup. Late information on these has come to us from an Iroquois pottery worker. He identified them as prototype pieces, none of which Wright approved for inclusion in the line. We must be careful as we examine the Iroquois line, questioning whether or not an authentic item could have been made in this color. With so many molds, so many colors, so many years, and so many workers, the possibility of any item in any color exists for as least as long as a mold remained.

Marks changed from time to time and we have never been exactly certain of dating on them. Wright had not been pleased with what we believe to have been the original mark and it was changed for that reason. He felt the replacement mark had more eye appeal but since there are several early marks, it is difficult to put each in any real sequence. One suggestion which seems to have merit is that the number on the bottom line of mark 6 and 8 relates to the quarter of the year when the piece was made. Mark study, however, remains confusing and all marks here remain as we found them in 1990.

It appears that Iroquois Casual was not singled out for distinguished design awards but a letter to me from the Des Moines Art Center relates that when the center opened in 1948, Eliel Saarinen, the important architect and designer, suggested that it be used in the dining room there. When the center changed its eating area much later, they put several settings away for archival use. Casual has found its place in permanent collections of many major museums.

Almost without exception, collectors of Wright's work use Casual for their dinner service day in and day out reserving the classic but fragile American Modern for special occasions. By combining colors, a table of Iroquois can dress up to white tie formality, or reduce itself to tailgate party use. Seasoned collectors surprise themselves as they contrast colors and new collectors, given a few pieces of each color, can combine them in ways that appeal to different occasions, different seasons. In his own way, and with many approaches, Wright accomplished color and style in harmony with the form follows function principle as he designed, restyled, and redesigned Casual. All will agree that the American table is infinitely more interesting because Wright set it with such care.

Iroquois Casual platter, redesigned teapot, tumbler, advertising ashtray, covered pitcher, original mug, redesigned butter dish, redesigned creamer, gravy with stand cover, and redesigned covered sugar.

143

ON PRICING IROQUOIS CASUAL

As we look at Iroquois pricing we must be aware that this is the Russel Wright line which collectors *use*. We all have admired American Modern and have collected it from the first, but it is Casual to which we turned as we found we could trust it in everyday refrigerator/oven/table uses. Its reputation for durability has been proven in countless kitchens, yesterday and today.

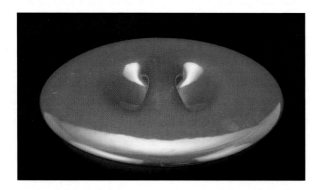

10" original covered casserole.

There are color favorites, to be certain. Aqua, that brilliant turquoise, is rare, but it would be a favorite even if it were not so. Its color, much less restrained than other of Wright's colors, makes a bold statement and Casual collectors have given it the "medium green" status of Fiesta. All pieces of it are difficult to find, but the rare pieces in this rare color, teapots, butter dishes, casseroles, as well as single salts and pepper mills, are especially important. Even ordinary items in this rare color are valued highly. Most of these same comments apply to brick red, which seems even more rare than aqua, though it lacks its vibrancy. The pricing on both of these colors has gone into orbit over the last few years — but it continues to sell even at record breaking prices. Cantaloupe, not quite so rare, is still a difficult color to find and is so beautiful that it enjoys a scarce-to-rare position. We find parsley more favored than before, perhaps reflecting the popularity of greens in the '90s color charts. Oyster remains an important blending color and charcoal attracts those whose taste runs to darker colors. Pastel sets of lemon, lettuce, pink sherbet, and ice blue continue to make for beautiful informal tables when mixed and matched.

Original design, before restyling, remains very popular with some collectors, but others prefer redesigned items, particularly cups, which are much easier to use than are the original ones. There is room for a lot of personal preference with Casual, but there are limitations. You should not be able to find original shapes in the late colors. One must choose between color and design (if you can limit yourself to one set of Casual). As with American Modern, however, what "should not exist" often does because of the existence of molds, color availability at the factory, and the practice of workers customizing items for their own use. We are still lacking a definite time frame for each color, necessary to our complete understanding of the line. From the first, we hoped that marks study would give us that information. It has not done so yet, though there are active studies in process.

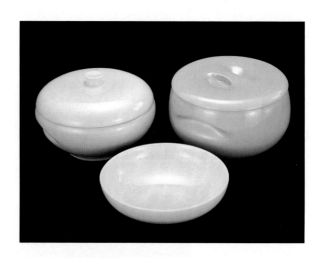

**8" two quart covered casserole,
8" four quart cookware casserole,
36 ounce open vegetable bowl.**

Location continues to influence values and condition is important. Knife marks seem to be the most common wear problem. Factory blemishes seem few and durability has proven to be as good as it was advertised to be. Color variances have made for difficulty in mail ordering Casual.

Avocado is positioned at the low end of the scale. Neither ripe apricot or nutmeg is as popular as ice blue, lettuce, pink sherbet, and lemon. Oyster, white, and charcoal hold high end pricing. Add 200% for cantaloupe, aqua, and brick red.

PRICES FOR IROQUOIS CASUAL

Bowl, fruit, 9½ oz., 5½"	$10.00 – 12.00
Bowl, fruit, redesigned, 5¾"	$12.00 – 14.00
Bowl, salad, 52 oz., 10"	$25.00 – 35.00
Butter dish, ½ pound	$65.00 – 100.00
Butter dish, ¼ pound**	$200.00 – 250.00
Carafe/wine/coffee	$100.00 – 200.00
Casserole, 2 qt., 8"	$25.00 – 40.00
Casserole/deep/tureen**	$150.00 – 200.00
Cereal, 5"	$10.00 – 12.00
Cereal, redesigned, 5"	$12.00 – 15.00
Coffee pot, covered	$125.00 – 150.00
Coffee pot, AD, covered	$75.00 – 100.00
Cover for 4 qt. casserole	$20.00 – 25.00
Cover for open/divided vegetables	$25.00 – 30.00
Covers for soups/cereals*	$20.00 – 25.00
Cover for water pitcher	$30.00 – 50.00
Cream, family style**	$40.00 – 45.00
Cream, redesigned	$15.00 – 25.00
Cream, stacking	$15.00 – 18.00
Cup/saucer, A.D.**	$125.00 – 150.00
Cup/saucer, coffee*	$15.00 – 20.00
Cup/saucer, redesigned	$18.00 – 22.00
Cup/saucer, tea	$10.00 – 12.00
Gravy bowl, 12 oz., 5¼"	$12.00 – 18.00
Gravy, redesigned cover becomes stand**	$150.00 – 175.00
Gravy stand	$10.00 – 15.00
Gravy with attached stand*	$50.00 – 85.00
Gumbo flat soup, 21 oz.	$30.00 – 35.00
Mug, 13 oz.*	$60.00 – 85.00
Mug, restyled*	$70.00 – 75.00
Pepper mill**	$150.00 – 200.00
Pitcher, covered, 1½ qt.	$120.00 – 150.00
Pitcher, redesigned	$150.00 – 200.00
Plate, 6½", bread/butter	$5.00 – 8.00
Plate, chop, 13⅞"	$30.00 – 50.00
Plate, dinner, 10"	$10.00 – 12.00
Plate, luncheon, 9½"*	$8.00 – 10.00
Plate, party with cup**	$75.00 – 85.00
Plate, salad, 7½"	$9.00 – 12.00
Platter, oval, 12¾"*	$25.00 – 35.00
Platter, oval, 14½"	$35.00 – 40.00
Platter, oval/individual, 10¼"**	$60.00 – 75.00
Salt & pepper, stacking	$20.00 – 25.00
Single salt, redesigned**	$100.00 – 150.00
Soup, 11½ oz.	$15.00 – 20.00
Soup, redesigned, 18 oz.	$20.00 – 22.00
Sugar, family size stacking*	$30.00 – 45.00
Sugar, redesigned	$25.00 – 30.00
Sugar, stacking	$15.00 – 18.00
Teapot, restyled*	$175.00 – 200.00
Vegetable, open, 36 oz., 8⅛"	$20.00 – 25.00
Vegetable, open or divided (casserole), 10"	$35.00 – 40.00

Rare **, Scarce *

COOKWARE, ALL REDESIGNED

All items are rare, but the covered fry pan and the covered sauce pan are seen more often than are the other items. The casseroles can be confused with the regular line, but the weight of cookware items will be heavier when compared.

Asbestos pad	$25.00
Basketry for cookware	$35.00
Casserole, 3 qt.	$175.00 – 185.00
Casserole, 4 qt.	$185.00 – 200.00
Casserole, 6 qt.	$200.00 – 225.00
Dutch oven	$225.00 – 350.00
Electric serving tray, 17½" x 12¾"	NPD
Fry pan, covered	$200.00 – 250.00
Percolator	NPD
Sauce pan, covered	$165.00 – 175.00

Original coffee pot.

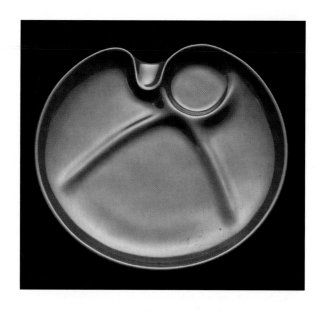

Hostess plate/party plate.

Plates: dinner, luncheon, salad.

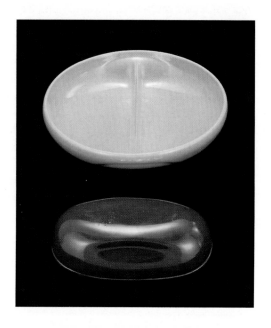

Divided open casserole
and original butter dish.

Gravy with fast stand and
covered gravy bowl on liner.

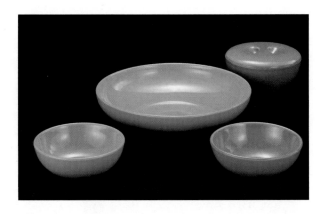

Open vegetable bowl, 10", covered soup,
and cereal bowls.

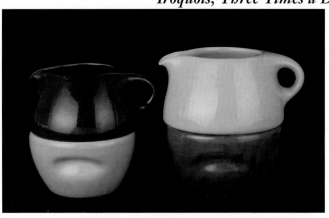

Stacking cream and sugar,
family size cream and sugar.

Iroquois Casual gravy with top
which becomes a stand.

Advertising sign with original
brochure and cookware.

Iroquois advertising ashtray used as
holiday greeting in 1952. Very rare.

Original Iroquois Brochure

America's
most
versatile
true
china

FAMOUS
Iroquois
CASUAL CHINA
by *Russel Wright*

◆ COOK, BAKE 'N SERVE CHINA ◆ REPLACED IF IT CHIPS
OR BREAKS* ◆ SOLID COLORS ◆ DECORATIONS ON COLOR

PINK SHERBET

CANTALOUPE   SUGAR WHITE

LEMON   ICE BLUE

America's
only
SOLID COLOR
CASUAL
China

NUTMEG BROWN.   RIPE APRICOT

LETTUCE GREEN   CHARCOAL

A gay spectrum of colors is yours for the choosing with Iroquois
Casual . . . enabling you to dress your every table to the occasion. Select your favorite color, add a pattern or contrasting
color—and discover a wonderful new versatility in dinnerware.

The Famous IROQUOIS CA[S]

Iroquois Casual, meeting the high quality standards
for which Iroquois is famous, is so ruggedly durable,
even in rough, tough everyday use, that it carries
this amazing warranty: If any piece of your Iroquois
Casual service for four or more breaks, chips or

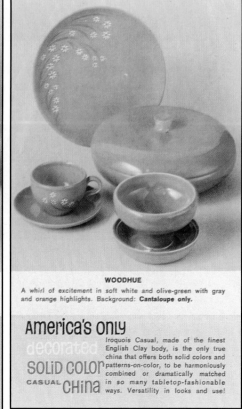

Cooking is Fun . . .

Entertaining Easy with Iroquois Casual

A roast is magnificent (tasty warm, too) served complete with
garnish on the **electric platter.** Buffet fare can be cooked on the
china stove and kept hot between helpings. These and the
saucepan will serve you so many ways . . . and eliminate the
extra pots-and-pans-cleanup from your household routine forever!

PEPPER TREE

Drama created by contrasts in the treatment of line and the
combination of orange and pastel green. Background: **Lemon only.**

[CAS]UAL CHINA Replacement Guarantee

cracks—for any reason—in the home within the first year of purchase, it will be replaced . . . free!* This guarantee assures
you carefree, lasting enjoyment of your Iroquois Casual service.
America's most versatile china is America's most outstanding
dinnerware value.   *In accordance with warranty.

SHEPHERD'S PURSE

Delicate traceries in soft and subtle shades of beige, yellow-
green and white. Background: **Ripe Apricot only.**

Cooking is Fun . . .

Each of these special Iroquois Casual cooking units
adds a new dimension to hostessing and everyday meal
preparation. With the **Dutch oven,** you cook and serve
main dish, soup, stews in sumptuous fashion. The **fry
pan** gives eggs dramatic stove-to-table presentation.

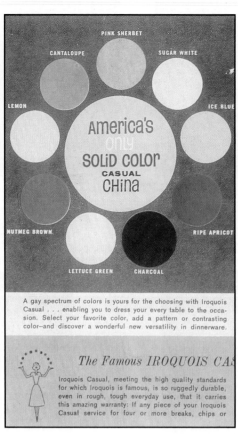

WOODHUE

A whirl of excitement in soft white and olive-green with gray
and orange highlights. Background: **Cantaloupe only.**

America's only decorated SOLID COLOR CASUAL China

Iroquois Casual, made of the finest
English Clay body, is the only true
china that offers both solid colors and
patterns-on-color, to be harmoniously
combined or dramatically matched
in so many tabletop-fashionable
ways. Versatility in looks and use!

WHITE VIOLETS

Romantic blossoms tenderly tinted in white with violet and nile green. Background: **Ice Blue only.**

bake roast
fry broil

Iroquois Casual China by famous designer Rus⟋ her talents in preparing and serving food at

True china to cook in—on top of the stove or in the oven—tor those recipes that look and taste their best when they go direct from stove to table in smart shapes and exclusive serving pieces that make table setting, serving, storing so beautifully simple.

GAY WINGS

A flight of fancy in variations on a theme of pink, accented by muted green stems and leaves. Background: **Pink Sherbet only.**

⟋el Wright is the true homemaker's china . . . designed to complement ⟋actively . . . catering completely to gracious dining and hostessing.

Bake, roast, fry, broil and boil in this true china with never a care because it's so ruggedly durable . . . replaced free if it chips or breaks* . . . completely dishwasher-and-detergent-proof.
*In accordance with warranty

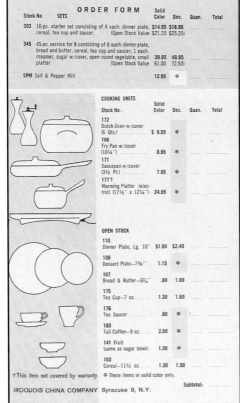

ORDER FORM

Stock No.	SETS	Solid Color	Dec.	Quan.	Total
303	16-pc. starter set consisting of 4 each: dinner plate, cereal, tea cup and saucer. (Open Stock Value $21.20 $25.20)	$14.95	$18.95		
345	45-pc. service for 8 consisting of 8 each: dinner plate, bread and butter, cereal, tea cup and saucer; 1 each: creamer, sugar w/cover, open round vegetable, small platter (Open Stock Value 61.00 72.50)	39.95	49.95		
SPM	Salt & Pepper Mill	12.95	✳		

COOKING UNITS

Stock No.		Solid Color	Dec.	Quan.	Total
172	Dutch Oven w/cover (6 Qts.)	$ 9.95	✳		
106	Fry Pan w/cover (10¼")	8.95	✳		
171	Saucepan w/cover (3½ Pt.)	7.95	✳		
177 †	Warming Platter (electric) (17½" x 12¼")	24.95	✳		

OPEN STOCK

Stock No.		Solid Color	Dec.	Quan.	Total
110	Dinner Plate, Lg. 10"	$1.90	$2.40		
108	Dessert Plate—7⅜"	1.15	✳		
107	Bread & Butter—6⅞"	.80	1.00		
175	Tea Cup—7 oz.	1.30	1.60		
176	Tea Saucer	.80	✳		
183	Tall Coffee—9 oz.	2.00	✳		
141	Fruit (same as sugar bowl)	1.30	✳		
103	Cereal—11½ oz.	1.30	1.50		

† This item not covered by warranty ✳ These items in solid color only.

IROQUOIS CHINA COMPANY Syracuse 9, N.Y.

Subtotal:

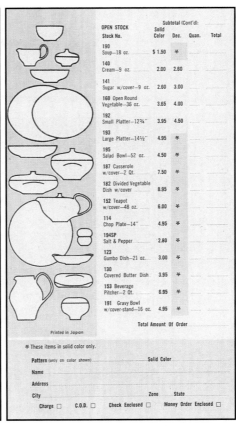

			Subtotal (Cont'd):		
OPEN STOCK Stock No.		Solid Color	Dec.	Quan.	Total
190	Soup—18 oz.	$ 1.50	✳		
140	Cream—9 oz.	2.00	2.60		
141	Sugar w/cover—9 oz.	2.60	3.00		
160	Open Round Vegetable—36 oz.	3.65	4.00		
192	Small Platter—12¾"	3.95	4.50		
193	Large Platter—14½"	4.95	✳		
195	Salad Bowl—52 oz.	4.50	✳		
187	Casserole w/cover—2 Qt.	7.50	✳		
182	Divided Vegetable Dish w/cover	8.95	✳		
152	Teapot w/cover—48 oz.	6.00	✳		
114	Chop Plate—14"	4.95	✳		
194SP	Salt & Pepper	2.80	✳		
123	Gumbo Dish—21 oz.	3.00	✳		
130	Covered Butter Dish	3.95	✳		
153	Beverage Pitcher—2 Qt.	6.95	✳		
191	Gravy Bowl w/cover-stand—16 oz.	4.95	✳		

Total Amount Of Order

Printed in Japan

✳ These items in solid color only.

Pattern (only on color shown) _____ Solid Color _____

Name _____

Address _____

City _____ Zone _____ State _____

Charge ☐   C.O.D. ☐   Check Enclosed ☐   Money Order Enclosed ☐

Top row – lettuce green redesigned
mug, pink sherbet original mug.
Middle row – early nutmeg tea cup and
saucer, brick red redesigned cup and
saucer, ripe apricot after dinner cup and
saucer.
Bottom row – lemon yellow coffee cup
and saucer, glacier blue prototype coffee
cup and saucer.

Pepper tree cereal bowl,
covered sugar and cream.
Shepherd's purse cup, saucer, and
cereal bowl on Simtex table cloth.

All rarities. Iroquois after dinner coffee pot with
basketry handle, after dinner cups and saucers,
Leacock symbols cloth.

Cantaloupe restyled teapot and covered pitcher.

Redesigned mug, 2 qt. covered casserole, soup bowl, redesigned butter dish, cream, stacking salt and pepper, sugar.

ALL-OCCASION CHINA
Durable Iroquois Casual... you'll buy for special-occasion elegance...use every day in every way. Genuine china so durable you can cook, bake and serve beautifully in its smart shapes and coordinated serving pieces. Completely dishwasher and detergent safe. Iroquois is the only American-made solid color genuine china—and is guaranteed 3 full years against breaking, cracking...even chipping!* You can't buy more value for your dinnerware dollar at any price.

*Replaced free in accordance with warranty

AMERICA'S ONLY SOLID COLOR GENUINE CHINA

SUGAR WHITE   TURQUOISE   MUSTARD GOLD   BRICK RED   ICE BLUE   LETTUCE GREEN   RIPE APRICOT   LEMON   PINK SHERBET

Original brochure substituting turquoise for aqua and mustard gold for avocado yellow.

Awash in rarity! 26 A.D. cups and saucers, coffee pot and A.D. coffee pot.

Aqua cream, sugar, stacking salt and pepper, restyled butter dish, gumbo soup.

Aqua covered divided vegetable bowl.

Cantaloupe 2 qt. casserole, covered divided vegetable, aqua divided covered cassserole, aqua stacking salt and pepper, restyled gravy.

Original Iroquois Brochure

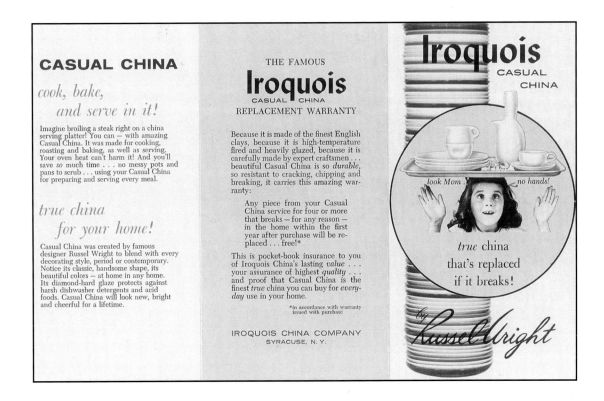

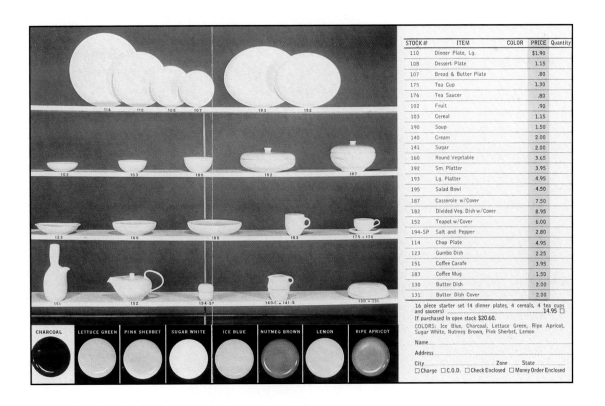

Table setting of nutmeg, ripe apricot, and avocado. Illustrates mix and match feature.

Early original brochure.

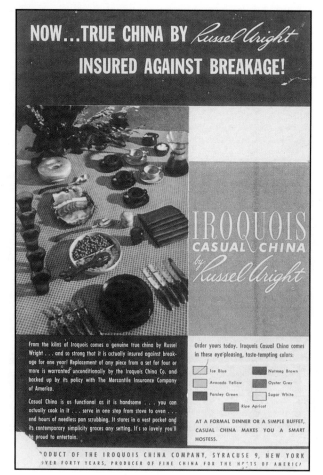

Denby Stoneware coffee server. Imported from England.

Emily Post tells how to make barbecue "Company Coffee"

This is the neighborly way to entertain your friends—with a thick steak sizzling on the charcoal, and plenty of tasty Nescafé to satisfy the *coffee* hunger outdoor cooking seems to intensify! Here's how Emily Post serves Nescafé out of doors:

"At a barbecue," says Mrs. Post, "Nescafé Coffee may be made in a colorful pottery server, and kept warm on a candle coffee warmer. Pottery mugs with easy-to-grasp handles may replace ordinary coffee cups. They are filled by the host or hostess, or by the guests themselves."

Follow the recipe at the right to get the *full* richness of Nescafé Coffee. And keep the server filled, to be ready for second cups as the firelight fades and conversation warms up!

"COMPANY COFFEE"

Put a teaspoonful of Nescafé (more or less according to strength you and your guests prefer) and a coffee cup of boiling water in your coffee server for each cup of coffee wanted. Close the lid to let coffee steep for a moment before serving. This brings Nescafé coffee to the peak of its delicious flavor.

NESCAFÉ INSTANT COFFEE 100% PURE COFFEE

SEND FOR FREE BOOKLET BY EMILY POST—"Coffee Etiquette." This 16-page booklet tells you how and when to serve coffee . . . shows colored photographs of attractive table settings. For your free copy, send your name and address to Nescafé, P. O. Box 5, New York 46, N. Y.

Tastier Nescafé®—Made to Satisfy Your Coffee Hunger!

Better Homes and Gardens **September, 1955 ad illustrating
Wright's "last word" in the controversy over cup handle referred to on page 138.**

Color drama in stove-to-table china
designed with an air of excitement by Russel Wright

Cook and serve in rugged Iroquois Casual, true china made of imported English clay. Dishwasher-and-detergent-proof, it goes directly from stove to table in streamlined shapes and rich colorings. Choose white or solid colors alone or combined with any of three delicate, decorative patterns. (Pattern shown above: "Shepherd's Purse").

Decorated 45-piece service for 8, *(if sold separately, 72.50).* **49.95**

Both decorated or solid color 45-piece sets include 8 each: dinner plates, bread-and-butters, cereals, cups and saucers; 1 each: creamer, sugar bowl with cover, open round vegetable dish, small platter.

Solid color
45 piece service for 8

39.95

If sold separately, $61
(Shown above, "Apricot")

Lemon

Ice blue

Pink sherbet

Lettuce green

Charcoal

Cantaloupe

"Pepper Tree"

"White Violets"

Open stock, save 20% from regular prices until March 31st

	Regularly	Sale		Regularly	Sale
Dinner plate*	1.90	**1.52**	Rd. vegetable*	3.65	**2.92**
Salad plate	1.15	**.92**	12" platter*	3.95	**3.16**
Butter plate*	.80	**.64**	14" platter	4.95	**3.96**
Cup/saucer*	2.10	**1.68**	2 qt. casserole	7.50	**6.00**
Fruit dish	1.30	**1.04**	Teapot	6.00	**4.80**
Cereal bowl	1.30	**1.04**	Butter dish	3.95	**3.16**
Soup bowl	1.50	**1.20**	Pitcher	6.95	**5.56**
Creamer*	2.00	**1.60**	Salt & pepper		
Sugar bowl*	2.60	**2.08**	mill	12.95	**10.36**

Starred items available in decorated patterns at slightly higher prices

Iroquois china cookware.
Cook-and-serve and keep food hot between helpings! Iroquois Casual china cooking units are easy-to-clean china in white and solid colors.

6 qt. Dutch oven	9.95	**7.96**	Electric stove	24.95	**19.96**
10¼" fry pan	8.95	**7.16**	17" Electric warming		
3½ pt. saucepan	7.95	**6.36**	platter	19.95	**15.96**

China, 4th Floor
At all 5 Bloomingdale stores

Mail and phone orders filled on 3.01 or more, exclusive of tax where required. Orders outside delivery sent express collect. A 30¢ charge on each C.O.D. order. Write Bloomingdale's, Box 1549, Grand Central, New York 22, N.Y.

Iroquois Casual abbreviated pattern listing and color selection represents the selection available at Bloomingdale's in 1956. Notice absence of signature.

Casual advertisement showing basketry items. Note fruit and snack server adaptation.

Bringing Sterling Restaurant China Home

Wright's work with the Sterling China Company, a supplier of restaurant china, was done in 1949. The story of that association and the work which he did there is uncomplicated, lasting only for about a year and confined, for the most part to shape work. The pattern work with which Wright was involved was his own custom work, derived from his shapes but including some patterns that would have been part of a whole business concept for which he alone would have been responsible. There were fewer Wright patterns. On the other hand, Sterling had many customers and they supplied them with custom patterned lines, often unique to one account. Most of the patterned Sterling dinnerware which we find today has grown out of Sterling's own design department.

Sterling benefitted from its association with Wright for it allowed the company to secure a place for itself as a supplier for home dinnerware. Not all such firms were able to make such a transition, but Wright's affiliation was intended to facilitate that move. Such an adaptation would never replace the standard institutional ware production which Sterling enjoyed, but it did add to the total production which they were able to achieve.

Never before had Wright been bound by pre-existing principles to which he must adhere, as was necessary in this line. His Sterling work centered around standard sizes and uses, a conformity which institutional usage imposed. To his credit, he questioned, but never forced his own concepts on Sterling when he found those concepts at odds with standards or prices which were established in the industry. He understood competition and its limits and never insisted upon his creative ideas where they would have forced Sterling to assume a bad position in dealing with its accounts. The teapot discussion remains the best example. Wright believed the 10 oz. teapot was too small, not generous enough, a larger one would encour-

age Americans to enjoy a more leisurely meal, he believed. Sterling responded that a larger pot would weaken the tea and that their experience was that "This is the size that sells. All are made, but the 10 oz. size is the volume item in teapot size." They added that the restaurants which used their product were not interested in promoting leisurely meals. Good service with a quick customer turnover was important to restaurants they supplied. With no argument, Wright restricted the size of the teapot and the coffee bottle. His own thoughts on more elegant meals with relaxed dining procedures in fancier settings would have to wait for another time, another client. With Sterling, he was willing to set aside his own judgements in order to achieve a functional, attractive design which would work well in institutions as well as in the home. Sterling, hoping for a product which would enable them to enter the home furnishings market while still producing custom work for the restaurant trade, worked easily with Wright, pleased with the basic business arrangements and the accommodations each would make to achieve this newness in restaurant ware.

The Sterling line was found to be easy to use and Sterling's clients were attracted by the dual uses for items, cutting their costs. The warm colors and flowing lines combined for the innovative effect Sterling had hoped and though Wright's association with them was for only a year, they continued to use his shapes plain, or with decoration of their own, for many years. Wright, himself, turned to them in whole concept work which he did for his own clients as often as such accounts came his way.

Glaze quandaries, problems which had and would become his most difficult ones, started early and soon slowed production. Doris Coutant, already well acquainted with Wright's ways and experienced beyond most in lengthy trials, was sent to deal with the glazes and to represent Wright to his best advantage while sorting through the confusion of glazes. Straight forward colors were tried, rejected by Wright, tried again. The process dragged on. Not recognizing his own demands as excessive, he complained that the trials were taking too long and chided all concerned that this should have been an uncomplicated procedure. What resulted was a small range of low key colors, exactly correct for utilitarian usage and most of which fell into Wright's preference for earthy background colors for food: ivy green, straw yellow, suede gray, cedar brown, shell pink. A stranger in the earthy color listing, pink seems not to have been made in large amounts. White, an institutional standard, for customer's insignias, logos, advertising, or decorations, was a Sterling requisite. With no Wright decorations, except for the custom work referred to, his own involvement with the line ended. If Sterling's customers wanted decoration (and they often did), Sterling could add that, paying Wright royalties on his shapes and glazes only. Collectors have found wonderful patterns, some so wonderful that they have been tempted to credit them to Wright instead of Sterling's art department, but they are not often able to do so. Surely, though, many of Sterling's own air-brushed patterns are very nice, collectible in their own right. One writer spoke of "just right cups," decorated with carnations, from the Carnation Milk Company restaurants. Another writer, finding the cups very special bought many pieces — doing so to get the cups. A dedicated collector told of carrying a box full as "carry on" in a flight home from a trip. Collectors today choose their own favorite pieces, not limiting those choices to these great cups.

After Wright's contract with Sterling expired, they continued to produce his line, and some items have been found in colors not attributed to Wright. In that case his royalties accrued from the shapes, not the glazes.

Since most collectors are not restaurateurs, piece identification has been difficult and adapting the shapes to home use has left some with questions. For those who are just now locating those items, we must repeat some basic characteristics. Plates were made in five sizes: 11½" service plate (a place plate, put on the table when a guest is seated, and which may be removed when the dinner plate, full, is served or upon which the dinner plate may rest). Collectors have found this oversized service plate a great "party plate" sized right for outdoor meals. The dinner plates were a generous 10¼", luncheons 9", salad 7½", and the bread and butter plate 6¼". The plates were wonderfully designed to accomplish a depth barely discernable as the slow curving edges rose from the center of the plates. Spilling was reduced when servers carried too many plates as

they walked. A rolled edge at the rim of the plate hid the foot and gave servers a good grip, as useful as a handle would have been. That rim is narrow, but integrally important to its function.

The tea cup has its handle jiggered on and extends from the rim of the cup down to the side allowing for a good grip. That design gives it a larger look than an ordinary institutional cup, but it remains the standard 7 oz. size. The saucer, with the same deep characteristics as the plates, protects against spilling during service. A slightly larger mug, shown here, is not part of the file listings, a Sterling addition, but collectors like it, agreeing with Wright that a leisurely cup of coffee puts a fine finish on a meal.

After dinner cup and saucer, rare.

The demi cup (after dinner cup), completely different in style from the tea cup is generously sized for its use, but it holds 3½ oz. only. The handle, molded on to the top of the cup, curves downward and inward, stopping before it reaches the body of the cup. From the first, collectors have called these the "pony tailed cups." They are very rare but all colors have been found, though the Sterling white seems even more difficult to find than are the Wright colors. The use of after dinner cups seems unusual in restaurant quality dinnerware.

The Iroquois-type pinch lid for the sugar bowl trades finger grip depressions for the more traditional knob. More easy to use, it rested better upon the table and stored better in the kitchen. The rounded bowl itself had no handles.

The cream pitcher is handled and incorporates the same lines as the tea cup. Wright gave this piece his special attention to achieve a lip which cut down on drips as it was used. It holds 9 oz.

Individual creamers were of two sizes for different uses. The smallest, a 1 oz. size, was served with coffee or tea while the larger was 3 oz., to be used for cereal or dessert. Their flowing shapes set them apart from standard restaurant creamers but they are easily overlooked on a table of dishes. Creamer collectors find them as important as do Wright collectors.

The same rolled "cushion edge" found in the plates is repeated in the fruit bowl which also was intended as an all purpose bowl and worked equally well used for individual vegetable servings.

Sauceboat, bouillon bowl, fruit bowl, and cup and saucer.

Bouillon bowls were rounded with small lug handles extending outward and slightly downward from the rim. As graceful as a cream soup, the lug handles made it easier to handle, less easy to break. Most establishments could conjure many uses for the bouillon bowls.

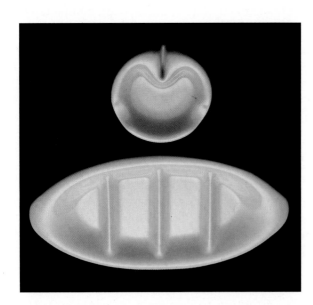

Ashtray and four-compartment relish.

The relish server, 16½" long but narrow, had four compartments making it a practical piece for buffets, smorgasborg's, or salad bars, all new dining concepts to Americans in 1949. It could be carried to the table full of condiments, its high partitions preventing spillage. Serving spoons and forks rested easily in the deep sections. The piece is not signed, but it is so unique that a quick look at the picture here will identify it easily. It has become a favorite with collectors, understandably.

Platters.

Just as there were many plates, there were many platters — four of them — and they were designed with the same cushioned edge, serving several purposes. The smallest platter remains the most difficult to find.

The coffee bottle, one of the most admired pieces in the Sterling line, could be used for coffee or tea and the size followed the potteries insistence — 10 oz. tall, and slender. The handle is integrally molded. A cover which must be removed for pouring seems a safety feature. With no knob, its cover has two finger depressions. Holding two cups of beverage, it takes up less table space than an ordinary coffee pot. This coffee bottle is a little gem, and most collectors, whether they drink coffee, tea, or neither, want one in their collections.

The designated teapot, with a handle molded into the body, follows the same depressed cover style but its design discouraged dripping while it allowed for easier draining or drying in the kitchen. This cover remains safely in place when pouring. When seen without its cover, this size can be mistaken for a cream pitcher, but the size is 10 oz., a bare 1 oz. larger. Be careful!

The sauce boat, in which Wright seems to have been given a free hand, is a departure from what had come before. The handle curves downward from the top, turns slightly toward the cup body and stops, forming the half handle style found in the demi-cup. You will not confuse the two items for the sauce boat holds 5 oz. and was used for serving sauces, syrups, and such. Ounces will be your best guide as you sort out these Sterling pouring pieces.

Sterling's soup bowls were deep bowls, said to be designed to keep soups warm for a longer time than did flat soups. They hold a generous 14 ounces and did double duty for serving many items requiring a larger container. As you consider soups, keep in mind that the bouillon had handles, the soup did not. A third soup must be considered; the covered onion soup. It held 10 ounces and followed the design of other covered items with its finger grip cover. Without its cover, you will not confuse it for only the sugar bowl holds the same amount.

Where salads were served as the main course, a generously sized individual salad bowl was included in the line. It also was designed to prevent the spillage of dressings or "fixings" and its 23 oz. size allowed it to be used for many other purposes.

With the customary cushion edge rim, the slender

Dinner plate, salad plate, and celery.

celery dish sloped slightly at the edges, forming handles integrally, much the same as had the American Modern butter dish. The celery is 11" long.

What can we say about the *ashtray*? What hasn't been said about the ashtray? It enjoys a position among Wright's most outstanding designs and collectors who will not allow smoking in their homes want Sterling ashtrays. Its shape follows that of the entire line with its flowing, rounded curves. With a matchbook holder cut into the folds, it is sensuous and seductive, usually marked, but not always. You will recognize it when you see it, however. When collectors first saw it they wondered what this strange piece could be. Soon they wanted one in every color. Has any one found a pink ashtray? None has been reported.

The water pitcher was one item which had to be redesigned for the original seemed not to please servers. The original, bulky and straight sided with a molded handle, held two quarts. It may be that filled with water, the piece was difficult to manage with one hand. The redesigned water pitcher was a modified tilt jug, almost aero-dynamic, certainly more graceful and less chunky, more eye appealing, and with better leverage.

Understandably, plates and cups, in daily use by restaurants will show use. The exception, of course is the 11½" service plate which was not a requisite for some institutions. Those were not ordered in the same amounts as were the other place setting items and there are less of them found. After dinner coffee cups, not ordered by many of Sterling customers, were made in fewer amounts. Fewer of us will find them.

If Sterling's dinnerware had difficulty in cross usage between homes and restaurants, that difficulty might be traced to the lack of serving items. Certainly adequate for institutional use, the line was shallow for application in the home.

New collectors must be aware that much Sterling is not marked. In some cases, incised signatures filled in with glazes show little or no mark, probably explained by the use of old molds. Several of the items are small, leaving little room for the signature. Stickers were used in many cases. Wright's association with the firm was not long, but Sterling's production of the shapes continued over many years. Items produced after his contract had expired do not always carry the signature. Our recognition of Wright's shapes will help as we sort through this production.

Wright did a great deal of custom work which involved dining rooms for industrial or retail concerns, restaurants, and businesses with total concepts. One example of that work is that which was done for the Shun Lee Dynasty Restaurant in New York City in

1965. A small amount of the dinnerware which he designed for that restaurant has been found and it is known that it was manufactured by Sterling. The shape was called Polynesian and we have examples of a few of the items to show here. There are other shapes, some not seen, but of which we are aware. They include: sake bottle with stopper, 9" plate, tea cups with handles and without handles, rice bowl, double sauce server, covered compote, dessert dish, various sized platters, 15" chop plate, soup server, after dinner cups and saucers, a 10 oz. teapot, a 24 oz. teapot, and a 32 oz. teapot. This line was first seen in black with a white ruffled edge but it has now been found in coral, brown, and seafoam. Perhaps more colors exist. While it would not be surprising to find glassware and cutlery used with this Shun Lee dinnerware, none has been reported. No large amount of Shun Lee can be expected to have survived for there was simply less of it made. As we became aware of this Shun Lee product, we hoped that we could expect more restaurant patterns resulting from Wright's own client work. We were on dangerous ground, however, and from the first, felt it important to confirm any possible findings of Wright's patterns with the Syracuse files. Such a verification was found in a line with an underglaze decal of children and Oriental dancers as well as one with a very simple naturalistic theme. The shapes were unfamiliar to us, but there was enough documentation in the files to be certain that it was a line Wright called Chinese. We first assumed a Sterling Shape Chinese

was Wright's but it is now believed that these were two lines and that Sterling's Chinese line was separate from Wright's client Chinese line.

For now, it seems best to confine our concept of Polynesian to that work which Wright did for the Shun Lee Dynasty restaurant, reserving the name Chinese (Wright's) to that work which has been found with Oriental designs and which we can attribute to him but designed for an unknown account. A late account has reported a Sterling plate in hot pink with a white border resembling the Shun Lee line, differing in that it shows a fancier edging. This plate is said to be stamped with Wright's signature and the Sterling identification. We cannot add to that information. Narrowing our concepts of Wright's Sterling work, it must be reported that Newport Tree patterns have been found, none with Wright's signature, unfortunately. It now seems unlikely that Wright was involved with that line beyond keeping a reference to it in his file which may have meant only that he admired the line.

Two Polynesian platters or plates.
Sterling Palm Frond patterned platter.

The most useful facts that Sterling collectors can return to are these: Wright's contract with the pottery dates from 1949 but he drew royalty on the line for many years as Sterling produced it for their clients. Patterns or decorations, except for those mentioned or pictured here, are not verified in spite of what may appear to be typical of his work. The gray/red air-brushed leaf pattern shown here on the redesigned pitcher is said to have been a favorite of Andy Warhol's. Several other Sterling patterns, done for their own clients are also

Large bowl, believed to be Chinese shape,
client patterned plate, and small bowl.

pictured here. There are certain to be many more.

When I first wrote about the Sterling line, I advised collectors to haunt old restaurant supply houses to look for obsolete stock. Many did, and came away with car loads, if not truck loads. I believe those sources have been exhausted for a long time. Eager collectors bought the unpatterned items in record amounts. Many have turned their attention to Sterling's patterns on Wright's shape, and it now seems if one finds a Sterling pattern too lovely to resist, it should be bought. We can never be certain as to the amount of any one design Sterling customers ordered and you may be looking at the last of a little.

ON PRICING STERLING DINNERWARE

Collectors continue to confuse Wright's few designs with Sterling's many designs, but some seem not to care, choosing Sterling's air-brushed patterns because of their excellent application of pattern. Clearly, shell pink and ivy green are the favored colors. Add 50% for pink, but retain green at the high level below until the color establishes itself in the '90s spectrum with a bit more authority. Signatures will be found on most items made during the time when Wright was associated with the line. Items in his shape and glazes made after his association was discontinued will show the Sterling imprint, but not his name. Collectors have not objected to including such examples into their sets. The most obvious escalation in today's market is the increase in pricing in the water pitchers. Watch these closely. Pitchers, ashtrays, and coffee bottles appeal to one-of-a-color collectors and they can be expected to command higher prices as dinnerware sets are achieved and one-of-each collecting has an effect. Both Chinese and Polynesian items are found in very limited amounts and are more costly. Finding an ashtray for the first time can be a memorable experience. It is one of several classic Wright pieces and it has not increased in value as one might have expected. The backlash on smoking may have hurt its value. One consultant advised that collectors should decide upon the plate size that they like best and not try to collect all the sizes. Considering the weight of the pieces, the size of some markets, and where your car is parked, all are important if your enthusiasm for Sterling extends beyond his advice. The major deterrent to a Sterling collection is the limited amount of serving items available, a drawback to the line then and now. If you are not a purist, try using Iroquois parsley for serving items. All of the glazes have held up well given their institutional usage, but one should study the plates for knife scratching.

Sterling's patterns are numerous and consultants are reluctant to break down favorites, but the black palm frond on pink has been a favorite from the first and remains so. The prices below reflect the undecorated line.

PRICES FOR STERLING DINNERWARE

Ashtray*	$70.00 – 75.00	Plate, dinner, 10¼"	$10.00 – 15.00
Bouillon, 7 oz.	$14.00 – 16.00	Plate, luncheon, 9"	$9.00 – 14.00
Bowl, salad, 7½"*	$14.00 – 18.00	Plate, salad, 7½"	$8.00 – 10.00
Bowl, soup, 6½ oz.*	$15.00 – 18.00	Plate, service	$16.00 – 20.00
Celery, 11¼"	$20.00 – 30.00	Platter, oval, 7½"	$13.00 – 15.00
Coffee bottle*	$100.00 – 125.00	Platter, oval, 10½"	$5.00 – 18.00
Cream, individual, 1 oz.	$10.00 – 12.00	Platter, oval, 13⅝"	$20.00 – 30.00
Cream, individual, 3 oz.	$12.00 – 14.00	Relish, divided, 16½"	$50.00 – 65.00
Cup, 7 oz.	$10.00 – 15.00	Sauce boat, 9 oz.	$20.00 – 22.00
Cup, AD, demi, 3½ oz.**	$35.00 – 45.00	Saucer, 6¼"	$5.00 – 7.00
Fruit, 5"	$7.00 – 8.00	Saucer, AD, demi**	$12.00 – 14.00
Pitcher, cream, 9 oz.	$14.00 – 16.00	Soup, onion, 10 oz.	$20.00 – 25.00
Pitcher, water, 2 qt.**	$115.00 – 120.00	Sugar, covered, 10 oz.	$22.00 – 25.00
Pitcher, water, restyled**	$150.00 – 165.00	Teapot, 10 oz.**	$100.00 – 125.00
Plate, bread and butter, 6"	$4.00 – 6.00		

**Rare, *Scarce

Three oz. cream and one oz. cream.

Custom, two-tone, gray and white, redesigned water pitcher; straw original water pitcher; ivy coffee bottle; suede individual teapot; ivy after dinner coffee cup and saucer.

Redesigned water pitcher, teapot, fruit bowl, and coffee bottle.

Covered sugar, sake bottle, original water pitcher, and handled cream pitcher.

Sterling Polynesian dinner plate, saucer, and teapot believed to be Chinese shape, Polynesian chop plate.

Teapot, cup, coffee bottle, ashtray, individual cream, bouillon.

Rare after dinner/demi cups and saucers.

Chinese coffee pot, 8¼"; and teapot, 5¼".

Sterling redesigned water pitchers, Sterling patterns. Pitcher in foreground shows Andy Warhol's favorite pattern.

165

Sterling Polynesian/Chinese variation.

Wright's client work done for the Shun Lee restaurant.
Marked with signature as shown in marks section. 12½" x 5¾".

Wright's bouillon and
cup flank Sterling's
own mug, 3³⁄₁₆" x 4 ³⁄₈".

Sterling design for Harold's Club in
Reno. Wright shape.

Shell pink Sterling covered sugar (with smaller than
usual cover), ivy green covered bouillon.

Sterling's pattern Carnation Company plate, Polynesian cedar brown plate, individual ivy green cream, wood rose cream pitcher.

Sterling Patterns on Wright Shapes

Dinner plate with restaurant logo, has mark 12 on back.

Sterling popular palm frond design, shown with unlisted mug.

White ashtray with palm tree design, has mark 12 on back.

Wood rose pattern.

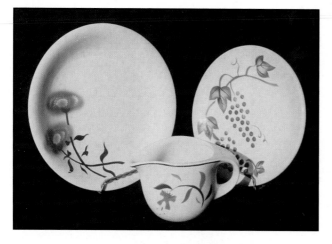

Sterling patterns, including Carnation Milk Company pattern.

STERLING

Presents

THE EXCLUSIVE

Russel Wright

DESIGNED

VITRIFIED

HOTEL AND RESTAURANT

CHINA

PRICE LIST
STERLING-RUSSEL WRIGHT* WARE

Item	Size	Price Per Dozen
Plate	6¼"	$ 5.70
Plate	7½"	8.00
Plate	9"	10.50
Plate	10¼"	13.40
Plate	11½"	17.10
Tea Cup	7-oz.	8.40
Tea Saucer	6¼"	5.10
AD Cup	3½-oz.	6.30
AD Saucer	5⅛"	4.70
Fruit	5"	4.70
Bouillon	7-oz.	7.60
Oval Platter	7⅛"	8.00
Oval Platter	10½"	12.50
Oval Platter	11¾"	15.60
Oval Platter	13⅝"	24.70
Celery	11¼"	25.10
Relish	16½" each	5.00
Individual Cream	1-oz.	5.70
Individual Cream	3-oz.	6.80
Cream Pitcher	9-oz.	17.10
Covered Sugar	10-oz.	17.10
Sauceboat	5-oz.	17.10
Ash Tray	6"	12.00
Onion Soup	10-oz.	9.50
Onion Soup Cover		7.60
Soup Bowl, 6½"	14-oz.	9.50
Salad, 7½"	23-oz.	11.40
Water Pitcher	2-qt.	22.80
Tea Pot	10-oz.	19.00
Coffee Bottle	10-oz.	17.10

THE STERLING CHINA CO.
EAST LIVERPOOL, OHIO

*PATENTS PENDING   PRINTED IN U. S. A.

Original Sterling brochure.

Original price list on back of Sterling brochure.

The Hope of Highlight

Wright's Highlight line, produced by the Paden City Pottery Company in 1948, was distributed by Justin Tharaud, an experienced marketing agent. The Paden City Glass Company had been chosen to coordinate glass items as companion pieces to the line, establishing it as an entirely new concept in dinnerware. The pottery was officially named Highlight and the glass was to be named snow glass. It promised to add elegance and refinement to Wright's work.

The line seemed to have difficulty from the beginning for various reasons. It is to the credit of all concerned that it survived sampling for Wright and Tharaud began to quarrel early. Tharaud, recognized as an arbiter of high style and master of sales and distribution, had standard contracts with self-protective clauses much like Wright's own. Each had demands to bring to negotiation. Tharaud was to have the exclusive rights to sales. Highlight was to be sold at a lower price than either American Modern or Casual and Wright must agree not to design another dinnerware as long as his royalties averaged $10,000.00, beginning with the first year of production. More significantly, Tharaud insisted upon a clause which would allow him to approve of each item before it went into production, a concession not usually allowed a distributor. Arguably, this clause may have had strong reflections on the line as it developed and it seems likely that it was responsible for its several problems. Wright was to agree to the production of white, or to alter color if the new glazes were not readily accepted by the public. He had wanted a flat fee of $15,000.00 on submission of designs, whether they were approved or not. Tharaud would not agree to this concession and Wright, for reasons not explained, dropped his demands. An agreement was reached, but troubles between the parties began immediately after the contract was signed. The correspondence indicates that both, with healthy egos, allowed personal differences to overshadow the success of their work.

The correspondence was among the most peevish in the files. Each would tell the other that they were the well established authority in this matter (even as each insisted on assuming a role in the specialty of the other). "Let me tell you!," "Let me know when you are serious." "You called me, I didn't call you." These are among the words written. Inter-office conversations were likely to have been even more accusatory, more inflammatory. Repeatedly, Tharaud would be told that he had violated Wright's contract clause which provided his signature to be the largest printing on the page. Repeatedly, Tharaud deflected these claims, responding that because he, too, was well established and had name recognition, his endorsement was worthwhile. Nothing escaped the attention of either and trouble had reached a fever point before production began. It is true that each was an expert, but it is also true that each extended his expertise beyond its limits. It was no surprise to the design community that a schism developed early and continued for the life of the design.

In Wright's defense, he was probably right in feeling that Tharaud had involved himself in design detail of which he had little knowledge. However, with the approval clause which Tharaud had extracted, complaints were too late. Business matters were not attended to in a timely matter, Tharaud's responsibility, Wright claimed. Tharaud's replies indicated that he could not possibly attend to business matters until production procedures were in place. Each allowed his own expertise to be compromised as he busied himself with affairs best left to the other. The situation deteriorated with each encounter, each exchange of letters. Molds needed to be made, new mills to grind glaze colors were to be purchased, new spraying equipment was required and if Highlight became as successful as American Modern and Casual had been, new buildings at the pottery would be needed. The line itself suffered as those most concerned engaged in personal attacks (all this at a time when the mails were the standard form of communication). Time dragged on. In serious trouble, the production waited and advertising and sales were in client's hands before details of design and production were agreed upon.

Costs were higher than either party had expected and the line quickly became competitive with American Modern and Casual. An early price cut to keep the line in accordance with contract agreements left neither party pleased. It cut into profits and royalties, not to mention the fact that such an early cut reflected upon the line's reputation. Wright blamed Tharaud for the situation and questioned his competency. Tharaud countered that the design was faulty. Neither profited as they had expected.

Not engaged in the disputes, the Paden City Pottery, glad to be working when potteries were closing, enjoyed the prestige of producing a Russel Wright design. When Highlight won the 1951 Museum of Modern Art Home Furnishing exhibit, the pottery enjoyed reflected honor. The Merchandise Mart in Chicago and the Museum of Modern Art co-sponsored Highlight in their Good Design exhibit the same year and it won the Trail Blazer Award given by the Home Furnishings League. Paden City Pottery had reason to hope for the long production time which Wright's other designs had enjoyed. They ignored the discord between Wright and Tharaud and kept working where they could.

Highlight drew its name from the appearance of the white clay showing through the glaze at the rims and edges of the pieces. With sophisticated and sensual shapes, it was elegant. The understated softness of its lines achieved for Highlight the position of the most suave and refined of Wright's dinnerware lines, perhaps among the highest styled American dinnerware lines of the time.

It must be said that Highlight had an urbane quality, not for every one, not for every day. It was Wright with sophistication, and those with artistic tendencies took to it at once. If it borrowed features of the Sterling line, it adapted them in a formal way, with no compromise in elegance.

The glazes were as skillfully conceived as were the shapes, all favorites of the designer. The original colors were blueberry, nutmeg, pepper, and citron, a palette not found in dinnerware at its selling price. Dark green and white were late 1951 colors with less of those made than the original colors. White was snow glaze, but there seemed to be no time to give an appropriate name to dark green. First made in a soft matte glaze, a later adaptation adjusted the glaze to a glossier sheen, showing less of the highlighted edges. Wright's original concept of a soft matte finish was, and remains, more refined.

Snow glass, made by the Paden City Glass Company, added to the line in a way that made it more innovative than any other line on the market. The body of the glass appears to be crystalline with tiny milk glass flecks resembling snow particles randomly suspended in it. It is very different, textured in appearance as well as in feel and hard to miss. Other look-alikes are easy to identify once you have seen snow glass for it is more dense than others and there are no ground bottoms on it. Seen side by side, Wright's glass is easily identified, but if you are not able to compare items in this way, shape will identify snow glass. Look-alikes are not undesirable to collectors for they are able to substitute bowls and serving items never found in the Highlight line.

Paul Lobel designed one of these similar lines and Mary Ryan, Wright's early client, sold it as Benduro. Made in several colors, it is the white, Snowflake, which is similar to the Wright snow glass. We now know that Ben Seibel also designed a textured white glass similar to the Wright line. Prototypes for snow glass were done by the Fostoria Glass Company. They have a thinner body, darker than snow glass. Fostoria considered the texture to be unsanitary and would not produce it for Wright. In 1942 Raymor advertised a textured glass very much like snow glass. Made in Mexico, it came in a 5 oz. juice glass and a 10 oz. cocktail glass and was very popular. This would have preceded snow glass and Wright's concept may have been influenced by the textured import. None of these are Wright's, none should be so costly, though they have a place on an incomplete Wright table of Highlight.

The approved snow glass listing was to include:

**Platter, snow glass tumbler,
snow glass look-alike sauce boat.**

three sizes of tumblers, salad plates, saucers, fruit bowls, covers which resembled plateaus, (making them useful as small trays or platters), a two-pint pitcher, a round vegetable bowl, and shakers. Not all of these items have been found, leaving us to question whether or not the line might ever have included all the items.

When the Paden City Glass company closed its doors in 1953, Wright was left with no replacement for this glass. By this time old tensions between Wright and Tharaud were renewed and each blamed the other for not having aggressively sought out a replacement glass company. Tharaud felt this was Wright's responsibility. Wright, by now disaffected with the entire situation, claimed that he had very little to show for his work on the line and was unwilling to expend more time and effort. Making the best of a bad situation, they turned to the pottery for snow glaze, a ceramic white glaze not included in the line before, but which had been anticipated at the time when initial agreements were signed. All of the former glass shapes, as well as those pieces which had been made in the colored glazes were made in snow glaze after that time. Problems, however, seemed irreversible and though the files indicate that there were additions and redesigns, much seems to have been lost in the battles between the two. In a last effort to sell, Tharaud cut prices below that of American Modern and Wright found himself in competition with himself. By 1953, both parties released claims against each other and except for royalties which Wright was owed, their contract and agreements ended.

The photograph on page 174 may be the two-pint snow glass pitcher. With such amorphic lines, it is different from other look-alikes. You will also find a large plate with all of the characteristics of snow glass except that we find no listing of this piece in the files. Our fingers are crossed on these. Any documentation pointing to or against inclusion of these in Wright's work will be welcome.

If the 1950s conflicts described above were not enough, Highlight continues to divide us, as collectors, much as it divided Wright and Tharaud. That situation derives from information found in the files and reported here. The file information, dated 1953 indicates that the pottery line was expanded to include pottery items as replacements for the glass items. At that time, serving items, including the shakers, butter dish, soups, and pitcher were redesigned. Few of these have been found in their original design, and none are known to exist in the redesign listing. Details of this redesign are explicit and drawings and detailed descriptions are given. The butter dish illustrates the point. Distinction is made between an Eastern version and a Western version.

Found! The Highlight butter dish from all angles.

Such information with specific documentation, seemed reasonable as we first looked at the line but after a few years of collecting, we were left with unanswered questions. What, we asked ourselves, would explain this? Where were the teapot, covered pitcher, the mug, and casserole, the rest of the original listing? How could it be that we had collected for this length of time and had found none of these items, original or redesigned. Some gave up hope, believing that they were never made. Others disagreed, believing that the file documentation could not have been so misleading. We differed, searched, and reasoned, with no explanation that could be accepted by both sides of the controversy. It remained true that if our listings are accurate, we should have findings. At the same time, how could the files contain such specific details about pieces that may never have been made? Why would prestigious awards be given to an incomplete line? Our questions continued to divide us, but in 1990 we heard reports of a pair of shakers. Score one for the believers. In 1995 a butter dish was reported. Score two. Can we expect to find more? It seems likely that we may, though the amount may be very, very limited. Was the production lost in Tharaud's insistence that he approve each item before production? That may be, but we continue to search, though with less expectancy. We have been forced to consider that details in the files, though accurate, may not apply to general production, perhaps only proto-

types, samplings, a run at the most, provided for Tharaud's approval. The butter dish may be one of one, but it restores our confidence and we continue to have hopes, but less of them.

Certainly we did not expect to find Highlight in the light blue matte glaze which was reported in 1990. Much lighter than blueberry, it is not supported by file reference. Still, the cups and saucers which were found are marked with the Justin Tharaud/Wright signature/USA mark. We would account for it as sampling or runs if enough had appeared. Have you seen more? We found no other colors, no additional pieces. Could this blue be a maverick blueberry? Answers would be guesses, but it seems likely.

Highlight is not often found in mixed colored sets as the colors neither blend nor contrast to the degree which allows for that practice. It was not advertised as stackable, unbreakable, or easy to use and care for. Not thought to become popular with those of us in the stew and soup crowd, Wright directed Highlight to the eclair circle. It was promoted as an elegant, polished dinnerware service with no apologies or explanations. It made a statement which was much different than that found in Wright's other work and he seemed not to have encumbered the line with his own social concerns. It remains that Highlight, with problems of its own, still presents functionalism with emotion, pristine and polished to perfection.

ON PRICING HIGHLIGHT

Highlight's comeback from controversy over the disputed serving items seemed like wonderful news but no new findings have verified the remaining missing items and the place-setting pieces seem to be few and even farther between. It remains the most difficult to find of the Wright-produced lines. Consultants all agree that they cannot find it in enough numbers to assemble sets and that buyers now are collecting it in smaller sets to serve four or so people for breakfast or a special dessert. Dealers report that they sell all that they can buy, but they cannot buy more to replace their stock.

Color information generally favors blueberry and pepper, with citron being the least popular. Be aware, however, that citron is not the acid green of Modern, certainly not the muddy green of Casual. Citron is a much better color and dealers who thought it might

never find a home have found that there are those who appreciate the statement which a Citron table achieves. The dark green is the most difficult color to find and coming on enough of it to use is almost impossible. Nutmeg falls into an in-between position with collectors while white seems not to be as favored in Highlight as it has been with Wright's other whites.

Snow glass is difficult to find an *any* condition and expensive even if cracked. Not all the accepted items have been found but continue to look for them. Put Snow Glass shapes in your recall and you will be better able to identify them as Wright's work and not that of several other very similar lines. Consider those similar lines if they come your way at a fair price, for you may need them to replace pottery bowls and servers that have not been found.

Finding the Highlight butter dish has raised hopes that other pieces will come out of the cupboards. We continue to be expectant. It seems likely that if these pieces exist, we will find them in the middle of original sets. Look for them there. In view of the fact that so much time has passed since our original listings, it seems best not to include pricing on those items. Obviously, such a piece could come to us for a song, unrecognized. If recognized, its value might sky rocket.

These prices apply to mint quality items. Snow glass cracks more easily than it chips. Such damage should be considered and would hurt value, but such a piece would still be important to a collector.

** Items listed, but not found

Bowl, vegetable, oval ....$65.00 – 75.00	Pitcher, covered** ....NPD
Butter dish ....NPD	Plate, bread & butter ....$8.00 – 10.00
Casserole (bain Marie)** ....NPD	Plate, dinner ....$25.00 – 30.00
Cover for soup** ....NPD	Platter, large, oval ....$55.00 – 75.00
Cream ....$35.00 – 40.00	Platter, small, oval......................$45.00 – 50.00
Cup ....$25.00 – 30.00	Platter, small, round ....$55.00 – 60.00
Cups/saucers a.d. demi** ....NPD	Relish server** ....NPD
Divided vegetable** ....NPD	Shakers, pair (2 sizes) ....$50.00 – 75.00
Dish, salad or vegetable, round ......$65.00 – 75.00	Soups/cereal bowls (2 sizes) ....$30.00 – 35.00
Gravy boat** ....NPD	Sugar bowl ....$35.00 – 50.00
Mug** ....NPD	Teapot** ....NPD

LATE POTTERY ADDITIONS

Covers for vegetable bowls..............$50.00 – 60.00	Saucer ....$8.00 – 10.00
Cover for sugar bowl ....$35.00 – 45.00	Sherbet/fruit dish ....$20.00 – 22.00
Plate, salad ....$25.00 – 30.00	

SNOW GLASS

Bowl, salad/vegetable, round.$175.00 – 200.00	Sugar cover/tray ....$75.00 – 100.00
Candleholders ....NPD	Tumbler, ice tea, 14 oz. ....$125.00 – 150.00
Sherbet/fruit......................$55.00 – 75.00	Tumbler, juice, 5 oz.......................$125.00 – 150.00
Plates/salad ....$100.00 – 125.00	Tumbler, water, 10 oz. ....$125.00 – 150.00
Saucers ....$35.00 – 40.00	Vegetable, oval with cover/tray platter**..NPD
Shakers, pair ....NPD	

Possible snow glass
two-pint pitcher.

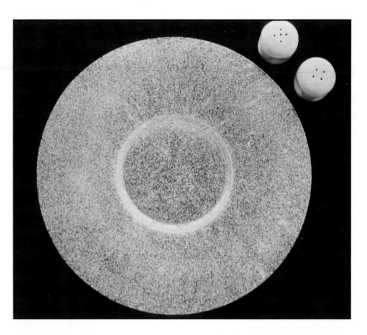

Possible snow glass plate. American Modern shakers.

Dark green, large platter; nutmeg oval vegetable
bowl; blueberry cup and saucer; citron sugar; blueberry creamer; pepper cup and snow glass saucer;
blueberry fruit bowl; citron redesigned cereal bowl.

Sugar and vegetable bowls shown with
pottery covers which replaced snow glass
covers.

One of several Paden City
look-alikes. *Not* a Wright design.

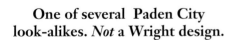

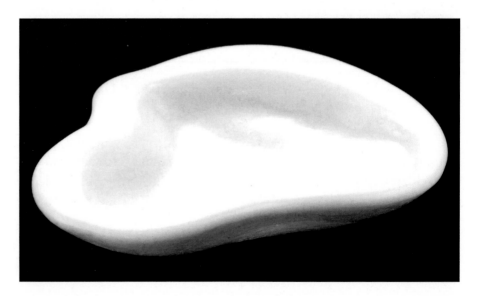

Highlight blueberry place setting.
Pinch cutlery and Leacock table cloth.

Highlight soup/cereal bowl, snow glass fruit,
look-alike '50s style textured bowl.

Highlight cream and sugar cup with snow glass
saucer, soup/cereal Simtex harvest cloth,
Snow Glass look-alike bowl.

Original Highlight advertisement.

Russel Wright

ADDS NEW SNOW GLAZE
TO *Highlight*
DINNERWARE

OPEN STOCK IN

Black Pepper

Blueberry

Nutmeg

Citron

Snow Glaze

Prompt Delivery

Distributed exclusively by

Justin Tharaud & Son Inc.
129-131 Fifth Avenue, New York 3

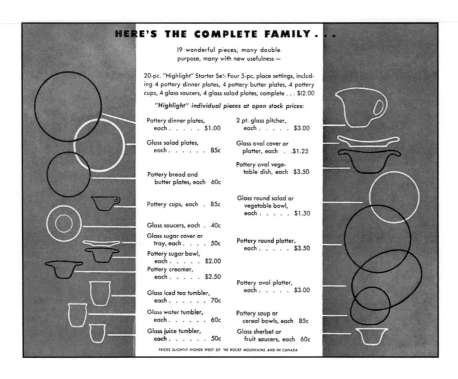

Original brochure showing all 19 pieces.

Highlight advertisement to the trade.

White Clover, Pattern for the First Time

Water pitcher, shakers, dinner plate, and cup and saucer.

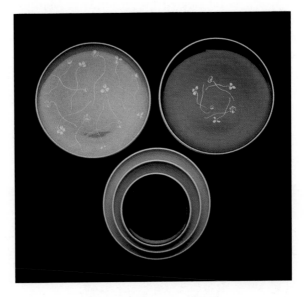

White Clover plates.

Many of us who have studied Wright's work and considered his design practices have questioned the turn to pattern which he made in 1951 when he designed Harker's White Clover. With 12 years of dinnerware design behind him, years in which he favored solid colors and resisted any sort of surface ornamentation, some important change, some new convictions, some unexplained considerations must have influenced his decision to work with pattern. It may be helpful to speculate. The American Modern work, experimenting with an altogether new concept in dinnerware design had been overwhelmingly successful. Iroquois had proved that dinnerware could combine good design and durability. Taking on the restaurant and institutional market with his Sterling designs, he added a new dimension to commercial dinnerware, bringing it into the home. Highlight, however incomplete, brought elegance where informality had gone before. Let us be as resilient as he. Perhaps pattern added a challenge. By incorporating pattern into his work, by accomplishing it with an entirely new treatment, it may be that he felt he could change the face of pattern as it was seen at the time, adding a Wright version that would be new and refresh-

Fruit, two-quart covered casserole, cereal/soup, gravy, and vegetable bowl.

ing. With confidence that it would be as well received as his other award-winning lines, he seemed to believe he could make another mark with this new Clover. Fighting fire with fire had always made sense.

And this new Clover did exemplify a different pattern treatment than any of the decalled lines of the mid-century market. It treated pattern as part of the glaze itself, incising the clover forms through the colored surface, exposing the white glaze beneath it. The sgraffito treatment was very different from traditional patterns and Wright showed that he could manipulate pattern as he had manipulated glazes. Some pieces were sprinkled, unexpectedly with four leaf clovers and other pieces were left solid, with no pattern. It all added interest. Add to this, the fact that by 1951 Wright was involved in his life-long love affair with the earth and all that grew there. We know from his other writings that his Garrison weekend work, as he cleared the grounds at Manitoga, influenced his week's work when he returned from there. It seems likely that White Clover was influenced by those outdoor experiences. His daughter, Annie, remembers long train rides home from Florida with Wright sketching patterns for White Clover. He filled his leisure with his work and having always put "self" into his work, it is not strange to find it here.

Made in golden spice, meadow green, coral sand, and charcoal and accompanied by a General Electric

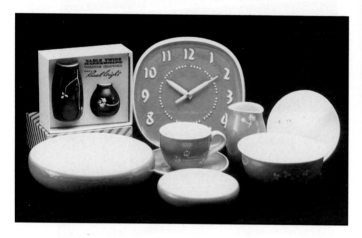

White Clover shakers, clock, vegetable bowls, cup/saucer, cream, fruit bowl, and covered sugar.

clock to match, the palette was typical of glazes Wright preferred. Soft, warm, easy-on-the-eye colors, they did not shock or detract from the svelte shapes. The line was advertised as acid-proof, detergent-proof, craze-proof, chip resistant. As his other lines, it stacked easily on a kitchen shelf and you were told that it could go into the oven with your favorite recipes. Wright even provided a favorite recipe of his own for shrimp and egg casserole. If you bought the dishes, you were given the recipe on a brochure which he designed. We are able to show a color photograph of this interesting original work.

The shapes were distinctly different from his older shapes, less amorphic, with more of a country look than an informal look. Flat pieces were banded in white glaze. A locking lid on the pitcher prevented spilling accidents while pouring. The salt shaker was taller than the pepper but most stores accommodated buyer's traditional shaker concept and sold them both ways. The sugar

bowl was sold as a covered individual ramekin from the beginning. More pieces, with more double usage would have followed, without doubt, but short production, no restyling, no redesign work amounted to a basic line.

Clover won awards as had his other designs. The Museum of Modern Art acquired a set for their permanent exhibit and gave it their Good Design Award. In spite of that, trouble soon developed.

Wright found himself in competition with himself

**Top row: Divided vegetable dish and pitcher.
Bottom row: Vegetable bowl, fruit, and cereal/soup.**

once more, with predictable results. Modern and Casual, so well established, were still selling for a lesser price, a high hurdle for White Clover and one it could not surmount.

A more central problem existed, however. Marketing practices, so carefully established had broken down with Highlight's production and it seemed Wright may have felt he could "go it alone" with no national distributor, an unfortunate decision. Sales were left to those which Harker could develop. Except for showrooms and salesmen's samples which Harker had in place, the line was not well promoted. National advertising was limited and the magazine advertisements were not as artistic as before. There were fewer of them, fewer in color. Store brochures, though carefully conceived by Wright, were not available in the amounts necessary to promote the line as it should have been. Wright complained, but with no distributor of his own, it did little good. The entire marketing scheme was wrong, contrary to practices which had worked so well for so long. Harker felt that the line should be promoted as difficult to find, as had been American Modern during the war years, and initially took orders for meadow green only, adding other colors as interest mounted. Salesmen were instructed to develop only one account in a town and much was made of exclusivity, a mistake. The line suffered. Clover never achieved the attention given to Wright's other lines and poor marketing was directly responsible for that situation. In 1951, introduced in a limited way to a limited number of accounts, it was not able to overcome the troubles it found in its own planning.

Customer reaction developed quickly and by 1953, with all the colors available, buyers complained that the 9" plate, the largest plate in the starter set was without pattern. Wright agreed with the customer, complaining that a starter set claiming to be decorated but with only the cup showing pattern, was sure to cause dissatisfaction. Harker countered that the 10" decorated dinner plate was too expensive to make and sell in the 16-piece starter sets. After protracted correspondence, the pottery reluctantly agreed to decorate the 9" plate, but warned that it would add to its already over-budget production costs. By early 1954 two different 16-piece starter sets were available with one including the 9" plate, the other, more expensive by $1.00, included the 10" decorated plates.

West Coast accounts, Wright believed, would add to sales volumes but Harker would only agree to sell to those accounts if they ordered box car amounts. Few would do so. Wright offered to add new items to the listings but Harker refused to accept them, claiming that kiln space for the plates was more than they usually allowed and added that the special cartons used on starter sets had added unnecessarily to their costs. They believed Wright's royalties were too high, especially in view of their own expenses. He countered by saying that he was not aware of these special needs which they claimed had derived from the design and had he known earlier, he would have modified the design to remedy the situation. To alter the price structure after so many sales had been made could force the failure of the entire line, he said. There was no meeting of the minds and the line stumbled forward.

By 1955, however, bankruptcy seemed a distinct possibility and Harker, acting alone, reduced the price of White Clover, affecting Wright's royalties directly. Starter sets were sold specially priced at $7.95 in the East and $8.95 on the West coast. Harker's records showed that their shipments had not added to more than 60% of their expectations on open stock and fell to a little less than 40% on starter sets. Accounting for a large part of the situation was the fact that the pottery industry was in an irreversible decline with most plants working at 70% of their capacity in spite of wage disputes with workers. Harker joined all the Ohio River potteries in a fight for life, but little could be done. Deeply affected, the pottery discontinued the production of White Clover shortly after the reductions were made.

Harker was no less imaginative than were other potteries and they used Wright's glazes on various pieces of their own production, often with better results. They seemed to be more adept in combining metal fixtures with plates and bowls, making serving items with extended uses. A salad set, using the open vegetable bowl and the cereal bowls is an example, as are several tidbit trays. Cake lifters were favorite Harker pieces and they dipped them in Wright's colors, paying royalties as they did so. Given the small size of the White Clover line, Harker's skill at producing companion pieces filled needs for which no item was designed and collectors use them now, as original buyers did then. Be aware though, that these are not rare, unlisted items. Wright drew royalties on the glazes and shapes of the items involved, but adaptation of the pieces was the work of others.

Colors in White Clover will be found as more uniform than in Wright's other lines. The shortened production time did not result in variances for the most part. You will find the signature in place, but it is often difficult to see as the glaze coating on the white underside of some pieces obscures the mark. In solid colored items, where signatures are difficult to read or non-existent, remembering the shape will help. Rarely, pieces have been found with no signature and items intended to be plain have been found with design in place. In such cases, we must credit creative potters who "custom designed" items for their own use.

Because Wright's work had dominated the dinnerware industry, the commercial failure of White Clover was difficult for him. The experience was industry-wide, however, and imports were responsible for pottery closings up and down the Ohio River. Retrenching practices were the sign of the times and some of the pessimism had spilled over into the designer's optimism. The line was never able to develop as fully as Wright had hoped.

Clover adds to our understanding of Wright's design theory as we find that he could incorporate pattern, adapt it in a new way, and develop a line which retained the uncluttered clean lines of his other dinnerware. It would be a mistake to consider this line as the equal of American Modern or Casual, but its place in Wright's work remains a significant one. Comparison with other patterned items of the 1950s shows its significant superiority.

HARKER WHITE CLOVER

Collectors buy White Clover in sets of one color, glad to find it in any color. Choice, however, indicates that charcoal is the favorite, but Clover's colors are 50s colors and all are welcome with collectors as America finds itself reliving the 50s again. Serving items, high-end pieces are important to Russel Wright collectors whether or not they search for enough to set a table, but those items are often difficult to single out from "lots" which dealers will not break. Collectors find themselves buying a table full of dishes to obtain the desired items. The clocks have not lived up to early expectations, probably because they are difficult to harmonize in our kitchens. Most clocks work well but many of today's households skipped the 50s in their rush to Country. Perhaps their time will come yet.

Ashtray, Clover decorated....................$40.00 – 45.00	Pitcher, covered, Clover decorated,
Casserole, covered, Clover decorated,	2 qt...$75.00 – 100.00
2 qt.. ....$45.00 – 55.00	Plate, barbecue, color only, 11" ....$20.00 – 25.00
Clock, General Electric ....$55.00 – 60.00	Plate, bread & butter, color only, 6"........$5.00 – 6.00
Cream, Clover decorated ....$18.00 – 20.00	Plate, chop, Clover decorated, 11"......$25.00 – 28.00
Cup ....$12.00 – 15.00	Plate, dinner, Clover decorated, 9¼"...$14.00 – 16.00
Dish, fruit, Clover decorated ....$10.00 – 12.00	Plate, jumbo, Clover decorated, 10" ..$16.00 – 18.00
Dish, vegetable, covered, 8¼" ....$40.00 – 45.00	Plate, salad, Clover only, 7⅝"...............$8.00 – 10.00
Dish, vegetable, open, 7½"..................$20.00 – 25.00	Salt & pepper, either size, pair ....$30.00 – 35.00
Dish, vegetable, open, 8¼"..................$27.00 – 30.00	Saucer, Clover only ....$3.00 – 4.00
Gravy boat, Clover decorated.............$25.00 – 35.00	Sugar, covered (individual ramekin) ......$25.00 – 28.00

Harker White Clover cereal on Simtex Harvest Variation cloth.

Original White Clover advertisement.

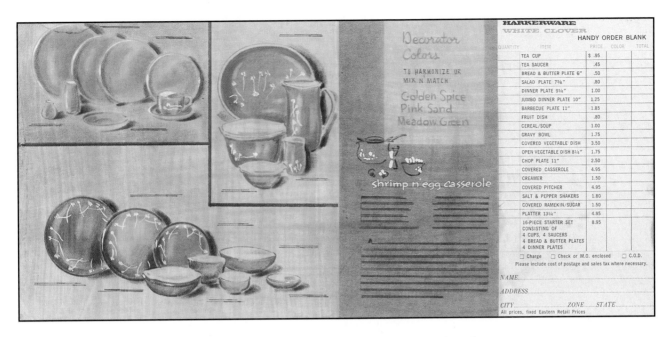

HARKERWARE
WHITE CLOVER
HANDY ORDER BLANK

QUANTITY	ITEM	PRICE	COLOR	TOTAL
	TEA CUP	$ .95		
	TEA SAUCER	.45		
	BREAD & BUTTER PLATE 6"	.50		
	SALAD PLATE 7⅜"	.80		
	DINNER PLATE 9¼"	1.00		
	JUMBO DINNER PLATE 10"	1.25		
	BARBECUE PLATE 11"	1.85		
	FRUIT DISH	.80		
	CEREAL/SOUP	1.00		
	GRAVY BOWL	1.75		
	COVERED VEGETABLE DISH	3.50		
	OPEN VEGETABLE DISH 8¼"	1.75		
	CHOP PLATE 11"	2.50		
	COVERED CASSEROLE	4.95		
	CREAMER	1.50		
	COVERED PITCHER	4.95		
	SALT & PEPPER SHAKERS	1.80		
	COVERED RAMEKIN/SUGAR	1.50		
	PLATTER 13¼"	4.95		
	16-PIECE STARTER SET CONSISTING OF 4 CUPS, 4 SAUCERS 4 BREAD & BUTTER PLATES 4 DINNER PLATES	8.95		

☐ Charge   ☐ Check or M.O. enclosed   ☐ C.O.D.
Please include cost of postage and sales tax where necessary.

NAME
ADDRESS
CITY   ZONE   STATE
All prices, fixed Eastern Retail Prices

Original mockup of Harker White Clover brochure.

Harker showroom display.

Harkerware White Clover Brochure

Brochure front.

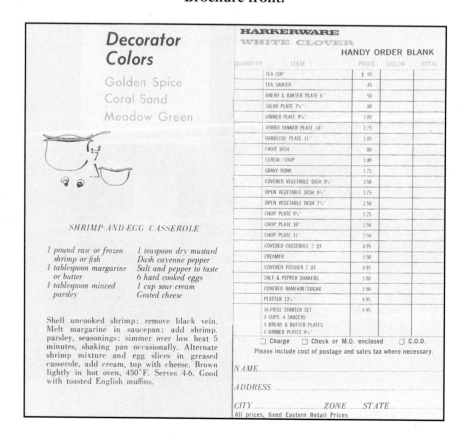

Inside of brochure.

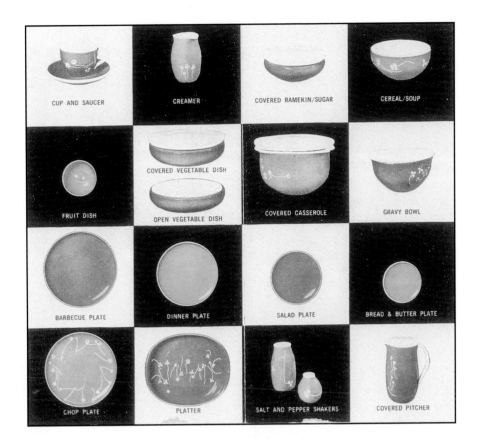

Back of brochure.

Harker and Steubenville adaptations of Wright's designs. *Not* part of his lines, they illustrate uses to which items could be put.

Ad for G.E. ceramic wall clock styled by Russel Wright.

Knowles Esquire, the Designer's Favorite

Wright's White Clover experience left him gun-shy of pattern, but he understood that customers were asking for decorated dinnerware after years of preferring solid colors and he respected the need for change if it could be accomplished without compromising his own honesty of design. It seems likely, also, that he believed the mosaic of his ceramic work was not complete. Not having found acceptance in his Harker work, it is possible that he chose to approach pattern from another angle, different from that on the market and different from Clover. Having worked all of his years filling voids where he could, it is logical that he recognized this challenge and moved to accomplish excellence in this very different way.

Aware of the deep financial problems swirling in the American pottery industry he knew that any further dinnerware designs must be restricted by the practicalities of production as they existed in 1955. Where possible, any new design must conform itself to the existing limits of the manufacturer. Expansion, research, development, all had to be in place for Japanese imports had proven to be even more competitive than feared and it was no longer possible to expect potteries to enlarge or retool to accomplish a new production.

Wright was challenged, but making the most of his opportunities, he designed a generous sized line to be executed on clear and serene pastel glazes, not the earth tones which he had favored in the past. The line was to be Knowles Esquire, with a matte finish in beige, white, pink, yellow, and blue, incorporating an underglaze rubber stamped pattern with an overglaze gold stamping. Items were back stamped, identifying the line, design, and signature where room provided. The patterns were Seeds on a yellow ground; Grass, broken stems on blue; Queen Anne's Lace on white; Snowflower on pink; Botanica on a beige base; and Solar on white. Each pattern, as conceived, was to be done on its own background color with no mix or match qualities in pattern or color. Collectors have found them exactly as described, in spite of our early suppositions that workers would have made adaptations in pattern and color in small amounts for their own use.

Both shapes and patterns borrowed from the Oriental influence. It is possible that his recent work in Asia added to his long-standing interest and admiration in the clean spare lines, efficiency, and economy of ornamental detail. Esquire sought out those influences, defined by Wright in delicate detailed patterns, very lightly applied, even difficult to distinguish, but perfectly suited to the pastel bodies upon which they were applied. Naturalistic traceries, they are not reckless in any way, but rather, seem to have been blown on to the shapes with a cool wind, resting there serenely. Undecorated versions were an Antique White, said to be architecturally simple and a "Classic for modern purists," Fontaine, a tan shade, and Mayfair, a blue tint.

With 20 or so pieces, the line was a large one because of the diverse patterns, but also because

Antique white shakers, pitcher, deep compote, plates, cup and saucer, and covered sugar.

185

Wright adapted his concern for double usage to items in the line. The deep compote, designed as a fruit bowl, served equally well as a soup tureen, floral centerpiece, or salad bowl. The cover on the serving bowl, with its genesis in Highlight covers, could be used as a hot plate, a butter plateau, a multi-purpose piece. Used as a cover, the fit was not good. The sugar, generously sized and with the suggestion of a footed piece, could hold its own in candy or nuts on a coffee table. In groups of four or more they were well suited to hold individual servings of desserts.

In spite of the designer's intent to conform to existing conditions, many shapes and patterns were considered by Wright, by the pottery, and even clients as the Esquire developed. Changes were being affected constantly, in an effort to meet client/customer approval in a difficult market, in a difficult time.

Problems began almost immediately. Sears and Montgomery Ward, the giant mail-order firms who were expected to feature Esquire, refused to carry the line. Photographic representations of the delicate patterns were too difficult to reproduce in a catalog format and the glazes were likely to "wash out," with little true representation. Those who would order from catalog pages could not see the delicate patterns and the mail-order houses expected that the line would not sell well for that reason.

Both Wright and Knowles were taken aback and Wright offered to reduce his royalties in an effort to find a distributor who would carry the line. He further agreed to drop open stock marketing in favor of packaged sets to be accompanied by a simple wood serving tray (one per set). In spite of that, no distributor could be found and as early as 1957, Wright was willing to offer Esquire to accounts who would be allowed to use a back stamp printed to include the account's name as well as his signature. Still careful of his name and the prestige which had accrued to it, he reserved the right to see and approve of all sales literature, so screening out any inference that he designed other patterns which an account might carry.

Club plans as well as home sales plans were considered. Jewel Tea and Stanley Home products as well as grocery market chains such as Grand Union were investigated with the hope that Esquire could be best sold if seen in informal home settings. The S&H Stamp company agreed to promote Esquire as premiums but they were not successful in that effort, for the same reasons that Sears and Montgomery Ward had cited. S&H had to take a price cut on about 1,000 sets on order to move it.

Bad news followed bad news and customer complaints were registered. Knife scratches ruined the glaze, it was reported. Knowles believed that to be a glaze problem and correspondence indicated that the lack of uniformity of glazes had not been achieved as late as 1959 and the company indicated that they were "forced to ship quite a range of finishes in order to make out at all." Wright was convinced that sales people did not actively promote the line, but salesmen who had sold the line to retail accounts reported that while first sales were good, they found that shops and stores still had it on hand six to eight months later. Even with this poor report, Knowles said it still fared better with retailers than with the catalog sales for which it had been intended. Accusations and suggestions flew, but with no effective sales organization available, Wright was soon told that Knowles and their clients must take reductions in prices.

It was his natural instinct to preserve the integrity of the line and he offered all he could do to set things right. He offered new designs, but Knowles replied that they were overstocked and had few orders. They added that they had "worn out any good will that Esquire had accrued" and that they were completely "stuck with 300 sheet editions of the decals." They proposed to run a low priced sale to move the existing stock and "would probably let the line run its course and move on to other shapes and decorations."

Wright extended himself and sent sketches of many new patterns, each carefully drawn and accompanied by suggested glaze colors. He tried to breathe new life into the line, but no new patterns were accepted and his personal search for a distributor not rewarded. Some samplings may have been done but it is unlikely that even short runs were made. Knowles was unwilling to proceed. Seeing no future for the line, the pottery decided that changes would not help and that they could not proceed with the production. Willing to make any reasonable concession, Wright tried to reverse this decision but the answer was clear. White, Fontaine, and Mayfair were produced in small amounts, for a short time, but Esquire had come to its own end in 1962.

With this problematic production, distribution, and sales, Esquire still made an important addition to the body of Wright's dinnerware lines as we see it today. The glazes were new to Wright and their purity of pattern was new to the industry. The shapes were elegantly achieved and admired by the artistic community then and now. Walter Dorwin Teague, recognized as important in the design community, borrowed Esquire for a table setting he was displaying, in spite of the fact that he had many of his own lines which he could have used. Wright, himself, chose Botanical, not

Grass as previously reported, for a "special occasion" set at Dragon Rock and, in 1960 he tried to find replacements for it with no luck. Rejected by the group for which it had been intended, the line received accolades from those who knew design best. That it would not photograph well was the worst that could be said about it.

With such limited production and distribution, and with little or no advertising, this Esquire line remains elusive but there is a body of unexplained information which collectors have tried to understand. That has not been easy to do. Strange items have been found which do not seem to be part of the Esquire line, but so similar in concept, they suggest that they may have been the result of attempts to make Esquire more commercially

successful. These fringe findings include the "Knowles Wright Shape," pictured here in a black and white photograph. While we still cannot add much positive information about this shape, it seems possible that it may have been the result of some of Wright's failed attempts to restructure the Esquire line. Items found in this shape are backstamped "Mary and Russel Wright/Sovereign Potteries." The glazes have been reported in a speckled pastel pink or blue.

Earlier information has been that Wright's sister and her husband who lived in Canada had connections with Sovereign Potteries there. Wright kept a lively correspondence going with his sister and it was not uncommon for him to suggest to her that they "look into" a design feature or production. Always concerned for economy in design as well as in life, it certainly would be in character for this to have been given to his Canadian family to make of it what they could. No personal involvement or business arrangement is mentioned in the files but we are aware that when Mary Wright's Country Gardens had been rejected by Bauer, Wright consulted with Sovereign as a possible manufacturer and it would seem that he was acquainted with Sovereign's work. Whatever this involvement, or the extent of production, very little of it has been found and those findings have been, for the most part, Canadian findings.

Another pattern back stamp adds confusion to the Knowles line. A dainty spray of pink flowers offset to the side of a plate has been found signed by Wright. While it does not bear the Knowles mark, it is unmistakably the same treatment, back stamped in gold with the signature, the words "Lexré Elegance" and "Fantasia" written on the third line. The mark is very like the Knowles mark, the pattern very similar in detail, and it may be that this was one of the rejected patterns which Wright proposed as an addition to the Knowles line. With only the plate shape found, we cannot be certain that this fits in the Knowles production, but it does seem likely that this is the right context in which we should look for it. Where one pattern exists are there not others? Probably so, but probably not many. Any such shapes or patterns would be welcome in a collection, welcome to collectors who look for findings or documentation to place and support the few references which we find in Wright's files.

Knowles "Wright Shape."

Rare sauce boat signed Mary and Russel Wright by Sovereign Potteries. Knowles "Wright Shape."

ON PRICING KNOWLES ESQUIRE

Several years ago the Knowles line seemed promising as collectors with artistic tendencies viewed and admired it. That position seems not to have changed. The Knowles lines are classic ones and attract those who admire dramatic presentation. The casual touch seems to have been left behind as Wright studied the shapes. The patterns, however, have not become more popular now than they were when they were first made. Antique white, Fontaine, and Mayfair, the solid colors, are difficult to find but appear to be more desirable. Most agree that the white is the favored color, showing the fine lines without the distractions of the indistinct patterns. Fontaine and Mayfair are rare, but desirable for the same reasons. Grass and Botanical continue to be the favorite patterns, with Solar a difficult to find runner-up. Respected as "fine china" by original buyers, it is usually found in good condition, but it should be inspected carefully. Knife marks show and gold detail has frequently been lost. Serving pieces continue to be desirable, surprisingly expensive, and often difficult to buy except as part of a small set. This is another line where two sets may need to be joined to make a complete set. One of the most difficult to find of Wright's dinnerware lines, there are fewer collectors. Reserve the higher pricing for the solid colored items.

Dinner plate, 10¾"	$12.00 – 15.00
Salad plate, 8½"	$8.00 – 10.00
Bread & butter plate, 6"	$5.00 – 6.00
Fruit, 5½"	$8.00 – 10.00
Soup/cereal, 6¼"	$14.00 – 16.00
Cup	$8.00 – 10.00
Saucer	$3.00 – 4.00
Serving bowl, oval, open	$30.00 – 35.00
Serving bowl, round, open	$30.00 – 35.00
Cover for above	$20.00 – 30.00
Platter, oval, 13"	$25.00 – 45.00
Platter, oval, 14¼"	$35.00 – 45.00
Platter, oval, 16"	$55.00 – 75.00
Cream	$14.00 – 16.00
Sugar, covered	$25.00 – 30.00
Shakers, each	$15.00 – 20.00
Pitcher, 2 qt.	$150.00 – 175.00
Vegetable bowl, divided	$55.00 – 65.00
Sauce boat	$25.00 – 35.00
Centerpiece server	$75.00 – 150.00
Teapot	$175.00 – 250.00

**Knowles Wright shape marked Mary and Russel Wright
by Sovereign Potteries.**

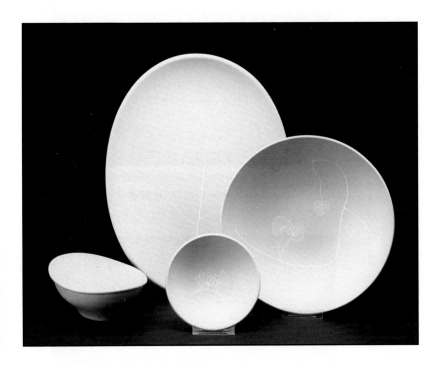

Botanica platter, covered sugar, vegetable bowl, fruit dish.

Botanica platter.

Solar divided vegetable bowl and teapot.

Solar oval vegetable bowl.

Snowflower tidbit server made from three dinner plates. This is an adaptation, not an original design.

189

Drawing of Queen Anne's Lace pattern.

Queen Anne's Lace covered vegetable bowl.

Queen Anne's Lace centerpiece bowl.

Queen Anne's Lace sugar, creamer, and teapot.

Knowles Queen Anne's Lace pattern.

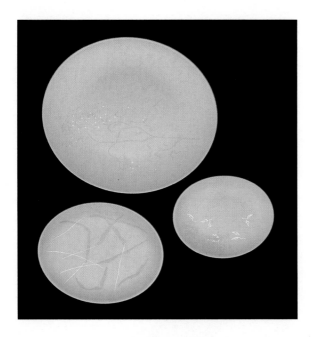

Queen Anne's Lace dinner plate, Grass salad plate, and Seeds bread and butter plate.

Seeds water pitcher.

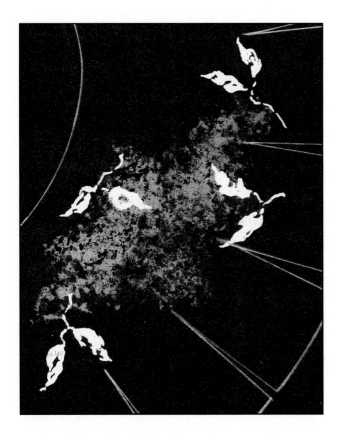

Seeds drawing.

Knowles Seeds pattern.

191

Grass shakers and
Snowflower soup/cereal.

Knowles Grass pattern.

EVERYTHING'S SET

for talented entertaining and graceful family dining when you start with this **Esquire** collection, designed by Russel Wright. You'll love the fluid, elegant shapes, the textured satin glaze with its sturdy diamond-hard finish, and the soft antique white of the **Queen Anne's Lace** design traced in muted ochre and starred with glittering gold.

1.10

1.40   .85

Dinner Plate, 10¼"; Salad Plate, 8¼"; Bread and Butter Plate, 6¼"

1.95 Cup and Saucer   10.50   Tea or Coffee Pot

3.85   Sugar Bowl

Cream Pitcher
2.50

Footed Bowl (soup and
1.40 cereal), 6¼"

Footed Bowl (fruit and
1.00 dessert), 5½"

7.25   Round Covered Serving
        Bowl, 9¼"

Pitcher, two quart 8.80

5.50   Low Open Serving Bowl, 12¼"

13.25   Centerpiece Server, 22"

6.20   Oval Platters; large, 14¼"; medium, 13"   4.40

Deep Compote, 7½" tall,
11.00   12½" wide

Sauceboat, 4¼" tall,
4.95 6¼" wide

Salt and Pepper
3.00 pair

Original brochure showing Esquire shapes.

Original brochures for Esquire's Grass, Seeds, Antique White, and Queen Anne's Lace.

Queen Anne's Lace platter, Seed's plate and pitcher, Grass covered serving bowl, Seeds serving bowl, Grass shakers, Queen Anne's Lace compote.

193

Naturalistic Bauer, Everyone's Choice

Russel Wright's art pottery, done for the Bauer Company in Atlanta, Georgia, enjoys a privileged position with collectors. It is important to those who look for his work wherever they can find it, but it is equally important to those who confine their interests to American art pottery. Since it is the single work Wright did in that area, it is difficult to find, expensive when found, and is often included in large collections from which it seldom moves.

Wright's contract with Bauer dates from 1945, six years after he had gained national attention with his American Modern dinnerware designs. Magazines with national distribution featured his work and readers as well as manufacturers were ready to follow where Wright's work took them. More than 27 companies had contacted Raymor, his original distributor, with the same proposal. All, wishing to duplicate Steubenville's good fortune, wanted to develop a Russel Wright line for themselves. Not at a loss for clients, he wished his work to extend beyond dinnerware designs. It should not have surprised anyone that he looked to art pottery, adding ceramic accessories to his work. Bauer was a prominent producer of art pottery and they challenged Wright by proposing that they develop a line not to include dinnerware, but to broaden the base of their own production by the inclusion of a modern type of art pottery. Wright, they believed, would add stature to their production. In agreement, Wright put all his skills and care, as well as an inordinate amount of time, in assembling this small, but distinctly different line.

It seemed important that Bauer was sufficiently tooled to do the work they proposed. Additionally, they expressed no desire to market the line themselves, allowing that function to be done by the experienced Raymor company.

The working agreement called for Wright to submit designs from which Bauer would select 20 items, the initial line. Bauer agreed that Wright's ceramic consultant, Doris Coutant, would work with their own ceramic engineers, developing production details based on the pottery's policy and Wright's concepts. Wright was to work with Raymor on sales materials, advertising, promotion, and other distributor functions. Rejected items were to revert to Wright, but he agreed not to place another art pottery line on the market, nor would he cause another such line to go into production for a year. After that year, he was restrained from working on another art pottery design as long as Bauer's sales amounted to $150,000.00 a year. Bauer agreed not to make items similar to his in shape, nor could they use his glazes on any of their other work without his consent. In the event that they did use his glazes, his royalty was to be 2% on those items. Royalty on the 20 items he would submit to them was to be 4% on first quality, 2% on second quality items which would be sold at a discounted price. Bauer allowed him the unusual concession of reviewing a statement of his account. This precaution, not seen in other Wright contracts, may point to an increased attention to the financial accounting of firms with which he worked. If Bauer ever found themselves in bankruptcy, his designs were to revert to him and could not be sold to pay their creditors. The pottery agreed to pay him monthly payments of $6,000.00 from July 1, 1945, until the line was no longer sold. This seemed a ransom price at that time, but it speaks to the willingness of Bauer to go to extremes to be associated with him. The payments were to continue for as long as the line was sold and he received monies even as he was working on items for consideration, a grant which probably had an unforeseen and adverse effect on the line.

The pottery items were beautifully conceived. The heavy clay, contrived into shapes became rock-like vessels providing a natural setting for plants and flowers. The lines were curved and flowing, allowing the flowers or plants to make a strong contrasting statement. Ridged bottoms on vases were used to hold flowers in place, a built-in flower frog arrangement. The shapes became a background for the plants, and they allowed for emphasis upon the contents, not upon the container. Where attention was directed to the vase or bowl, it was called a "Gallery Piece." Time has made that a reality, but in 1946 it was to seem an over-statement.

Wright's proposed colors were earth colors which, by then, he seemed to own. They were entirely suitable for the handmade look he hoped to achieve with this line. Flowers, he stressed, were to be the focus of these pieces and he wished that nothing be done to lose that focus. The proposed colors, not all of which we have found but all of which were probably sampled, were jonquil yellow (said to have derived from ancient Chinese ceramic colors), dirty yellow, lemon yellow, Atlanta brick (a warm terra cotta), cinnamon, bronze (a copper treatment), gun metal (the iridescent black shade), pale moss green, dark moss green, potlatch green, celadon green, Georgia brown (a deep dark earthy color), Raymor turquoise (a bright blue aquamarine shade), aqua (a delicate pale shade), true blue, rust, bubble white, a figured white, and a glossy white. Some glazes were rich and shiny, others more textured, even lace-like. His plan called for many of these colors to be used in dramatic contrasts, suggesting hand artistry. Carried to the varieties of these colors, the line would have extended far beyond the original 20 items. The parties agreed that the items should be sold in the $1.25 – 10.00 range!

Glaze trials began at once and problems incumbent upon them were not new problems for Doris Coutant. She ran over 1000 glaze trials and spent a year trying to please Wright, with little success. As trials were made and rejected, monthly payments to Wright added costs to the development of the line. Bauer seemed equally difficult to please and months of painstaking trial and error research was done in an effort to control all the chemical elements involved, to combine material and color for the special effect sought, to contain costs for the pottery. Combining the handmade look which Wright required with the practicality of mass production overwhelmed Bauer and their affairs went from bad to worse.

Raymor's Irving Richards, less abrasive than the exacting Wright, went to Atlanta, hoping to smooth the waters separating Wright and the pottery, but he returned to tell Wright that Bauer had felt him to be too demanding, involving himself in manufacturing details which were not his concern. Wright's self concept was offended and he denied this position, claiming that he had compromised his opinions, and would continue to do so, in the interest of the product.

The affair deteriorated as glaze trials continued and Doris Coutant tested and mailed countless results to New York. Wright, at odds with the testing, and overwhelmed with other work, often responded that the Bauer ceramist and Doris would have to use their best judgements. It was too involved, he said, and he had spent far too much time on this small line. The correspondence at Syracuse reflects these responses, but letters, dated only a few days later expressed his displeasure with one glaze, his preference for another.

Unable to please himself, or others, he was not willing to allow them the free hand he had extended. From the first, Coutant and Bauer were unable to achieve the glaze formulas he insisted upon, and the factory found them impossible to control. Uniformity and consistency, necessary to mass production and sales could not be achieved, with colors varying from piece to piece. The use of two glazes on the same item made it impossible to foretell results. The glazes ran in alarming and unexpected ways, with thick concentrations often at the base of items. Bubbles of glaze burst open as pieces were fired. Drips dropped and no two were alike. Bauer complained that all of this was of second quality and that such variances would affect reorders. Unwilling to face the fact that these unusual silica glazes could not accomplish the effect he desired, Wright insisted that experiments continue. They did until Bauer put a stop to them. Herb Brusche, president of Bauer during this sampling period, told me that this line would have ruined their kilns in six months if work on it had continued. Bauer was better acquainted with production requisites amd more aware of the cost of all these trials than was Wright.

The line was sent to Bauer's showroom in New York in January 1946 with disastrous results. Original reaction, based on a conservative art pottery market, was not good. "Too modern," "Too extreme and unappealing," "Not consistent with the tastes of our customers," they said. Not one of Bauer's 600 accounts placed an order. Raymor advertised the line with all its expertise and that may account for the few orders which were received later. Advertising announced that these glaze drips and runs and the burst bubbles were *intended*, that such variances achieved the textured appearance developed by ceramic engineers at the university level. These were not flaws. This treatment was one seen before only on ancient Chinese ceramics, trade papers quoted. In an effort to explain it all away, every aspect of the line was addressed.

#1 pillow vase, #18 tapered oval vase, #6 vase, #4 jug vase, #19 bulb bowl, #9 mantelpiece bowl. This shows the different treatment of similar glazes: figured white, glossy white, and bubble white.

Production was abandoned late in 1946, a disappointment for all. Sales had not responded to Raymor's advertising and orders for the last six months of 1946 were for $43,000.00. In 1947, in an effort to reduce the remaining stock, Bauer offered the line at reduced prices with no credits or returns. Sales from the first six months of that year added to $5,000.00. All seemed overwhelming for the Wrights for this work was done at the same time that Mary Wright's Country Garden dinnerware was being developed by Bauer. It did not fare better, rejected by Bauer and the buyers when it was shown in the gift shows.

Wright did not consider this Bauer experience a defeat and often referred to the possibility of another art pottery line, but it seems likely that none of the parties concerned had the inclination to enter into such an extensive and complicated study. At a time when he might have returned to it, the art pottery business was in deep trouble, facing the same foreign import competition which was threatening the dinnerware industry.

Reasons for the failure of this Bauer production were rooted in glaze problems, as explained, but there were other considerations. Bauer, paying Wright as he designed the items, allowed costs to escalate beyond their expectations and expenses ran rampant as experimentation was extended. Finding Wright difficult to please and his glazes impossible to achieve, the compa-

ny found itself in a bad position. Without doubt, Bauer was hurried to recover losses involved in the experimental process, but allowing imperfect pieces to be shown to the trade, apologizing with advertising which was contrived, at best, seemed not to work to the advantage of either party.

The number of items, given the extensive use of color combinations, would have amounted to a very large line. We still cannot be certain that items were sampled in the colors in which they were to be produced, nor can we be absolutely certain that an item was restricted to the designated colors. Fortunately, we have Wright/Bauer documentation as a guide and we can add information to it that has been supplied by collectors who have found wonderful Bauer pieces. Items should be marked with the designer's signature on the unglazed bottoms but the original agreement included the use of stamps or stickers. Items have been found with glazed bottoms on which the Wright signature is all but obscured by thick glaze. Given the extensive experimentation, it can be expected that we will find documented items in uncommon glaze combinations. If you find an item which you believe to be a Bauer piece, but it is unsigned, study it for a number. Examples with prototype or experimental glazes, have surfaced and some are impressed with a number which corresponded to the numbers listed here. Finding such pieces has added interest to our understanding of this work, exciting today's collectors in spite of 1940s rejections.

All of this experimentation, even with limited production, may mislead new collectors. Though more of this work exists than the troubled history would indicate, it has never been found in the amounts collectors would like. Even a piece here or there is a great find to advanced collectors but a piece or two will not satisfy a Bauer collector for long. Standing alone, a piece is impressive, but several massed, make a strong statement. Art pottery collectors are as anxious to find these pieces as are Russel Wright collectors and this cross-collecting has added to the prices which Bauer brings. It has gained importance in spite of factory damage which is usually found. Values seem not to be affected. Bauer is a Russel Wright line which should be bought as found if one is to collect it.

The items, with base color and inside glaze colors, were approved as follows but it is likely that this is only basic information and that the experiments, samplings, and runs would add to this amount.

CATALOG NUMBER	DESCRIPTION	MAIN GLAZE	INSIDE GLAZE
#1A	Pillow Vase	Figured White	Aqua
		Jonquil Yellow	Georgia Brown
		Atlanta Brick	Rust
		Aqua	Georgia Brown

Slender and graceful, holding a few cut flowers. Especially suited to a narrow shelf or a bookcase. Narrow at the top, more bulbous at the bottom.

#2A	8½" Vase	Figured White	Figured White
		Jonquil Yellow	Jonquil Yellow
		Aqua	Georgia Brown
		Gun Metal	Gun Metal

A slender vase holding stems of average length. The top is cut at a slight angle permitting the flowers or leaves to flow in a natural, graceful angle.

#3A	5" tall Vase, narrow top	Gun Metal	Gun Metal
		Figured White	Figured White
		Jonquil Yellow	Jonquil Yellow
		Atlanta Brick	Rust

Corsage vase, intended to hold a corsage after wearing. Small narrow opening at the top with wide base.

#4A	9" tall Vase 24" diameter	Bubble White	Georgia Brown
		Jonquil Yellow	Georgia Brown
		Bronze	Bronze
		Aqua	Georgia Brown
		Atlanta Brick	Gun Metal

Large, heavy earthen jug, irregular and almost primitive with lines like a handless pitcher. Designed to lend emphasis to large floral clusters. Top opening is small, cut off at a right angle.

#5A	20½" tall Floor Vase 5¾" base	Figured White	Georgia Brown
		Jonquil Yellow	Georgia Brown
		Georgia Brown	Georgia Brown
		Atlanta Brick	Rust

A large oval vase designed to hold a large crop of long-stemmed flowers or branch cuttings. Narrow top, wide base.

#6A	10½" Vase	Bubble White	Georgia Brown
		Jonquil Yellow	Georgia Brown
		Georgia Brown	Georgia Brown
		Atlanta Brick	Gun Metal
		Aqua	Georgia Brown

Tall oval table vase.

Naturalistic Bauer, Everyone's Choice

#7A	17" long Bowl	Figured White	Figured White
	9½" wide	Figured White	Bronze
	Bowl	Jonquil Yellow	Bronze
		Georgia Brown	Turquoise
		Aqua	Bronze

Centerpiece bowl for flowers or fruit. Intended to hold short stems in a rock-like setting, platter-like.

#8A	6½" long,	Figured White	Raymor Turquoise
	Ashtray	Figured White	Bronze
		Jonquil Yellow	Bronze
		Georgia Brown	Raymor Turquoise
		Aqua	Bronze

Pinched at one edge.

#9A	24" long	Figured White	Figured White
	4" wide Bowl	Jonquil Yellow	Bronze
		Gun Metal	Bubble White
		Georgia Brown	Georgia Brown
		Atlanta Brick	Atlanta Brick

Mantelpiece bowl, narrow for use on mantel or window sill. Side walls are thick and heavy, rock-like in appearance.

#10A	4" square small Ash Bowl
	Colors not found in file information.

#11A	13" Bowl	Figured White	Gun Metal
		Jonquil Yellow	Bronze
		Gun Metal	Bubble White
		Aqua	Bronze

Centerpiece bowl, free-form with sculptured appearance. Heavy clay with sides flowing up and curving down with rhythmic abandon, a vase in an entirely new guise. Early collectors called this the "Floppy Pancake," but soon changed it to the "Manta Ray Bowl."

#12A	4½"	Figured White	Georgia Brown
	square	Atlanta Brick	Rust
	Flower Pot	Jonquil Yellow	Georgia Brown
		Georgia Brown	Georgia Brown

Small square flower pot, often grouped in three or more, some times combined with 12B.

#12B	7½"	Georgia Brown	Georgia Brown
	square	Figured White	Georgia Brown
	Flower Pot	Atlanta Brick	Rust
		Jonquil Yellow	Georgia Brown
		Georgia Brown	Georgia Brown

Larger version of #12A.

#13A	7" tall	Figured White	Georgia Brown
	Flower Pot	Jonquil Yellow	Dirty Yellow
		Atlanta Brick	Rust

Tall flower pot appears to be of one piece but combines the saucer with the pot as a single unit. Dirt which seeped to the saucer from watering would go into unseen saucer shape. Pot and saucer are separated by a groove. The usual drainage hole is in the pot. This was a very different approach to the usual pot and saucer.

#14A	Candlesticks	Georgia Brown	
		Atlanta Brick	
		Aqua	
		Jonquil Yellow	
		Figured White	
		Bubble White	

Tall candlesticks, sold in pairs, but equally important as a single candlestick. Findings have shown sizes to vary in small ways. They are 10¾" – 11" tall, 2" top opening, and 3¼" – 3½" at bottom.

#15A	Long Bowl	Figured White	Figured White
		Jonquil Yellow	Jonquil Yellow
		Atlanta Brick	Atlanta Brick

Advertised as a space-saving bowl, combining a center ample for fruit/flowers and greens with candleholder ends achieved by folding a solid slab of clay.

#16A	7½" wide	Bubble White	Georgia Brown
	Vase or Planter	Jonquil Yellow	Jonquil Yellow
		Atlanta Brick	Gun Metal
		Aqua	Georgia Brown
		Bronze	Bubble White

Large vase/planter for growing foliage. Full and wide proportions contoured to hold spreading roots.

#17A	11" long	Gun Metal	Bubble White
	Bowl	Figured White	Bronze
		Jonquil Yellow	Bronze
		Aqua	Bronze
		Atlanta Brick	Gun Metal

Low bowl in the shape of a hard boiled egg cut in half. Designed to hold bulbs but would be suitable as a large ashtray.

#18A	12" tall	Bubble White	Aqua
	Vase	Jonquil Yellow	Jonquil Yellow
		Aqua	Bronze

Off-center oval vase to hold branches and stems.

#19A	8½" long	Figured White	Bronze
	Bowl	Jonquil Yellow	Bronze
		Aqua	Bronze
		Atlanta Brick	Gun Metal
		Georgia Brown	Raymor Turquoise

Another bulb bowl, round and deep.

#20A	10" square	Bubble White	Georgia Brown
	Pot	Georgia Brown	Georgia Brown
		Jonquil Yellow	Jonquil Yellow
		Aqua	Georgia Brown
		Atlanta Brick	Gun Metal

Very large container for leaves, branches, evergreens, or berries. Suitable for flowering shrub arrangements. This seems to be a larger version of the #12 flower pots.

Note that we still have not found an item number for the unidentified small ashtray with the side folded in, incorrectly identified as #8 ashtray on page 125 of 1990 book, nor are we certain of the colors in which it was made. In this writing, we refer to it as "8B" in an effort to separate it from the other small ashtrays in the line. In addition to this you will find what is certainly a saucer with a glazed and signed underside. Not listed, it is an addition to the line as we have come to know it and may be a prototype.

ON PRICING BAUER

Bauer art pottery is popular and pricing here reflects the interest it holds with art pottery collectors as well as Russel Wright collectors. Rare items and rare color combinations still find their way into advanced collections but new collectors keep demand steady for more commonly found, more affordable items. Certainly, the demand continues. Condition seems not to be any more important in 1997 than it did in 1990 but that applies to factory damage. A chip or a chunk, of course, decreases value. Pricing here reflects colors in which items are usually found. An unusual color treatment, a prototype piece or an experimental glaze item, all should be priced higher than the listing here.

#1A pillow vase	$500.00 – 750.00	#12A flower pot, 4½"	$350.00 – 500.00
#2A 8½" vase	$500.00 – 600.00	#13A flower pot, 7"	$550.00 – 650.00
#3A 5" corsage vase	$450.00 – 500.00	#14A candlesticks pair	NPD
#4A 9" irregular jug vase	$600.00 – 900.00	#15A centerpiece bowl, candlestick	
#5A 22" floor vase	$950.00 – NPD	ends	$650.00 – 700.00
#6A 10½" vase	$600.00 – 800.00	#16A 7½" tall vase/planter	$600.00 – 750.00
#7A 17" long, 9" wide		#17A bowl, half egg shape, 11"	$600.00 – 800.00
centerpiece	$875.00 – 1,000.00	#18A vase, oval, 12"	$750.00 – 850.00
#8A 6½" pinch ashtray	$400.00 – 450.00	#19A bulb bowl round/deep, 8½"	$650.00 – 850.00
#9A mantelpiece bowl, 24"	$850.00 – 900.00	#20A square vase, 20"	$600.00 – 800.00
#10A 5½" ash bowl	$300.00 – 350.00	8B unlisted ashtray (see text)	$350.00 – 400.00
#11A centerpiece bowl, 13"		Unlisted saucer (see photos)	$350.00 – 400.00
(Manta Ray/pancake)	$1,000.00 – 1,100.00		

The following two photographs are from the collection
of B.J. Smith and Jack Brooks. Photographs by Robert Bozarth.

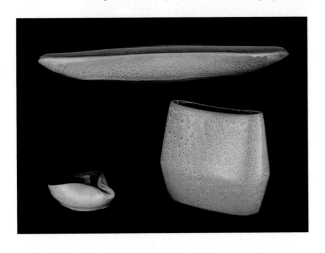

#9 bowl, #8 ashtray, #1 pillow vase.

#3 corsage vase, #18 oval vase,
#12 flower pot.

These four photographs are from the collection of Jose Machado, Alvin Schell, and Annie Wright.
Annie's photo includes the unidentified item. The #12 flower pot is from the collection of William Strauss.

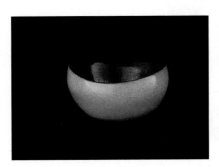

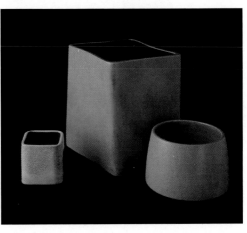

#2 vases, #17 bowl, #8A ashtray.

#19 bulb bowl.

#12A square flower pot, #12B tall
flower pot, #16A planter.

#15 candleholder bowl,
unidentified item, #10 ashtray.

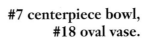

#7 centerpiece bowl,
#18 oval vase.

Bauer #1 pillow vase and #3 corsage vase.

Corsage vases in gun metal and experimental green, jonquil yellow candlesticks.

Corsage vase.

Candlesticks and #4 jug vase.

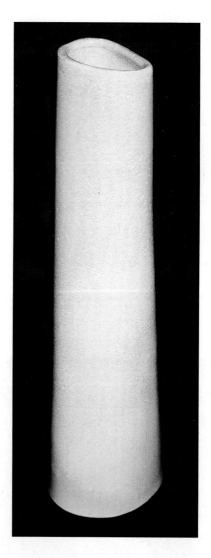

One of two known floor vases.
This one owned by Russell Wright,
Silsbee, Texas.

#18A 12" vase, #7A centerpiece bowl, #10A ash bowl, #10 ashtray. All on Silver Lace cloth.

#3 vase, #12A flower pot.

A variety of shapes showing the diversity of glazes.

#15 candleholder bowl, #8A ashtray, unidentified ashtray, #2 vase (background).

Centerpiece Manta Ray bowl in rare black glaze as well as figured white.

#19 mantelpiece, canoe-shaped bowl, #18 vase.

#11 bowl, #3 corsage vase,
#1 pillow vase, ashtray/pipe bowl,
#13 flower pot.

A New Look at Cutlery

When we first looked at Wright's cutlery which included his silver as well as stainless steel, we had to clear misconceptions because of sketchy and incomplete Syracuse file material. The study of Wright's personal files added to and corrected much of that misinformation and, in 1990, we believed we understood the story of this body of his work. That involved our understanding of Pinch, the important cutlery line in his work.

We first found Pinch advertised to accompany Wright's Highlight Paden City line and we came to call it Highlight. Then our understanding was changed when different advertising referred to it as American Modern. We should not have been surprised. Wright was accomplished at using more than one term for the same subject. It appears that Wright, with no other cutlery line in production, promoted its use with both of the dinnerware lines. Because of its troubled production history, it is likely that he could not consider other options and advertised it as it pleased him, choosing it to accompany either line, as its production allowed.

We should continue to identify it by its proper name of "Pinch," but we can call it American Modern with propriety and no one can contradict if we call it Highlight. A small, but adequate line, it consisted of teaspoons, soup spoons, tablespoons, forks, salad forks, ice tea spoons, knives, oyster forks, butter spreaders, berry spoon, cold meat fork, sugar shell, and gravy ladle. Most items have been found, but not in large enough amounts to please collectors.

In 1990 we were able to add to Wright's cutlery lines. Collector findings had included a different stainless pattern, also made by the Hull Company and signed by Wright. In no time, a third pattern surfaced and we were overwhelmed with the possibilities of three stainless steel patterns. The personal files identified these newer lines as "Lily" and "Threads." Not all Wright associates agree on these late lines, or their production, but it seems wise to go down on the side of documentation and findings.

Before a stainless contract with Hull was signed, Wright turned to The National Silver Company, hoping they would agree to work on a line of his design. They were not interested since their work focused on hollow ware pieces, not the sort of line which Wright proposed. It was to be an important rejection to the designer.

Twenty-four-piece service (six sets of four pieces) in original box with brochure and "lifetime guarantee."

The Pinch contract was given to Hull and as early as 1951 Wright and Hull were differing over production problems. To be fair, the designer made every concession reasonable in order to achieve production but Hull seemed plagued by internal problems and one deadline fell, replaced by another, then another. Early on, a Hull subcontractor insisted upon his own contract with Wright and this put Hull in a middle position which they felt was untolerable. Wright, with no real desire to engage another firm in the arrangements, agreed. However, Hull seemed not able to shake the third party and work slowed. The negotiations broke off with the designs reverting to Wright.

By 1952, both parties had again agreed to proceed but Wright stipulated that he be paid the royalties originally agreed upon and added, significantly, that the items be produced in six months. Hull soon pleaded the lack of availability of materials. Wright, once more, withdrew the contract and turned to The National Silver Company hoping they would reconsider their former position. They refused. Still believing Hull to be his only choice for the line, Wright allowed them to continue.

Business practices remained troubled. Royalties were not paid when due and they could not be depended upon to act as they agreed to do. Finally, he wrote "We have bent over backwards in a manner not at all in keeping with the standards of our profession and our status in the field of industrial design to an extent that we have never gone with another client and at fees too low in signing an agreement to help you. May we please hear from you?" For a time, he did not hear from them and with labor problems adding to what appeared to have been bad management, Hull moved their operation to Japan. Not surprisingly, word soon came that their problems were behind them and they were ready to produce Pinch. Wright, wary and out of patience, registered his design with the Japanese Patent Office to avoid any conflict of ownership, and found himself in a legal contest in a foreign country.

He granted Hull permission to resume production. Again, for reasons of which we are not certain, they were unable to continue. In spite of the fact that they could not keep up with work already assigned to them, they asked for other designs, one with a wooden handle or a plastic design. Completely exhausted by their erratic production, Wright washed his hands of them, believing it to be in his best interest to involve another supplier as quickly as possible. In the end, however, Wright had no choice and extended Hull even more concessions to produce Pinch, Lily, and Threads. Our

documentation ends with that reference, but our findings tell us that Pinch was made, in amounts less than the contracts proposed, and it seems probable that Lily and Threads were made in short run amounts. Hull was never able to sustain the production amounts that Wright expected.

Highlight/Pinch stainless steel — slotted spoon, cake lifter, serving spoon, dinner knife, butter knife, dinner fork, salad fork, soup spoon, teaspoon, ice tea spoon.

Pinch remains Wright's important cutlery line. It came at a time when silver or silver plate was the only cutlery in use. Wright knew a good thing when he designed it. This may account for the many chances he gave Hull. Well received by buyers, this new stainless steel was lower in price to sterling or silver plate, making it attractive to modernists who were watching budgets and others wishing for less than formal silver. It had a soft brushed stain finish, making a distinct statement for modernism, but not an obtrusive one. All items showed the pinch at the base of the handle. It was lighter in weight than silver, but sales people offered the information that it was tapered to achieve better balance. Tarnish proof, it carried a lifetime guarantee of service. Wright's open stock policy made it possible to buy now or wait till later. Buying a service for eight gave you a storage chest with a reversible unit which became a cocktail tray. Lily and Threads might have become popular in their own right if their limited production had been extended. All of this work is typical of the emerging sense of Modernism afoot in the 1950s, but its softer statement sets it apart from other modern lines on the market in its day.

Macy's, Wright's reliable retailer, introduced Pinch and it was an immediate success with buyers, many of whom could never find enough of it. The six-piece set sold for $6.95. Separately, the chest was $7.95. The Museum of Modern Art awarded it its Good Design Award in 1953. Success would have been certain if Hull had been able to follow through with production. Pinch backstamps are of two different styles and both identify the same line, differing only in that some was made in this country and some in Japan. American pieces have Wright's signature, the words "Hull Stainless," and a patent number. Those made in Japan are worded in the same way, but include the word "Japan," as required by law. Both carry Wright's signature. The knives are signed at the base of the blade and include a patent number.

Buyers used the line interchangeably from the first and collectors continue to do so, glad to have any of it to use. The Pinch knife remains the difficult to find piece. Buyers at the time were accustomed to hollow handled knives and did not like the molded Pinch knife, choosing a substitute knife from Hull's production. If Wright had been able to accomplish good working relations with Hull, there is no question that he would have redesigned these knives. Market research, which would have reflected this dissatisfaction, was not achieved. Those collectors who have found the knives have strong opinions. Some think it a great piece, fitting a grasp just right. Others agree with 1950s buyers and, though they are glad to own them, they don't want to use them. One first time collector shared the story that she bought the knives and used them until she was asked to help with a drive for the benefit of flood victims. In a spurt of generosity, she sent them off to others. There must be more such Wright stories.

The National Silver Company continued to be on Wright's short list of possible clients for cutlery. In 1954 they prototyped a set of sterling silver flatware as well as a tea set of Wright's design. Rena Rosenthal, whose accessory sales featured work done by the finest artists and artisans of the time, advertised the cutlery in the leading magazines. It seems likely that orders did not reach expectations for the line was never made commercially. Prototyped in sterling, the single set belongs to Wright's daughter Annie. The silver tea service belongs to Herbert Honig, Wright's business manager and friend.

This silver cutlery was, without question, the most modern cutlery design made in this country at the time. Offering a wide variety, the items which were to have included a tea spoon, dinner fork, knife, soup spoon, salad fork, oyster fork, butter spreader, berry spoon, gravy ladle, pastry server, coffee spoon, ice tea spoon, tablespoon, cold meat fork, sugar shell, butter knife, bouillon spoon, and salad serving fork and spoon. This design is the prototype for the silver plate set produced and sold by the Metropolitan Museum of Art in New York City in sporadic offerings from 1987 to 1990. Their rights to the flatware design had been donated by Wright himself.

In 1987, when it was first advertised in the Museum's Christmas catalog, it seemed too good to be true, and it soon was. Supply never kept up with demand and some buyers would be told that it was no longer available. Soon, however, other offerings were made and some orders were filled, but many other collectors were disappointed. In spite of a great deal of interest, little was made, and it seems likely that reports of production problems were true. What was made is the exact National Silver line, but abbreviated to place settings with a few serving items differing only in that it was produced in brass and nickel silver and heavily silverplated with nine microns of silver. The dinner knife blade was stamped in stainless steel for added strength. This Museum service can be considered original issue since none was ever produced in 1954 and the line languished until the museum made it available. It is marked MMA 1987 Korea or MM 1990 Japan.

In addition to the silver plate pieces Wright's small cube salt and pepper shakers were produced by the Metropolitan. They were made in sterling as well as silver plate. Still in the line, they are wonderful additions to any collections, marked MMA 925 93 in sterling, MMA 93 in silverplate. All include the copyright symbol. My last writing on this amounted to what might have seemed blatant advertising, good news for collectors, I believed at the time, but too few were able to acquire enough to use.

The Syracuse files refer to other work which would have included plastic handled stainless, done for the Englishtown Cutlery Company in 1947 – 1949. That company agreed to do two sets of four to seven piece place settings in stainless or stainless with plastic handles. This would have been early work and Englishtown, just recovering from a fire, was not yet in full production. Wright stipulated that they would have his exclusive service and could use his name for this work, but they were bound to pay him $5,500.00 if they could not produce in 11 months. If they became insolvent, they could not sell the use of his name. Shortly after the contract was signed, Englishtown asked for a six month extension on production of the plastic handled ware and Wright agreed to that. They experimented with several sets, finally admitting that they were unable to continue. The affair went to arbitration and Wright was given a cash settlement. No examples have been reported.

In addition to the possibility of plastic handled cutlery, the files encouraged us to look for pearl handled pieces. These were said to include a knife, fork, spoon, butter knife, and soup spoon. This work would have been very early work dating from his Accessory Company work and is described in mimeograph sales sheets which was probably in-house advertising devised and executed by Mary. Lists were accompanied by very simple line drawings, descriptions, and prices. In addition to these place setting pieces, the list included 5½" curved caviar spreader, 6½" swizzler (for "long" drinks), 5" lemon fork, 5" sardine fork, 5" relish spoon, and 5" straight caviar spreader. Sizes, only slightly different, are described in the files.

Accompanying this cutlery were a 8", 7", and 6" white pearl shell plate made of mother of pearl and said to be "the jewelry of the table." Suitable for individual servings of hors d'oeuvres, jelly or jam, and baked shell fish entrees, they were claimed to be oven proof and the sales sheets indicate their use as ashtrays as well. Decorative accessory items extended the line to centerpieces, vases, and bookends. All shells were left rough on the back with highly polished surfaces. Buyers were offered the line in a black shell treatment as well as the beautiful white shell finish. This archival information has not been enriched by collector findings. Surely not marked, and probably more fragile than the descriptive details indicate, there may be little left after 50 years or so, but continue to look. We have a photo to show that prototypes were made.

This chapter of Wright's work leaves blanks in our collecting as we find products designed and developed, business details described, products not produced or produced in limited amounts. The fact that he was interested in cutlery from his early days in 1935 over the next 20 or so years underlines the frustration he experienced with suppliers. Many of today's collectors, anxious for examples of this cutlery, are willing to search through boxes of old stainless steel, hoping for a knife, happy to find a spoon. Many dealers, having found a set or a partial set, are unwilling to break it into the original open stock option which Wright favored. For that reason, Wright's stainless can represent more than pocket change. Unfortunately, the MMA production was too limited to satisfy demand and, we believed that it would be some time before sets purchased from them would again come on the market. Recently, however, items from that production have been seen in advertisements in antique trade papers. It surely did not take long for what came around to come around again!

ON PRICING CUTLERY

My questions on cutlery pricing brought consistent answers: "Expensive!" One consultant wrote that a service for eight could represent the down payment on a car! Those who sell it explained that the value of cutlery is in a set large enough to use. Condition is important, but the nature of the material has preserved the good condition for the most part. Pinch is the first choice with collectors, the other lines not seen often enough to price. Never found in amounts to please collectors, it all seems even more rare than it did in 1990, but stories abound of those who religiously check and find it in Good Will stores. To collect Wright cutlery, it seems, you need a lot of money or a lot of patience.

PINCH

Knives	$100.00–150.00	Soup spoon	$100.00–120.00
Fork	$ 75.00–85.00	Ice tea spoons	$100.00–125.00
Spoon	$75.00–88.00	Butter spreaders	$100.00–110.00
Salad fork	$75.00–85.00	All serving items	$125.00–150.00

Lily and Threads should be 15% to 20% below the Pinch items. They are more rare but not enough can be found to use in table settings. There may be investment value in these lines if more appears.

METROPOLITAN SILVER PLATE

It may be too early to realistically value this line but a small set including service for four with bouillon spoons, butter knives, and a pair of the dice shakers has been advertised. The asking price was $475.00. It may not be an indicator of value or price, but it allows us a bottom line around which we may be able to make judgements. This is another area that warrants a watchful eye.

Threads, John Hull Cutlery.

Part of an earyl Pearl line done by Russel Wright Accessory Company.

Early cutlery advertisement.

National Silver Sterling flatware. Recently produced in silverplate and sold at the Metropolitan Museum in New York City.

Pinch/Highlight/American Modern
stainless steel flatware.

Pinch American Modern gravy ladle,
slotted spoon, cake lifter, serving
spoon, cold meat fork.

Lily cutlery.

Putting Plastics in their Place

In 1944, with the war behind them, Americans found themselves on the threshold of the synthetic materials revolution. The promise of release from many demanding household chores was enticing and the new products met a market that rushed to greet them. Changes were immediate, as we had hoped, but not always for the better, and not always permanent. Wright, also expecting miracles from the laboratories of science and industry, had examined these new materials before many of us were aware of them and he quickly saw limitations. It would take some time and some experience for many of us to understand the complexities of these new products for ourselves.

At the close of World War II, there were many opportunists who looked at war-time materials, hoping to adapt them to household usage. They did not wait for grass to grow under their feet and the market was soon full of poorly made, poorly designed products all selling at what would soon seem to be too much money. Such was the case with plastic dinnerware. It seems fair to say that the best properties of this synthetic material were often lost in the rush for sales. Consumers would soon learn that and plastic dinnerware would be given a bad name, a difficult position to overcome.

Wright's early involvement dates from 1944. The American Cyanide Company in New York tested a synthetic product, patented it, and called it Melamine. Initially, he was impressed, believing that its manufacture would involve less time and materials than had ceramics. Given those advantages, the product could be brought to customers at less cost. He was certain that he could work with it to design dinnerware which would be durable and easy to care for, all principles important to him. At that early time, and with enthusiasm, he signed a contractual agreement with American. On a cost plus basis, he was to design a test group of institutional plastic dinnerware on which he would own the patent. American was to pay costs, direct, criticize, and instruct him in the use of their materials in this dinnerware. (It is important to understand that American was the chemical company perfecting the properties of the material.) Once the pilot set was developed, they agreed to assist Wright in locating sources who would be interested in manufacturing it. He, on the other hand, would retain the rights, titles, and possession of designs if they or any other manufacturer, produced the line. Other manufacturers would be compelled to turn to him for the use of Melamine. American, or any other manufacturer using it, would pay Wright the price of each designed item, $800.00 and 2% of gross billings. The designed set which American would help him develop was to be called Meladur. America renamed the material Melmac.

With plans made, Wright was impatient for development. Once that was accomplished, Wright expected immediate acceptance, but reaction was measured, causing Wright and American to believe that they might have been ahead of the market. Manufacturers, while interested in Wright's pilot set, seemed to be "sitting it out." waiting to see if he could make a commercial success of this new material.

After four years, with no manufacturer, American asked Wright to terminate their agreement and to agree to a lapse of options. Angry, Wright replied that the agreement was valid and if American had others who would produce the line, those manufacturers were contractually bound to buy the designs and pay him royalty on them. American responded, saying that they had been interested in it as an experimental project only, and that since they had no plans to use the resulting designs, they did not intend to buy them. Ownership was questioned, with American claiming rights since the experimentation work was theirs. Wright holding the patent, argued that the design work, separate from the material, was his and he believed that it set the standard on which all Melmac dinnerware would be made. With no agreement, the matter went to arbitration. A fine line was drawn and American was instructed to relinquish their right to Meladur.

In possession of legal right to Meladur, Wright found himself well positioned. He turned to General American Transportation's plastic dinnerware division with his designs and an agreement was signed. Restrictions upon marketing prevented General from using his name without his permission. Once that was given, he reserved the right to review all of their advertising. With these restrictions, his standard contract applied. General was to produce a "furnished set" and they quickly arranged to do so. It is not clear, nor is it quite understandable, but for reasons of his own, Wright soon lost interest in this production for which he had fought so hard. It may be that he recognized that the product was flawed and constant daily institutional usage (the area for which he believed Melmac was best suited) would result in dissatisfaction. His Sterling experience acquainted him with restaurant industry requirements, and he knew those to be very competitive and profit oriented. He may have doubted if they would remain interested in dinnerware which would show use

in a short time. In 1953 he relinquished his rights and titles to Meladur, selling them to General for a lump sum payment of $15,000.00. They were to be the sole owners of the designs and modifications and could produce, use, add to the designs, or modify them as they chose but when the existing stock was sold, his name was not to be used on Meladur, regardless of the manufacturer at that time. General did continue to make the line after Wright had withdrawn from its production.

Meladur dinner plate, salad plate, soup bowl, and cup and saucer.

Meladur was made in pink, mint green, yellow, and blue. The refined product, General said, was less than one third the weight of ceramic restaurant ware and possessed qualities which allowed a cup to stay positioned even when the saucer was tilted at a 70° angle. It was their claim that it could be used in warming and would outwear ceramic pieces four to one. You may expect to find a 6 oz. fruit bowl, a 9 oz. cereal, 12 oz. soup, 5¾" bread and butter plate, 6¼" dessert plate, 7¼" salad plate, 9" dinner plate, 7 oz. cup and saucer, 10" service plate, 9½" compartmented plate. It may not be asking too much to find other items for the experiments on this line were many and conducted over a long time. Consideration was given to the design of coffee cup covers, egg cups, small platters, and footed drinking glasses. None of these have been found, but they are, for the most part, small items with little room for marking and may have escaped attention. On the other hand, some seem unlikely items in institutional usage and may never have been made. Expect to find Meladur marked with Wright's name if it was made before he sold his rights. An unsigned piece, or an item

Meladur plates and bowls.

not listed here, would be the work of General, produced after he terminated his contract with them. Most collectors value the signature but will add documented Wright items to fill out collections.

Within two years America caught up with Wright and he found himself overwhelmed with requests for another Melmac line. Other manufacturers had rushed to produce and in 1953 Wright joined them with a new line. Residential, which was to be produced by Northern Industrial Chemical, was formulated and designed to be used in homes, not institutions. Almost at once, in 1953, it won the Good Design Award from The Museum of Modern Art, repeating the award the following year. By 1957 it was the best house-to-house selling dinnerware in the country, breaking records with sales of $4,000,000.00. Homemakers, by now obsessed with the easier living Wright's products promised, were delighted to own dinnerware that was guaranteed not to break. Wright made the most of old marketing procedures and it was sold open stock, advertised as ideally suited for gift giving and promoted in pasteboard boxes holding one place setting. His endorsement had come to mean a great deal to buyers and sales were good from the first. The line was so popular that Northern increased its one year warranty with a ten year warranty.

Set of Residential in original packaging.

Strangely, we again find the designer was unhappy. Royalties, he believed, were not enough. Northern, with such an outstanding sales record, was accused of not promoting sales as they should have. Out of patience with him, Northern told Wright that these complaints must stop or they would discontinue the production of Residential and replace it with another

Melmac line, done by another designer. Their claim was that the line resembled his Sterling line to such a degree that their sales were hurt in competition with it. Northern went further, claiming that they had been patient with the design as it had evolved from concept through experimentation to production and that it had not been their intent that he should design pieces for them which would meet his artistic standards with no regard for the constraints of time and money. Stung by these threats and accusations, Wright fired back that if they dared to replace him or his work, he would sue and claim royalties on any line they produced, his or that of others. Only the success of the dinnerware kept the adversaries working together and they continued, with Wright studying all options, still hoping to add to his royalties.

Residential was different from other Melmac lines in the 1950s, largely because Wright insisted upon improving the design, and the quality of the product, adding any element that would set it apart from other lines. The new material challenged him and finding that he could work with it to achieve an amorphous design, was exciting. For a time he was able to set aside old doubts.

Experimentation with the material had resulted in a body that appeared cloud-like with two colors, overlapping, showing the base color in places, the cloud overlay in others, achieving an effect not duplicated in other Melmac designs. Residential items were made in bread and butter plates, salad plates, dinner plates, cups and saucers, lug soups, fruits, two vegetable bowls, shallow or deep, a platter, covered sugar and creamer, covered vegetable, divided vegetable, tumbler, and a covered onion soup. Tumblers were a later design, resulting in fewer of these popular items. From the first, buyers were told to use these items interchangeably as they could be adapted to different uses. With shapes entirely new, the original colors were sea mist, gray, and lemon ice. Black velvet, a black with a scattering of aluminum dust, white, light blue, copper penny, a brown treated with copper dust, and salmon, an orange red were all added later. As with Wright's ceramic lines, not all retailers carried all of these colors. The line was nationally advertised and widely distributed but it was in heated competition with the work of some of the most popular designers of the '50s. Belle Kogan, George Nelson, and others soon designed aggressively marketed lines.

While he recognized the positive qualities of Melmac, Wright was never able to shake his first feelings that the material was innately impaired. Sooner or later, he believed, the manufacturers of this dinnerware would have to answer to the fact that pieces lost sheen, knife marks scratched surfaces, coffee stained, and sanitary conditions were questionable. Dishwashers, in limited use at the time, would be hard on it, he was certain. Later, buyers would come to see this product as he did, but in their early euphoria, many looked the other way.

In 1954, still chasing options for Residential, still hoping to perfect its quality, Wright turned to Home Decorating Service to distribute a variant of it. Made on the same shape, it was not clouded, and added floral patterns to the plain Residential items. The color selection offered in opaque colors included: white, turquoise blue, salmon, and pink. The Home Decorator patterns involved a difficult process, using a color overlay with different parts of the pattern on different items. Informal, it was felt that it added interest to the plain Residential.

Believing that pattern, however difficult to achieve, would be popular, Wright designed Flair with a different shape and a different design treatment which Home Decorators would make and distribute. The year was 1959. Flair, with a light, fragile body, almost translucent, achieved a quality of delicacy and fineness not found in comparable dinnerware. The designs, themselves, were carefully conceived and executed. Golden Bouquet had white or golden stems on a cloudy white ground. Spring Gardens featured blossoms of pink and blue on green stems. Ming Lace, a favorite from the first, had actual leaves of the jade orchid tree imported from China tinted and permanently molded into the white body. A version of Ming Lace has been found using green leaves while another shows brown leaves. Woodland Rose, a more formal floral design was used on an eggshell back ground. Arabesque, a formal pattern, swirled two tones of gold or gold and turquoise on eggshell. As in the decorated Home Decorator work, theme variants were used on different items. Buyers loved Flair and collectors today believe it to be very good, an example of what could have been done with Melmac if price had not been so important.

However discouraged he was with Melmac dinnerware, Wright seemed to have an intuitive recognition of the enduring position for which Melmac was suited, the refrigerator. In 1957 he combined a limited amount of dinnerware pieces with refrigerator storage pieces involving a new product made of polyethylene which he named Fortiflex. Designed for the Ideal Toy Company, it was an altogether different product. Soft, without the rigidity of Melmac, it made no pretense of being fine, clearly intended to be used for the refrigerator to table function. Bowls conformed to the sizes of frozen food packaging eliminating another bowl for serving purposes. Both

Mold maker's prototype. Feeding dish, fortiflex dish on Leacock symbols cloth.

Ideal and Wright were hopeful that a line developed by Wright would attract customers and encourage them to believe that Fortiflex was superior, either in design or quality, an effort was made to separate it from low-end refrigerator storage items because of special design.

Wright advertised that it would have no direct competition because there was no such complete refrigerator-to-table group on the market. All of the usual Wright features were put into place in articles which took on the mantel of "news" because of the recent development of synthetics. It could be stacked easily, taking up less room. It was easy to care for, unbreakable, and in addition, Fortiflex was "freezer proof" with covers that snapped on and stayed in place, safely avoiding spills.

All concerned were pleased with the color names he designated: mint, carnation, snow, blue mist, shrimp, and citron. Fortiflex never met the claims Wright made for it or hoped for it and little has survived. So soft that it bordered upon being pliable, it was almost flimsy, difficult to handle, and spills resulted more often than expected. Plain, aesthetically devoid of interest, most pieces sold slowly and when purchased, probably did not survive for long. It won no awards and was not on the market for long. The item listing remains as it was found in 1990 and consisted of a salad bowl, covered left-over bowls in two sizes, a covered butter dish, juice decanter, a dish for freezing food, a salad dessert dish, large water jug, salad fork and spoon, and two sizes of tumblers. Clearly the rarist of Wright's synthetic work, its collectability derives from that position.

A happier account can be told of Ideal's production which followed and included the wonderful plastic line of toy dishes made in exact copies of American Modern. Not made of Fortiflex, but of stronger material, young cooks could handle them without fear of breakage or spillage. Sears offered them in service for four in their 1959 Christmas catalog, priced at $3.76. The color assortment is very close to the ceramic colors. You will find them there accompanied by silver and crystal (clear plastic) which were not Wright's designs. The pieces were irresistible to parents who owned American Modern and to children who could claim to have dishes "just like mommy has." They were exactly scaled, exact miniatures and were such a success that in their catalogs two years later Sears offered a choice of a serving for four or six. These later sets have been less desirable since the colors, orange, tan, bright yellow were not as "true" as the original sets. They were found in the catalogs in 1961 and 1964 but the record stops there. Popular in the '60s, they remain so today. In 1964 American Made Plastics Company in New York City assumed all Wright designs which had been done by Ideal and we can add no more details to this work.

A contract exists in the files which indicates that Wright did work for Mallory and Randall which involved plastic materials. Since we are not certain of the presence of a signature, it is possible that our only identification would be the manufacturer's name. The files list Thermo cups and tumblers with metallic accents, gold spangles, diamond dust, gold threads, and Oriental characters. With such '50s treatments, these, if found and documented, could be important to those who look for that style.

Wright joined the plastics field early and reluctantly turned to it several times, hoping to add interest, incorporate different treatments, and to bring integrity to the product. His synthetic designs have been the first of this sort to which collectors have turned. Most believe his work includes significant examples of a phenomena that lasted for a short time, resulting in a relatively small amount of good quality plastic dinnerware. It is true that it symbolizes the '50s as few other products do and there are many of us who still live our days in a '50s world. Additionally, most of us can make room for a "picnic set," adding to the occasions for which Wright's dinnerware seems appropriate. I repeat, "Bakelite and Celluloid may have to move over to make room for Melmac."

SYNTHETIC DINNERWARE LINES

Attempting to reconcile the different remarks which consultants offered on these lines is difficult. Some saw little current interest, others said it sold easily if one had a service which included serving items. Another wrote *important* in several different lines. You may need to measure your own market and adjust these prices according to the sophistication of your collecting/buying/selling.

All agreed that the Flair line is the premium line and they believed Ming Lace to be the important pattern with either green or brown leaves. It has almost achieved rarity. Arabesque continues to be popular, leaving the floral patterns in the lower range given here.

Whole sets in any line were said to be attractive to collectors, but a piece here or there might rest awhile in a dealer's inventory.

Meladur, rare and difficult to find, continues to be expensive. Most must settle for examples.

Children's items are considered too important to leave to today's younger cooks.

Residential, often over-used and scratched or stained, is found most often. In fact, one collector found 24 white covered onion soups, but that was so unusual that phones rang for several days.

Condition means everything in these plastic lines and no matter how impressive the signature one should resist the impulse to buy any items not in very good to fine condition.

Not all consultants believed that they had enough experience to value these lines so our figures do not represent the broad range we would like. However, they come from those who have sold or seen items sold at these prices. Our lesson would seem to be that if a person is interested in this work, these are the prices he will accept. If not, they do not apply to him.

MELADUR

All Rare

Cereal	$8.00 – 10.00	Plate, dinner, 9"	$8.00 – 10.00
Cup	$7.00 – 10.00	Plate, salad, 7¼"	$8.00 – 10.00
Fruit	$7.00 – 8.00	Plate, service, 10"	$10.00 – 15.00
Plate, bread & butter, 5¾"	$4.00 – 5.00	Saucer	$3.00 – 5.00
Plate, compartmented, 9½"	$12.00 – 15.00	Soup, 12 oz.	$10.00 – 12.00
Plate, dessert, 6¼"	$5.00 – 6.00		

HOME DECORATOR, RESIDENTIAL, FLAIR

Flair items at high end of range.
Copper penny and black velvet are rare, add 50%.

#701 Cup	$6.00 – 8.00	#709 Vegetable bowl, oval, deep	$15.00 – 18.00
#702 Saucer	$2.00 – 3.00	#710 Platter	$20.00 – 25.00
#703 Dinner plate	$8.00 – 10.00	#711 Cream	$10.00 – 12.00
#704 Salad plate	$8.00 – 10.00	#712 Covered sugar	$12.00 – 15.00
#705 Bread & butter plate	$3.00 – 6.00	#713 Covered vegetable bowl	$25.00 – 30.00
#706 Lug soup	$10.00 – 12.00	#714 Divided vegetable bowl	$20.00 – 25.00
#707 Fruit	$13.00 – 15.00	#715 Tumbler	$15.00 – 18.00
#708 Vegetable bowl, oval, shallow	$15.00 – 20.00	#716 Covered onion soup, ea. piece	$16.00 – 18.00

IDEAL ADULT KITCHEN WARE

All very rare

Bowl, salad	$20.00 – 25.00	Dish, salad/dessert	$10.00 – 15.00
Bowls, left-overs with covers	$20.00 – 25.00	Jug, water, large	$50.00 – 55.00
Butter dish, covered	$45.00 – 50.00	Salad servers (fork & spoon)	$35.00 – 45.00
Decanter, juice	$30.00 – 35.00	Tumblers, 2 sizes	$20.00 – 25.00
Dish, freezing	$18.00 – 20.00		

IDEAL CHILDREN'S TOY DISHES

Covered items add 50%.

Boxed sets	$150.00 – 250.00	Serving pieces	$20.00 – 25.00
Place setting items	$10.00 – 12.00		

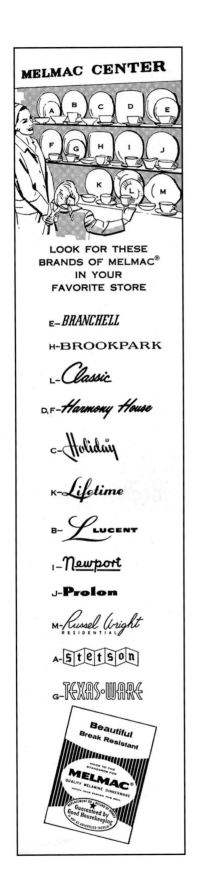

Good Housekeeping, July 1957,
a menu of Melmac designs,
all based on American development.

Good Housekeeping, July 1957.
American ad for Melmac *after* Meladur
rights had been sold by Wright.

219

Table setting: copper penny Residential, Hull Pinch cutlery, American Modern pilsners.

Original Melmac Dinnerware Brochure.

Dinnerware made of MELMAC gives outstanding service and economy because it is molded of one of the hardest synthetic materials known. MELMAC dinnerware is made by a group of manufacturers whose skill, integrity and high standards assure you that this fine material has been carefully processed to give the greatest possible satisfaction in use.

"RESIDENTIAL" *by Russel Wright*

DISTRIBUTED BY:
RICHARDS MORGENTHAU CO., New York

MANUFACTURED BY:
NORTHERN INDUSTRIAL CHEMICAL CO.
Boston, Mass.

MELMAC is a registered trade-mark of American Cyanamid Company, New York 20, N.Y., supplier of MELMAC Molding Compounds to manufacturers who fashion high-quality dinnerware in a variety of designs and colors. American Cyanamid does not manufacture dinnerware as such.

Printed in U.S.A.

dinnerware

. . . . . . *molded of* ®
melmac

break resistant . . . beautiful
—with these unique features

Guaranteed by
Good Housekeeping

Here's why you'll find MELMAC dinnerware is a good buy...

- It is remarkably durable and long-lasting. It will not crack or chip in normal household use. It takes the worry out of handling — even by children.

- The beautiful colors of MELMAC dinnerware are light-fast. They cannot chip off because they are molded in, from surface to surface.

- MELMAC dinnerware is easy and safe to wash by hand or machine. It will not soften, warp or bend under heat.

- Standard household soaps or detergents do not harm the surface or the color of dinnerware made of MELMAC.

- It's so practical you'll use it for every meal, every day...so smart-looking you'll use it for special occasions, too.

These are the reasons why MELMAC *dinnerware is already the choice of hundreds of thousands of women. You'll be proud of your set —proud, too, of the wise purchase you've made!*

How to get the most—in long service and lasting beauty—from your set of MELMAC dinnerware.

A Few Do's—*Do* wash with standard household soaps or detergents. Never use scouring pads or powders — you don't need to!

Do give your MELMAC dishes the periodic care you give fine silver and china. Should discoloration occur from coffee or tea, rub cups briskly with dishcloth and soap . . . or immerse them in (or fill them with) a solution of one of these cleansers*, following the manufacturer's directions:

DIP-IT (Economics Laboratory, St. Paul 1, Minn.)
M-E CLEANER (Maid-Easy Cleansing Products Corp., Mount Vernon, N. Y.)

If you use an automatic home dishwasher, these detergents are suggested*:

FINISH (Economics Laboratory, St. Paul 1, Minn.)
THANX (Calgon, Inc., Pittsburgh 22, Pa.)

And A Few Don'ts — *Don't* use MELMAC dishes for cooking or warming food.

Don't expose them to flame – they might char.

Don't use abrasives to clean MELMAC dishes.

Follow these simple rules and your MELMAC dinnerware will stay new-looking for years!

*The above trade names are not cited to indicate brand preferences. Similar compounds, working on the same principles, would doubtless achieve the same beneficial results.

Residential sugar, soup, and divided vegetable bowl.

Residential platters, dinner plate, salad plate,
bread and butter plate.

Residential cream, covered vegetable bowl,
and covered onion soup.

Residential black velvet cup and saucer,
vegetable bowl, soup, soup on saucer,
divided vegetable, and dinner plate.

Residential tumbler shapes.

Late Residential items made after Wright's contract
had expired. Cup and saucer, sugar/tumbler,
tumbler, redesigned sugar.

Advertisment for Residential.

223

Copies of Residential Mock-ups

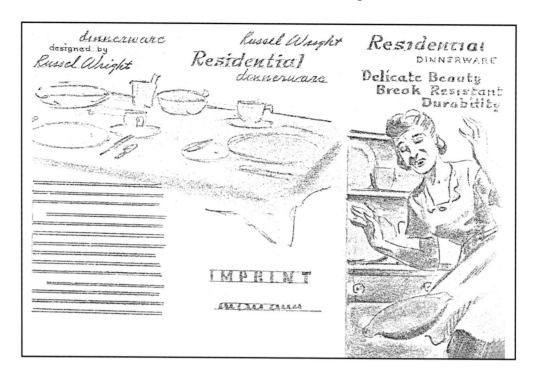

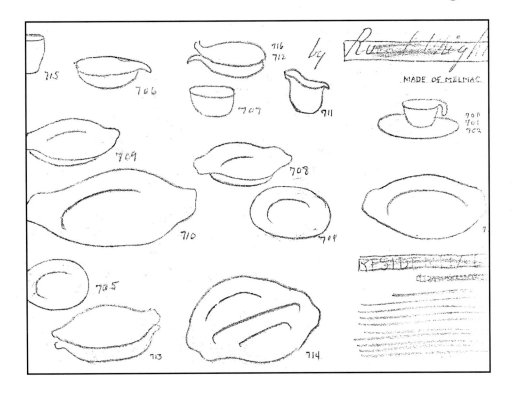

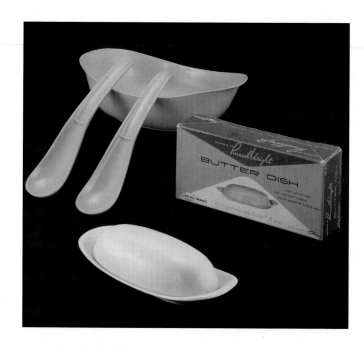

Ideal salad bowls, servers, and butter dish
with original box.

Ideal Fortiflex.

Flair solid color.
Covered sugar, platter,
dinner plate, and cream.

Flair solid color.
Fruit, oval vegetable bowl,
and cup/saucer.

Flair Ming Lace cup and saucer.

Flair Ming Lace.

Flair Golden Bouquet.

Flair Arabesque.

The following are original brochures showing the Flair patterns of Ming Lace, Golden Bouquet, Arabesque, Woodland Rose, and Spring Garden. The last photo shows an open brochure illustrating the Flair shapes.

Home Decorator's Patterns

Home Decorator's plate,
children's Ideal Toy American
Modern plastic dinnerware.

**Ideal Toy Children's
American Modern plastic dishes.
"off color" set.**

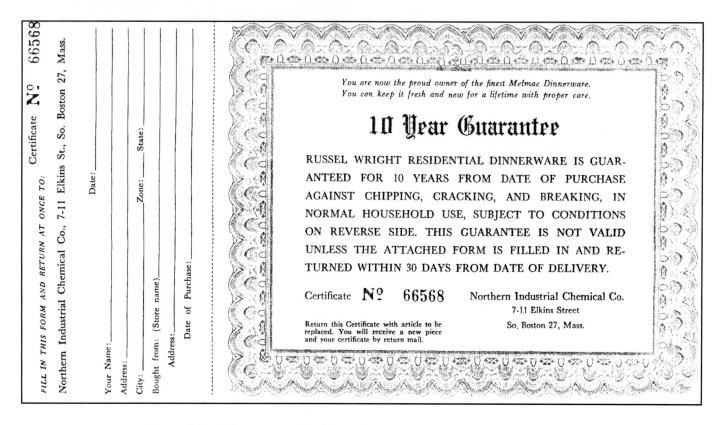

Russel Wright 10-year Melmac dinnerware guarantee certificate.

Glass with Class

Wright's work with glass began early in his career and extended itself throughout his working life. Some of his most interesting early work centered on designs which were table top glass items, specifically designed to accompany his various dinnerware lines.

The 1990 study of this work began with a picture of his early sherry pitcher, dating from his Russel Wright Associate days and it clearly illustrates the combination of different materials in harmony with the major component. Such a combination substituted for pattern, and added ornamentation and interest to an otherwise ordinary item. As he was able, Wright found glass accessory items into which he could incorporate this principle.

In 1945, six years after American Modern dinnerware introduced the world to his table top designs, many manufacturers were contacting Wright, hopeful that they could reap some of the profits which The Steubenville Pottery had shown were there for the designing. Century Metalcraft, interested in producing a crystal line to accompany American Modern was one of these and negotiations went so far as to produce a contract, but no product resulted. Two years later the contract was sold to American Crystal but they, also, failed to produce as far as the archival material indicates. In spite of that, it seems likely that one or both of these companies experimented with designs for Wright's approval and the fact that American Crystal produced a list as well as a publicity picture for a salad fork and spoon with glass handles, indicates that some amount actually resulted. (While we cannot be certain, these may be the salad servers mentioned in the metal section and attributed to that work.) The listed items included punch set, tumblers in three sizes for juice, water, zombie, centerpiece bowl, salad plate, cup and saucer, cheese board, salad servers, tray, and coasters.

**Russel Wright's Flair tumblers.
Shown as part of a Modern table grouping.**

In 1941 Wright established a working relationship with The Imperial Glass Company and they produced a line which was called Flair to be included in his American Way program. In the program listing, it was said to have been made in five colors to harmonize with American Modern dinnerware. Cross-referenced, it was not the extended line which evolved as the American Modern line. It was, however, the first of what would be a longer list of seeded, textured glasses which seemed to interest Wright.

Flair had a granular surface, a smooth interior. Contradictory information on sizes of Flair has not been resolved, primarily because so little of it has been found and identified that it has not been possible to establish these sizes with accuracy. American Way files and the Syracuse files identify sizes as 14 oz., 11 oz., 6 oz., and indicate that a finger bowl and 8" salad plates were included in the line. Since these copies were distributed to clients, it would seem that these may be the correct sizes. The personal files point to slightly smaller sizes in addition to a 3 oz. juice glass and they do not include the finger bowl or salad plate. Still not found in any colors but crystal and pink, the early information told us to expect yellow, smoke, turquoise, amber brown, and crystal. You will be fortunate to find a Flair tumbler in *any* color, but do not let this conflicting color information confuse the granular seeded pattern.

Rough texture on the outside with a smooth interior is typical of Wright's work. Mexican glass, very similar, very similarly shaped is the reverse of this positioning and it has confused us in the past. An ice bucket, reported, has not been verified and is not listed in the files as an item which was made. Advertisements show finger bowls and underplates also not listed in the files and it would seem likely that actual production was much less ambitious than Wright's planning; the line was less colorful, with fewer items and a short production time. Buyers, it is believed, did not take to it for it was not pristine, perhaps not sanitary. In spite of this, collectors value Flair beyond Wright's other glass; it is important to our understanding of his work with glass since it predates experimentation and production of other textured glass styles which seemed to be important to his work over a long period of time.

Wright's glass designs for American Way are found in the Way listings and we know that work was done for The New Martinsville Glass Company but we have little information to add to that fact. It is hoped that the inclusion of Ameri-

can Way listings here will identify more of this work.

Raymor, ever the aggressive distributor, turned to The Appleman Bent Glass Company in 1946, hoping to find a manufacturer to produce a small line of bent glass serving piece glass items to accompany the American Modern line. Raymor's limited list was an interesting one. Out of that came work involving a textured, seeded glass with a powdered glass applied to a "flesh" colored base. Raymor approved this production, rejecting a type which would have involved a swirled or silver mirror pattern. Those items which Appleman would produce would be limited to a relish rosette, 6" plate, chop plate, highball tray, dinner plate, cocktail tray, ashtray, bread tray, 18" boat shaped bowl, double jelly dish, olive relish dish, candleholders, and salad plates. Approved colors, different than the typical Wright colors, included apricot, amethyst, and green as well as milk glass. None of this work has been reported, but the Syracuse files indicate that production began and product resulted. Perhaps we need to look again at seeded glass in these shapes, particularly if it is found in combination with wood, rattan, reed, cork, or other natural materials. Given Raymor's wide distribution, this glass must be around today, unrecognized.

What we are certain of is that Appleman made bent glass warming trays with electrical connections that allowed for constant heat, keeping food warm when taken to the table. These are not marked with Wright's signature, but they do bear the Appleman name and are authentic Wright designs. Produced in two oblong sizes, as well as a round shape, they are usually found with blond wood handles. Black handles have also been found.

The Fostoria Glass Company was approached by

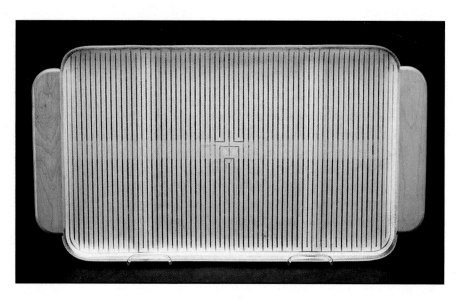

Appleman electric warming tray.

Samples of unproduced Fostoria Glass.
Courtesy of Huntington Museum of Art.

important to us as we trace common characteristics to which he returned to often in his work, each different, but in a related way. Annie Wright's personal collection further illustrates her father's interest in textured glass. In her collection are prototypes less granular than the production which we associate with Flair, with the Fostoria prototypes, or Paden City snow glass, but they emphasize Wright's interest in this type of glass.

Before we leave the Fostoria/Wright involvement, we should be aware of an advertisement sent just as this document was being edited. Undated, it shows a table set with the Wright prototyped silver flatware,

Wright and asked to develop a textured, seeded glass, presumably to accompany Wright's Highlight line. They prototyped it to Wright's specifications but never produced it commercially, feeling that it was unsanitary, too difficult to clean and keep clean. When this contract was first examined, I questioned the late David Dalzell, then the president of Fostoria, and he explained this situation to me. Believing that there was no reason to continue my search, I turned my attention to Wright's work with the Paden City Glass Company who actually did do textured glass work to accompany Wright's Highlight line. However, had I looked further, invited myself to dig into Fostoria's research and development area, at a time when the plant was in operation, I would have found samples, perhaps prototypes of this work. Another collector, at the time of Fostoria's closing, did so.

You will find examples of that work at the Huntington Museum in Huntington, WV. Again, even an "empty contract" provided us with information on Wright prototypes. What would have resulted amounted to small bowl, low bowls of several sizes 12 oz., 9 oz., and 5 oz. as well as a 4 oz. cocktail, and a 6½ oz. old fashioned glass. All were to have had sham bottoms with lines similar to his late Theme Formal line. Wright had worked with Rutgers University in experiments as he developed his concepts for this line. Plans were to produce a dense glass of uneven surface texture in colors as well as white. Rutgers described a bowl testing as "opaline," a term Wright was to use later in the Theme Formal line. Others felt the word "alabaster" was more descriptive. While none of this work was produced, his continuing interests in this sort of glass is

Magazine copy showing Wright's unproduced National Silver. Glassware pictured may be Fostoria prototype.

the cube silver shakers, and pictures plates and stemware which appear to be wheel cut in a design that is geometric and difficult to describe. All is described as Wright designed. Neither I, nor those who know Fostoria best, can identify this but we are picturing it for what it is worth. It may represent prototype work, or it may represent Wright's customary use of altering materials or wording to add interest. In either case, it adds to our understanding. Remember, though, that the president of Fostoria denied any Wright work.

Wright's association with The Old Morgantown Company was a more positive one and much of the information concerning it comes from Jerry Gallagher whose research of Morgantown glass is considered a scholarly study. Gallagher has written The *Old Morgantown Glass Book* and has given permission to relate his interesting details of this important Wright glass. The account begins with the work of this well-respected glasshouse, with a strong reputation for fine quality glass products, highly styled, certainly ahead of the curve in glass design. They agreed to produce what would become the companion glassware to the American Modern dinnerware line. Raymor had made the original contact and, initially, Morgantown was reluctant to take on the line. They were working at peak capacity, overbooked with orders. Still, a line which would accompany the popular American Modern line was tempting. The negotiations with Joseph Haden, the president of Morgantown led to the firm's largest private mold production and they were overwhelmed with the acceptance of the line. It was so successful that they were compelled to build larger furnaces to handle orders. Three shops were kept very busy for several years working on this line. A friendship between Wright and Haden based on common understanding of the excellence of quality of design and materials developed soon after work on the line commenced.

Wright had distinct opinions concerning the colors which would be most suitable, most complimentary, and would work well with any possible mix and match combination. It should not surprise us that he had some difficulty in communicating the results he desired. Gallagher reports that the line was "simple and plain in appearance but not in production." Haden, described as having a creative bent, himself, was intent upon working to Wright's specifications within the realm of practicality. Both saw the end results with the same vision and a good working relationship developed out of the mutual willingness to achieve a fine product.

Mr. Haden's son, Richard, gave the following account. "Russel Wright's line consisted of four different colors — unusual colors, to say the least — none of our regular colors — a chartreuse — light gray — pink,

which was good in the dinnerware — was not very good in the glassware — also a SEAFOAM blue —. My father was still in the business at that time, and Mr. Wright came to the plant on two or three occasions to get the details worked out, trying to resolve the colors that would be used. My father knew many, many colors but, when Mr. Wright indicated to my father that he wanted a SEAFOAM blue, that one just slipped him — that one, he couldn't figure out; Dad showed Mr. Wright different samples of blues that Morgantown had made at one time or another, but none of them were acceptable. Mr. Wright then said that he would send some color swatches of materials that would indicate the desired color." As the story is detailed, Mr. Haden was driving Wright to the Pittsburgh airport for a return flight to New York and it was raining "and they came upon a road sign on the highway — Russel Wright said to my dad, 'Now, Mr. Haden, the blue in the signboard is the identical color we want. You can see what it is RIGHT THERE — that's the color I want, EXACTLY.'" Richard reported that his father said later that all he had to do was remember what the signboard looked like.

Morgantown, with great artistic resources from management to workmen did accomplish Wright's colors in a way that pleased him. Wright, of course, was the owner of his designs and Morgantown never used the colors in any of their other production. Morgantown's colors, Wright's spectrum, called for coral (said to be difficult for the factory to achieve with uniformity), seafoam, chartreuse (achieved by adjusting Morgantown's topaz), smoke (sometimes called granite gray a

**Old Morgantown American Modern chilling bowl.
Very rare. 3" tall, 5¼" diameter.**

new color for Morgantown), as well as crystal.

All were produced in 1951 in these items: tumblers in three sizes, a 5¼", 15 oz. ice tea, a 4½", 12 oz. water, and a 3¾" 8 oz. juice. Five stemmed items included a 4¼", 11 oz. goblet, a 2¾", 5 oz. sherbet, a 2½", 3 oz. cocktail, a 4 oz. wine, and a 2", 2 oz. cordial. A dessert dish is small, a 2" x 4" bowl. Very soon after the original items went into production other items became part of the line: a 7" pilsner; a chilling bowl, 3" tall and 5½" wide holding 12 oz.; as well as a 3½" double old fashioned glass. Collectors continue to confuse the very similarly sized wine and cocktail. The wine is slightly taller while holding 1 oz. more. All sizes given here are as accurate as is possible when measuring handmade glass. They have been altered from our 1990 sizes to conform to measurements in Morgantown records. Your own measurements should be "filled to the brim." Color is our best indicator for it is true that the shapes are not distinctive and the tumblers do not stand out as do the stems.

Unsigned, most of this glassware lost its stickers many years ago. According to the personal files, Wright wrote to Morgantown, wanting to add to the line, to accessorize American Modern by adding salad plates, a candy dish, fruit bowls, ashtrays, and a tray with relish compartments. No reply was found and none of these pieces have been reported. That does not mean that some experimenting was not done. Please refer to the photo of the old fashioned glass here. Our 1990 photo was incorrect and I apologize.

The warm glowing coral with its pink tint seems to compliment and bring out the best of all the dinnerware glazes and it is a favorite with collectors. Seafoam accents many ceramic colors beautifully. Smoke blends earth-tones with monochromatic style and chartreuse adds a surprisingly soft accent wherever it is found. Crystal is rare.

We cannot leave Wright's American Modern work without referring again, this time in a more direct manner, to the contradictory terms for items and colors which Wright employed with largess. Photos here will show (if they will reproduce) a box which contained American Modern seafoam goblets, found in their original wrappings. The box describes the contents as SERV'ELEGANCE and is accompanied by the signature. The return address is the Morgantown Glassware Guild in Morgantown, WV. It was sent to Russel Wright Serv'Elegance, 143 S. Williamsbury, Birmingham, Michigan. Elsewhere on the box is another label with the Serv'Elegance return address directed to a customer in Wisconsin. Nowhere have I seen the word SERV'ELEGANCE, but single boxes are not printed and packages are not sent to addresses that do not exist. It implies that

Wright's glass work was even more involved than we had known it to be. Research continues.

The Imperial Glass Company produced the glass designed to accompany Iroquois Casual, dating from the

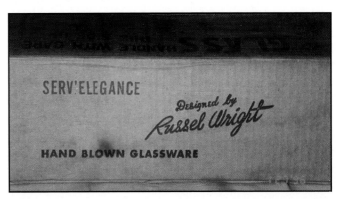

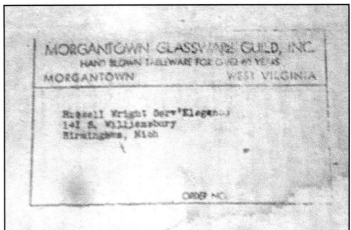

**Mystery! Unusual packaging
for Russel Wright's Morgantown stems.**

time when Casual was redesigned in 1951. The line is not a complicated one, as Wright proposed it. Three tumblers, 14 oz., 11 oz., and 6 oz. were called Pinch because of the pinched-in depression low on the sides, extending to an inch or so below the top. Colors, as accepted by Wright, were to include verde, smoke (a warm brown, not the grayed brown of Morgantown), seafoam, cantaloupe (a light amber), chartreuse, ruby, pink, and crystal. Little has been found in ruby or cantaloupe. When Imperial was closing its doors, selling remaining stock including samples and experimental items that were in their morgue, I found ruby and cantaloupe in the research and development section. Not a lot, and more expensive than the other colors, they still were sold for a song in comparison to collector's prices. I have made a real attempt to account for the amount of ruby which has been found and believe it to be less than 50 pieces. That may be an overstatement for collections change hands, but I do not believe this is much of an overstatement. Whatever the numbers, they are small ones.

Enough ruby has been seen to note a slight variation in the almost pigeon blood red. A recent conversation with Lucille Kennedy, who is acknowledged as the authority on Imperial Glass has explained that ruby was not made commercially, though there was much experimentation. She indicated that Imperial hoped to achieve the red which Viking had made so successfully, but could not achieve uniformity, actually throwing much of it away. Three experienced collectors who have searched and found Pinch have reported finding a blue, described as an ice blue and an aqua blue. It is impossible to place them in Imperial's production, but it is unlikely that they have been mistaken for look-alikes. We are left wondering if these, also, have been morgue experiments or if glassworkers poured blue molten glass into Pinch molds. Ruby may have to move over to make room for these new blues, but, for now, we must consider blue as an unlisted color.

There is a variation in the thickness in Pinch tumblers, some very heavy, some less so. That would appear to be a redesigned feature, with the lighter, less heavy line replacing the original thick body. Heavy tumblers are usually found with ground glass bottoms. Variances are problems to new collectors and the lack of uniformity confuses us as we try to sort out Pinch from its look-alikes, which are several. Attention to the soft depression in the Imperial Pinch beginning low on the bottom of the tumbler and extending to less than an inch from the top will help to define it, contrasting it with sharper edges in Fostoria and Heisey production. The heavy, sturdy quality of Imperial's work contrasts with that of others also. Pinch is more likely to scratch than to chip.

Before Imperial closed, I had contacted them to ask if the Russel Wright line was larger than we had known it to be, questioning specifically as to whether or not stems had been made. The reply stated that they had made no stems in his lines. I answered all questions concerning Imperial stems with information from an old Imperial catalog #79 which shows a stem line in the right colors, but identified as "Dawn," believing that collectors findings could be attributed to that line. Since then, Imperial stems with Wright stickers on them were found but remained unidentified until the personal files were researched. They were pictured there and identified as "Twist." Charitably, these *could* be called footed tumblers since the twist is low on the foot of the stem. Imperial called them "footed tumblers" and dated them from 1949.

Twist was made in sizes to hold ice tea, water, juice,

and old fashioneds and have been found in smoke, seafoam, coral, and crystal. Be careful as you examine Twist. Imperial made the most of this short line and included other items of their own design into the production after Wright's contract had expired. I cannot add to this regarding permission or royalty payments, but it seems certain that only the four items were approved by Wright.

There is another chapter to Imperial's Twist line, however. We now know that they produced another Twist line, more '50s in appearance, with several stems and unfamiliar colors. Those who study catalogs and advertisements should not confuse these lines. Vases, said to be Wright's, have been found and my original position was that they may have been look-alike designs. With no confirming file information on them, no Imperial catalog reference to them, and shaped in a manner that would have made it possible for glassworkers to alter the tumblers while the glass was in a semi-molten condition, that explanation also seemed likely. However, more, not in great numbers, but enough to make me return to the question, have been found. It seems, that we may not yet be able to take any absolute position on these vases, waiting for more findings. If the numbers increase, it would suggest that this was beyond the work of a few factory workers. In the event that the numbers found do not increase in any large amount, the possibility remains that they may have been experimental, closed out of the research and development room at Imperial.

With such wonderful glass designs to his credit, it remains difficult to understand Wright's work with Bartlett Collins, a machine-made glasshouse in 1957. Bartlett Collins placed its products in chain stores, early discount houses, and sold them in sets at prices that made it possible to throw away a partial set and buy a new set for not much money. Not only did Wright agree to design the shape, Oklahoma, but he agreed to do pattern work on the line. The quality of the glass was poor and the designs were unlike anything we might associate with Wright. To his credit, he would not allow his name to be used on stickered tumblers, nor would he allow them to use his name in advertising, distancing himself from the line, while enlarging it in a patterns-on-request arrangement. The line called for constant updating — their new name for "redesign." They told him to spread on gold lavishly. Their customers loved gold, they said. Wright, holding his nose, we suspect, turned out tumbler sets one worse than the other and in rapid fire order. Gay nineties, cowboys, drunks with lamp post supports, barber shop quartets, bottoms up — these and many more with as many themes as he, or Bartlett Collins could imagine were turned out — none characteristic of his work or his standards. It must be said that he knew the appeal of this over-done, over-decorated treatment, but it can also be said that he had stood against it for all of his working life. Did he believe he could enter this market and "manage" it? Perhaps. Was he able to do so? Certainly not. What seems more likely is that he recognized that profits drove royalties.

One pattern has emerged as a favorite with collectors. Eclipse is a polka dot design with overlapping moons of gold and color. The important word is "overlapping," eclipsing, for Bartlett Collins, after he discontinued work for them, continued to produce a similar line with moons which did not overlap as well as a look-alike overlapping moon pattern in different colors than those used on Wright's work. Eclipse, made in huge quantities, has all but disappeared as collectors rushed to buy it at reasonable prices in the mid '80s. Not rare, it still takes some effort to find and buy in the '90s. Sunburst, a pattern with rays of color in vertical shoots, is also a restrained pattern as is Asterick, a sunburst of color. These are the pick of the lot. They were made in yellow, turquoise, green, and flamingo pink combined with gold. All patterns were on the Oklahoma shape and included more sizes than we first believed. The latest information shows the list to include (in order of size, and with fractional differences) 7" zombie, 5" highball, 4" double old fashioned, 3½" old fashioned, 3" cocktail, 2½" tumbler of unknown purpose, a 3½" juice, and a 2" shot glass. Ice tubs and other bar-related items were made to match. I am told that ice tubs with black and gold moons are seen most often, though they were made in other colors. Most collectors have made room for Eclipse and Sunburst, but have resisted the impulse to buy the rest of the line. The association was a short one and Bartlett Collins moved on to new designers while Wright, it seems sure, took a free breath. Recent catalog findings indicate that after Wright's contract expired, tumblers were made with gold moons which have a crackled appearance, as were some which substituted white for gold. Additionally, the Eclipse moons are shown on shapes other than the Wright Oklahoma shape. In spite of this, there is no reason to believe that Wright's work extended beyond the Eclipse decoration as we have known it on the Oklahoma shape.

Wright's work with glass was extensive and does not end with this account. The Paden City and Yamato lines add detail and elegance to Wright's glass products. Paden City snow glass is discussed in the Paden City chapter since some of the items in that line were place setting items. Yamato Theme Formal/Theme Informal is discussed in the chapter which relates to that unproduced work.

ON PRICING GLASS

Consultant's pricing on Wright's glass production found large differences. Availability as well as color choices vary regionally and you may need to use these prices as a guide as you establish your own values. I have come to believe that pottery people are not glass people and it seems that glass, very important to some, is not so to others. Most dedicated Russel Wright collectors, however, want it *all* and the prices here indicate the importance of this glass to those who have a Wright attitude.

The Morgantown Modern production remains popular on the West Coast with seafoam, coral, and even chartreuse selling well. Smoke seems less so and crystal even less than smoke. Others, in the South, agree with those regional favorites but believe that crystal is as important with collectors as are the colored items. Stems continue to be more important than the very plain ice tea, water, or juice. Middle America appears to believe that the 1990 prices should hold in today's market but demand on both coasts point to increased activity, increased prices.

Flair, the seeded glass with which Wright seemed preoccupied, continues to have that effect on collectors as well. Few have enough of it to use, but all look for it, hoping for examples, taking any they can find. Difficult to separate from look-alikes, the defining feature is a smooth interior, a seeded outside. Pricing here is for crystal and pink. Any other color, as described in the glass chapter, would be rare and more expensive.

Imperial's Twist is very difficult to find and not easy to sell in small amounts. Collectors want to use these glass designs and Twist is seldom seen in amounts which add to a service for eight.

Pinch remains the important, usable glassware. Very durable, it is easily sold, especially in groups of six or eight. Seafoam has become difficult to find while cantaloupe is scarce and ruby remains very rare.

Bartlett Collins in the Oklahoma shape is difficult to keep in stock on the West Coast and continues to be popular around the country as a whole. Eclipse is the favored pattern and prices have escalated surprisingly, probably because this line sold for a song when collector's first became aware of it and it held a lower price for several years. A sharp eye will still find it at garage sale pricing.

OLD MORGANTOWN/MODERN

Ice tea, 5¼", 15 oz. ....$25.00 – 30.00	Cocktail, 2½", 3 oz......................$25.00 – 30.00
Water, 4½", 12 oz. ....$25.00 – 30.00	Wine, 3", 4 oz.............................$25.00 – 30.00
Juice, 3¾", 8 oz. ....$20.00 – 25.00	Cordial, 2", 2 oz. ....$35.00 – 40.00
Double old fashioned, 3½" ....$30.00 – 40.00	Chilling bowl, 3", 12 oz. ....$100.00 – 150.00
Goblet, 4½", 11 oz. ....$35.00 – 40.00	Pilsner, 7" ....$125.00 – 150.00
Sherbet, 2¾", 5 oz. ....$25.00 – 30.00	Dessert dish, 2" x 4" ....$35.00 – 45.00

IMPERIAL FLAIR

Rare

Ice tea, 14 oz..............................$50.00 – 65.00	Water, 11 oz. ....$50.00 – 65.00
Juice, 6 oz. ....$45.00 – 50.00	

IMPERIAL PINCH

Add 100% for cantaloupe. All ruby NPD.

Ice tea, 14 oz..............................$30.00 – 35.00	Water, 11 oz. ....$25.00 – 35.00
Juice, 6 oz. ....$30.00 – 35.00	

IMPERIAL TWIST

Rare

Ice tea ....$35.00 – 50.00	Old fashioned ....$35.00 – 50.00
Juice...$35.00 – 50.00	Water..$35.00 – 50.00

BARTLETT COLLINS
ECLIPSE AND OTHER PATTERNS

Cocktail, 3" ....$10.00 – 15.00	Zombie, 7"...................................$20.00 – 25.00
Double old fashioned ....$18.00 – 20.00	Juice..$10.00 – 15.00
Highball, 5" ....$16.00 – 18.00	Ice tub ....$40.00 – 45.00
Old fashioned, 3½" ....$16.00 – 18.00	Set of 8 in metal carrier $150.00
Shot glass, 2" ....$20.00 – 22.00	

APPLEMAN WARMING TRAYS

Round ....$75.00 – 100.00	Small oblong ....$75.00 – 100.00
Large oblong.............................$75.00 – 100.00	

American Modern Old Morgantown sherbet,
goblet, cocktail, wine, and cordial.

Old Morgantown American Modern
old fashioned glass. Very rare.
3⅛" tall, 5¼" diameter.

Old Morgantown American Modern dessert dish.
Difficult to find. 1⅞" tall, 4" diameter.

Old Morgantown American Modern
items: wine, goblet, iced teas, pilsner,
water, dessert dish, and sherbet.

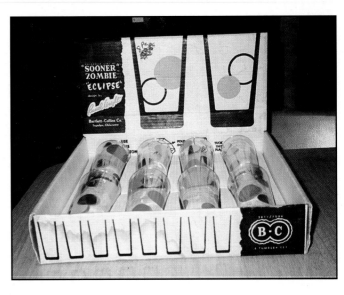

Bartlett Collins Eclipse glassware.
Flamingo cooler; green, double old fashioned; yellow old fashioned; turquoise ware; flamingo juice; green cordial; turquoise shot; and black ice bucket.

Bartlett Collins Eclipse zombies in original box.

Fun for all

Serve delicious ice cream sodas in these gay 14-oz. containers. Modern version of the old-fashioned tumbler was designed by Russell Wright. Glasses are decorated with colorful discs and chip-proof gold rims. Brass-plated metal holders have graceful handles. $4 ppd. the set of four glasses and holders. Thomas-Young, Webster Groves, Mo.

Bartlett Collins Eclipse ice bowl, double old fashioned, zombie, shot glass.

House & Garden, December 1958.

**Bartlett Collins Asterick
on Oklahoma shape.**

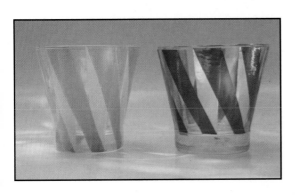

**Bartlett Collins
on Oklahoma shape.**

**Pinch tumblers. 14 oz. seafoam and ruby,
11 oz. chartreuse, 6 oz. verde.**

**Imperial Pinch ruby tumbler and
unidentified "Coin Spot Type."
Tumber documented by Annie Wright
as her father's design. Bandana cloth.**

241

Imperial Flair tumblers.

Enlarged photo of Imperial label
illustrates seeded Flair texture.

Flair tumblers, 3" tall,
and bowls, 5½" wide.

Imperial Twist footed tumblers. Stickers
attached, measurements not determined.
Old fashioned, ice tea, water, and juice.

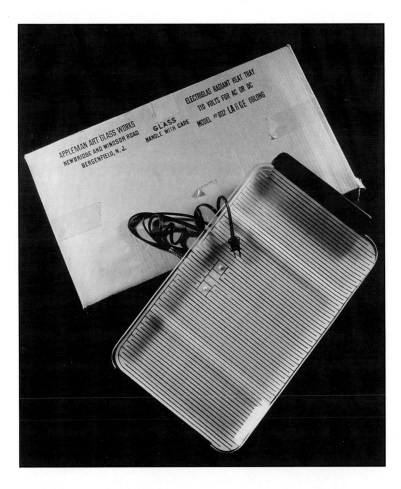

This early glass bottle probably had a cover or stopper. It represents Wright's combination of materials.

Appleman Art Glass serving tray, 12½" x 20 ¾".
Made in a smaller size as well.
Both available with black or blond handles.

Sherry pitcher made under the early Russel Wright Associates label.

Appleman Art Glass electric serving tray, 17".

Table service in Residential black velvet, shows American Modern pilsners.

Fabrics, Background Material

In 1990 with new linen information coming to us from Wright's personal files, we had cause to reconsider his linens, to see that his work in that area was more extensive, more interesting than we had imagined it to be. Collectors since, with that new understanding, made good use of it, coming up with even more new findings. All this allows us to add a good number of photographs to this writing, further identifying some linens and indicating additional patterns and colors which should alert us as we search for Wright's linens.

Some basic facts remain. Our understanding of the companies, the sizes, or contractual specifications continue to be as we have found them, but colors, styles, and designs as well as some information on Wright's materials sold as yard goods can be added. The study is more detailed than we had believed it to be.

At the early time when Wright was planning for the American Way, in 1940, he contacted The Ellison and Spring Company who would provide a solid colored line of table fabrics which would either accent or blend with his American Modern Line. Limited to the table, they were to be scarves, runners, table cloths, and napkins. The color range, as he proposed it, would be quaker blue, coral, turquoise, rust, yellow, and spring rose. Advertised as the perfect background for the American Modern dinnerware, they were also said to achieve a more refined look, less busy and confusing than traditional cloths, many of which were floral patterns. Not a large line, and not one which collectors have felt confident in identifying, it is likely that these solid colors were so easy to use that many simply wore out. Since the colors are so typically Wright's colors, however, surviving pieces may be recognizable. Look for:

12" x 18" mat
12" x 24" scarf
12" x 36" runner
16" x 36" runner
16" x 45" runner
52" x 52" tablecloth
52" x 70" tablecloth
12" x 12" napkins
15" x 15" napkins

Certainly these early solid colored items were paper labeled, and would have shown the manufacturer's name as well as an American Way identification logo, but is is unlikely that those remain. The Ellison and Spring label may be sewn into the selvage edge and that, combined with color may help as you identify these linens. It would seem that any solid color cloth with that label should be given serious consideration.

Wright's work with The Leacock Company began in 1948 and was detailed, with a good amount of linens done in patterns and styles very typical of the work collectors have come to recognize. Once more, the colors which identify these Leacock linens are Wright colors and they, also, were intended to coordinate with American Modern dinnerware. Patterns would include names such as Crosshatch, Brush Strokes, and Abstracts. The names themselves help us identify them. Several color combinations and several geometric plaid variants are part of this work. Napkins, some in patterns, others solid colored, allowed them to be used with any cloth. Table covers were 54" x 54", 54" x 72", and 63" x 80", and were made of sturdy sailcloth. Those found have held up well and seem to have a solid close weave that has survived in spite of years of wear. Others, of the same pattern have some rayon content and these have not fared so well. The rayon pieces seem to pucker on the selvage edge and are not as neat as the sailcloth pieces. On the other hand, the rayon cloths found seem to hold their color, not fading as easily as did the sailcloth ones.

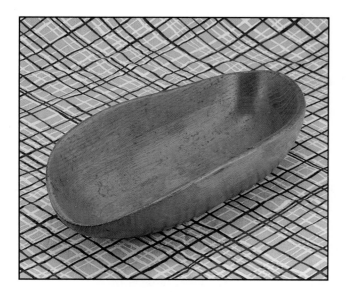

**Mary Wright's wooden bowl
on Leacock Crosshatch.**

Other Leacock sets included Silver Lace, an ivy pattern with background colors of pink, gray, aqua, taupe,

and raspberry ice. We have a beautifully cared for Silver Lace cloth with matching napkins photographed. Symbol, another especially handsome cloth, was advertised in colors that must have delighted Russel and Mary as they conceived their names: root green, endive, earth green, pink copper, brown, aqua, turquoise, chartreuse, and gray. Bandana, a red and white print whose name describes it best was the most informal of the group. Silver Lace, Symbol, and Bandana were made in 52" x 52" and 52" x 78" sizes. Wright's work with Leacock extended to a solid colored line also and though we do not have colors or sizes, the information in his personal files indicates that he intended these solid colored items to compliment Casual colors. As with the earlier Ellison work, check the selvage edge for the manufacturer's label.

While the Leacock plaid sets have become popular with collectors, a plaid line made by The Simtex Company is equally sought after, more often found. The contracts date from 1950 and call for colors and styles so similar to those of Leacock that it seems likely that Simtex picked up designs which Leacock rejected, or that Wright altered in small ways. The cotton fabric used by Simtex was of good, sturdy quality, guaranteed to be color fast and the Museum of Modern Art honored the line, naming Simtex Modern plaids as the best fabric designs of the season. Sized 52" x 52", 54" x 72", and 60" x 80", and accompanied by napkins, Simtex added interest by advertising that these napkins could be used as "Matkins," place mats, of course. Using the same colors as had his other cloths, the Simtex plaids were colorful, intricately woven or otherwise detailed in ways that set them apart from the usual 1950s cloths. Spice, a combination of earthy colors in large bold block plaid was striking, one of the most popular.

Focusing on a harvest theme, several other interesting cloths brought a new look to America's table. Harvest Moon, Square Dance, and Halloween Party typify this line. Square Dance is a woven shepherd's check pattern in two tones of seafoam. Harvest Hayride is an oversized plaid of rayon and cotton and the rayon was said to give it the sheen of damask while the cotton added the element of homespun. With colors described as "Apple Orchard colors," deep greens and browns blended with soft yellows and grays, Hayride is a real departure in table linens. Thanksgiving Dinner, another plaid, incorporated large squares of greens, grays, and browns, or a blending of curry and gray. Harvest Moon Dinner, a lattice pattern with large squares is found in harvest colors — gold, curry, and gray. There were other cloths in this Harvest line and each cloth was made in several different color combinations, generally of larger block squares than were the other Simtex plaids. In 1951 The Museum of Modern Art honored the line and today it is a treasure to collectors. The label should be found sewn into the edge of the cloth.

Patchogue Mills did two woven cloths for Wright in the 1949 – 1951 time span. Geometrically patterned, they were said to have been woven on Nottingham looms. That work also included a line of "summer rugs" made in throw rug sizes of 27' x 50', colored blue, green, or turquoise. Larger, room sized rugs, in 9' x 6', 9' x 12', and 9' x 15' were patterned, achieved by weaving various colored yarns in random sequences. These Patchogue fabrics were probably country styles, but the descriptive information seems to indicate that the quality was good. The fact that the firm had a showroom in New York City would indicate that they were a substantial firm and it is difficult to explain why Wright would not allow his name to be used in advertising, but the fact remains.

Other fiber rugs, also called "summer rugs" were made by the Waite Carpet Company. Made in a 27" x 54" throw rug and room sized 9' x 6', 10' x 12', as well as a 9' x 15' over-sized, they were sold in green rattan, red, and blue. None have been reported and it seems likely that they may have been used on summer porches or sleeping porches, probably worn out in such use.

These rugs, difficult to find and with no pretense of fineness or refinement, were different in many ways from the floor coverings which had been used in most homes of the time. Wall to wall carpeting was not commonly used and floors, often beautifully polished, were covered with large oil painted, stenciled patterned rugs, heavy, ornate, over-done. When Wright entered this field, he really believed that there was a simpler, more honest alternative and he was willing to put that concept and his informal rugs to the test. In an attempt to achieve pattern in a random use of colored yarns, he reshaped old Jacquard looms to obtain this effect and was able to achieve pattern of a different sort. Plaids, basket weaves, and tweeds resulted, and since Wright had planned them as neutral backgrounds for the furniture in a room, they added smartness and neatness to what had been clutter.

As early as 1950 Wright worked with Comprehensive Fabrics Company to promote a "Designs for Easier Living" project which would allow them to make fabrics to his specification. If the patterns met his approval and theirs, he would add new colors, new patterns, and supervise their production. They were to be allowed to use his name and would pay royalty on his designs. The working arrangement was short lived, but *McCall's* magazine advertised draperies in an advertisement that year.

Other such work followed, however. From 1952–1957, work was done for The Tilbury Fabric Company. Wright was to design cotton material and slip cover fabrics in printed patterns. He submitted nine designs and they rejected all of them. Ten more were sent and only one of those was selected. The time involved in such work was costly and Wright felt that Tilbury did not explore the designs or the qualities which they possessed, sure that better examination would result in the inclusion of more selections. He also felt that they were attempting to influence his talents beyond his acceptability. With designs and approval at a standstill, the matter was sent to arbitration. Wright was so distrustful that he cautioned them not to "show these (rejected) patterns around," reserving the right to submit them to others. The matter was settled in his favor and Wright did make the most of a bad situation by using the designs with other clients.

In 1955 Simtex sold their plaid line to a company named Edson who used the patterns in fabrics for slipcovers and bedspreads. Wright enlarged the pattern selection at that time and we know that he designed chintz drapery fabric for them, not all of which was typical of his work. Cabbage rose patterns, his associates say, were very popular and Wright made the most of that popularity. These were said to be "jumbo sellers." His royalties continued through the change of manufacturers and Edson marketed these fabrics through Spiegel catalogs. Other yard goods work was done for The Everlast Company but detailed information on it has not been available.

It is important to us as collectors to recognize that there was a good bit of this yard goods design, some more typical of his work, some less so. There is simply no way to identify much of it unless color seems to shout at us, and it often does. It did so to me one Sunday at a fairground sale in Missouri. Draped off the side of a pick-up truck was a piece of very '50s patterned material. Like nothing described above, the colors were Wright's colors. I looked at all the edges for a signature, with no luck. When the dealer told me I could have it for $1.00, I had to take it home. There is some rayon content to it and it has all the qualities all the colors of work Wright would have done. If he did not, someone else, influenced by his colors, had a hand in it. Until I spoke with others who were fabric collectors, I thought such an experience was strange, one unique to color, suggestability, the excitement of an outdoor sale, and a one dollar price tag. I was wrong. Others have told me of these strange, but happy combination of Wright's colors found on bedspreads and draperies in unlikely places, meaning that it could happen again — and again, with luck. I had my bedspread made into a tablecloth, but I have now heard from others who used theirs as placemat material. Whether or not Wright designed these mavericks, he would have approved of the double use we have made of them. We learned that lesson well.

Cohen, Hall, and Marx were early producers of vinyl fabrics and Wright was ready to explore that market as early as 1946. He agreed that they were to have the exclusive use of his name and that he would design only for them. No copies were to be developed and submitted to others. He chose 10 designs for them, but for reasons having to do with their own affairs, they did not produce. After a two-year relationship, with no product result, Wright claimed that he was owed $4,000.00 and wanted his designs released so he could submit them to others who could proceed. Once more, the affair was sent to arbitration and it was settled in his favor.

Later, in 1951, he contracted to do vinyl table mats for the Aristocrat Leather Company. He agreed that they could use his name, but stipulated that these designs, the mats themselves, would be taken back, and the use of his name prohibited if the quality of the work fell below the standards he required. The outcome of this work has not been determined by documentation, nor is it further described.

Another vinyl table mat contract involved the Hedwin Corporation, but it met with no better result than those which had come before. Wright was to design eight mats of thermo plastic material, not imitative of natural material (no look-alike leathers, rattans, bamboo, etc.). They gave him a minimum guarantee of $3,000.00, a sum with which he was not pleased and within a short time they complained that he was too slow in submitting designs. Convinced that they were "fast sale operators," he also believed that they took parts of his designs and used them on other patterns of their own, paying him no royalty on them. It had been done before, and he was suspicious of Hedwin. A first-rate company, he added, would use a national distributor rather than rely upon their own sales department. He added his own opinions about that department's efforts, also. Finally, he claimed that the prices they were charging for these mats were too high, that he had enough experience to know that overpriced wares, even if of excellent quality would grow old on a retailer's shelves, never selling at high costs. These were important concerns to him, vital parts of the relationships which had been developed in his agreements with clients and he felt he must take a strong stand on them for royalties do derive from sales. The affair went to

arbitration which was settled to his satisfaction. Hedwin was forced to recall all the objectionable merchandise which Wright claimed used portions of his designs, and they were required to replace it with the designs he had submitted. The association, surprisingly, survived and the royalty structure which evolved out of these new developments paid him for portions of his designs as well as complete designs. He became Hedwin's color consultant and all would have ended well except that the line did not sell well and the contract was voided in 1954. Only three lines have been documented: Spencerian (which we can guess to be a scroll effect), Venetian, and Loop Dot. We still have no other information, nor has any of this work been reported. It does seem reasonable, however, that with the amount of mats produced, some will be found. Even an original box may not be too much to expect.

Our 1985 notation that work done for Frank and Saden remains only a reference and no other information has been available.

An association with DuPont allowed them to sell products designed by him to their many clients. These would have been synthetic fabrics with leather effects suggestive of reptile and pony skin as well as an imitation saddle leather to be used as upholstery fabrics. A process of "color conditioning" was said to combine the exact colors necessary to achieve these effects. DuPont called the material "Fabrilite" and described it as fabric supported plastic upholstery material. The saddle leather automobile seat covering was the most popular of the work done for them. Given the scope of DuPont accounts, it is likely that there was a good bit of work involved in this contract but there is little information in the files concerning details or customers.

An important guide stands out as we examine these various ways with which Wright worked with these unmarked fabrics and synthetics. Color, more than any other quality, points to his work. We should look for the colors which were those he chose for his dinnerware lines and if we find them singly or in concert with others, particularly in cases where a plaid results, our ground is more sure. As we look at this work, it is important to remember that the problems which he had with manufacturers centered on his dissatisfaction with the quality of the work they produced, not the materials they used. It is safe to say that he did not regard synthetic fabrics as less important than natural fibers, not altering his designs because of the background upon which they were to be used.

248

ON PRICING LINENS

The most easily recognized of Wright's linens are the Simtex Modern and Harvest plaid cloths. Made in several variant plaid patterns, we will be more certain of identity if we concentrate on the colors that harmonized with Modern or Casual. Leacock plaids follow that rule also, adding variant patterns in abstract to geometrical designs. Once your eye has concentrated on these colors, you will recognize a Wright cloth easily.

Condition, once more, remains the important factor as we look for these cloths. Fading or worn patterns diminish value as would a crack/chip/craze in dinnerware. All sizes are collectible, of course, but the 54" square size seems easiest to find, probably because these were kitchen-table sized. Rarer than the cloths, are the napkins which were solid colored or banded in a coordinating color. Those which duplicate pattern as do the Leacock cloths are more identifiable. Though they remain difficult to find, matkins are worth the search. Bedspreads in 3" plaid squares have been reported. Much of Wright's linen work may never be accurately identified since a good bit of it was included in yard goods production.

My personal linen collecting has often had results if I remember to look for cloths where dinnerware collections are found. There is no way to minimize the dedication of original collectors and where there is dinnerware, there is often linen, glass, and even cutlery.

Cloths:
54" x 54" ....$50.00 – 75.00
54" x 78" ....$125.00 – 150.00
63" x 89" ....$150.00 – 175.00

Napkins $15.00 each
Matkins $25.00 each

Add 25% for cloth and napkins as a coordinated set.

Original paper tags from linens.

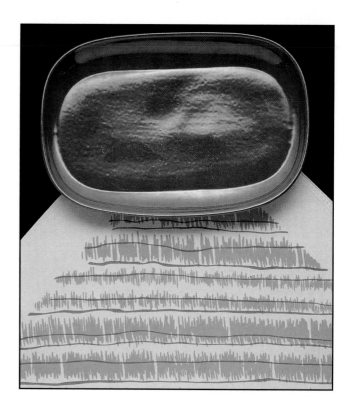

Leacock Brush Strokes cloths in cedar green and seafoam gray. Shown with American Modern canteloupe vegetable bowl.

Leacock Abstracts cloth shown with American Modern platter.

Leacock table linens — Abstracts, Brush Strokes (original label), and Symbols.

Simtex Harvest variation.

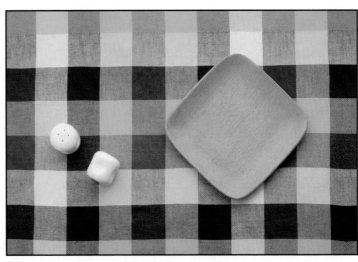

One of the Harvest themes from Simtex.

Simtex Harvest cloth shown with
American Modern celery.

Simtex Harvest Sundeck Plaid.

Unknown cloth. Represents the
naturalistic theme which Wright
used in many of his works.

Highlight dinnerware on Silver Lace
cloth.

Harker dinner plate on unusual colored
Simtex Modern cloth.

Simtex table cloths showing different
color combination.

Better Homes and Gardens, May 1951, ad for Simtex Modern Spice.

Early Simtex Modern Advertisement.

Good Housekeeping, **October 1951.**

Mary, her Work and Support

Russel Wright, with few social skills and a complicated sense of business practices, was the beneficiary of great fortune because of others who entered his life, influencing it in ways that were vital to his success: Frank Duveneck, prominent art instructor in Cincinnati; Norman Bel Geddes, important designer turned mentor to Wright; Irving Richards, practical and discerning friend and partner; Herb Honig, trusted business manager; a hand-picked staff of excellent designers whose loyalty could be counted upon. There were others but none of these was as important to his life and career as was his wife, Mary Einstein.

The marriage, coming as it did in 1927, brought balance to a life too often out of control as Wright's accomplishments brought success beyond his dreams. It was a good marriage because Mary worked to make it so.

She sublimated her own work as well as her own aspirations in an effort to sooth matters that her husband riled, opening doors of the smart shops who would carry his line in a retailing world with which he was not acquainted. His enterprise found refuge in his wife's stability. They shared the same interest in modernism and appreciation for his work came naturally to Mary. They laughed at their common interest in the language, conjuring names for animals and glazes which indicate the light touch she brought to his rigid nature. Adopting his social concerns, she became an early activist in his work.

More experienced with finances, she played an early business manager/sales representative at a time when his show was a one man act. In addition, her money helped Wright's career survive during times when sales were few. While he produced the wonderful small animals and his early decorative items, it was Mary who showed them to the best shops. With a good eye for market trends, she directed him toward the design of table top accessories, a turning point in his career. Respecting her advice, he directed his early work to his extensive spun aluminum line and Mary devised advertising, wrote orders, and kept books. She financed the production of American Modern dinnerware and it was she, working with Irving Richards, who structured and managed the important Raymor firm. She and Richards wrote textbook principles of marketing and carved out business practices to which Russel would return many times in his career. She made speeches, participated in store demonstrations, collaborated with

Mary Wright's Klise Frosted Oak tray with holes for napkins and compartments for drinks or bottles. American Modern wine, double old fashioned, and pilsner.

Wright in writing *A Guide to Easier Living*, affirming her approval of his philosophy as well as his products. She was tireless in her husband's behalf. I have said it before, "Mary sold Russel with style," but it should be added that she sold him with sincerity as well.

In the American Way files, it was said that "Mary Wright's claim to fame is that she is married to Russel Wright." Feminists of the 1990s would be outraged, but Mary seemed not to have corrected the reference. Her own work had been respected by the design community and she collaborated with very important designers in the Way program. Never ignoring her own skills, his priorities became hers. The dimension of their marriage grew because Mary tended it so well.

Much of what we know of her work derives from Russel's American Way sources for she made distinctly important contributions to that flawed program. Her work there shows imagination and confidence as well as a willingness to experiment with new materials and ideas. As you compare her work in the listings of that program, you will see that her designs stand out as very sophisticated on one hand, very craft-oriented on the other. Different styles testify to her various interests and skills and you will find her working with established and important designers, not a position granted to a novice. Her early work, not often seen, identifies her private design world as one of fantasy, whimsy, delightfully different from the strict attention to form which was the Mecca of the times. She was salsa to the sameness that was evolving in design. The sorrow of her professional life was the work which she did on Country Garden dinnerware. It was rejected by Bauer after a great deal of work on her part and a considerable amount of experimentation by the pottery, a real disappointment for her.

The Country Garden line was to have been produced by Bauer in Atlanta in 1946, and work on it was being done while Wright's art pottery line was in development there. It is important to understand that Mary, with the help of Doris Coutant, Russel's ceramist, was trying to accomplish glazes which could be mass produced and sold at a margin of profit which Bauer insisted upon. This was difficult to achieve since an intrinsic part of the design was a handmade look, not easily accomplished on a low budget.

Wright, with glaze problems of his own, could not, probably by virtue of his own personality, leave Mary's work to those who were developing the line. Doris Coutant sent a great deal of correspondence from the factory in which she addressed the circumstances which

Country Garden patterned chop plate, dinner plate, sauce boat, sauce plate, patterned 6" plate, cream, sugar with spoon cover, cup and saucer, and divided relish.

concerned both Mary and Russel. Wright typically replied by saying that these were his wife's concerns and that he should not be bothered by matters which did not involve his own work. Typical of this correspondence were statements: "While I think all the trials are excellent, white stands out. It is a snowy-looking color and I really prefer it, but I suppose the others are softer. However I shall leave it entirely up to you and Mrs. Wright to decide which to use." He believed the background color of the brown was "a little too dark. Try to lighten it with a gray cast. My reason for this is that it will combine better with the green (in the event that this color is selected). Get your directions as to what to do with it from Mrs. Wright." Claiming to be "crazy about the green and like its metallic cast, I prefer the stone, but do not like either of these very well; they are too common. I really think Mrs. Wright should consider changing it to a bright, dark, Persian-blue color which would be more saleable, I believe. These dark greens suggest Victorian jardinieres and spittoons! I do not want you to send me any more yellows." and "Pink? How did pink get in here?" Always admonishing Coutant that these were Mrs. Wright's concerns and that questions should be addressed to her, Mary's copies of these letters were always detailed with his suggestions and one could suppose that, in addition to her own problems, she may have been forced to put a good face on her husband's interference. Certainly, the documentation shows that Mary's inclination was to compromise where the line would benefit. Reading between the lines, it seems sure that Bauer's relationship with the Wrights and the detailed tests they demanded was strained beyond that which we have described.

Still experimenting with glazes about which they were unsure and items with names not certain, Bauer showed Country Gardens at the Atlanta Housewares show on May 12, 1946. There were few orders. With costs which had exceeded expectations, Bauer believed that it could not be made and sold at a competitive price on the Eastern market and refused to continue work on the line. Mary was very distressed, understandably, and offered to work with Bauer in any way possible but they could not be persuaded. Work came to a standstill. She consulted attorneys and finally tried to interest other manufacturers, but in the end she was unable to save the line.

As it had been planned, Country Garden glazes would have been white, green, pink, beige, and brown. There had been too little time for the Wrights to let their imaginations play with more interesting descriptive names for the colors. The original pieces as listed in the files were to be dinner plate, bread and butter plate, cup and saucer, fruit, cream and sugar, and sauce boat. A two-cup as well as a five-cup pitcher were known to have been sampled but several serving pieces, abstract and with no real identification were also sampled. Some of these have been found and some have come to us in amounts which suggest that small runs may have been made. Items which appear to be jelly dishes, vegetable bowls, gravy boats, bread trays, pitchers, ladles, vinegar and oil cruets, and a skillet server have been found as have other items with unspecified usage. Our listing remains open ended as salad spoons have been found. Who has the forks? Unfortunately, we can only access Mary's work through her husband's files, and we are left with less than complete information except as his work crossed hers as it did in this Bauer work and as it had done in his American Way program. Our impression is well grounded, however, in the belief that Country Garden is much more extensive and important now than it was in 1946.

Mary's American Way work appears not to have been influenced by Russel except that all of that work had been approved by him. With Raymond Loewy, Mary designed a group of aluminum serving pieces manufactured by Everlast Aluminum. This was a line of heavy gauge aluminum buffet items, said to ensemble with any home setting, modern or traditional, using naturalistic floral patterns, hyacinths, lilies of the valley, crocus, dogtooth violets in a Spring Flowers line. Our listing comes from Wright's personal files. It is certain that there was some production, but items may not have been signed except for the American Way sticker. Aluminum is still new to the collecting world and we may still find examples of this Everlast work. Look for these items in sizes not documented:

Large rectangular tray
Small rectangular tray
Square basket with handle
Deep round basket with handle
Flat round basket with handle
Flat round tray with two side handles
Deep round bowl, no handles
Shallow platter, narrow edge with two handles
Coaster

A "Fallen Leaves" group, similar but with a native American leaf pattern was made in the above items but added:

Ice bucket with ladle and strainer
Oak Leaf relish
Single Ivy Leaf bowl
Double Ivy Leaf bowl
Candlestick

Mary extended her Way contributions to include lovely delicate basketry. Annie Wright shares that years after the Way had been discontinued, Russel wanted a firm in the Carolinas to do work from sketches Mary had made, but that seems never to have been accomplished. Way files indicate that her basketry work was done by the Penobscot Indian arts and crafts group in Maine. Joined by Peter Cabot and Princess Goldenrod as design collaborators, a line was developed which was said to have been a secret Penobscot technique passed from one generation to another. Certainly unusual pieces resulted in several sizes and would have been used as decorative container pieces, sewing baskets, knitting baskets, and the like. Given descriptive names, probably by Mary, herself, all had sweet grass handles which gave them a lasting scent. Baskets were called Red Strawberry, White Strawberry, Black Blackberry, and a Maroon Cherry. A knitting basket was made in the form of a red cross, an important symbol of women's work in 1941's war time. It was done in natural colored string and cane, large enough to hold the longest knitting needles. A wonderful assortment resulted from this Penobscot work and knowing of Wright's inclination to store ideas for future work, we believe it may have influenced his use of basketry to hold serving dishes in his Iroquois dinnerware, not yet in production.

Ceramic work for the Way in a floral accessory line was done for the Maddox Company in Los Angeles. Made as accessory serving items to include at least an ashtray and bowls for jams, jelly, or nuts, they were shaped and colored to reflect a yellow daisy or a yellow, blue, or brown pansy. Certainly stickered by the American Way, they were probably not signed by Mary. We could expect to find the Maddox mark, however. Perhaps we need to take a longer look at California flowers.

Early work, before 1941, resulted in some of the most beautiful linens described in the Wright files. Not made in the amounts of Russel's fabrics, collectors have not found them in any amount, but a better acquaintance with the wonderful patterns may yet lead us to her work in this field. The earliest of these was a table cloth group, Kitchen Garden. Sized 54" x 54", it was done in red, yellow, and two tones of green covered with radishes, onions, carrots, string beans, peas, squash, tomatoes in rows with a large head of lettuce in one corner and a cauliflower head in the opposite corner. This cloth, coming at the time when it did may be said to show Russel's influence for he had designed an exhibit for Campbell's Soup at the 1939 World's Fair and did drawings of dancing vegetables to be used as part of that exhibit. Fruit Orchard, in the same size, was made in sky blue (Russel advised that this was not the best color, nor the best name), lavender, and turquoise. Showing full branches of fruit trees against blowing clouds, it should attract attention when seen. Sea Garden, of similar size, was made in turquoise (the best color, her husband said), dusty pink, yellow, and purple. The marine design showed shells of sea horses, urchins, shark eggs, coral, and seaweed in a random pattern. All of these cloths were made of fine Belgian linen and, if not faded when found, should be of better quality than any of Russel's cloths, perhaps even more interestingly designed. Another Way cloth done in collaboration with several designers was made by Leacock and it featured a marine garden, similar in concept and perhaps derived from Sea Garden. A 52" cloth, we have no description except that it was made of a spun-glo fabric (suggestive of rayon content) in red, coral, turquoise, and yellow. Napkins were white with colored borders to match the cloths and came in generous 17" squares. We have photocopies to illustrate these cloths, and in contrasting them with Wright's own plaids, we are able to see the qualities which Mary brought to her husband's work.

As had Russel, Mary worked with wood. Her American Way work was designed with Three Mountaineers of Asheville, NC, as the manufacturer. She collaborated with Miles Aborn and Douglas Maier to design a

Mary Wright early wood bowls.

wooden accessory line. That work includes peanut dish, tobacco leaf tray, cheese board and spreader, individual nut dish, acorn salt and pepper*, apple bucket*, footed 17" maple bowl, ashtray and snuffer of cherry with lead lining, cigarette box with acorn knob of cherry as well as another with three compartments*, cigarette case, hurricane lamp with wood base, hurricane lamps with tin reflectors in three sized bases, 6¾", 8⅝", 10"*, cherry fruit bowl, and a cheese cutter of stainless steel with a cherry handle. Though the three designers worked together on this line, Mary is known to have been the principle designer on the items which are starred. You may find examples of these items, seemingly lifted from the Way production and attributed to Russel.

Working with The Klise Manufacturing Co., Mary designed wood items for the American Way program. Our listing remains confused since file documentation refers to items not listed, and marked items, unlisted but seeming to have been part of this work, have been found. We are left with the conclusion that the line was a larger one, out of which an American Way listing was derived. Those items which are known to exist are:

> Square cheese board, round center
> Rectangular cheese board
> Large square salad bowl
> Individual square salad bowl
> Rectangular salad bowl, plastic handles
> Rectangular salad bowl, no handles
> Cigarette box
> Individual square plate
> Bread tray
> Salad fork and spoon
> Pine cone shakers
> Relish bowl with three glass inserts

With what seems to be incomplete records on this early work by Mary, it is not possible to give sizes on these items, but the Klise quality sets this work apart from much of the inexpensive wood to be found today. Not so fine as Oceana items, they are immediately recognized as better than ordinary. The glass inserts used here were furnished by the Imperial Glass Co., indicating good quality in glass as well as wood. Signed with Mary's burnt signature, these items come to us as birch or maple with various finishes.

Leather accessory items designed by Mary were very early works which were included later in the 1941 Way listings. Unsigned, research reference mentions that these were done by "a designer of whom Russel Wright approved." This leather work was given a light treatment because of the themes around which it centered, but it is very sophisticated, very fine, very expensive work. Dating from a Depression-driven market in the mid 1930s, it came at a time when Wright was head-over-heels in aluminum. Without question, the line was not marketed aggressively, for Mary's energies were directed toward Wright's emerging success. Involving the use of expensive, exotic leathers, the listing would include cigarette boxes, cigarette cases, lighters, match box covers, and a pair of bookends.

The cigarette boxes drew their design from fruits and vegetable shapes, pears, pineapples, apples, eggplants, onions, and tomatoes. All were done in leather covered Philippine mahogany, each fruit or vegetable given individual treatment. The pear, 5½" overall was made of tan pigskin with a dark green calfskin leaf and fur stem. The pineapple, over sized at 7½", held more than a package of cigarettes. It was covered with mustard-colored gold tooled pigskin with olive green calfskin leaves. The apple, 5" tall, was covered with red moroccan leather, apple green vealskin leaves with a brown suede stem accented it. The eggplant, slightly larger at 5½" over all, was covered with eggplant colored skin, contrasted with a tan ostrich stem and a chartreuse green suede leaf. The onion, covered with white gold tooled skin with pale green suede shoot, was a larger piece, 7½". The tomato, with tomato red skin and dark green rosette, was 5". Ashtrays were companion pieces to the cigarette boxes, covered with matching leathers and fitted with a chrome grill top which could be removed for cleaning. They were made to match the pear, apple, and tomato.

Smaller cylindrical cigarette boxes were 3½", covered with assorted leathers in different pastel colors, and had a match striking knob. Snail bookends were heavy, 5 pounds and 4" tall. They were made of gold tooled moroccan leather, laminated with a heavy marble dust composition.

Cigarette cases were equally elegant, using the same leathers treated in different, even more exotic ways. These pocket pieces were 6" x 4" x 1". An African frogskin case was said to have a padded, upholstered top of frogskin while the sides and bottoms were made of matching kid skin in beige or brown. A water snake cigarette case, similarly sized, shaded subtly from brown to black with a wide band of snake skin circled the curved width of the case. Brown cowhide covered the other surfaces. Pony fur covered the largest of the cases, 9½" x 5½" x 1½", almost vanity sized. With a top completely covered with brown and white pony fur, the sides were brown cowhide.

Delicately covered, this work would have been fragile, handled often, and probably would have damaged easily. Using delicate leathers unheard of outside the jewelry field where some had been used in watch straps, these pieces were elegant and costly, lavish and luxuriant. They were designed when the country was in deep financial trouble and that may account for the few examples found. Neither of the Wrights had name recognition when Mary designed these pieces and it is not likely that the work is signed. Her carefully cared for items may still exist, but we would probably need to turn to those who sell vintage clothing for examples.

Mary's story was a happy one in that she worked so closely with her husband out of choice and she took reflected recognition from the success that he achieved. While her personal work deserved more attention than came her way, I have not heard that she expressed unhappiness over that except for her Country Garden experience. The Wrights shared many pleasures. His ways became her ways, his interests were hers. Never able to instill a sense of light-hearted joy in her husband, she did not abandon her own and her laughter shows through the descriptive adjectives with which she sprinkled his work. "Blond Maple" was her term which the industry used to describe Wright's furniture and it was she who described the dark and heavy furniture of the time as "Brothel Style." No doubt Russel dictated and Mary edited as they wrote *The Guide to Easier Living*. She did some personal writings of "may have been, might have been" narratives, simple but charming, keeping them for her own pleasure, and she did some small paintings for the same reasons. Mary's shortened years did not allow her artistic life to be developed as it deserved.

Her disappointment when Country Garden was refused was real. She learned of her illness at about the same time and it seemed that she would not have another turn. Much of her last energies were spent fighting breast cancer and trying to make something of her Bauer work, but neither of these were to be.

After her death, Russel worked to promote her work as she had promoted his. He wrote to several potteries in hopes of finding another manufacturer, sending price lists, photographs, and cases of the samples which he had on hand. He offered to have new molds made and where items were not seen to be acceptable, he offered to design new items. He asked for no guarantees against royalties and further agreed to release her patents and supply her glaze formulas with any pottery who would proceed with the work. None would do so. Finally, he contacted Sovereign Pottery, in Hamilton, Ontario, Canada, a firm with which his sister had ties. Some small amount of Sov-

ereign work has been found signed "Mary and Russel Wright, Sovereign Potteries." It is very different from Mary's Country Garden but is the original Knowles "Wright Shape." The Sovereign work has been found in small amounts, usually by Canadians and is a speckled pastel pink or blue. Wright's associates guessed that Sovereign used some Country Garden shapes, some Knowles "Wright Shapes" and applied their own glazes. While little of it is suggestive of Mary's work, it seems significant that Russel did not rest until he was able to secure her name on a dinnerware line. Other work, as yet not explainable, shows dinnerware in colors similar to Country Garden, but with unfamiliar shapes. A skeleton leaf tracery decorates it. It is signed "Russel Wright for International China Co., Alliance, Ohio" in gold lettering. Since we have no reference for Wright's work with this company, it seems probable that this follows his pattern of trying to accomplish some lasting evidence of Mary's work.

Mary's death in 1952 left Wright with many working years ahead of him and with no close companion upon whom he depended for the emotional support and understanding he needed. His way was harder because of that and he found himself alone with his 3-year-old daughter, overwhelmed with success and sadness.

Mary and Russel Wright.

ON PRICING MARY WRIGHT ITEMS

Mary Wright's items are very interesting to dedicated collectors who believe that her work is as important as her husband's and often find the same influences in their similar designs. Little of her work was distributed nationally, in spite of the fact that she accomplished a good amount. With the exception of Country Garden samples and some wood items, little appears on the market and pricing is often left to dealers who use the "what I paid for it" principal. Her Country Garden items have achieved "ball-park" pricing, but you could get as good an argument over them as you would get at a ball game. The certainty is that it is expensive.

With a sampling that is less broad than we would like, these prices are "sold" prices, not estimated. The names by which you will find items listed are names given them by collectors. The correct names seem more rare than the items.

Mary's wood is usually priced at about half of Russel's wood but it is true that it does not touch the beauty of his Oceana line. In spite of that, Mary Wright items are highly sought after.

No linens have been reported.

CONTRY GARDEN EXAMPLES

Large serving bowl ....$150.00 – 200.00	Skillet server ....$250.00 – 300.00
Ladle ....$100.00 – 150.00	Pitcher, 5 cup............................$300.00 – 325.00
Cup and saucer ....$100.00 – 125.00	Pitcher, 2 cup............................$200.00 – 250.00
Sauce boat, deep ....$150.00 – 200.00	Plates, 6" ....$65.00 – 70.00
Sauce boat, medium ....$200.00 – 250.00	Plates, 8" ....$100.00 – 125.00
Sauce boat, shallow (rarer) ....$225.00 – 275.00	Platter ....$150.00 – 175.00
Sugar with spoon cover ....$175.00 – 200.00	Fruit bowl ....$75.00 – 85.00
Cream ....$75.00 – 100.00	Soup...$85.00 – 100.00
Butter pats ....$85.00 – 100.00	Divided relish ....$150.00 – 200.00
Butter plateau ....$250.00 – 300.00	Jelly dish....................................$75.00 – 100.00
Cruet, each ....$200.00 – 250.00	Bread tray ....$115.00 – 125.00
Hinged-lid casserole ....$300.00 – 350.00	Decorated items NPD — Unidentified items NPD

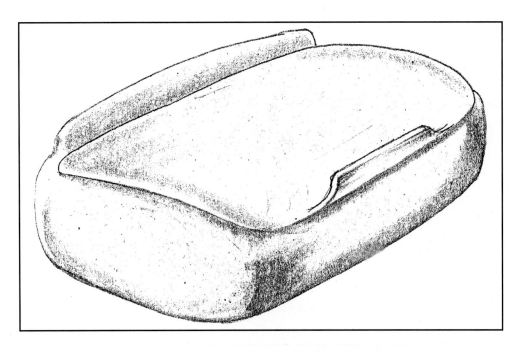

Mary Wright original drawing of Country Garden covered bowl.

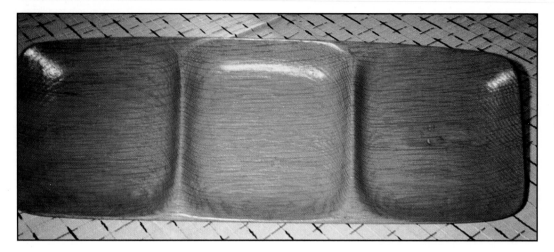

Mary Wright relish tray,
18" long, 6½" wide.

Mary Wright tray,
34¼" long, 8¼" wide.

Mary Wright chrome and cork
ashtray. Russel Wright shakers.

Country Garden. Skillet/server, 12" x 16", hinged lid casserole, oil or vinegar decanter, sugar spoon/sugar bowl, butter plateau, dinner plate, bread and butter plates, cup and saucer, 1½" individual butter plateau, 6" butter plateau.
All very rare.

Country Garden sauce boat.

Mary Wright Country Garden individual coffee pot, Bauer underplate.

Country Garden butter plateau and ladle. Early wood tray all by Mary Wright.

Country Garden stack set without cover, cruet, large serving bowl.

Bauer pottery, Country Garden beige cup and saucer; bluish-white cereal bowl; beige-white divided, handled serving bowl; green covered sugar; pink creamer.

Mary Wright Country Garden three-compartment relish and large butter plateau that also slides across the top of relish, handled divided serving bowl, medium size pitcher, large salad bowl with salad spoons, covered sugar and creamer on tray.

Everlast aluminum made in collaboration with Raymond Loewy for the American Way. Ice bucket, Oak Leaf relish, Ivy Leaf bowl, and Double Ivy Leaf bowl.

Three Mountaineers wood line designed for American Way.

**Leather group designed for
Russel Wright Accessory Company.**

Mary Wright exotic leather accessories.

**Klise Frosted Oak.
King-size cigarette holder with rawhide handle,
bread tray, Pine Cone shakers, serving tray with Lucite handles.**

Klise Frosted Oak.
Covered jelly on tray, wood tray
with glass inserts held glasses,
napkins, ashtrays, and bottles.
Side holes for napkins. Double
covered jelly on tray, and relish
tray with glass inserts.

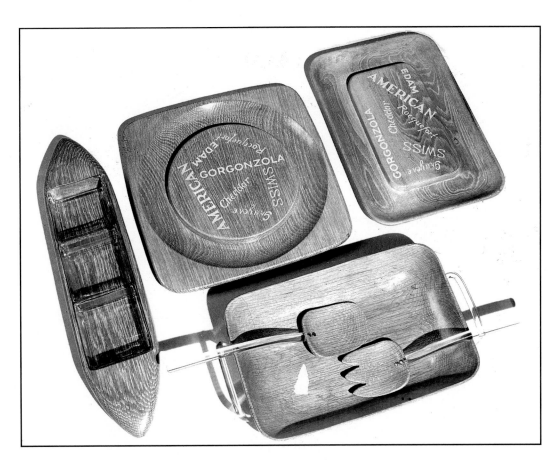

Klise Frosted Oak.
Relish boat with glass inserts, square cheese board, rectangular cheese board,
rectangular salad bowl with Lucite handles, salad fork and spoon with Lucite handles.

Various Mary Wright tablecloths.

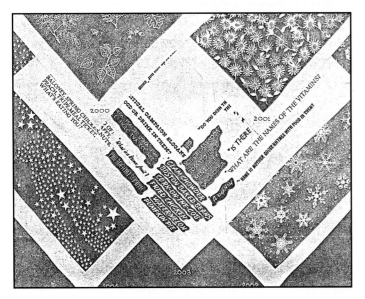

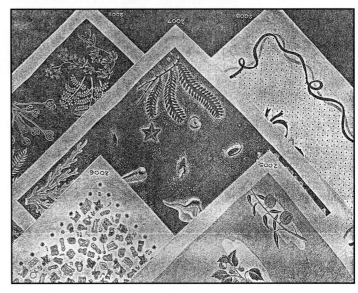

Elegance in the '60s

By the early 60's Wright had moved beyond his own design work and had put his skills to use by involving himself with government work centered upon an Asian handicrafts project in which he traveled to third world countries, helping them to develop small cottage industries. He seemed well suited for such a position for the fires of his old creed still burned.

Such a project renewed him in a personal way also, for he was not yet ready to abandon his own work but by this time most American potteries were closed and only a few handmade glasshouses remained. It seemed unlikely that the American ingredient which he had advocated for so many years could be still incorporated into his work. He took a chance. With a grand plan, not yet completely conceptualized, he turned to Asian suppliers.

Using refinements applied to old fragments of designs never fully executed, he developed a grand ensemble group combining polish and elegance as well as informal and casual qualities. He divided the ensemble into two sections in order to achieve these results and gave them the descriptive names of Theme Formal and Theme Informal. Yamato in Japan was to do the actual work on the lines, subcontracting where the various materials were beyond their capabilities. Schmid International, an importer with an established reputation, was selected to market the line internationally while Raymor, still unsurpassed on the American market, would be responsible for domestic sales.

Conceived to be a total package, the Themes were designed to furnish items to serve any dining or entertaining need a customer might have. Theme Formal would be used in elegant table settings, Informal, on those occasions which were more casual. He coordinated texture, color, and design with item listings which were said to fit into any home, traditional or more modern, with newer furnishings or ones already owned.

Theme Formal was an ensemble combining porcelain, glass, and lacquerware, an approach Wright had not taken before except in the short-lived and troubled Highlight line where he had used glass to compliment the pottery. As that had been formal, this new Theme was similarly elegant. The porcelain, a translucent snow white, was clearly the finest ceramic product with which Wright had worked. Also planned was an alternative white with a spaced white on a gray double dot. With soft sheen and elongated curves, the lines were enticing, sophisticated, and refined. Showing no pretense of his early informal lines, the slender finial knobs added detail and interest. The Oriental influence is strong in this line, gracefully extending the lines, accomplishing beauty for its own sake. The companion glassware is opaline, self shaded from a depth of white at the base, fading to a blue-white opalescent cast extending to a rim edge deepened in white again. It is elegant, very different from any of Wright's other glass work and unlike any glass of its day. It was said to be hand blown. With an elongated hour-glass shape, the sham base is deep, forming a stem which meets the base of the bowl midway in the piece. Its shape is very similar to an Imperial shape, not Wright's, but from a similar time span. Formal, with opalescent qualities, is not likely to be confused with the colors of the Imperial work, however. It will be found only with the

**Yamato opaline glasssware for Theme Formal line.
7" highball, 6" water, 4" wine, and 3¼" cordial (original label).**

white opaline treatment.

Also part of the Theme Formal line is a Bakelite group, with iridescent linings making it strikingly different from any American product you are likely to see. Done in shrimp with a copper lining, green with a bronze lining, and black with a blue lining, these items are signed and include the words "Shinko Shikki." They extend the use of the porcelain line and when combined with it would amount to a handsome contrast. The listings which were found in Wright's personal files may not be as accurate as we would like but they indicate what was actually planned in the Formal production. What "might have been," almost "was," and enough has been found to allow examples, very important to collectors.

The porcelain work suggests:
    10½" dinner plate
    8" salad plate
    6½" bread & butter plate
    Cup/saucer
    8½" soup plate
    After-dinner cup & saucer
    5½" consomme/cream soup
    4⅝" fruit dish
    15⅞" platter
    11" baker
    1½ qt., 8½" covered casserole with ladle slot
    Gravy
    8" teapot
    10" coffee pot
    Cream pitcher
    Covered sugar
    12" oval platter

In 1965 a five-piece place setting was to be priced at $3.75. A Formal coffee pot has been found with stylized floral decoration and another with a Playboy Bunny mark. I have no real information to bring to these findings except that they would appear to have found other lives outside of the original planning, perhaps adapted to custom work for a client.

We are aware of four sizes of glassware:
    8 oz., 5" goblet
    12 oz., 7" highball
    6 oz., 7" wines
    3 oz., 3¼" liqueur/cordials
These very '50s looking tumblers were to be priced at $1.50 in the good old days!

Note: New information adds the possibility that an epergne, 7⅞" x 10½", was planned. It was not included in original listings nor has it been reported.

Lacquerware items have been listed to include:
    Place plate
    Soup/dessert plate
    Soup/salad bowl
    Covered rice bowls
    Salad serving bowl
    Salad fork and spoon

Theme Formal has still been found only in white. The porcelain seems more elusive than the Theme Formal glassware. Bakelite examples exist but they are rare and precious. Few findings of any of this line have been made.

Photo from 1965 China Glass & Tablewares showing Theme Formal group. White porcelain teapot, coffee pot, creamer, covered sugar, cup and saucer, Bakelite cover and rice bowl on porcelain soup plate, Bakelite place plate, glass, wine, and liquer.

Intended for opposite use, more casual and less formal, Theme Informal was not so elegant, not so graceful, but just as carefully executed as its counterpart. Wright promoted it as a line with a country look, setting it apart from the Formal porcelain. Ceramic stoneware was highly fired to add durability to the concept. It was made in dune, a mottled sand color with heavy white speckling which gave the items a textured appearance. Ember, a black/brown with orange speckling showed the same self detailing and was the color which Wright favored. Some items have been found with a lighter brown replacing the orange speckle as well as a prototype orange with tan speckling. Achieved by the use of an Oriental oil spot glazing which releases the iron in the glaze, allowing it to come to the surface, a "Bristol effect" adds a random pattern to items.

Wright had used a version of this process in his early Iroquois work, but in Informal, the effect was accomplished with more contrasting results. All items were very close to prototypes, but enough samples to supply showrooms were certainly made.

The Theme Informal stoneware listing from the files included:

> Dinner plates
> Salad/dessert plates
> Bread & butter plates
> Mugs
> Cream
> Sugar
> Stacking vegetable bowls
> Oval platters
> Rice bowls/individual casseroles
> Soup/salad bowls

No measurements on this Informal line have been available.

Hand-blown optic glassware joined the Informal unit. Generously scaled, it is believed to have been made in several sized tumblers. With stickers lost, it is difficult to identify and very little has been found. It was made in warm amber and a soft smoky green with horizontal optic detailing. Intended for production were:

> Tumblers in 3 sizes measured 3½" x 3½"
> Salad/sessert plates
> Individual salad/dessert bowls, 5" x 1¾"
> Bowls, 7¾" x 1⅕", may have been intended
>   for salad when salad was the main course

Both tumblers and bowls have now been found bearing the gold metallic sticker with white lettering. Without these stickers, however, items may seem almost ordinary, difficult to separate from other optic lines. Our pictures on these are last minute desperation photos from a hurried collector with a helpful nature. They seem too good to omit, in spite of photographic quality.

Not surprisingly, wood was a component in this concept. American elm, given a natural finish which exposed the grain, added interest to the undecorated bowls. They were to have been made in individual salad bowls as well as a salad serving bowl. Without question, these were also stickered, if produced.

With only showroom sampling, Wright's hopes were high and he expected large orders, following the same reception his other lines had met. The Themes were presented at the New York showing in 1965 but were not received as Wright had expected. Dinnerware buyers, a group until now solidly behind any offering Wright chose to introduce, felt it to be out of touch with the market of the time. Too few orders were taken to make production practical. The little which has come to us represents that small production for sampling, and a limited amount of Formal which had been made to fill original orders, expected to be written at the showing. It is not possible to measure the exact amount, but it is certain that it was minimal. Schmid relayed the message that Yamato would not produce and that existing orders must be filled with samples taken from the showroom. There is no evidence that the short runs were ever duplicated or that the line was ever exhibited at another show. Wright, unable to proceed as he had hoped, had to drop plans, discontinue agreements, and close affiliations with those concerned with manufacturing and sales.

Wright found himself in a difficult position, one not familiar to him. For many years he had been the advocate of modern design. His work had become significant in American furnishings for many years and he had espoused the causes of those for whom he designed. He believed he knew Americans, perhaps better than they knew themselves, and asked himself how he could have been so wrong when he had always been so right. He had been, for many years, an American icon and it was hard for him to understand that there had been a change in the 1960s. Civil rights, war resistance, and very different lifestyles all had emerged as important to the American conscience. Wright had thought that there would be a return to elegance, a natural trend for difference after a long love affair with informality, but the direction had changed while he had looked the other way. He found himself, as many of his generation did, face to face with new ways of stating old ways. Values had been reevaluated and it was difficult for him to understand the concerns of young people of those times, to find a place for himself with America's children. He did not wear his new position easily. He had lived and worked ahead of his time, always championing those for those whose lives he hoped to improve. Never retreating from those personal concerns, it surprised him that he had misread the '60s. He joined his generation in wondering how he had missed the mark.

He seemed not to recognize that his own concepts were being restated in different terms. Rejection seemed personal because he had put so much of his own person into his work. We wish that he had been able to recognize the sincerity of purpose in the decade which disappointed him, but he may not have been able to do so. Many did not. It would have pleased him, if he had lived, to see that '60s activists would grow to embrace his spirit, search for his designs with the same enthusiasm as had their parents. What a difference a few years make.

271

ON PRICING THEME FORMAL

This unproduced group of Wright items has been the most difficult to price with a degree of certainty. The few examples seem to have circulated early and consultants believe they may have been recirculated several times since. We now believe that the frenzy that surrounds the lines has settled down and some comparative pricing can be done. Most collectors have had to be satisfied with examples but your imagination will allow for use outside the limits of a table setting. A Formal lacquerware bowl could hold nuts or candy and a glass would impress a guest if used as a morning eye opener full of juice. Do not expect to find a great deal of this work. Its rarity defines the high pricing it commands.

THEME FORMAL DINNERWARE

Bread & butter plates ....$50.00 – 75.00	Bowls ....$100.00 – 125.00
Salad plate ....$75.00 – 100.00	After-dinner cups and saucers ....$150.00 – 175.00
Dinner plate, 10" ....$75.00 – 100.00	Coffee pot ....$600.00 – 650.00
Cups and saucers ....$100.00 – 125.00	Other items NPD

THEME INFORMAL DINNERWARE

Dinner plate, 10" ....$100.00 – 150.00	Mug ....$125.00 – 150.00
Bread & butter plate ,6" ....$65.00 – 75.00	Platter, oval ....$150.00 – 175.00
Salad plates, 7" ....$95.00 – 125.00	Covered casserole (rice bowl) ....$200.00 – 225.00
Cup & saucer ....$100.00 – 150.00	Cream ....$175.00 – 200.00
Fruit bowl ....$75.00 – 100.00	Covered sugar ....$200.00 – 250.00
Soup bowl ....$75.00 – 100.00	

THEME FORMAL LACQUERWARE

Plates.............................$125.00 – 150.00	Other items NPD
Rice bowls.....................$175.00 – 250.00	

THEME FORMAL GLASSWARE

Goblet, 8 oz., 5" ....$150.00 – 200.00	Cordial, 3 oz., ¾" ....$175.00 – 225.00
Highball, 12 oz., 7" ....$150.00 – 200.00	Wine, 6 oz., 7" ....$150.00 – 200.00

Theme Formal Shinko Shikki
lacquerware bowl and plate.

Theme Formal Shinko Shikki lacquered Bakelite.
Covered rice bowls and salad plate.

Theme Formal cream, teapot, and sugar.

Theme Formal fruit bowl, 4⅝".

Theme Formal lacquerware plate,
bowl, covered rice bowl.

Theme Informal tumbler.

Theme Informal mug/saucer, dune rice bowl,
dune ember cover.

Theme Informal tumblers, salad/dessert plate, bowl.

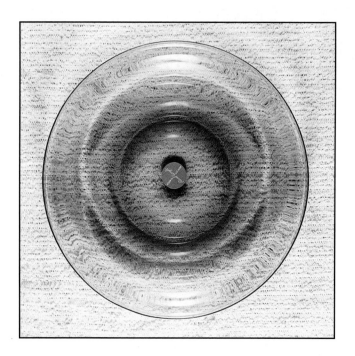

Theme Informal salad plate.

Theme Informal covered casserole
on prototype orange sand plate.

Theme Informal tumblers and bowls.

Theme Informal table showing dune and ember place plates, mugs, saucers, stacking vegetable bowls, oval platter, cream, and sugar. Pinch cutlery.

Theme Informal ember glaze treatment.

275

Theme Informal ember stacking vegetable bowls, dinner plate, mug, cream, sugar, covered individual rice bowl, Informal wood salad bowls, glassware.

Theme Informal rice bowl, Formal goblet, Formal rice bowl, Formal cup/saucer, and Informal fruit and saucer.

Yamato Theme Formal cordial. Very rare. 3¼" tall, 2" diameter.

Theme Informal dune covered individual rice bowl/casserole, vegetable bowl, soup bowl on Informal glass salad plate, tumbler, wood salad serving bowl.

The Best of the Rest

It is important not to limit our understanding of Wright's work to the general listings which we have covered. Many designs were one of a kind for clients, some times, but not always signed. Other work, also custom designed involved whole concepts for restaurants, showrooms, corporate offices, institutions. This work may or may not bear his markings, leaving collectors with the right look, wondering whether or not it is Wright work. These whole-concept themes would have involved table top items — dinner ware, linens, crystal — but could extend to furniture, disposable products, logos, any item involved in customizing a site, an item, a concept. Contracts, when supported by findings or actual documentation in the personal files as well as the Syracuse files are helpful, but the extent of custom work for a client is not always defined. He was said to have had 11 accounts for store displays and showrooms running on a continuing basis at one time with results not always accepted. His designs submitted to the client, might be accepted in part, the rest saved against future use. Clouded by uncertainty, it would seem that these designs are still being identified and that more may remain to be found. Some client work which we can positively identify can be listed, however.

By 1932, with his success waiting only for the Depression to end, Wright's work was acknowledged as fine. He had designed the mahogany chair with the pony skin seat and scooped out arm that was singled out and included in the Museum of Modern Art International Chair Exhibit in 1938. It went on to furnish a conference room at the Museum of Modern Art for many years.

An early example of custom work which brought him attention in 1934 was his design of the Wurlitzer Baby Grand Piano. Made of walnut with polished copper trim or in ebony with bright chrome hardware, it was the first modern piano made for commercial sales. A device in the back held music and allowed for it to slide back and forth for the benefit of the near- or far-sighted. The keyboard was very low so that the pianist's hands could be seen while playing. This beautifully executed piece did much to put Wright's name before the public and brought a great deal of attention to the young designer, so in need of this sort of acknowledgement. He also designed at least two small table radios for Wurlitzer.

In 1940, Wright joined with other designers to do work for the Caseine Company of America's Borden Division. His plans for a "do-it-yourself" collection were sold in cooperation with the Stanley Tool Company and included such diverse items as a tea cart, cigarette box, tables, lamps, hostess tray, bookcases which made a wall unit, and a drop-leaf bedroom vanity which included a clothes hamper in the design. These designs came with detailed instructions on how to assemble them and finish them with wood, metal, fabric, or imitation leather. At this early time, and with this less than significant production, Wright allowed the use of his name. A Silex coffee pot and "stove" to be used with it have not been identified, but it must have been made.

In 1944, five years before his Sterling contract, Wright was interested in restaurant ware designs and agreed

Wright's Wurlitzer piano, first piano of modern design.

to design such a line for the Shanango Pottery Company. The contract called for a one year association, suggesting that product sampling, perhaps runs were made, but there is no evidence that production followed. None of this work has been found. Nor has similar work which was to have been done the following year, 1945, for the Buffalo Pottery Company. In this association, prototypes were made but when they decided against the production Wright asked them for his examples, warning them not to pursue any other similar line. In so doing, of course, he preserved the designs for his own use in later work and eliminated any attempt by others to copy or redesign his work. We may still find examples of the work submitted to these two restaurant pottery firms.

In early work with metal furniture, Wright's agreement with Colgate Aircraft Corporation included in-house furniture as well as outdoors designs. This work would reflect a 1945 change in Wright's earlier, 1941 Old Hickory concept of outdoor furniture. Restrictions on this Colgate contract would have allowed Wright to retain ownership of the designs until he was paid $16,000.00 in royalties. At that time, title and possession would pass to the manufacturer. The use of his name was allowed. None of this work has been reported.

Amtra Trading Company, in 1946, returned his designs when they rejected his work on a streamlined iron. There is no record that he used the designs with other clients.

With little reference in the files, we still know that Wright agreed to design hassocks for the Baker Lockwood Company in 1947. Details lead us to believe that production was done. Wright submitted 18 designs for approval and said that his name could be used if they allowed him to make the final approval of the line. They, on the other hand, extracted promises that he was not to design another line of hassocks, hassock chests, or hassock record cabinets. Our information ends there.

With no mention in the files, a collector has found door bell chimes in the original box and another has reported a coffee mug marked with Wright's name as an advertising piece for Instant Maxwell House coffee. The mug was made in Japan, with the script signature.

More certain is the Samson line done for Shwayder Brothers Corporation. The working agreement lasted from 1949 to 1954 and included Samsonite luggage and vanity cases as well as tables with adjustable heights signed on the rim edge. The metal folding lawn chairs which collectors have found are part of this work, but we now know it to be more involved than we expected

Advertisement for Samson folding armchair designed by Russel Wright.

to find it in 1990. At least three versions of these chairs have been found. One is a solid color, with back supports that become side bars below the seat. Photographs of it with a school desk indicate that it was intended for that usage. The other is colored, with white arms and legs. These were made in patio coral, chartreuse, azure, and green, and had arms wide enough to hold glasses or ashtrays. All of these would fold for easy storage. These chairs were marked on both the bottom and the back of the chair with the following information:

> Samson Chairs
> Made in U.S.A.
> Shwayder Bros., Inc.
> Samson Folding Tables
> Samsonite Luggage
> Detroit Denver
> Patent #2155522
> designed by
> Russel Wright.

They sold for $7.95! Often worn from exposure, questions have been asked about restoration. I have little experience but I have been told that paint repairs with a coat of hard wax produce more acceptable results than I had expected.

One reader says that the metal chairs are so anatomically designed, so comfortable that dealers will not sell them! By adding the fact that a third metal chair was a rocking chair may loosen up some of the more ordinary ones for you and me. Since the 1990 study, I met a gentleman who told me of chairs described as very much like these and made of bent plywood which were used as "school chairs." He was certain of that description since he worked at a school at a time when it was being remodeled and saw many of these chairs, identical to the metal ones, being thrown away. Because he had seen the Russel Wright signature, he believed them to be too good to ignore and kept *one*! Fortunately for us the story doesn't end there. Wright pictured these wood chairs in a patio setting, described as made of birch, with a natural finish on black enameled tubular steel legs. Coming without dated information, but shown with Residential dinnerware, the chairs probably date from 1954, or shortly before. There are examples which Wright kept for himself at his home at Dragon Rock.

In 1955, Wright designed indoor furniture for Sydney Chairs Inc. Chairs were to be sold in pairs and the line would also include a sectional sofa which included a corner piece as part of the sofa, a one-piece sofa, and a mechanical contour-type chair. The contour chair was prototyped, perhaps produced, but in a very limited amount.

The Mahama Importing Company details add humor to Wright's custom work. In 1955 he agreed to make an adapter for opium lamps, aladdin lamps, and designs for lamps to use denatured alcohol. They were to be made in Japan or Hong Kong and he planned to enter into a limited partnership with Mahama in this work. Contractually, both would make an equal investment with Wright supplying the design and Mahama producing white metal based lamps with brass fittings. Of the profits, Wright was to receive 60%. Mahama agreed to use their sales organization but Wright was to act as sales consultant. Their portion of the "seed money" was never funded.

Wright, having contributed the designs was sure that he had been "out done" in some way, and sought out the advice of his attorney. A red flag went up at once and the attorney urged him to put the matter behind him. The term "opium lamps," the lawyer said, raised serious questions and if he persisted in the affair, Wright would be well advised to discontinue referring to them as such. The use of opium was against the law, he was told, and it was equally illegal to design narcotic devices. Granting that their use might include that of a cigarette lighter, the attorney advised Wright to discontinue trying to think up exotic names for them as conversation pieces. Collectors who recognize that this practice of "thinking up exotic names" was almost a parlor game for Wright may understand that the attorney also recognized that practice and advised against it in uncertain terms. In the event that Mahama returned to the agreement and supplied their portion of the necessary capitol (there were significant contradictions in the percentages involved), Wright was advised that a partnership was to be avoided in favor of a corporation. Unable to take suggested criticism, Wright, calling upon his talent with words, at once claimed that these were designed for modern outdoor lamps, not cigarette lighters, and certainly not opium pipes. No one, he declared, had any intent of doing anything illegal. Mahama, perhaps alerted, did not meet with him again, did not return his prototypes, and did not meet the financial arrangements to which they had agreed. Wright did take them to court, asking for $2,000.00 which he felt a fair sum for the work he had done. No judgements were made and it seems likely that Mahama had understood the legal ramifications sooner than did Wright, disappearing as quickly as possible.

A popcorn warmer for Lodge Electric Company was designed and redesigned, indicating production. We have no dates and no information on markings, but any popcorn warmer bearing the name of the manufacturer should be investigated.

Lamp work, of a limited nature, was done in 1949 for the Amplex Corporation when he agreed to redesign a "Swivelite lighting fixture." This contract is interesting in that he did not design the original but in redesigning it, he allowed Amplex to use his name in their advertising.

Paper Novelty Manufacturing Company in 1949 – 1950 asked Wright to design a line of paper Christmas ornaments. These would have been signed with tags or directly on the ornaments themselves. This small amount of production may have been lost over the years, but, with '50s frenzied collecting, we may still find examples. Since many collectors are interested in holiday items, and others are interested in collecting paper goods, it is possible that we need to widen our search.

By 1950 Bowes Industry had contracted to produce a line of paper table service. The agreement extended for a year and it is certain that sampling was done. Wright agreed to exclusivity if sales were $2,500.00 a year but if sales were better, his payment was to be larger. Bowes, fearful that war-time shortages would affect their business did not proceed with production but

Wright was paid for his work for them. It is doubtful that any of these items remain.

Early in 1951 Wright worked with The General Electric Company to design three clocks. One was the clock which became part of the Harker White Clover line and it will be found with his signature. The others would have involved wood, brass, crystal, aluminum, or Bakelite. They prototyped several in an attempt to decide on the line but it is uncertain as to what may have resulted. Wright was not happy with the association, believing they were overly concerned with costs.

For two years, in 1950 – 1952, Wright was working with the Sloan Babcock Company to produce vinyl in hard surface flooring. An abstract wallpaper, in deep, intense colors was also part of the work.

By 1957, he had signed a contract to do work on a vinyl floor covering for American Olean. These involvements with vinyl illustrate his continuing interest in the possible uses of synthetic materials.

Finding himself with no original pieces of his wood Oceana line in 1954, Wright wanted to have casts made of the items and to reissue the line in Lucite. He would have called the line Celomat. Some prototypes were done and some small amount of this may be found, but none was ever made commercially.

Wright and Raymor were contacted by a company named Ravenswood, in 1955 looking for designs in brass decorative accessories. Wright, with the recognition that his own spun aluminum work had peaked, continued to be interested in aluminum, feeling his pioneering work with that metal had been so extensive that he "owned the market" and that others, if not copying it, were trading on the type of designs which he had first produced. Both Raymor and Ravenswood, however, hoped to persuade him to turn his attention to brass, with which he had not previously worked. He was not convinced and said that while that metal had been used extensively in the Orient and Europe, he believed the American market might be "short." His opinion was that brass was trendy and was quick to add that he "had watched the market for 25 years and felt brass was too costly," involving more work detail and leaving less profit. However, he agreed to proceed if more royalties were paid. The contract was signed and production resulted. Unmarked by Wright, these should have Ravenswood identification, though none have been reported. Given Raymor's broad distribution capabilities, there should be a good amount of this brass and since collectors are just beginning to consider themselves as "Raymor collectors," we can expect more information on this Ravenswood line.

With an uncertain dating, Peerless Electric Company produced a fryer cooker, corn-popper, shis-kabob, and a well and tree serving platter as well as an electric broiler and oven. A Bak-O-Matic electrical tray as well as a Toto Chef Unit for baking were said to bake, make coffee, and cook at the same time. A broiling unit, named Broil King brought outdoor summer preparation into the kitchen year round. Difficult to design, Wright, never-the-less, worked with electrical advisors, creating function while preserving form. These were said to be signed, but they have escaped notice by collectors. I have seen Bak-O-Matic trays but those I have seen did not have Wright's signature.

Similar work for a baker, broiler, and a cart for serving was done for Sharon Steel. The results of this contract are unknown, but considering the fact that the president of Sharon was also interested in tubular casual furniture, in particular a folding chair and side table, leaves collectors hopeful that some sample work was done.

In 1955 Wright, working with Philip Vandoren Storn, a representative for U.S. Plywood, joined other prominent designers who were submitting plans for "Do-it-Yourself" furniture items. It is still possible that we will hear of a U.S. Plywood buyer who actually put together a design and now realizes that it had a connection with Wright.

By 1958, Wright had returned to electrical unit design and was working for the Cornwall Corporation. Several items resulted, the most often found an anodized thermo-electric hot tray, 12" x 23". Finished with copper, silver, or gold texture with wood or plastic handles, it is signed. Also produced was an electrical appliance with a ceramic insert which could be used as a cook and serve unit, a well and tree server, a vegetable dish, and warming oven. With a great deal of planning, Wright was pleased with the work and entered the Thermo-Tray in a competition for the best contributions to design in household furnishings in 1961. The working arrangement with Cornwall appears to have been a good one but we have no report of additional items.

By 1960, with fewer contracts to work on, Wright redesigned the Hunt Foods catsup bottles and worked on many different packaging projects for them. The relationship appears to have been a good one, but it is not likely that we will ever know much about the work.

Also, in 1960, a plastic ring box was designed for the Arden Jewelry Case Company.

Working for Cresca, a food distributor, Wright redesigned their labels, but was asked to do product design also. That work would include a picnic carrier, a bottle opener, and cork screw. It was 1961 and the files are not clear as to whether or not Cresca agreed to production. Prototypes, however, were presented for their approval.

Cresca labels designed by Russel Wright.

Furnishings for his homes were often designed for his use only, though they were showcased in articles concerning his work. A chrome gadget attached to a chair allowing it to swing to desired positions served as end table usage, holding a telephone, a drink, and a deep ashtray with water in the bottom to keep cigarette smoke at a minimum could be easily removed for cleaning. His Park Avenue apartment included a wonderful coffee table, concealing a radio-record player with storage space for records or reading material. The top slid out on each end adding table space while revealing the radio and phonograph.

With little proof, but a great deal of conviction, I believe that Wright left us some personal work, done for his own pleasure or for private studies. It seems logical that it would include ceramic experimentation, done in workshop environments which would be available to him on a student or experimental basis. Any material which would involve much fabrication might be dismissed, but if he were given clay or other materials with properties which allowed for handwork, it seems that he would have worked with it to explore ideas for his work, perhaps for his own gratification. That sort of work would necessarily be one or few of a kind and would be impossible to identify unless he signed it RW, as he did in some few cases.

Wright would not have expected that his work would be caught up in a collecting world so soon, but he would have been pleased. He would be disappointed, though, if we had collected the designs, but missed the message. He had declared democracy for our generation, and our children have become influenced by his beliefs and work. Our days have been richer, our self-esteem higher for his pointing out that we deserved a better life. Our living became easier, as he had predicted. He told us that life could be "just great" and he did what he could to make it so. In the end he found his own pleasure in the woods and he encouraged us to follow him there — some of us did, and were glad for it. His work has been copied, adaptations have derived from it, and much has been influenced by it, but his own place has not been transcended. He was a designer for America, introducing, selling Transitional Modernism as no one had done before, setting standards which remain important. Sui generis.

Ad for Cornwall Corporation's
electric hot tray.

1932 Wurlitzer Lyric radio,
made of Melmac. Redesign of earlier radio.

RUSSEL WRIGHT DESIGNS

RUSSEL WRIGHT, aided and abetted
by his clever wife, adds these radios,
done for Wurlitzer, to his list of
achievements in industrial design.
Upper left. "Ram's Horn", midget
radio, dark walnut and bird's-eye
maple. Below this, at left, is "Portable". Brown and café au lait spray-
ed cork, aluminum grilles, handle
and dial. Next. "Wrap Around" in
rosewood and zebra wood. Left.
Modern console, ebonized wood and
harewood. Above. Combination
radio and phonograph, ebony
and harewood. Macy's. Accessories:
Russel Wright and Modernage

Telechron wall clock. White and clear plastic.
Also produced in blue, red, black, and green.

Drafting stools, probably custom work for an
individual customer.

Early casserole with rust colored ceramic pieces made
by Gladding McBean, rattan frame.

Custom package design.

Samson outdoor furniture.

Samson folding chairs by Shwader Bros. Wooden folding chair, black tubular steel frame, 30" tall, 24½" wide. Metal folding chair, 32" tall, 25½" wide.

Broil King by Peerless Electric Company.

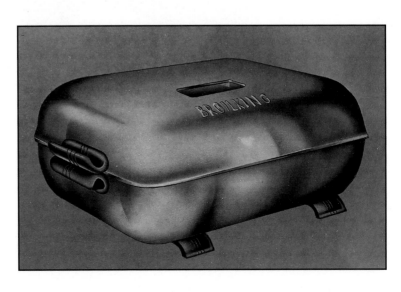

285

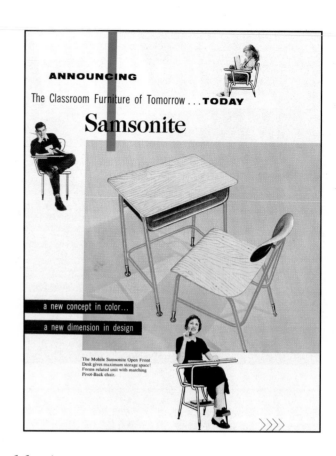

Samsonite school furniture.

Cornwall Thermo Tray.
Gold finished warming tray with
wooden handles. Original box
and instruction sheet on bottom.
Sheet gives questions and
answers such as "If my child
touches the surface, will it burn?
Answer: no."

Wright's American Way, Another World of Modernism

In my 1990 writing, some small amount of information concerning Wright's American Way program was included. As I approached this writing, I believed that many collectors, with advanced Russel Wright collections, were able to look beyond Wright's product work, into the world of Transitional Modernism to which he had introduced us. My own collecting, still Wright-oriented, had begun to broaden, to show examples of this work or that school, other designers. At the same time, phone calls came asking for information on Wright items which I could not identify as his. Calls were often insistent for they had bought these items at department stores which featured whole rooms of his work. The clue to these identities, of course, was that this was American Way work and the buyer had misunderstood Wright's involvement with the project. Each call further convinced me that buyers then, collectors now, do look beyond Wright into the larger field of modernism. He encouraged us to take a longer look when he organized his American Way program in 1940.

In a speech given in 1940 as the exhibits opened, he expressed his motivation for the Way and the promise he believed it held. "As America grew so fast, Europeans began to laugh at us and our culture because it wasn't like theirs. So, in the past few generations we have developed a disgusting interest in pretentious European culture and manners and traditions, a disgusting self-consciousness culturally unknown to our forefathers. American women, I think, have been particularly responsible for this condition. They have developed a habit of looking over the fence at their neighbor, of keeping up with the Joneses, of aping New York and of copying Paris — a tragic lack of respect for themselves and their own. In the past ten years I have traveled considerably to many parts of our country. In each city or town I've usually been entertained by some family. I appreciate the hospitality and generosity of all my hostesses, but I have nevertheless found all of them pitiful in one respect — ad lib. Now,

I've been talking about National self respect and individual self confidence. What does all this have to do with the American Way program of merchandise now being shown downstairs? Well, you see, these outstanding designers for the past few years and at the beginning of 1940, some of us got together and talked about it. We reasoned that with growing national pride, the time was ripe for a consolidated and cooperative effort to interest the American woman in the work of the artists and designers of her own time and her own country. We reasoned that the development of a good way of living in American homes — that the development of pride and respect for the American home was as important as anything else culturally to our country." Wright's social philosophy, just becoming understood, was spelled out for all who would listen. We were in good company. He was as ambitious and creative with his social concerns as with his design work, seldom separating them. He had used his speeches as philosophical essays, promoting American design with the same enthusiasm as he promoted his teapots.

The program, intended to offer the very best of American design/craft/manufacturing work, was presented in room units in leading department stores. In so doing, he hoped to lend direction to the modern design movement. All work would require Wright's acceptance before inclusion in the program, developing a more inherently American design and relating it directly to the American market. Presenting his case, Wright gave three ways by which he would judge good modern design: Form must be practical, comfortable, efficient. Material must serve its use with surface, weight, and strength able to meet the demand made of it. Fabrication must be economically efficient with balance, durability, and security important. By the use of honest, inherently American items, it would allow customers of average means to look into America's past and future, with the hope that these designs would take root in our soil. With these insights he carved out his own career and influenced much of America's post war production. That the Way did not succeed was unfortunate, but that it had been conceived pointed to a new beginning in the troubled times of pre-war 1940.

As conceived, artists/designers would sell their work directly to the Way which would distribute and resell it. Proven craftsmen were to be given designs, supervised and approved by Wright. They were to do their work under his direction, carefully monitored and assembled in New York close to 39th St. and 5th Ave. where they were given space to promote and display the work they did. The concept would have combined the work of both groups, incorporating them

into the complete program. Both the craftsmen and the designers were expected to refresh their lines twice a year following a seasonal change. Manufacturers and stores were to be responsible for stimulating customer interest, joining Wright in the direction of publicity. Distribution was to be done nationally. Aiming for exclusivity, a plan was devised to allow for a one-account-at-a-time scheme which would make certain merchandise available exclusively in one outlet in a city for a limited time. Wright, who knew the value of cooperation with consumer groups, museums, and the like, made personal appearance tours, spoke on radio programs, and released publicity announcements frequently. Invitations for the opening were sent out from Macy's in New York where Eleanor Roosevelt invited customers to the formal opening on September 21, 1940. There was every reason to believe that success was in hand.

There was soon recognition, however, that the scheme, however well considered, would fail and it did within the year, some work never even having found its way to the market. The onset of World War II complicated the demands on production and distribution and administering the project soon proved to be overwhelming. Supply seemed to be difficult to direct and demands, calling for different items in different locations, made orders hard to fill. Uniformity of the product was difficult to maintain and problems seem to develop where all had seemed so simple. Of course, the war in Europe changed American markets, but the practical concerns of managing such an ambitious program were too much for Wright who remained committed, but who chose to continue with his own design work at the same time. He was ten years in paying for costs incurred in the Way, but his own business practices benefited from the experience and he had expanded his interests into the best of design/craft work at the time. I have written that he was not a "bitter-ender," and he was not. It would be wrong to suppose that the Wrights were not disappointed, however.

Wright's organization of the Way divided the country into geographical locations with artists, designers, and manufacturers closely associated with retailers who would carry their work. All was to have been marked with Way information, but some added the artist/designers name also. Planned to exhibit the work of about 65 people, the number grew to almost 100, and you will find familiar names in the listings here. Much of Wright's own work was included. His spun aluminum buffet accessories, American Modern dinnerware, Klise Oceana, his lamp line, Imperial's Flair tumblers, furniture work for The Old Hickory Company as well as

Sprague & Carlton, and the Sears and Roebuck knock down designs were all part of the program as was work done for the New Martinsville Glass Co.

Additionally, seven pieces of marble decorated accessories done by the Vermont Marble Company in Proctor, VT, included a console dish, candlesticks, a vase, and bookends. All Wright designs, they were offered in Travertine and Rose, said to be a rose-beige. Another vase, ashtrays in three sizes, a covered urn, and bookends were made in an olive and gray, combined to give a colored marble effect.

Gold aluminite serving pieces made by Everlast Aluminum are important to our understanding of Wright's Way work. He carved original models for the pieces out of alabaster in an effort to insure an elegant flowing form. It was heavier than other aluminum, a gauge previously used for airplane and automotive parts. With a pale gold finish, much like the finish which we have come to associate with annodized aluminum, it did not require polish, did not peel, chip, or corrode. This product is discussed in the Metals chapter.

In an effort to simplify production and distribution, Wright divided the country geographically. Believing the information will be easier to access if divided according to type, I have altered the listings in that way. You will find all the ceramic work under that heading, the glass under its own heading, etc. The following list is abbreviated to allow descriptions, but not stock numbers. Designers/craftsmen, artists/manufacturers where identified, are included, as well as dimensions where possible. Though the Way was terminated after the first year, many of the products continued to be produced by those responsible for them and, as we look for Modernism, some will cross our path, it is certain.

METALS

Designer: Robert Gruen, source: Kenilworth Plating Co., Berwin, IL.

Extra heavy gauge pewter accessory items, excellent in proportion and line, not bizarre. Tray, sugar and creamer, shakers, candy box, nesting ashtrays, round cigarette box.

Designer: Harriet Lyle Veazie

Sculptured figural pieces of copper or aluminum, intricately formed to give the pieces the feeling of precious jewelry, but used as decorative accessories. Typically Southwestern subjects. Tiny mouse, mabbit, colt, two sizes of horses, cowboy with lariat, cowboy with horse, pelican (snow bird), gay bird (hop head), century plant, barrel cactus, prickly pear, prairie dog.

Designer: Rebecca Cauman, craftsmen: The Arthurdale Association of Mountaineer Craftsmen. Arthurdale, WV.

The Association, sponsored by Mrs. Franklin D. Roosevelt, crafted kitchen items combining pewter and earthenware: honey jar, pewter cover with bee handle; cookie jar, pewter cover with humming bird handle; casserole, pewter cover with pea pod handle. All pieces made of oyster white earthenware.

Designer: Mizi Otten, source: A. R. Kanne, New York, NY.

Hand-wrought brass decorative accessories done by former designer at Wiener Werkstatte of Vienna. Breaking away from traditional forms, asymmetrical forms to ensemble with modern interiors. Deep vase, low bowl for fruit or flowers, ashtray also used for flowers.

Designer: Raymond Loewy, source: Everlast Metal Products, NY.

Gold and silver Aluminite drinking accessories.

for the first time OCT 9 9 1940
115 South Avenue
ROCHESTER, N.Y.
Leading
American design talent combines
to provide a background
for the American way of living.
AMERICAN-WAY announces
the contemporary furnishings
you will want and can afford

furniture... fabrics... dinnerware... table linen... lamps... giftware... handcrafts... glassware

...only American-Way products carry this label in the store

watch for the designer's name

AMERICAN-WAY design by

The AMERICAN-WAY program of related homefurnishings designed by sixty important artists and industrial designers is available in many stores and featured by the following:

Wm.Filene's Sons Company,Boston,Mass.
G.Fox & Co.Hartford,Conn.
R.H.Macy & Co.Inc.New York City
The Whitehouse,San Francisco,Calif.
Joseph Horne Co.Pittsburgh,Pa.
Strawbridge & Clothier,Philadelphia,Pa.
J.L.Hudson Company,Detroit,Mich.

The Higbee Company,Cleveland,Ohio
Gimbel Brothers,Inc.Milwaukee,Wisc.
Bullock's,Los Angeles,Calif.
J.N.Adam & Co.Buffalo,N.Y.
Meier & Frank Co.Inc.Portland,Oregon
W & J Sloane,San Francisco,Calif.

America Designs, Inc., 4 East 39th Street, New York City

House and Garden, September 1940.

Careful proportioning and precision workmanship give pieces the feel of a modern silversmith's gold and silver hollow ware. Heavy gauge, some with crystal and walnut trim. 17" round relish with three-part glass insert, 15" round beverage tray, high-ball beeker, old fashioned beeker, whiskey cup, coaster, cocktail shaker, vacuum ice tub, covered cheese dish, ice tub set.

Designer and source: Bernita Lundy, San Francisco, CA.

Made of tin, tinted with brilliant metallic colors. Child angel candle holder and a Noel shrine for wall hanging.

Designers: Walter Sobotka, Henry P. Glass, Source: Molla, Inc., N.Y.

Hand wrought iron garden furniture in Modern style, painted black or white. Detachable sailcloth or fabricoild covers, arm chair, side chair, table. Another group (glass) used iron rods formed into "hairpin bends." Arm chair, side chair, bridge table, square table, dining table, upholstered chair, settee, round table 36", 30", 24", lamp table.

WOOD

Designer: Scheiding, source: Premier Mfg. Co., Chicago, IL.

Serving accessories, all items in "Daisy" or "Celery." Canape trays 10", 12"; cheese boards, 12", 15"; salad plates 8", 10"; jelly jars; scalloped salad bowls with servers; round edged bowl, 11", 13"; square relish tray; hostess tray; individual bowls, 6"; nut bowl, 11".

Designer: Charles Rudy, source: Klise, Grand Rapids, MI.

Famous sculptor carved original models replicated by Klise. Made of elm, they were whimsical, interesting, and amusing, singly or in groups. Named Rudy Bears: Standing Bear, Sitting Bear, Leaning Bear.

Designer: V. V. Huff, craftsmen: The Woodcarvers.

Handmade figural pieces made in western poplar. Original rodeo pieces carved by Huff, replicas hand carved by skilled carvers. Steer, cow, pony, roped steer, cowboy, lying calf.

Designers: Douglas Maier, Miles Aborn, Mary Wright, source: Three Mountaineers, Ashville, NC.

Listing is included in the Mary Wright chapter. Douglas Maier, a New York architect, designed the cheese board with names of the cheeses burnt in. Interestingly, the author's cheese board has Mary Wright's signature burnt on the back. The birch acorn salt and pepper shakers, as discussed, were later found in an original box identifying Russel Wright as the designer.

The Way files, however, attribute them to Miles Aborn. Mary Wright is singled out as the designer for the apple bucket, hurricane candle holders, and the pop-up cigarette box.

Designer: Hardy Davidson, Swannanoa, NC.

Whittled solid wood ducks, hand painted achieving an unpretentious sincerity setting them apart from trite decorative gift ware. A set of three Red Head Ducks as well as a set of three assorted species were made.

Source: Wood Arts Co., Waynesville, NC.

Complete table settings in hand-turned, scalloped edged pieces made of birch with the wood turned down to a very thin edge. Designed by the woodworkers themselves. Small plate, 8" plate, large plate, berry plate, cheese and cracker board.

Source: D. L. Bryant, Monmouth, ME.

Baskets, Table Mat and runners woven of wide strips of skinned or rough Birch Bark.

Source: Richard Taylor, Suffern, New York.

Primitive styled wood carvings done by farmers in a tradition that had been handed down by generations. Heavy oak and birch tree trunks carved into serving pieces: Salad Bowl with spoon and fork and a Scoop said to serve as a centerpiece.

Designer: Michael Hare, source: Bailey & Co., Bend, OR.

Hare, architect, well known for University of Wisconsin Theatre and Art Center did buffet serving items in yellow pine, said to have used molding and bold form. Salad bowls, 14", 12"; individual nut bowl and scoop; candlesticks, set of three; relish server, 3 compartments; serving tray, 13" x 18"; cheese board and spreader; salad fork and spoon; seasoning set with detachable containers for mustard, salt, and pepper.

Designer: Peter Cabot, Source: Penobscot Arts and Crafts, Penobscot, ME.

Functional wood baskets emphasizing construction of Indian craftsmanship. Baskets with or without handles.

Source: Green Mountain Wood Crafters, Charlotte, VT.

Table accessories with very thin and tapered edges. Carved and hand turned of native lumber. Salad bowls, large, medium, individual; round platter; salad fork and spoon with heavy carved handles in two sizes; salad fork and spoon with flat handles in two sizes; cheese board; cheese spreader; scoop; shakers; frying pans, 9", 8", 7"; pineapple server; footed stand; condiment sets; oil and vinegar bottles; shakers; peanut set with spoon.

Designer: Emrich Nicholson, source: Clyan Hall, Corona del Mar, CA.

Redwood serving pieces studded with copper nail heads. Nicholson designed the New York World's Fair flags. Items: bowls 11", 14"; salad servers; rectangular serving tray; compartment trays with pink glass inserts 5 compartments, 3 compartments; nut bowl with mallet; long candle holder.

GLASS

Designer: Scott Wilson, source: United States Glass Company, Pittsburgh, PA.

Handmade glass called "Crystal." Two-handled vase in two sizes, sugar, cream, glass dinner bell, salad bowl.

Designer and source: Dorothy Thorpe, Glendale, CA.

An internationally known museum quality designer, Thorpe offered a footed vase with primrose design and a rectangular vase with cala lily design.

Craftsman: Frederick Jackson, Malaga, NJ.

Solid glass animals pressed into the original early American cast-iron molds giving the impression of huge, brilliantly colored jewels. Discarded, colored medicine bottles were melted down to produce colorful figural items, said to possess design qualities which fit well with contemporary designs. Large turtle, light or dark green, blue; small turtle in same color selections; frog, blue; chicken, green.

Designer: Joseph Platt, Source: Duncan Miller Glass Co., Washington, PA.

Done in a European style, prosaic pieces of glass shaped as if frozen folds of cloth. Star leaf: vases, 8", 10"; rose style, 7½"; crown style, 8"; flower bowl, 11"; 13"; candlestick 2"; plate, 14". Clover leaf vase, 9½"; 12"; footed flower bowl, 10½"; footed cake salver, 13". Draped: square or oval vases, 9", bowl, 15"; leaf relish, 8"; individual leaf ashtray, 3"; oval salad bowl, 14"; oval flower bowl, 14"; oval sandwich plate, 16"; shallow salad bowl, 15"; six-compartment relish, 15"; crimped mayonnaise, 5½"; ladle.

CERAMICS

Designer Lester Gaba, source: Le Pere Pottery Co., Zanesville, OH.

Figural pieces called "Beach Nuts" by the creator of the famous "Cynthia" mannequin seen in department store windows. Figures are sun-burned bathing beauties, male and female figures. Many orders taken for these pieces were said to threaten the records for popularity of items of this sort. Girl and beach ball, beach ball catcher, boy standing on arms, boy doing back flip, sitting girl, girl bent over, hand on ground.

Source: S. A. Weller Pottery Co., Zanesville, OH.

Vases and bowls in Turkish red and turquoise. Leaf vase, spiral vase, leaf bowl, grape bowl, melon bowl.

Designer: Eugenis Oershoy, Source: Zanesville Pottery Co., Zanesville, OH.

Previous work exhibited only in museums and art galleries, these sculptured small ceramic dogs were her first entry into commercial market. Whimsical figures: French dog, bull dog, spaniel, pekinese, rolling dachshund.

Designer: Nura, Source: Zanesville Pottery Co., Zanesville, OH.

Nura's work both in sculpture and painting had been popular in museum exhibits here and abroad. She has established an appealing, amusing style presenting her work commercially for the first time. Rolling kitten, demure kitten, bogging kitten.

Designer: Bernita Lunda, source: Zanesville Pottery Co., Zanesville, OH.

"Water baby" figures reminiscent of Kewpie dolls. Interestingly used as "water babies" among flowers in a low bowl. Baby with starfish, baby with sea shell, baby crawling.

Designer and Source: V. M. S. Hannell, Chesterton, IN.

Handmade pottery crude, inexpensive, and unpretentious with primitive, peasant quality not confined to any design period. Two versions: transparent glaze over red clay resulting in earthy orange color, thin milky white glaze over the clay. Some pieces partially glazed with a beautiful deep Persian blue — an unusual treatment in American pottery. Pieces finished in both glaze treatments, most with blue added. Candle boat, salad bowl, porringer, sugar, cream, mug, large pitcher, cigarette box, flat dish, calf, colt, dog, pig, cat, sheep, rooster, hen, goose, man.

Designer: The Griffiths, Source: Brown County Kilns, Brown County, IN.

Serving items showing floral designs in natural colors with incised lines on cream background. Plate and jug with tulip design, porringer with ivy.

Designer and source: Glen Lukens, University of Southern California, Los Angeles, CA.

Lukens, said to be entering the commercial field for the first time, having previously sold only to museums and art galleries. Decorative accessories with startling texture and color contrasts. Clays and glazes secured, prepared, and ground by the designer. The results were said to be used as a jeweler would a precious stone. Square bowl, 11" x 11", turquoise, crackle inside, unglazed terra cotta outside, named "Water of the Sea"; round weed bowl, yellow or green drops of glaze inside, outside unglazed terra cotta; ashtray, yellow or green drops of glaze inside, unglazed terra cotta outside; ashtray, turquoise crackle inside, unglazed terra cotta inside.

Designer: Antonin Raymond, source: La Mirada Pottery, American Ceramics, Los Angeles, CA.

Egg-shell thin and very delicate, ceramic pieces showing successful union of design and craftsmanship by internationally known architect. Demi-tasse cup and saucer, cream, sugar, pitcher, tumbler.

Designer: Peter Cabot, source: Walter Howatt Kilns.

Wall plaques inspired by Thornton Wilder's "Our Town," representing typical New England scenes in full color. "Town Courtship," "Coming Out of Church," "Hay Wagon," "The Wharf."

Designer: Dorothy Warren O'Hara, source: Walter Howatt Kilns.

Important designer contributed the well known "Pigeon Vase," expected to take its place among American heirlooms. Natural bisque outside, transparent glaze inside.

Source: White Cloud Farms, Rock Tavern, NY. Cooperative family group of farmer-craftsmen turned potters between harvests. Demi-tasse cups and saucers in dull pale green glaze. Saucers said to be unique with a raised base lifting it from the table for ease in handling.

Source: Rountree Pottery Co., Blue Hill, ME.

A cooperative group supporting a local community. Clay is dug from near-by mountains, the glazes dug from the sea. Typical of Peasant Pottery in Europe. Jam jars with various fruit handles, sugar and cream, demi-tasse cup and saucer.

Craftsmen: Jamestown Colony Clay Products.

Traditional Pinch-bottle sets with jug and drinking vessel cover. Finished in an iridescent metallic finish accomplished with long immersion in wells with high mineral content. Wide neck (night table set), narrow neck (wine set).

Source: Jugtown Pottery, Jugtown, NC.

The firm asked that the design background be kept anonymous. Hand crafted, thrown by hand on a potter's wheel. Casseroles, ramekins, soup tureens, pie plates, and more to be used for cooking as well as serving. Typical are a rich orange, achieved by using a transparent glaze over the native red clay, a deep but brilliant brown, dull green frog skin. In addition, a glaze similar to an old Chinese blue as well as an oyster white. Many pieces had been exhibited at museums. Orange: tea set; pot; sugar; creamer; cup; saucer; platter plates, 11", 9", 7"; pitcher and cover; pie plate; pie plate with chicken; soup bowls; soup tureen. Brown: pitcher and cover, oversize cup, bean pot and cover. Yellow: crock frog

skin, vase with four handles. Turquoise with oxblood: large vase. Turquoise: cigarette bowl, vase. Black: pitcher.

Designer: Douglas Maier, source: Waco Pottery.

Waco's craftsmen made a night table bottle and cup as well as a waffle set composed of a batter pitcher, syrup pitcher, sugar bowl, and plate. Items combined dull terra cotta with a shiny transparent glaze covering the handles and interior surface.

Designers: J. Mattson and Maggie Mud, source: North Dakota School of Mines.

Styled in the American Indian tradition, pieces were fired in modern kilns making them less fragile than most Indian pottery. Pieces in various earth-colored glazes from black to terra cotta. Low bowl (Mud), plate, shallow bowl, round (Mattson).

Source: Oregon Ceramic Studio, Portland, OR.

Dining accessory items, characterized by textural combinations and brilliant glazes. Turquoise glaze over rough pink terra cotta, a plum and dark midnight blue. Items had dual usage. Relish wheel; beer stein with snake design; also used as vase; cookie jar with spruce or maple top; waffle set composed of pitcher, sugar shaker, syrup jug; dessert set, large bowl, four individual bowls; duck sculpted of rough terra cotta with varicolored jewel-like drops of glaze; covered flask; bowl, terra cotta with cream lining; blow fish shakers in ivory crackle glaze; lamb with tiny daisy heads applied-cream bisque and coral.

Designer and source: Ann De Carmel.

Collector's pieces of museum quality design, done by a master potter, here offered in lower prices. Large orange bowl, brown vase with deep orange border, green vase, small and large green low bowls.

Designer and source: Frances Sherber.

Another of the country's master potters with pieces sold previously only by museums, art galleries, and decorators. Because of anticipated distribution, prices were lowered. Green Leaf: 6", 10", 12"; 12" with bowl, 16". Cigarette box, footed vases, bowls, tall vases, flared vases, chicken vase, peacock vase (with Charles Williams), hippopotamus (with Williams), plate with birds.

Shape designer: Douglas Maier, pattern designers: Petra Cabot and Euphame Mallison, Source: Fulper Pottery Co., Trenton, N.J.

Dinnerware in Clover reproduced by hand from original painting by Mrs. Cabot. Utilitarian pottery in peasant style. Ensembled with Ellison & Spring table linens. Amethyst Terra Rose. Transparent glaze applied over reddish clay body on Douglas Maier shape. Rich amethyst glaze unevenly applied. Ivy Leaf (Mallison) with leaf on plates only. Undecorated items are varying

American Way Mallison plate. Shape by Douglas Maier. Pattern by Petra Cabot and Euphane Mallison. Source: Fulper Pottery Company.

sand tones. Items: Plates 9", 7½", 6"; cup, saucer, 5" fruit; 14" chop plate; 9" salad bowl; sugar & cover; creamer; small covered casserole; large covered casserole; relish compartment; mug; large pitcher.

Source: Santa Clara Indians, New Mexico.

Rooted in traditional Indian lore, the pieces are free in design. Made in Santa Clara black glaze as well as in natural red color with transparent glaze. Items: Cienega salts, tiny donkeys and miniature Indians for small table decorative accessories; bird sticks carved out of jointed branches and painted brilliantly to be used for garden or flower pot decorations; pottery in six bowls, larger sizes with twisted handles.

FABRICS

Designer: Ann Krusnan, source: Textile Art Craft, Chicago, IL.

Table linens, mats, napkins, and runners in evergreen print.

Designer: Ada Worthington, source: Cape Cod Fish Net Industries, North Trure, MA.

Fish-net tablecloths in neutral colors for informal use. Made of linen threads.

Source: Mrs. Charles Tucker, Providence, RI.

Handwoven table mats of raw silk with delicate aluminum threads running through the weave.

Designer: Joseph Platt, source: Cabin Crafts, Dalton, GA.

Bedspread designs using chenille on cotton in designs from modern to traditional. Pastel colors conformed to the correlated color scheme of which the

Way approved. Platt, an important industrial designer, designed the settings for *Gone with the Wind* and Rebecca Bedspreads in patterns with small varicolored flowers in swag frames in five colors, a broad chenille band with looped corners, two-toned in five colors, another without border.

Source: Oregon Ceramic Studio.

In addition to pottery, linen table mats and napkins using first home grown Oregon flax. Woven on hand looms with an open-work pattern.

Source: Louisville Textiles, Inc., Louisville, KY.

Drapery material in various designs, as well as solid colors.

Designer: Tony Antolini, source: Hillandale Fabrics, NY.

Established buyer of floor coverings, designed hand-loomed cotton material for drapery and upholstery purposes. Plaid checked patterns with summer porch affinity. Hand-loomed, colorful washable rugs in room size as well as occasional sizes.

Designers: Frances Miller, Audrey Buller, Julian Levi, Scott Wilson, Herbert Bayer, George Giusti, source: Cyrus Clark Co., New York, NY.

Drapery fabrics in ceylonese nino, cretonnes, voile, chintz, sailcloth, sateen.

Designers: Marguerita Mergentime, Scott Wilson, Madame Majeska, Russel Wright, Source: Ellison & Spring, New York, N.Y.

Table linens in cotton and rayon American Beauty (Mergentime), Carnation (Wilson), Bamboo Leaf (Wilson). Napkins with colored borders to match cloths. Note: Wright's work is discussed in the text.

Designers: Marguerita Mergentime, Katharine Burton, Scott Wilson, Mary Wright, source: Leacock & Co., New York, NY.

Tablecloths of Spun Glo cotton and rayon in Checkerboard (Mergentime), Violet (Burton), Hawaii (Wilson), Plaid (Wilson), Field and Garden (Majeska). Napkins white with colored borders. Note: Spun-Glo was a registered name. Mary Wright's work is discussed in the text.

Designer: Marguerita Mergentime, source: McCrossen Weavers, Santa Newe, NM.

Tablecloths and napkins in two color combinations, asymmetrical with broad bands crossing only in one corner. two sized cloths, 16" square napkins.

Source: International Looms, New York, NY.

Yard goods material in mohair and cotton frieze.

Designers: Madelyn Smith, Dan Cooper, source: Magee-Laflin Mfg., New York, N.Y.

Water repellent sailcloth suited for wrought iron, rattan, or hickory upholstery use as well as summer drapery fabric. Solid color and peppermint stick (Smith). Ribbon plaid sailcloth in plaid prints for upholstery or drapery (Glass).

Stylist: Madelyn Smith, source: Van Arden Fabrics, New York, N.Y.

Two-toned fish-net fabric to be used for inexpensive window treatment.

Designer and source: The Hamton Guild of Handcrafts, Southhampton, LI.

Non-profit group making woven hemp rope table mats by hand. Their work is said to be used in many smart homes on Long Island. Harmonized with American Modern, Jugtown Pottery, Fulper's Clover. Various colors tied in contrasting threads, matching napkins.

Source: Cohn Hall Marx Co., New York, NY.

Yard goods for drapery and slip cover purposes. Plaids and jacquard, cotton and rayon faille, novelty cotton screen print. Note: This work is in addition to work which is described in text. No designer is listed for this work.

Designer: Isobel Croce, Source: Beacon Looms, Inc., New York, NY.

Pastel cotton plaid curtains of open weave which forms a plaid. Rayon mesh curtains, textured. Both said to take the place of "glass curtains" and draperies. "Two in One" concept.

SYNTHETICS

Designer and source: Norman Beals, New York, NY.

Sculpted serving pieces in Lucite. Working by hand and with blow torch, the designer accomplished pieces with uneven edges, seeming to be framed in glowing light. Relish rosette; salad bowl; salad fork and spoon, twisted; ice bucket; ice tongs, twisted; long and curved hors d'oeuvres tray; cylindrical cigarette box; vase.

Designer: Madelyn Smith, source: Asher & Boretz, New York, N.Y.

"Leatherette Upholstery Goods " in "American Way" colors. Light quality, drillcloth and heavy quality, sateen.

Designer: Lily Berndt, source: Hermann Berndt Weavers, NY.

Leatherette table mats done on hand looms in snake skin and pigskin treatment. Doilies, runners.

Designer: Clarrisa Gross, source: A. R. Kanne, New York, NY.

Tropical plastic fruit with matching candlesticks. Made of Shellflex, a soft plastic, entirely new, textured and bubbly with soft coloration. Leaves, tendrils, and stems made of various metals. Alligator pear, bread fruit, pineapple, grapes, candlesticks.

FURNITURE

Designer: Gilbert Rohde, Source: Herman Miller Furniture Co., Zoeland, MI.

Furniture in straight grain walnut and quilted maple. Table, buffet, china, server, side chair, arm chair with wood backs, side chair, arm chair, upholstered. Bed, dresser and mirror, chest, vanity and mirror, bedside table, bench. Note: Wood not designated.

Designer: Gerald Johnson and Associates, source: Herman Miller Furniture Co., Zoeland, MI.

Maple bedroom units with drawerfronts covered in beige fabricoid, beds, dresser and mirror, chest, vanity and mirror, night table, bench, chair.

Designer: Allan Gould, Source: Ypsilanti Reed Furniture Co., Ionia, MI.

Simply designed group of rattan pieces. Beauty derived from material and good craftsmanship with no surface ornament. Some upholstered pieces were also available with split rattan backs and seats. The wheel lounge and sectional sofa have kapok filled, caterpillar type cushions. Sofa and chairs have spring seats and backs. Sofa, matching chair, wheel lounge, ottoman, sectional sofa (3 pieces), bridge chair, side chair, rectangular lamp table, lazy susan table, cocktail cart, square lamp table, bridge table, canopy for chase.

Designer: Helen Park, source: Ficks Reed Co., Cincinnati, OH.

Recognized summer furniture expert. Rattan group suitable for use in both modern and traditional settings. "New" were rain-proof table tops of varnished oak with boards separated by narrow openings for drainage. Some items said to be equally at home inside or outside. Matching chair, settee, bridge table, bridge chair, ottoman, coffee table, bar stool, bar on wheels, lamp table.

Designer: Robert Heller, source: Berkshire Upholstered Furniture Company, East Springfield, MA.

Sofa, love seat, matching chair, odd chair with cotton/hair cushions, cotton inner spring cushions, or goose down and feather cushions. Muslin covered.

Designer: Gilbert Rhode, source: Company of Master Craftsmen, Flushing, NY.

Entire line straight grain walnut with legs painted black. Desk/bookcase; bookcase; knee hole desk; coffee tables, large or small oblong; oblong lamp table; small or large round coffee tables; round lamp table.

MISCELLANEOUS

Designer and source: Mary Jean Lloyd, South Pasadena, CA.

Decorative gourds suggesting primitive Indian

design of the locale. unusual items, useful and entertaining. Penguins, four sizes; Bottles, three sizes; Covered boxes, three sizes; indian wall hanger, large or small; open gourd server; letter box with hinged door opening, two sizes.

Designer and source: Margaret Hatcher Studio, San Fernando, CA.

Wreaths and charm strings of dried vegetables of the region — gourds, pine cones, wheat, straw flowers and more. Natural earth colors, not gaudy. Wreaths in two sizes, charm strings, 36" or 23". Note: This listing is not complete as evidenced by a last minute finding of a Stangl bird with an American Way backstamp.

**Three Mountaineer's cover, divided box.
Typical of their work done for
the American Way.**

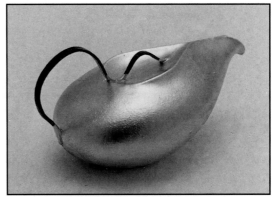

Wright's Everlast aluminite.

Russel Wright Chronology

This is to be considered as an incomplete listing. Dates are approximate.

1904	Born April 3 in Lebanon, Ohio
1921 – 22	Student at Cincinnati Academy of Art
1922 – 24	Law student at Princeton University
1923	Attended Columbia School of Architecture
1924 – 31	Engaged in stage and costume design
1927	Married Mary Small Einstein
1930	Established his own factory for the production of first metal serving pieces, Russel Wright Incorporated
1930 – 31	Experimentation and production of Spun Aluminum
1930 – 31	Irving Richards and Wright begin working relationship
1932	Lamp work by Russel Wright Inc.
1934	Work done for Wurlitzer
1934	Heywood Wakefield Furniture produced
1935	Conant Ball produced American Modern furniture
1935	Russel Wright Incorporated changed to Russel Wright Accessories
1935	Klise Woodenware made Oceana
1935	Approximate date of Plantene production
1936	Approximate date of Chase chrome work
1938	Designed American Modern dinnerware
1938 – 39	Steubenville Pottery agreed to produce American Modern dinnerware
1939	Joined with Irving Richards to form Raymor. Exclusive distribution rights for five years on home furnishings designs
1939	World's Fair work
1940	Ellison and Spring linens designed for American Way
1940	Caseine Co. of America/Borden Division Assemble-Yourself furniture kits
1940 – 41	American Way products shown in stores
1941	American Modern dinnerware received the American Designers Institute award for the best ceramic design of the year
1941	Old Hickory furniture produced
1941	Sprague and Carleton furniture produced
1941	Master Craftsmen furniture produced
1941	War brought metal production to end
1941 – 42	Silex Coffee items designed
1944	Shenango restaurant ware designed
1944	American Cyanide prototyped Meladur
1944	Raymor exclusive contract expired
1945 – 47	Century Metalcraft contract for cutlery and glass
1945	Bauer Art Pottery introduced
1945	Colgate Aircraft Corp. furniture
1945	Buffalo Pottery prototyped
1945	Aluminum Manufacturing Goods designed Mirro Stove to Table accessory line
1946	Mutual Sunset Lamp Company design work
1946	Amtra Trading company streamlined iron work
1946	Iroquois Casual introduced
1946	Chase chrome contract expired
1946	Cohen Hall Marx and Company designed plastic tablecloths and mats
1946	Mary Wright Country Gardens shown at Atlanta trade show
1946	Appleton Art Glass contracted to do bent glass items
1946 – 48	Acme Lamp contract
1947	Backer Lockwood Company Hassock designs
1947 – 49	Englishtown Cutlery designed plastic handled flatware
1947	American Crystal assumed glass contract from Century Metal craft
1947	Popcorn popper produced by Lodge Electric Company
1948	Leacock produced American Modern Linens
1949	Imperial made Twist footed glass items
1949	Frank and Saden table linens designed
1949	Redesigned swivelite lighting fixture for Amplex corporation
1949 – 54	Schwader Brothers/Samsonite Luggage metal folding furniture
1949 – 51	Patchogue Mills contract for woven cloth and rugs
1949	Colonial Premier Lamp contract
1949	Conant Ball introduced Birch finishes
1949	Sterling dinnerware produced
1949 – 50	Paper Novelty Mfg. Co. paper Christmas ornaments
1950	Statton Furniture contract
1950 – 51	Paper table service for Bowes Industry
1950	Simtex Mills produced Simtex Modern linens
1950	Comprehensive Fabrics drapery fabric
1950	Herbert Honig joined Russel Wright Associates as business manager

1950	American Modern Black Chutney and Cedar Green added to palette
1950 – 52	Sloan Babcock vinyl flooring and wallpapers
1950	Sterling Institutional contract dinnerware ended
1950 – 51	Bowes Industries designed paper table goods
1951	DuPont contract for vinyl produced approximate date
1951	Aristocrat Leather produced plastic table linens
1951	Imperial Glass Company made glassware to accompany Iroquois Casual
1951	General American Transportation produced Meladur
1951	Harker White Clover introduced
1951	Paden City White and Green added to highlight line
1951	"Guide To Easier Living" published by Simon and Schuster
1951	Received Home Fashions league Trail Blazer Award for upholstery fabric and table linen designs
1951	American Modern dinnerware line enlarged
1951 – 52	President of the Society of Industrial Designers
1951	Simtex Modern linens won Museum of Modern Art award for best design
1951	Patchogue Mills given contract for geometric patterned woven linens
1951	Fairmont Lamp contract
1951	American Modern glassware introduced by Old Morgantown
1951 – 52	Iroquois Casual dinnerware redesigned and new colors added
1951	Highlight dinnerware won Museum of Modern Art Home Furnishings Award and Trail Blazer Award by Home Furnishings League
1952	Museum of Modern Art awarded Harker White Clover its Good Design Award
1952	Mary Wright's death
1952 – 57	Tilbury Fabric company tests slipcover fabrics
1953	Paden City Snow Glass discontinued. Pottery items substituted. Additions and redesigns
1953	Wright sold Meladur rights to General American Transportation
1953	Hull produced stainless steel flatware to accompany highlight
1953	Hull stainless steel won Good Design Award from Museum of Modern Art
1953 – 54	Hedwin Corporation designed vinyl table coverings
1953	Northern Industrial Chemical contracted to design Residential dinnerware
1953 – 54	Residential won Good Design Award from Museum of Modern Art in both years.
1954	Consideration of Oceana models for use in Lucite called Celomat
1954	Home Decorating Service named to market a variant of Residential
1954	National Silver contracted to design flatware and various serving items
1955	Simtex sold their contract to Edson
1955	Ravenswood Aluminum contract for metal items
1955	Knowles Esquire line introduced
1955	Canteloupe and Glacier Blue added to American Modern dinnerware colors
1955	Assigned by I.C.A. to develop native handcrafts for local use in Cambodia, Taiwan, and Vietnam
1955	Sydney Chairs four promotional chairs including lounger
1955	U.S. Plywood Company Assemble-Yourself furniture kits contract
1955	Approximate date of discontinuation Paden City Highlight
1955	Approximate date of discontinuation Harker White Clover
1955	Imperial Glass Co. made Flair tumblers
1956	Seafoam, Chutney, and Cedar dropped as American Modern dinnerware colors
1957	Bartlett collins Glass company produced large line of decorated tumblers and barware.
1957	Ideal dinnerware produced in Fortiflex
1957	SS Sarna contract for 20 pieces of basketry, wood, aluminum
1957	Ideal toy dishes produced
1957	American Olean vinyl flooring contract
1958	Advisor on merchandising and selling to wood and basketry industry in Japan
1958	Cornwell corporation made small metal and wood table accessory line
1959	Flair dinnerware added to Northern Industrial Chemical line
1959	Patterned Iroquois introduced
1959 – 61	Southerland Paper made paper table goods
1960	Hunts foods packaging designs
1960	Jewelry case for Arden Jewelry Case Company contract
1960	Involved with U.S. Park System and Nature Conservancy in ecological programs for public lands
1961	Cresca Food company packaging design contract
1962	Knowles discontinued Wright's Esquire
1964	Duraware Corporation designed thermoplastic serving items
1964	American Made Plastics company assumes Ideal line
1965	Yamato Theme Formal and Theme Informal shown at New York Gift Show
1965	Polynesian drawings placed in Sterling files
1965	Chinese drawings placed in Sterling files
1967	Closed Russel Wright Associates Design Studio
1976	Russel Wright's death

Bibliography

The American Home. July 1936 Volume XVI. Page 19.

Brody, Barbara. *"American Civilization."* May 7, 1984.

Bates, Elizabeth Bidwell, and Fairbanks, J.L. *"American Furniture 1620 to the Present."* Richard Marek Publishers, 1981.

Battersby, Martin. *"The Decorative Thirties."* Walker & Company, 1971.

Bolger, Nancy. "What's Right about Wright?," *New York-Pennsylvania Collector*. November 1983.

Braziller, George and Bush, Donald J. *"The Streamlined Decade."* 1975.

Cheney, Sheldon and Cheney, Martha Candler. *"Art and the Machine, An Account of Industrial Design in the 20th Century America."* Whittlesey House, 1936.

China and Glass. "Important People." March 1946.

The Cincinnati Enquirer. "A Designer Forest." January 22, 1995.

Cochrane, Diane. "Designer For All Seasons," *Industrial Design*. March 1976.

Country Life. "Spring Sets The Style," March 1934. Vol. LXI #5 Page 66.

Craft Horizons. "A Tribute to Russel Wright." August 1977.

Current Biography. "Russel Wright." 1950.

Design Since 1945. Philadelphia Museum of Art, Catalog to accompany exhibit, 1983

Doblin, Jay. *One Hundred Great Product Designs*. Van Nostrand Reinhold Company.

Eckardt, Wolf Von. "Russel Wright," *Time*. July 1983.

Fehrman, Kenneth R and Fehrman, Cheri. "Collecting American Modern Ceramics, *Gentry* #8. 1995.

The Gift and Art Buyer. "Russel Wright." November 1934.

The Gift and Art Buyer. "Russel Wright." September 1934.

Gift and Art Buyer, August 1934.

Gift and Art Buyer. "Going On In The Trade." June 1937.

Greenberg, Cara. *Metropolitan Home*. "Metro." March 1990.

Hennesy, William J. *Russel Wright American Designer*. M.I.T. Press, 1983.

House Beautiful. "American Way." October 1940.

House Beautiful. "Meet Russel Wright." May 1945.

House Beautiful. November 1952, Vol. 94 #11, page 205.

House Beautiful. "A Designer at Home." April 1983.

Interiors. "Russel Wright." 1950.

Interior Decorator, December 18, 1939.

Kaplan, Michael. "Russel Wright Vitrified China by Sterling." *The Daze*. January 1996.

Kilbride, Richard J. *Art Deco Chrome The Case Years*. Chase Chrome Catalog, 1936 – 1937. 1988 Jo-D Books.

Lucie-Smith, Edward. *A History Of Industrial Design*. Van Nostrand Reinhold Co, 1983.

Lynes, Russel. "A Designer For the Machine Age." *Art News*. February 1984.

Men's Club. "Back to Mid Century Furnishings. July 1995.

New York Times. "Entertaining In a Smart Way." Russel Wright Accessories. November 20, 1932.

Poor, Henry Varnum."Design…A Common Language." *Craft Horizons*. 1951.

Stich, Sally. "Meeting Mr. Wright." *Colorado Homes and Lifestyles*. October, 1993.

Storey, Helen Anderson. "Aids to Informal Entertaining." *The American Home*. July 1933.

Times. August, 23, 1979.

Woman's Home Companion. "…any man can keep house." September 1956.

Wright, Russel. "A Guide To Being Modern." *Arts & Decoration*. February 1935.

Wright, Russel. "Bedroom Comfort." *House & Garden*. April 1938.

Wright, Russel. "Home Furnishings at the Fair," *Creative Design In Home Furnishings*, January 1939.

Wright, Russel and Mary. *A Guide To Easier Living*. Simon & Schuster, 1950.

Wright, Russel. "Gold Mine in South East Asia." *Interiors*. August 1956.

Many phone calls and personal interviews from 1978 to 1996 with Herbert Honig, Annie Wright, Irving Richards.
Personal correspondence with many who are credited in previous writings.
Collection of files left to the George Ahrents Research Library, Syracuse University, Syracuse, NY, by Russel Wright.
Personal files loaned by Annie Wright.

Helpful Internet addresses as they have been given to me:
http://www.derby.k12.ks.us/~rwright/wright.html

listsersv@home.ease.lsoft.com Follow this with "subscribe russelwright (your name) in message. This should be your real name, not your e-mail address or screen name.

I have been told that these groups are conversational and sources for buying and selling.

Other titles by Ann Kerr available from Collector Books:

COLLECTOR BOOKS

Informing Today's Collector

For over two decades we have been keeping collectors informed on trends and values in all fields of antiques and collectibles.

DOLLS, FIGURES & TEDDY BEARS

4707	A Decade of **Barbie** Dolls & Collectibles, 1981–1991, Summers	$19.95
4631	**Barbie** Doll Boom, 1986–1995, Augustyniak	$18.95
2079	**Barbie** Doll Fashions, Volume I, Eames	$24.95
3957	**Barbie** Exclusives, Rana	$18.95
4632	**Barbie** Exclusives, Book II, Rana	$18.95
4557	**Barbie,** The First 30 Years, Deutsch	$24.95
4657	**Barbie** Years, 1959–1995, Olds	$16.95
3310	**Black Dolls,** 1820–1991, Perkins	$17.95
3873	**Black Dolls,** Book II, Perkins	$17.95
1529	Collector's Encyclopedia of **Barbie** Dolls, DeWein	$19.95
4506	Collector's Guide to **Dolls in Uniform,** Bourgeois	$18.95
3727	Collector's Guide to **Ideal Dolls,** Izen	$18.95
3728	Collector's Guide to Miniature **Teddy Bears,** Powell	$17.95
3967	Collector's Guide to **Trolls,** Peterson	$19.95
4571	**Liddle Kiddles,** Identification & Value Guide, Langford	$18.95
4645	**Madame Alexander** Dolls Price Guide #21, Smith	$9.95
3733	**Modern Collector's** Dolls, Sixth Series, Smith	$24.95
3991	**Modern Collector's** Dolls, Seventh Series, Smith	$24.95
4647	**Modern Collector's** Dolls, Eighth Series, Smith	$24.95
4640	Patricia Smith's **Doll Values,** Antique to Modern, 12th Edition	$12.95
3826	Story of **Barbie,** Westenhouser	$19.95
1513	**Teddy Bears & Steiff** Animals, Mandel	$9.95
1817	**Teddy Bears & Steiff** Animals, 2nd Series, Mandel	$19.95
2084	**Teddy Bears, Annalee's & Steiff** Animals, 3rd Series, Mandel	$19.95
1808	Wonder of **Barbie,** Manos	$9.95
1430	World of **Barbie** Dolls, Manos	$9.95

FURNITURE

1457	American **Oak** Furniture, McNerney	$9.95
3716	American **Oak** Furniture, Book II, McNerney	$12.95
1118	Antique **Oak** Furniture, Hill	$7.95
2132	Collector's Encyclopedia of **American** Furniture, Vol. I, Swedberg	$24.95
2271	Collector's Encyclopedia of **American** Furniture, Vol. II, Swedberg	$24.95
3720	Collector's Encyclopedia of **American** Furniture, Vol. III, Swedberg	$24.95
3878	Collector's Guide to **Oak** Furniture, George	$12.95
1755	Furniture of the **Depression Era,** Swedberg	$19.95
3906	**Heywood-Wakefield** Modern Furniture, Rouland	$18.95
1885	**Victorian** Furniture, Our American Heritage, McNerney	$9.95
3829	**Victorian** Furniture, Our American Heritage, Book II, McNerney	$9.95
3869	**Victorian** Furniture books, 2 volume set, McNerney	$19.90

JEWELRY, HATPINS, WATCHES & PURSES

1712	Antique & Collector's **Thimbles** & Accessories, Mathis	$19.95
1748	Antique **Purses,** Revised Second Ed., Holiner	$19.95
1278	Art Nouveau & Art Deco **Jewelry,** Baker	$9.95
4558	**Christmas Pins,** Past and Present, Gallina	$18.95
3875	Collecting Antique **Stickpins,** Kerins	$16.95
3722	Collector's Ency. of **Compacts, Carryalls & Face Powder Boxes,** Mueller	$24.95
4655	Complete Price Guide to **Watches,** #16, Shugart	$26.95
1716	Fifty Years of Collectible **Fashion Jewelry,** 1925-1975, Baker	$19.95
1424	**Hatpins** & Hatpin Holders, Baker	$9.95
4570	**Ladies' Compacts,** Gerson	$24.95
1181	100 Years of Collectible **Jewelry,** 1850-1950, Baker	$19.95
2348	20th Century Fashionable Plastic **Jewelry,** Baker	$19.95
3830	Vintage **Vanity Bags & Purses,** Gerson	$24.95

TOYS, MARBLES & CHRISTMAS COLLECTIBLES

3427	**Advertising Character** Collectibles, Dotz	$17.95
2333	Antique & Collector's **Marbles,** 3rd Ed., Grist	$9.95
3827	Antique & Collector's **Toys,** 1870–1950, Longest	$24.95
3956	Baby Boomer **Games,** Identification & Value Guide, Polizzi	$24.95
3717	**Christmas** Collectibles, 2nd Edition, Whitmyer	$24.95
1752	**Christmas** Ornaments, Lights & Decorations, Johnson	$19.95
4649	Classic Plastic **Model Kits,** Polizzi	$24.95

4559	Collectible **Action Figures,** 2nd Ed., Manos	$17.95
3874	Collectible Coca-Cola Toy **Trucks,** deCourtivron	$24.95
2338	Collector's Encyclopedia of **Disneyana,** Longest, Stern	$24.95
4639	Collector's Guide to **Diecast Toys** & Scale Models, Johnson	$19.95
4651	Collector's Guide to **Tinker Toys,** Strange	$18.95
4566	Collector's Guide to **Tootsietoys,** 2nd Ed., Richter	$19.95
3436	Grist's Big Book of **Marbles**	$19.95
3970	Grist's Machine-Made & Contemporary **Marbles,** 2nd Ed.	$9.95
4569	**Howdy Doody,** Collector's Reference and Trivia Guide, Koch	$16.95
4723	**Matchbox®** Toys, 1948 to 1993, Johnson, 2nd Ed.	$18.95
3823	**Mego** Toys, An Illustrated Value Guide, Chrouch	15.95
1540	**Modern Toys** 1930–1980, Baker	$19.95
3888	**Motorcycle** Toys, Antique & Contemporary, Gentry/Downs	$18.95
4728	Schroeder's Collectible **Toys,** Antique to Modern Price Guide, 3rd Ed.	$17.95
1886	Stern's Guide to **Disney** Collectibles	$14.95
2139	Stern's Guide to **Disney** Collectibles, 2nd Series	$14.95
3975	Stern's Guide to **Disney** Collectibles, 3rd Series	$18.95
2028	**Toys,** Antique & Collectible, Longest	$14.95
3979	**Zany Characters** of the Ad World, Lamphier	$16.95

INDIANS, GUNS, KNIVES, TOOLS, PRIMITIVES

1868	Antique **Tools,** Our American Heritage, McNerney	$9.95
2015	Archaic **Indian** Points & Knives, Edler	$14.95
1426	**Arrowheads** & Projectile Points, Hothem	$7.95
4633	**Big Little Books,** Jacobs	$18.95
2279	**Indian** Artifacts of the Midwest, Hothem	$14.95
3885	**Indian** Artifacts of the Midwest, Book II, Hothem	$16.95
1964	**Indian** Axes & Related Stone Artifacts, Hothem	$14.95
2023	**Keen Kutter** Collectibles, Heuring	$14.95
4724	Modern **Guns,** Identification & Values, 11th Ed., Quertermous	$12.95
4505	Standard Guide to **Razors,** Ritchie & Stewart	$9.95
4730	Standard **Knife** Collector's Guide, 3rd Ed., Ritchie & Stewart	$12.95

PAPER COLLECTIBLES & BOOKS

4633	**Big Little Books,** Jacobs	$18.95
1441	Collector's Guide to **Post Cards,** Wood	$9.95
2081	Guide to Collecting **Cookbooks,** Allen	$14.95
4648	Huxford's **Old Book** Value Guide, 8th Ed.	$19.95
2080	Price Guide to **Cookbooks** & Recipe Leaflets, Dickinson	$9.95
2346	**Sheet Music** Reference & Price Guide, 2nd Ed., Pafik & Guiheen	$18.95
4654	**Victorian Trading Cards,** Historical Reference & Value Guide, Cheadle	$19.95

GLASSWARE

1006	**Cambridge Glass** Reprint 1930–1934	$14.95
1007	**Cambridge Glass** Reprint 1949–1953	$14.95
4561	Collectible **Drinking Glasses,** Chase & Kelly	$17.95
4642	Collectible **Glass Shoes,** Wheatley	$19.95
4553	Coll. **Glassware** from the 40's, 50's & 60's, 3rd Ed., Florence	$19.95
2352	Collector's Encyclopedia of **Akro Agate Glassware,** Florence	$14.95
1810	Collector's Encyclopedia of **American Art Glass,** Shuman	$29.95
3312	Collector's Encyclopedia of **Children's Dishes,** Whitmyer	$19.95
4552	Collector's Encyclopedia of **Depression Glass,** 12th Ed., Florence	$19.95
1664	Collector's Encyclopedia of **Heisey Glass,** 1925–1938, Bredehoft	$24.95
3905	Collector's Encyclopedia of **Milk Glass,** Newbound	$24.95
1523	Colors In **Cambridge Glass,** National Cambridge Society	$19.95
4564	**Crackle Glass,** Weitman	$19.95
2275	**Czechoslovakian Glass** and Collectibles, Barta/Rose	$16.95
4714	**Czechoslovakian Glass** and Collectibles, Book II, Barta/Rose	$16.95
4716	**Elegant Glassware** of the Depression Era, 7th Ed., Florence	$19.95
1380	Encylopedia of **Pattern Glass,** McClain	$12.95
3981	Ever's Standard **Cut Glass** Value Guide	$12.95
4659	**Fenton** Art Glass, 1907–1939, Whitmyer	$24.95
3725	**Fostoria,** Pressed, Blown & Hand Molded Shapes, Kerr	$24.95
3883	**Fostoria Stemware,** The Crystal for America, Long & Seate	$24.95
3318	**Glass Animals** of the Depression Era, Garmon & Spencer	$19.95
4644	**Imperial Carnival Glass,** Burns	$18.95

COLLECTOR BOOKS
Informing Today's Collector

3886	**Kitchen Glassware** of the Depression Years, 5th Ed., Florence	$19.95
2394	**Oil Lamps II,** Glass Kerosene Lamps, Thuro	$24.95
4725	Pocket Guide to **Depression Glass**, 10th Ed., Florence	$9.95
4634	Standard Encylopedia of **Carnival Glass**, 5th Ed., Edwards	$24.95
4635	Standard **Carnival Glass** Price Guide, 10th Ed.	$9.95
3974	Standard Encylopedia of **Opalescent Glass**, Edwards	$19.95
4731	**Stemware Identification,** Featuring Cordials with Values, Florence	$24.95
3326	**Very Rare Glassware** of the Depression Years, 3rd Series, Florence	$24.95
3909	**Very Rare Glassware** of the Depression Years, 4th Series, Florence	$24.95
4732	**Very Rare Glassware** of the Depression Years, 5th Series, Florence	$24.95
4656	**Westmoreland Glass**, Wilson	$24.95
2224	World of **Salt Shakers**, 2nd Ed., Lechner	$24.95

POTTERY

4630	**American Limoges**, Limoges	$24.95
1312	**Blue & White Stoneware**, McNerney	$9.95
1958	So. Potteries **Blue Ridge Dinnerware**, 3rd Ed., Newbound	$14.95
1959	**Blue Willow**, 2nd Ed., Gaston	$14.95
3816	Collectible **Vernon Kilns**, Nelson	$24.95
3311	Collecting **Yellow Ware** – Id. & Value Guide, McAllister	$16.95
1373	Collector's Encyclopedia of **American Dinnerware**, Cunningham	$24.95
3815	Collector's Encyclopedia of **Blue Ridge Dinnerware**, Newbound	$19.95
4658	Collector's Encyclopedia of **Brush-McCoy Pottery**, Huxford	$24.95
2272	Collector's Encyclopedia of **California Pottery**, Chipman	$24.95
3811	Collector's Encyclopedia of **Colorado Pottery**, Carlton	$24.95
2133	Collector's Encyclopedia of **Cookie Jars**, Roerig	$24.95
3723	Collector's Encyclopedia of **Cookie Jars**, Volume II, Roerig	$24.95
3429	Collector's Encyclopedia of **Cowan Pottery**, Saloff	$24.95
4638	Collector's Encyclopedia of **Dakota Potteries**, Dommel	$24.95
2209	Collector's Encyclopedia of **Fiesta**, 7th Ed., Huxford	$19.95
4718	Collector's Encyclopedia of **Figural Planters & Vases**, Newbound	$19.95
3961	Collector's Encyclopedia of **Early Noritake**, Alden	$24.95
1439	Collector's Encyclopedia of **Flow Blue China**, Gaston	$19.95
3812	Collector's Encyclopedia of **Flow Blue China**, 2nd Ed., Gaston	$24.95
3813	Collector's Encyclopedia of **Hall China**, 2nd Ed., Whitmyer	$24.95
3431	Collector's Encyclopedia of **Homer Laughlin China**, Jasper	$24.95
1276	Collector's Encyclopedia of **Hull Pottery**, Roberts	$19.95
4573	Collector's Encyclopedia of **Knowles, Taylor & Knowles**, Gaston	$24.95
3962	Collector's Encyclopedia of **Lefton China**, DeLozier	$19.95
2210	Collector's Encyclopedia of **Limoges Porcelain**, 2nd Ed., Gaston	$24.95
2334	Collector's Encyclopedia of **Majolica Pottery**, Katz-Marks	$19.95
1358	Collector's Encyclopedia of **McCoy Pottery**, Huxford	$19.95
3963	Collector's Encyclopedia of **Metlox Potteries**, Gibbs Jr.	$24.95
3313	Collector's Encyclopedia of **Niloak**, Gifford	$19.95
3837	Collector's Encyclopedia of **Nippon Porcelain I**, Van Patten	$24.95
2089	Collector's Ency. of **Nippon Porcelain**, 2nd Series, Van Patten	$24.95
1665	Collector's Ency. of **Nippon Porcelain**, 3rd Series, Van Patten	$24.95
3836	**Nippon Porcelain** Price Guide, Van Patten	$9.95
1447	Collector's Encyclopedia of **Noritake**, Van Patten	$19.95
3432	Collector's Encyclopedia of **Noritake**, 2nd Series, Van Patten	$24.95
1037	Collector's Encyclopedia of **Occupied Japan**, Vol. I, Florence	$14.95
1038	Collector's Encyclopedia of **Occupied Japan**, Vol. II, Florence	$14.95
2088	Collector's Encyclopedia of **Occupied Japan**, Vol. III, Florence	$14.95
2019	Collector's Encyclopedia of **Occupied Japan**, Vol. IV, Florence	$14.95
2335	Collector's Encyclopedia of **Occupied Japan**, Vol. V, Florence	$14.95
3964	Collector's Encyclopedia of **Pickard China**, Reed	$24.95
1311	Collector's Encyclopedia of **R.S. Prussia**, 1st Series, Gaston	$24.95
1715	Collector's Encyclopedia of **R.S. Prussia**, 2nd Series, Gaston	$24.95
3726	Collector's Encyclopedia of **R.S. Prussia**, 3rd Series, Gaston	$24.95
3877	Collector's Encyclopedia of **R.S. Prussia**, 4th Series, Gaston	$24.95
1034	Collector's Encyclopedia of **Roseville Pottery**, Huxford	$19.95
1035	Collector's Encyclopedia of **Roseville Pottery**, 2nd Ed., Huxford	$19.95
3357	**Roseville** Price Guide No. 10	$9.95
3965	Collector's Encyclopedia of **Sascha Brastoff**, Conti, Bethany & Seay	$24.95
3314	Collector's Encyclopedia of **Van Briggle** Art Pottery, Sasicki	$24.95
4563	Collector's Encyclopedia of **Wall Pockets**, Newbound	$19.95
2111	Collector's Encyclopedia of **Weller Pottery**, Huxford	$29.95
3452	Coll. Guide to **Country Stoneware & Pottery**, Raycraft	$11.95
2077	Coll. Guide to **Country Stoneware & Pottery**, 2nd Series, Raycraft	$14.95
3434	Coll. Guide to **Hull Pottery**, The Dinnerware Line, Gick-Burke	$16.95

3876	Collector's Guide to **Lu-Ray Pastels**, Meehan	$18.95
3814	Collector's Guide to **Made in Japan** Ceramics, White	$18.95
4646	Collector's Guide to **Made in Japan** Ceramics, Book II, White	$18.95
4565	Collector's Guide to **Rockingham**, The Enduring Ware, Brewer	$14.95
2339	Collector's Guide to **Shawnee Pottery**, Vanderbilt	$24.95
1425	**Cookie Jars**, Westfall	$9.95
3440	**Cookie Jars**, Book II, Westfall	$19.95
3435	Debolt's Dictionary of **American Pottery Marks**	$17.95
2379	Lehner's Ency. of **U.S. Marks** on Pottery, Porcelain & China	$24.95
4722	**McCoy Pottery**, Collector's Reference & Value Guide, Hanson/Nissen	$19.95
3825	**Puritan Pottery**, Morris	$24.95
4726	**Red Wing Art Pottery**, 1920s–1960s, Dollen	$19.95
1670	**Red Wing Collectibles**, DePasquale	$9.95
1440	**Red Wing Stoneware**, DePasquale	$9.95
3738	**Shawnee Pottery**, Mangus	$24.95
4629	Turn of the Century **American Dinnerware**, 1880s–1920s, Jasper	$24.95
4572	**Wall Pockets** of the Past, Perkins	$17.95
3327	**Watt Pottery** – Identification & Value Guide, Morris	$19.95

OTHER COLLECTIBLES

4704	Antique & Collectible **Buttons**, Wisniewski	$19.95
2269	Antique **Brass & Copper** Collectibles, Gaston	$16.95
1880	Antique **Iron**, McNerney	$9.95
3872	Antique **Tins**, Dodge	$24.95
1714	**Black** Collectibles, Gibbs	$19.95
1128	**Bottle** Pricing Guide, 3rd Ed., Cleveland	$7.95
4636	**Celluloid Collectibles**, Dunn	$14.95
3959	**Cereal Box** Bonanza, The 1950's, Bruce	$19.95
3718	Collectible **Aluminum**, Grist	$16.95
3445	Collectible **Cats**, An Identification & Value Guide, Fyke	$18.95
4560	Collectible **Cats**, An Identification & Value Guide, Book II, Fyke	$19.95
1634	Collector's Ency. of Figural & Novelty **Salt & Pepper Shakers**, Davern	$19.95
2020	Collector's Ency. of Figural & Novelty **Salt & Pepper Shakers**, Vol. II, Davern	$19.95
2018	Collector's Encyclopedia of **Granite Ware**, Greguire	$24.95
3430	Collector's Encyclopedia of **Granite Ware**, Book II, Greguire	$24.95
4705	Collector's Guide to **Antique Radios**, 4th Ed., Bunis	$18.95
1916	Collector's Guide to **Art Deco**, Gaston	$14.95
3880	Collector's Guide to **Cigarette Lighters**, Flanagan	$17.95
4637	Collector's Guide to **Cigarette Lighters**, Book II, Flanagan	$17.95
1537	Collector's Guide to **Country Baskets**, Raycraft	$9.95
3966	Collector's Guide to **Inkwells**, Identification & Values, Badders	$18.95
3881	Collector's Guide to **Novelty Radios**, Bunis/Breed	$18.95
4652	Collector's Guide to **Transistor Radios**, 2nd Ed., Bunis	$16.95
4653	Collector's Guide to **TV Memorabilia**, 1960s–1970s, Davis/Morgan	$24.95
2276	**Decoys**, Kangas	$24.95
1629	**Doorstops**, Identification & Values, Bertoia	$9.95
4567	Figural **Napkin Rings**, Gottschalk & Whitson	$18.95
3968	**Fishing Lure** Collectibles, Murphy/Edmisten	$24.95
3817	**Flea Market Trader**, 10th Ed., Huxford	$12.95
3976	Foremost Guide to **Uncle Sam** Collectibles, Czulewicz	$24.95
4641	**Garage Sale & Flea Market** Annual, 4th Ed.	$19.95
3819	**General Store** Collectibles, Wilson	$24.95
4643	**Great American West** Collectibles, Wilson	$24.95
2215	Goldstein's **Coca-Cola** Collectibles	$16.95
3884	Huxford's Collectible **Advertising**, 2nd Ed.	$24.95
2216	**Kitchen Antiques**, 1790–1940, McNerney	$14.95
3321	Ornamental & Figural **Nutcrackers**, Rittenhouse	$16.95
2026	**Railroad** Collectibles, 4th Ed., Baker	$14.95
1632	**Salt & Pepper Shakers**, Guarnaccia	$9.95
1888	**Salt & Pepper Shakers** II, Identification & Value Guide, Book II, Guarnaccia	$14.95
2220	**Salt & Pepper Shakers** III, Guarnaccia	$14.95
3443	**Salt & Pepper Shakers** IV, Guarnaccia	$18.95
4555	**Schroeder's Antiques** Price Guide, 14th Ed., Huxford	$12.95
2096	**Silverplated Flatware**, Revised 4th Edition, Hagan	$14.95
1922	Standard **Old Bottle** Price Guide, Sellari	$14.95
4708	Summers' Guide to **Coca-Cola**	$19.95
3892	**Toy & Miniature Sewing Machines**, Thomas	$18.95
3828	Value Guide to **Advertising Memorabilia**, Summers	$18.95
3977	Value Guide to **Gas Station** Memorabilia, Summers & Priddy	$24.95
3444	**Wanted to Buy**, 5th Edition	$9.95

This is only a partial listing of the books on antiques that are available from Collector Books. All books are well illustrated and contain current values. Most of these books are available from your local bookseller, antique dealer, or public library. If you are unable to locate certain titles in your area, you may order by mail from COLLECTOR BOOKS, P.O. Box 3009, Paducah, KY 42002-3009. Customers with Visa or MasterCard may phone in orders from 7:00–5:00 CST, Monday–Friday, Toll Free 1-800-626-5420. Add $2.00 for postage for the first book ordered and $0.30 for each additional book. Include item number, title, and price when ordering. Allow 14 to 21 days for delivery.

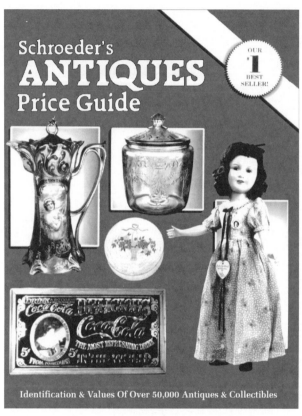